SENSING
THE
WORLD

SENSING
THE
WORLD

Moreland Perkins

HACKETT PUBLISHING COMPANY

The paper in this book meets the guidelines for
permanence and durability established by the
Committee on Production Guidelines for Book Longevity
of the Council on Library Resources.

Interior design by James N. Rogers
Cover design by Jackie Lacy

Printed in the United States of America

For further information, please address
Hackett Publishing Company, Inc.
P.O. Box 44937
Indianapolis, Indiana 46204

Library of Congress Cataloging in Publication Data

Perkins, Moreland, 1927–
Sensing the world.

1. Senses and sensation. 2. Consciousness.
I. Title.
BF233.P43   1983   153.7   83–10825
ISBN 0–915145–74–X
ISBN 0–915145–75–8 (pbk.)

To the memory
of
HENRY DAVID AIKEN

TABLE OF CONTENTS

CHAPTER SIX   Vision   205

CHAPTER SEVEN   The Sense of Touch   241

PREFACE

In Berkeley's language, the question from which this book arises is this one: Is what we immediately perceive by the senses something that depends for its existence upon our perceiving it and therefore something internal to our minds? My answer is, yes. However, I prefer to speak of immediate "awareness". And I think it a confusion to follow Berkeley and call the objects of immediate awareness "sensations". What we are directly aware of are sensuous qualities whose instantiation within us partly constitutes our sensory, conscious states. So I shall argue.

It is well known that some philosophers have challenged the sense of the question that motivates this work, doubting that 'immediately perceive' or 'directly aware' have sense, or have a sense worth anything to a clear-headed philosopher. Austin's *Sense and Sensibility* works at this project more ably than others. I find that work vagarious and the argument not persuasive. So I have not undertaken to criticize it but merely to make clear what I mean by (my preferred terms) direct and indirect awareness (consciousness). This meaning does not seem difficult to grasp. However it would certainly be a help if my readers were familiar with the early parts of the useful book, *Attention,* by Alan White, a brilliant practitioner of a craft like Austin's.

Unlike Berkeley, whose power to believe in the incredible is one of the wonders of the philosophical world, I am, like Locke, a merely commonsensical Newtonian who presumes that there are mind-independent objects which we succeed in a perceiving by sense. These objects, therefore, I hold that we *indirectly* perceive; also, that within perception the sensuous qualities belonging to us of which we are directly aware represent for us objective properties of physical objects before our sense organs.

Now compare this position with two other accounts of the same subject, and ask what difference the choice between them makes to a theory of perceptual knowledge. One might hold, with D. M. Armstrong (*A Materialist Theory of the Mind*), that perceiving is nothing but believing; specially caused and conscious of its causal origin, yet nothing but belief. Our original question can scarcely get a foothold on that slope. But this much seems clear: many rather simple perceptual beliefs about physical objects before our sense organs—such as "There is something

1

red"—will be without evidence. So an account of knowledge as justified (true) belief will not work. Whereas on my account, we should always have available as evidence for such beliefs what we are directly conscious of, e.g., an instance of sensuous "red". Consider a third account, Fred Dretske's in *Seeing and Knowing*. In addition to perceptual beliefs about the features of physical things before the sense organs, Dretske admits (for vision) things looking certain ways to us. These looks provide evidence for our beliefs. But according to Dretske we are not conscious of things looking certain ways to us: Dretske denies direct awareness of the looks of things. Yet he introduces what one would think are the sensuous appearances of physical things as the perceiver's evidence for his perceptual beliefs about the physical things he perceives. Roderick Chisholm, in *Perceiving* and elsewhere, defends a similar view. So here there is allegedly available a kind of sensuous evidence for all of our perceptual beliefs, as in my account, and by contrast with Armstrong. Yet someone might argue that an appearance of which we are not conscious cannot serve as evidence for a perceptual belief we should not have without the appearance.

In short, the conclusion one reaches concerning the question I try to answer in this book certainly makes *some* difference to one's theory of perceptual knowledge. These implications for theory of knowledge, however, I never discuss. In that way, the focus of this work is narrow, and its subject matter not primarily epistemological. Of course, since perception is a form of knowledge and this inquiry is philosophical, that perception is knowledge never ceases to be an important consideration. I could wish I had made no controversial assumptions about what this consideration comes to. But the wish would be in vain: I assume, for example, that knowledge requires something *like* belief, *some* form of attribution of a property, at least.

The chief antagonist to my position I call the "direct realist". (The phrases, 'direct realist' and 'indirect realist' I have taken over from James Cornman.) This antagonist plays an important role in the strategy of my argument. He shares with the indirect realist the recognition that in perception something holds our attention in a way that is both uniquely vivid and direct. He further recognizes that for each sense there are one or a few sensible properties of physical things before the sense organs which we perceive less indirectly than everything else we perceive before those organs: we do not perceive them through perceiving some other property of a thing *before* the sense organs. For example, we hear a fire engine by hearing the loudness, tone, timbre, etc., of the sound which the fire engine makes in the air. But we do not hear the loudness and tone of the sound in the air through hearing any other property belonging to something before the ears. Those properties the direct realist believes that we perceive directly. Whereas the indirect realist believes we perceive those properties indirectly, through becoming directly aware of sensuous qualities belonging not to things before the sense organs but to our own consciousness.

In developing his position with any detail the direct realist must choose his candidates for object of direct awareness by each of the senses, and choose the best candidate for each sense. My strategy is to give the direct realist the best run for his money I can: for each sense choose the best candidate for object of direct awareness, and then show that we cannot be directly aware of this candidate. Only after doing this am I prepared to argue that the object of direct sensory awareness for that sense must be interior to our conscious state itself. With this strategy, everything hinges on the nature of the property chosen as candidate for object of direct sensory awareness. Choice of the candidate must, therefore, he made with care. What is more, the nature of the property chosen must be carefully examined.

Touch presents rather a special case; and I deal with bodily perception in a special way. For all the others—smell, thermal perception, hearing, vision—this general situation emerges: the direct realist is faced with two alternatives in providing a specification of the nature of the property he chooses as candidate for object of direct awareness. Either the property is analyzed as a disposition to appear a certain way to the perceiver, or its nature must be specified by some relevant physical theory. But it turns out that choosing the first alternative will always be self-defeating for the direct realist. So he is forced to choose the second alternative. This means that a property which must, of course, be evidently a sensible property of some physical thing before the sense organs, and which must, furthermore, not be perceived through perceiving some other property of something before the sense organs, this property's *nature* must be understood as physical theory specifies it. For example, the tone we (allegedly) directly perceive must *be* a frequency of vibration of airwaves that strike the ear. All this has the following upshot: that a sensible quality that does not seem to be identical in its nature with a property whose nature is specified by physical theory must be shown to be in fact identical with such a property. The problem of reduction of an observable property to a theoretically specified property becomes, therefore, central for the argument. For these reasons, and somewhat regrettably for some of my readers—and in some cases for the author—more physics needs to be introduced than is customary in philosophical works on perception. Also, perhaps, more philosophy of science. Fortunately not all of the work on this problem needs to be repeated for each sense. The most sustained treatment of the problem of reduction occurs in the chapter on thermal perception, where the direct realist's candidate for object of direct thermal awareness, temperature, has loomed rather large in both scientific and philosophical discussions of reduction of observable properties to theoretically specified properties.

However, the sense which offers the most formidable obstacles to successful completion of this portion of my argument is surely the sense of touch. This was no surprise to me, since I had long believed that most philosophers inclined to representative theories of perception had arguments which failed when applied to touch. This seems to me to be true, for example, of the most recent defense of a position like mine, Frank Jackson's in his *Perception*. In any event it was with dismay that I discovered that the argument for touch had to be carried to the quantum mechanical level. I hope that a reader more competent than I am in physics will improve upon my argument for touch—or refute it, if that is what it deserves.

When I began writing this book I believed that it would be possible to maintain neutrality on the issue of materialism *vs.* some form of psycho-physical dualism. Indeed I thought that the difficulties materialism has to face could not be fully understood until the question I was asking had been decisively answered, since it is clear that the sensuous dimension of our experience poses an apparently formidable obstacle to materialism, yet how formidable this obstacle is depends upon how this dimension is conceived. And on the latter question differences of viewpoint among perceptual theorists have been extreme—as witness the contrast between, say, Armstrong and Chisholm, the first reducing perception to acquisition of belief, the second introducing an adverbial sensing which is no object of awareness. However when I confronted—in the last chapter—the full difficulties of making coherent the idea of a sensuous quality whose instantiation within consciousness depends upon consciousness *of* it, I found myself able to resolve the difficulties only by assuming that sensory consciousness is a physical process, hence that conscious states are brain states. To my surprise, therefore, it has turned out that the book as a whole constitutes an argument for materialism: if the defense of the book's major thesis is sound, and if this thesis can be made coherent only on the assumption of the truth of materialism, then materialism is true.

Of course, conversely, if materialism is false, and the coherence of indirect realism requires its truth, then indirect realism should be rejected. I have not undertaken in this work to resolve any of the well known problems that confront materialism. However, one observation seems worth making in this place. The chief reason for denying that sensuous qualities belong to the physical structures we perceive by sense is that ascription of those qualities to these structures can find no role to play within the explanation by physical theory of the behavior of these structures. However the science of human consciousness scarcely exists. And it is by no means now evident that the introduction of sensuous qualities into the characterization of conscious states will have no role to play in the explanation of human behavior. Even given such a role, a problem for materialism would of course remain, because of the macrostructural character of sensory states of the brain.

On a very small scale it is possible to assign a function to the sensuous qualities belonging to consciousness. I mean something more interesting than the function of serving as the direct object of sensory consciousness. Consider the perceptions in which the direct realist must be most interested: perceptions of those sensible properties of physical things before the sense organs which are perceived least indirectly among the things perceived before the sense organs. For example, hearing the loudness of a sound in the air. I construe the perception of this loudness to consist in the perceiver's involuntary attribution of objective loudness to something in the space before his ears (which happens to be vibrating air). For the moment I leave aside how one should analyze the loudness so attributed. The perceiver in this case is directly aware of a sensuous "loudness" internal to his consciousness. The more interesting function I assign to this sensuous quality is its serving as the sensuous content of the perceptual attribution of objective loudness to the sound before the ears. Hence in being directly aware of sensuous "loudness" we are directly aware of the sensuous content of our perceptual attribution of loudness to the sound before our ears. Being directly aware of sensuous qualities interior to consciousness is closely analogous to being directly aware of a thought that corresponds to the predicate of a nonperceptual judgment—to being directly aware of *what* one predicates in making such a judgment about some particular. But here the *what* that is attributed is a purely sensuous content. Within every perceptual attribution of a certain class of sensible properties to things before the sense organs there is a sensuous attribution, and it is of the content of the latter that we are directly aware. To so conceive the sensuous object of direct perceptual awareness is to assign to this object an important function within our conscious states. It does not follow that my account will make things easy for a functionalist theory of sensory consciousness. For what is perceptually attributed is attributed to something before the sense organs. Hence the sensuous content of such an attribution is ascribed to something before the sense organs, characteristically external to the perceiver's own body. How such an attribution of this sensuous content is achieved is not explained merely by saying that the sensuous quality is functioning as the content of an attribution. If a functional account of sensory consciousness is to be possible then it is our very capacity to attribute these sensuous qualities to things before our sense organs that needs explaining. The problem is analogous to the problem of explaining how nonperceptual beliefs, whose contents are conceptual rather than sensuous, manage to be *about* objects external to themselves. A functionalistic explanation of such conceptual attribution of properties to external objects would seem to have to take the form of a behavioristic analysis: an activated belief would be an activated disposition to behave in certain ways towards the object the belief is about, the *ways* of behaving manifesting *what* is believed about the object. However, there is a difficulty in producing such an explanation of the *sensuous* attributions we make in perceiving objects before our sense organs. Here I can only hint at the difficulty. The problem (without reference to the functionalistic account of consciousness) is discussed in the last chapter.

I have reached the following conclusions. (1) In perceiving the least indirectly perceived properties of things before the sense organs we perceptually ascribe causal powers to these properties. (2) The attribution of causally empowered properties is conceptual attribution. (3) Therefore, included within perceptual attribution of properties is conceptual attribution: this attribution is achieved through exercise of concepts. (4) Since ascribing to objects before the sense organs causal powers entails ascribing to such objects the power to aid or obstruct behavior by us in the pursuit of our goals, our behavior is capable of *manifesting* the attributions we have made of such powers. (5) Hence insofar as a perceptual state includes a conceptual attribution, so far the perceptual state may be specified as being what it is in virtue of being a state that founds a dispo-

sition to behave in certain ways toward the objects it is a perception of. (6) Our direct awareness of purely sensuous qualities
is not an awareness of any causal powers. (7) Our direct awareness of purely sensuous qualities determines what qualities we
sensuously attribute to objects before our sense organs. Therefore, (8), the attribution of *sensuous* qualities which figures
within perception does not involve the attribution of causal
powers. Therefore, (9), because of (4) and (5) above, it does
not appear likely that the perceptual attribution of purely sensuous qualities to objects before the sense organs can be explained behavioristically. Therefore, (10) it does not appear
likely that a functionalistic account of our perceptual attribution of sensuous qualities is possible.

I should warn the reader that the behavioristic account of
perceptual attribution of causally empowered properties to
which I have just alluded is not fully developed in this book,
nor is its defense. To do this is, to my mind, little less than to
develop a behavioristic theory of reference and meaning. This
of course would require another book, which I could not presently write.

Another problem that faces an indirectly realistic and representational account of perception is the following. First, on any
realistic account of perception, the analysis offered of those
properties whose instances are least indirectly perceived among
those things we perceive before the sense organs must meet these
two constraints: (i) It must be evident that the properties, as
analyzed, do belong to physical structures before the sense
organs. (ii) It must be plausible to hold that ordinary perceivers
do commonly acquire the perceptual knowledge *that* something
or other before the sense organs does have a property having the
nature specified by the analysis. The analysis of these properties
offered by a representational account of perception has to meet
this further constraint: (iii) It must make it possible to explain
how it is that the direct object of awareness, a sensuous quality
which cannot belong to the physical object before the sense
organs, can serve to represent for the perceiver a property which
does so belong. This last requirement is somewhat too severe.
As I have remarked, the causal powers of perceptually ascribed
properties are, on my account, represented by means of *concepts*
exercised within perception. So the sensuous quality is not required to achieve this representation alone. Nevertheless the role
of the sensuous qualities of which we are directly aware is a central one in the representation of objective properties of things
before the sense organs. So the third constraint is important.

My solution to the problem of analysis of the objective properties here at issue is to construe them as dispositions to appear
a certain way to the perceiver. But this has the effect of making
the sensuous quality which is directly perceived a somewhat
deceptive representation of the objective property indirectly
perceived. Hence there is, on my account, an element of illusion
in ordinary veridical sense perception. This I regret.

I have already remarked that although the results of this inquiry have implications for a theory of perceptual knowledge,
the primary motivation of the study is not epistemological. Is it,
then, ontological? If it were, the problem of materialism would
have to be taken more seriously than it is—although the results,
if sound, will impose certain constraints on ontological inquires.
How shall the reader construe the motivation? I think of it as
continuous with a scientific approach to sensory awareness. I
am moved by the various components of what I take to be a
straightforwardly factual question about sensory awareness of
the physical world before our sense organs: is what we are
directly aware of something *before* these organs or something not
before them? If not before them, then what is the most accurate
description of its (their) location, character and function? I
think of these as questions about the facts of the matter; as factual questions about the nature of perception. From this presumption it follows that the answers, if correct, should be of
interest to the scientific student of perception. Indeed, I hope
they are.

The first complete draft of this book was written during the
summer, fall and winter of 1974 and the winter of 1975. It was
entirely rewritten several times during the next five years, and
completed in December of 1980. While writing it I largely
stopped reading new work on the subject. When I began, I think
that no book had appeared in the analytic tradition in English
defending a representational, indirectly realistic account of sense
perception since J. R. Symthies' *Analysis of Perception* in 1956.
I felt somewhat uncomfortably old fashioned. While rewriting
the book, Frank Jackson's *Perception* appeared, and I did, in
time, read through it, to be amazed at how different a contemporary defense of a position so similar to mine could be. Although his book has not influenced mine, it has made me feel
less lonely.

When I began this work the philosophers writing on perception whom I had found most stimulating were D. M. Armstrong,

Roderick Chisholm, Fred Dretske, Wilfred Sellars and Alan White. I found White's *Attention* a great help in bringing to focus for me my own belief that none of the other philosophers had succeeded in rendering the structure of sensory *consciousness.* (Of course White's book is not primarily about perception.) Armstrong's little book, *Bodily Sensations,* seemed by far the most illuminating book on that subject ever written. And his ingenious attempt, in *A Materialist Theory of the Mind,* to reduce perception to belief, while taking very seriously the perception of secondary qualities, helped me to focus my attention upon the sensuous dimension missing in his account. And since I share with Armstrong the conviction that belief needs to be analyzed behavioristically, his taking so seriously this conviction, in its bearing upon perception treated as belief, has helped me to appreciate the acute difficulty of explaining sensuous attribution. Sellars' defense of scientific realism, together with his persistently worrying the problem of homogeneously colored, perceived surfaces, reinforced my own misgivings about the theories afield. Chisholm's and Dretske's careful attempts to include the sensuous dimension of our experience without embracing a representational account focused for me even more sharply the place where more work was needed. (The Dretske I speak of here is, of course, the author of *Seeing and Knowing.*) Because Chisholm's and Dretske's views come closer than most to my own, I have tried in the first portion of the chapter on vision to show where I think they go wrong. This is not easy, and I doubt that this effort, taken alone, is altogether successful. Here I must ask the reader to take into account not only what has come before but also what comes after, especially the last chapter, to complete the story.

Many philosophers working on materialism in the last two decades had an influence upon my perception of the need to take seriously the problem of the *possible* identity between directly perceived qualities and theoretically specified, physical properties of physical structures before the sense organs—and upon my feeling the need to take seriously the reduction problem for those sensible qualities. The names that come especially to mind here are U. T. Place, J. J. C. Smart, Hilary Putnam, Armstrong again, Richard Rorty, Sellars again, James Cornman, and Robert Causey. But many others have been read with profit. Those who have made materialism seem possibly true have also helped make it possible for me to be more comfortable than I otherwise could have been in finding myself forced to adopt a materialistic view of consciousness, in the last chapter, in order to make coherent for myself the idea of sensuous qualities whose instantiation depends upon our being conscious *of* them.

J. J. Gibson's long-standing project of developing what I take to be a fascinating, directly realistic psychology of perception has, throughout its course, stimulated me, first to emulate it, and later to criticize it, as I here explicitly do in the chapter on smell.

During the years spent writing this book, it happened more times than I want to number that it was not until a fair copy of the whole work was at hand, typed by others, that I could see the defects in what I had written. For their cheerful perseverance in expertly typing and retyping a book that seemed to promise never to conclude, I thank these secretaries in the Department of Philosophy: Linda Cook, Frances Di Carlo, Mary Luetke-meyer, Sheila Morgan, Debra Paden and Helen Wade.

One semester of sabbatical leave from the University, and two summer research grants from the General Research Board of the University of Maryland Graduate School, were especially helpful in enabling me to write this book.

Nevertheless, a very large part of the writings was done while teaching. That our department chairman, Samuel Gorovitz, was sympathetic to my need to minimize administrative duties was a great help, for which I am grateful.

Also, when evaluations of the finished manuscript were needed to facilitate publication, Raymond Martin, Stephen Stitch and Frederick Suppe generously read it through, for which I thank them.

For her vivid and sustaining presence, and her belief in the book, I thank my wife, Desirée Weidaw Perkins.

College Park
March, 1983

MORELAND PERKINS

Chapter One   INTRODUCTION

1. Direct and Indirect Sensory Consciousness
   of the Physical World

When we sleep without dreaming we are conscious of nothing.
To awaken is to regain consciousness, to become again conscious
of something: of one's body, of relationships between it and
other objects, of happenings around one, of thoughts and emotions. The form that our sensory consciousness of visible things
takes is seeing them; of audible things, hearing them; of tangible things, feeling them; of conditions of our own body, also
feeling them; and of tasty and odorous things, tasting and smelling them. Being conscious of our emotions and desires we also
speak of as feeling them. And we are conscious of our thoughts
in thinking them.

Sometimes we become conscious of one thing through becoming conscious of another. A man walks into his house and
sees on a table an open handbag; through becoming thus visually
conscious of the handbag he may become mentally conscious of
the presence of his wife somewhere in the house. He does not
perceive that the handbag is there by seeing or hearing his wife;
he becomes conscious of his wife's presence through noticing
the handbag. Although we do not ordinarily do so, we could
describe his situation by saying that after entering the house
the man is visually conscious of the handbag, that he becomes
(mentally) conscious of his wife's presence in virtue of being
more directly conscious of the handbag, and hence that he
is only *in*directly conscious of his wife.

Instances of sensory awareness of one item mediating a less
direct awareness of another are not limited to occasions, like the
present one, of achieving a merely mental awareness of the second item. Suppose that from his living room, where the handbag
is visible on the table, the same man now hears his wife's voice
coming from the kitchen. He does not discover that a sound has
occurred through hearing (or seeing) his wife; he becomes conscious of his wife's presence in the kitchen through becoming
conscious of the sound she makes in speaking from there. He is,
we might say, more directly conscious of the sound his wife has
produced than of his wife herself. Of his wife in person he is not

11

yet, we may say, directly conscious. However, whereas in seeing the handbag and thereby becoming aware of his wife's presence somewhere in the house he did not succeed in seeing his wife, so his awareness of her presence in the house could not yet be said to be sensory (because not visual), and so was merely mental, now, hearing her speak from the kitchen, he not only hears the sound she makes, he also, as we always say, hears *her:* his indirect awareness of his wife we conceive to be also auditory. But auditory awareness is sensory awareness; so when he hears her voice his indirect awareness of his wife is sensory awareness.

Indeed it is clear that this man's auditory awareness of his wife in part consists of his auditory awareness of the sound he hears. However, we are not so ready to say of that earlier moment before she spoke, when he first saw the handbag, that the merely mental awareness he then gained of his wife's presence somewhere else in the house consisted in part of his visual awareness of the handbag before his eyes.

If we have begun to accept this mode of describing instances of awareness as more and less direct, it will be natural by now to say that if this same man walks into the kitchen and sees his wife, then he has, at last, become quite as directly conscious of his wife as he had before been, first, of the open handbag and then, a moment later, of the sound of her voice. It does not now seem to be the case that it is through being conscious of something else that he can tell that his wife is there before his eyes, just as it does not seem that it was through being conscious of something else that he earlier noticed the handbag on the table or, a moment later, heard a voice. Without further critical reflection, we might naturally say that this man is *directly* conscious first visually of the handbag, then aurally of the human, vocal sound, and finally again visually of the woman herself—of whom he had, until at last seeing her in the kitchen, at first been only *in*directly conscious.

When, through feeling them, we become conscious of our own desires and emotions, or in thinking them we become conscious of our thoughts, it surely does not seem to us that we do so through becoming conscious of anything else: of these, too, we should naturally say that we are directly conscious.

Turning to the sense of touch: if someone uses a cane to feel the ground ahead of him, we readily admit that he becomes only indirectly (yet tactually) aware of that portion of the ground, for it is only in virtue of what he feels in the cane he is holding that he feels the character of the ground the cane is striking.

However, we naturally believe him to be directly aware of the cane, for we do not spontaneously believe that it is through being aware of something else that he is aware that the cane is in his hands, or that it is smooth or vibrating: we should now naturally say that he directly feels the cane.

Some philosophers have held that what we unreflectively believe about direct, sensory awareness of things before our sense organs is mistaken. They have held that we are *directly* conscious through our senses of no objects or events situated *before* our sense organs, but always only of items that are not before these organs—items, furthermore, which depend for their very existence upon our being conscious of them. According to this view, of everything before our sense organs of which we achieve sensory awareness we are always only *in*directly aware: we discover by sensory awareness of it that each such object or event is out there before our sense organs only in virtue of being directly aware of something that is not out there—an interior, sensuous item that depends for its existence upon our direct awareness of it. This philosophical thesis concerning our sensory consciousness of the physical world I shall call "indirect realism".

Other philosophers have held that, of however many sorts of things before our eyes and other sense organs we may be, in attending to them, only indirectly conscious, for each sense there exists before our sense organs at least one sort of thing of which we can and commonly do become *directly* conscious: of these physical objects and events—and of some of their features—we achieve sensory awareness without mediation through a more direct awareness of anything else. This thesis concerning our sensory awareness of things before our sense organs I shall call "direct realism".

In this study I shall try to show that indirect realism is the truth about sensory awareness. In the argument more emphasis will fall upon proving the indirectness of this awareness than upon proving its realism. Nevertheless, although in general discussion I shall simply assume the truth of realism, I shall treat no argument for indirectness of awareness (in regard to a particular sense) as complete until the realism of that form of awareness has also become manifest.

2. Two Different Contrasts between More and Less Direct Sensory Consciousness of the Physical World

I shall have frequent occasion to speak of two different contrasts between more and less direct sensory awareness of things. Only one of these figures in the definition of direct and indirect realism; however, consideration of the other contrast will often be useful in reaching conclusions concerning the one of primary interest, so it needs to be explained.

The contrast of primary interest is between indirect sensory awareness and (absolutely) direct sensory awareness. The indirect realist holds that it is only of things not before our sense organs (and which depend for their existence upon our sensory awareness of them) that we are ever directly aware.

However, the indirect realist may have an interest in making another contrast: between, on the one hand, those objects before the organs of a given sense our sensory awareness of which is not mediated by awareness of anything else located *before* those organs, and, on the other hand, all the other objects we perceive before those organs.

The indirect realist's interest in this second contrast arises from his interest in identifying the most plausible sort of object for the direct realist to propose as what we directly perceive before the organs of a given sense. The indirect realist will want to focus his critical examination of direct realism upon our sensory awareness of the sort of object before our sense organs which offers itself to the direct realist as the most plausible candidate for direct object of perception. For a single sense this class of objects will consist of all those before that sense's organs our sensory awareness of which is not mediated by awareness of other objects *before* those organs.

Before explaining these two contrasts between more and less direct sensory awareness a word is needed about a preliminary matter already touched upon. There are many ways of being conscious of an X through being conscious of another thing, Y; I shall be concerned only with the one in which both awareness of X and awareness of Y is sensory awareness. In the example discussed a few pages back, the man's indirect awareness of his wife is sensory (since it is auditory) when it is achieved through more direct, auditory awareness of the sound she makes; it is not sensory (because not visual) when it is achieved only through visual awareness of her handbag. (In the one case he hears *her;* in the other case he does not *see* her.) As remarked in describing these examples, corresponding to this distinction is the distinction between his auditory awareness of his wife being quite evidently constituted in part by his auditory awareness of the sound she makes, and his mental awareness of her not being so evidently constituted even in part by his visual awareness of the handbag on the table.

To help assure ourselves that both the more and the less direct awareness are instances of sensory awareness we can, therefore, stipulate that the only cases of indirect awareness of Y in which we are interested are those in which it is quite evident that the awareness of Y is at least in part constituted by the less indirect sensory awareness of X (the sensory character of the latter awareness being self-evident).

I now return to the two sorts of contrast between more and less direct awareness. The contrast of primary concern is this one: between, on the one hand, a direct sensory awareness of something *not* before the sense organs, and (mediated by that awareness), on the other hand, an indirect sensory awareness of something *before* those organs. The former is not only more direct than the latter: it is absolutely direct awareness of its object. If such a contrast is realized in every instance of awareness of an object before the organs of a given sense, then indirect realism is true of that sense—so far, however, only weak indirect realism. Full-blown indirect realism—the strong version—asserts that the direct object of sensory awareness, *not* before the sense-organs, depends for its existence upon the awareness we have of it. It is the strong version that interests me; but I shall treat it as a second stage in the argument for indirect realism to show that, given the truth of the weak form, acceptance of the strong form is required.

Of secondary interest, but important because attention to it will help us reach conclusions about the contrast just indicated, is the contrast between more and less direct, sensory awareness of things *all* of which are before our sense-organs. Here the contrast between our auditory awareness of a sound and of the source (producer) of the sound can serve as a paradigm: if the direct realist had to choose between sounds and producers of sounds for the (absolutely) direct object of our auditory awareness, then provided that he could plausibly construe sounds as happenings located before our ears, we should expect him to choose the sounds rather than their sources. (And I shall now merely assume that he can plausibly take sounds to be vibrations of the air. In a later chapter this identification will not be taken for granted.)

The reason we should expect this is that we believe that one hears what makes a sound through hearing the sound, but not vice versa; we know the direct realist wants an object of perception before the sense organs which is not perceived through perceiving something not before these organs: he must look for a sort of object (which could be an event) before the sense organs which is not perceived through perceiving anything else before those organs, and then argue that sensory awareness of this sort of object is not mediated by more direct awareness of anything else.

Hence both the direct and the indirect realist will be justified in testing the former's thesis, as applied to auditory perception, by trying first to ascertain what sorts of things before the ears are perceived without mediation through auditory awareness of something else before the ears, and by next asking whether or not our auditory awareness of these objects is absolutely direct, i.e., whether or not we can become aurally conscious of these objects without becoming aurally conscious of something else that is *not* before our ears.

What are the presumed facts about our auditory awareness of sounds, on the one hand, and about our auditory awareness of their sources, on the other, which warrant our treating the first as more direct awareness than the second?

(1) Whenever we do become aurally conscious of the producer of the sound, we do so through becoming aurally conscious of the sound, but never vice versa. (2) Our auditory awareness of what produces the sound is always in part constituted by our auditory awareness of the sound, but not always vice versa. (3) We can become aurally conscious of sounds without becoming aurally conscious of their sources, but never vice versa. (4) In the causal chain leading from the producer of the sound to our conscious, auditory impression of the sound, the occurrence of the sound always constitutes a causal link whose position in the causal chain is temporally closer to the occurrence of our impression of the sound than the sound-maker's activity is, i.e., the sound-maker by its action causes the sound to occur (and never vice versa) ; the sound's occurring in turn causes our ear to respond in certain ways; this response of the ear in turn causes us (through numerous further links) to become aurally conscious of the sound and (whenever we do become conscious of both) of its source.

These four propositions are not logically independent of each other. For example, (2), (3), and (4), taken together, may be regarded as providing an analysis of (1).

Analogous relationships will be found to hold between our

sensory awareness by other senses of other pairs of sorted objects and events located before the organs of these senses. Whenever analogous relationships do hold, I shall say that we have a more direct, sensory awareness of the sort of thing whose place in the structure is analogous to sounds than we have of the sort of thing whose place is analogous to the sound's source. However, there may be sensory situations in which we shall want to decide what the direct realist's most promising candidate for object of direct sensory awareness is and in which not all these relationships can be adduced as evidence. Then we shall need to settle for less ample criteria of the distinction between more and less direct sensory awareness of object and events before our sense organs.

Always, however, in returning to the contrast between direct and indirect sensory awareness which is of primary concern, I shall treat it as a matter of definition that if we can achieve sensory awareness of some sort of object before our sense organs only through sensory awareness of something not before them, where the latter awareness in part constitutes the former, then the latter is not only more direct than the former, it is absolutely direct sensory awareness of its object.

A possible sensory state of affairs which can be used to illustrate both of the contrasts just described is the following. Suppose that sounds are soundwaves. And suppose that we become aurally conscious of everything we hear before our ears except sounds only through becoming aurally conscious of sounds; and suppose that we do not become aurally aware of sounds in virtue of becoming aware of anything else out there before our ears. Hence among the objects and events before our ears which we hear in virtue of attentively listening, sounds are the most direct (or, the least indirect) objects of auditory awareness. Suppose, however, that we become aurally conscious of sounds only through becoming aurally conscious of "tonal" (and other) qualities belonging to consciousness itself, and that this awareness of subjective, "tonal" qualities in part constitutes our awareness of the sounds (soundwaves) before our ears. Suppose, finally, that these "tonal" qualities that belong to our auditory consciousness depend for their existence (their instantiation within consciousness) upon our being conscious of them. If all this were true, then we should have absolutely direct, auditory awareness of these "tonal" qualities; this direct awareness would mediate all auditory awareness of things before our ears; the latter awareness would therefore be indirect, and the strong version of indirect realism would be true of the sense of hearing.

3. Sensory Awareness, Attention, and Sensible Qualities

In discussing direct and indirect realism some philosophers not only prefer the word 'perceive' but seem to avoid using the words 'conscious' or 'aware'. I have reasons for not following them.

In this context the word 'perceive' is an abbreviation for the disjunction 'see or hear or feel or taste or smell'. Some philosophers believe that we sometimes see, hear, feel, taste, and smell things without noticing anything at all about them, indeed without becoming in any degree conscious of these things' presence. It is not uncommon for philosophers who believe this and write about perception to produce an analysis of the concept which leaves room for this sort of "perception." Consequently they sometimes provide an account of *un*conscious sensory "perception."

We may then encounter a "proof" of direct realism which is equivalent (though not always evidently so) to the following argument: "In driving along a road when my mind is preoccupied with its thoughts I may be quite unconscious of the road; yet I must see the road, since I keep my car on it. This is unconscious, visual perception of the road. However, it is clear that I do not perceive the road in virtue of being conscious of something else that is not before my eyes; for the only things I am conscious of are my thoughts, which distract my attention from the road and therefore can neither be that through my awareness of which I visually perceive the road nor constitute in any part my (unconscious) perception of the road. Therefore by vision I *directly* perceive the road. So direct realism is true of at least some instances of visual perception."

This purported proof of direct realism seems strange because direct and indirect realism have traditionally been conceived as opposed theses about the direct objects of our sensory awareness of the world, whereas in this argument the issue is decided by appeal to an interaction between person and environment involving no sensory awareness of anything. The argument has changed the subject.

The human interest that philosophers' claims about direct sensory perception have been widely felt to have—Berkeley's first dialogue is a famous example—arises from their pertaining to the character and place in the world of what holds so much of our waking attention. Nearly all of us have at some time been interested in these claims because the subject matter of debate clearly embraces so much of the subject matter of our conscious experience of the world throughout our waking life. Surely philosophers who conduct the discussion about direct and indirect perception in terms of unconscious perception have changed the subject. The classical debate concerning direct and indirect perception has no place on its agenda for the "indirect realist" who maintains that whenever by means of our eyes we take account of the green color of the grass, without being conscious of the grass or its color, we do so in virtue of taking account of the "green" sensum belonging to our mind, but without becoming conscious of this sensum. No more relevant is the "direct realist" who claims that *un*consciously seeing the grass requires no direct awareness of a subjective sensum. Direct and indirect realism should not be formulated as theses about unconscious perception. They are theories of our sensory consciousness of the world.

An important strategic advantage is gained from thus focusing upon sensory consciousness of the world. What one becomes in a sensory way conscious of in one's own body and in its environment coincides with what attracts or holds one's sensory attention there. (The attention of the "unconscious driver" described above is not held by the road, it is held by his own thoughts; so he loses consciousness of the road and becomes conscious only of his thoughts.) One can, therefore, always formulate questions about the objects of sensory awareness in an alternative way: What is it that attracts (holds) our sensory attention?

I have now a guide to the forms of sense perception which will concern me: they are those in which we look with attention at something, listen with attention to something, taste or sniff something with attention, or give our attention to what we feel through touch, through our thermal sense, and through our bodily sensibility. All these forms of perception are forms of *awareness* of things before our sense organs. It will sometimes be convenient, therefore, to refer by ellipsis to the forms of sensory perception—sensory consciousness—associated with such attentive looking, tasting, sniffing, listening, and feeling as "attentive perception." I shall no doubt often neglect to include the word 'attentive', but unless the context suggests otherwise, when I speak of "perception" or of any of its species I shall always mean to refer to *attentive* sensory perception, which coincides with our sensory consciousness of things.

The driver who is taking account of the turns in the road, hence seeing them, but allegedly without consciousness of them, illustrates only one way in which sense perception has been thought by some philosophers to be sometimes unconscious. Other philosophers have argued for direct realism by appealing to a different idea of a way in which sense perception allegedly fails to be conscious. Of course the objections just raised stand in the way of posing the opposition between direct and indirect realism in terms of any form of unconscious "perception." This second, alleged form of it has, however, as an idea, its own interest for us, and is widely enough defended to require mention in these introductory remarks.

Take vision: we are told that our common idea of seeing objects is not an idea of gaining knowledge of either the object or anything else. Knowledge may arise *from* seeing, but neither the idea of gaining knowledge nor of possessing it enters into our idea of merely seeing an object. It would not be unnatural to describe the allegedly unconscious driver as gaining through vision some knowledge of the road (knowledge not held in a conscious form), since, for example, his taking account of the curves in the road seems to entail that he knows they are there. But on the present view, knowledge, whether consciously or unconsciously held, never figures as part of what is achieved in merely seeing a road. Since knowing an object through vision entails knowing some feature of the object, this interpretation of our idea of seeing consists, on its negative side, in the denial that in merely seeing an object we gain knowledge of any feature of this object.

My present purpose in introducing this nonepistemic idea of seeing is not in order to criticize it but to use it to sharpen, by contrast, our present focus upon an important fact about sensory consciousness of things. Whatever application we may be able to find for the idea, just sketched, of "perceiving" objects without gaining knowledge of any feature of them or of anything, we can find no application for the idea of a person's having his sensory *attention* held by an object without its being held by some feature of the object: to become in a sensory way conscious of something before our sense organs—to have an awareness of it which takes the form of seeing it or hearing it or feeling it or tasting or smelling it—but without becoming in a sensory way conscious of any feature of it is not possible for us.

To be in a sensory way conscious of an object is for that object to hold, or at least for a moment to attract some degree of our attention. But it can do this only in virtue of some feature of it holding or attracting our attention. This, in turn, entails that we become in a sensory way conscious of this feature of the object, and this last entails that we know that the object has this feature.

It is true that a person may report that he became suddenly conscious of someone's presence in the room, but without being conscious of any visible, audible, or other sensible sign of the other's presence. One possible account of such a report is that it is mistaken: that the sensible signs of which the person did have a brief awareness were so fleetingly present for him (and so merely instrumental) that he immediately forgot them. However, if we treat such a report as literally true, then we cannot also conceive the awareness achieved of the other person's presence in the room as *sensory* awareness: there is awareness of no visible sign of the other's presence, awareness of no sound, of no tangible or thermal qualities, of no odors or tastes signifying the other's presence. Whatever causal role stimulation to the sense organs may have played in its genesis, this awareness is entirely mental, a mere thought (conviction) that there is someone in the room, no more.

No doubt, the fact that such a conviction "ought to" take the form of sensory awareness but either does not or does not seem to, makes having it an eerie experience.

The fact that objects and events before our sense organs attract our sensory attention only in virtue of sensible features attracting it, the fact that sensory awareness of a thing coincides with sensory attention to it, the entailed fact that sensory awareness of objects and events can be accomplished only through sensory awareness of sensible qualities—these facts can have an important bearing on the strategy of an inquiry aimed at getting the truth about direct and indirect realism.

Suppose I want to know whether *before* the organs of a given sense there is anything we directly perceive. It might be an object, it might be an event. Let me speak of both as "objects." Also let us suppose that if there is such an object, there is only one sort. Other sorts of perceptible objects before these organs are perceived indirectly. Therefore, if there is a sort of object before the organs of this sense which is directly perceived it is the most directly perceived (sort of) object out there. This means that perception of this object will mediate perception of every other object we perceive before the organs of this sense. But I am speaking only of attentive sensory perception. Hence, in speaking of what we perceive before the sense organs I am speaking only of what ("out there") we become in a sensory way conscious of. But we can achieve sensory awareness of an object only through sensory awareness of sensible qualities. And if, as assumed, our sensory awareness of a particular sort of object is not mediated by awareness of any other object before the sense organs, then the sensible qualities through awareness of which we become aware of this object must belong to it.

We can therefore identify the most directly perceived object before the organs of a given sense in this way: it is the sort of object that has in a sensible form at least one of the sensible qualities our sensory awareness of which mediates our sensory awareness of every other property we perceive (through this sense) which is instantiated before these sense organs. The sort of objects that have these sensible qualities will comprise the sort of objects that are most directly perceived before the organs of the sense being studied.

Therefore, in seeking the truth about direct and indirect realism concerning a given sense we can begin by looking for the sort of sensible property that is not perceived in virtue of perceiving an instance of some other property located before the organs of that sense. Whatever sort (s) of object before these organs has this property in a sensible way becomes the direct realist's strongest candidate for the direct object of sensory awareness. This sort of object will be a *successful* candidate if and only if it passes this further test: it turns out that we do not always achieve sensory consciousness of the key sensible property of this sort of object in virtue of becoming directly conscious of some other quality instantiated somewhere *not* before the sense organs. If this test is passed, then direct realism will be true of the sense being studied. If all the plausible candidates fail this test, then the weaker form of *in*direct realism is true of that sense. If, furthermore, all the qualities of which we are directly conscious by means of one sense belong to our consciousness itself, then the strong version of indirect realism is true of that sense.

Finally a word about my use of the word 'object' in such phrases as 'object of sensory awareness' or 'direct object of sensory awareness'. I use the word sometimes merely to mean whatever we are in a sensory way aware of. This may be a substantial object, it may be a process, action, or other sort of event. I shall also sometimes refer to an instance of a property as an "object of sensory awareness." When the instance is before the sense organs, where the property is instantiated will be reasonably clear from the context of discussion. When the property-instance is said to be not before the sense organs, what has the property poses a problem to be solved.

Although there have been some signs of the beginning of a change during the six years that have passed since I began writing this book, most analytic philosophers have not in recent decades been sympathetic either to indirect perceptual realism or to the representative theory of perception usually associated with it. For this reason, in the next chapter I begin my defense of both of these doctrines with an examination of a form of perception concerning which the case for indirect realism strikes me as intuitively most persuasive: perception of hurting, bodily parts. That chapter is intended not to prove my theses but to clarify them—and to give them initial plausibility. Certain crucial steps in the argument will there be treated as intuitively plausible, as if requiring no demonstration. These same steps, or rather the analogous steps in regard to other forms of sensory consciousness, will, however, be the subject of extended argument as I proceed beyond bodily sense perception and examine, one by one, several other senses. Even then not all the theses that need extended argument for their support, and extended analysis for their clarification, will receive either as they make their appearance in a single chapter concerned with a particular sense. Some problems lend themselves to more fruitful exploration in connection with one sense than with another. The argument, therefore, will be cumulative and will be completed only in the last chapter.

Chapter Two   FEELING ONE'S
BODY

1. The Strategy of this Chapter

In the early stages of reflection upon certain bodily sensations—pains, itches, tickles, and the like—we do not easily think of our having these sensations as ways in which we perceive our body. The explanation of that fact is largely to be found in this one: when attention is invested in one of these bodily sensations, what holds this attention is a quality that appears to belong to some part of the body but which we come to think of as specifying our conscious state. Upon reflection we are inclined not to believe that a pain or an itchy, tickly, or tingly quality belongs to the part of our body in which it seems to us, in sensing it, to inhere. For we believe that such qualities depend for their occurring in the world upon our feeling them—their instances exist, we think, only while we feel them. Upon reflection we do not believe that a genuine feature of a tooth or of a portion of skin can always depend, for its being this feature at a given moment, upon our feeling it at that moment.

If, however, in spite of this inclination of early reflection not to conceive such bodily sensation as a form of sense perception of the body, we do, upon second thought, so conceive it, then the purported facts, our belief in which had prevented us from thinking of sensation as perception of the body, will, if we continue to accept them as facts, make it very natural for us now to think of this perception as *in*direct. For we shall find ourselves acknowledging as the direct object of this perception of the body something which surely exists—an instance of a tingly or tickly or itchy quality, for example, or a pain—but which does not, we believe, exist *before* the organs of our bodily sense; on the other hand, we now acknowledge the ulterior object of this perception to be some bodily part, which *is* (most of it) before these organs (since the "organs" are sensory receptors embedded within the bodily part). We shall now find it natural, holding these beliefs, to say to ourselves something like the following:

"To feel a toothache is to become in a sensory but indirect way conscious of one's tooth, in virtue of being directly conscious of a pain. The pain genuinely characterizes one's conscious

25

state, functioning as this state's mode of representing the diseased condition of the tooth. The tooth that one thereby perceives is (most of it) located before the sense organs by means of which one perceives it, since these organs are embedded within the tooth. However, the pain, through one's attention to which one attends to the tooth, constitutes (part of) the conscious state in which one's attention is realized."

We shall also now find it natural to tell a similar story about indirectly perceiving several physical conditions of our skin in virtue of becoming directly conscious of tingly, itchy, or tickly qualities which specify the characters of our conscious states. We shall find this a natural way to think, I say, in case we come to believe that bodily sensations constitute perceptions of bodily parts, while we retain our earlier belief that in experiencing certain bodily sensations the qualities that most immediately command our attention belong to this attention rather than to its objects before the sense organs.

It is not difficult to find good reasons for holding that bodily sensation is a form of sensory perception of our body (though it is somewhat difficult to show that all the conditions necessary for the truth of this claim are satisfied). However, such is the resistance of many philosophers to accepting indirect realism that, once vivid bodily sensation has been conceded to be attentive perception of the body, it is commonly no longer granted that the direct object of this perceptual consciousness is a state of this very consciousness: indeed this description of what is to be granted reveals part of the ground of the resistance to it. And many artful dodges have been invented to avoid granting so much while not altogether ignoring the intuitive support for the position now denied. More art than I wish to exercise upon bodily sensation would be needed for me to give now a satisfactory proof that the direct object of our sense perception of the body is a condition interior to consciousness. It is not my purpose in this chapter to *prove* that we have only indirect sensory awareness of our own bodies.

This chapter has another objective: to give a preliminary account of the sort of indirectly realistic structure which I shall later try to prove to belong to the deliverance of each of several other senses. By analyzing bodily sensation as perception of the body, but by *positing* as the direct object of this perception a condition of consciousness itself, I set the stage for an early exploration of conclusions which I shall later try to prove concerning the other senses.

I choose to use bodily sensation in this expository way because, on the one hand, intuitively we find it natural to think of the direct object of this sort of awareness as internal to the awareness, and, on the other hand, it is useful and not too difficult to make the case for conceiving bodily sensation to be a form of perception of a physical object located before our sense organs. I want to take advantage of this plausibility of two basic conditions needed for the truth of indirect realism in order quite early both to confront difficulties and to exploit opportunities which indirect realism's defense encounters when the premise so difficult to prove, concerning the interior locus of the direct object of perception, is posited as true. Once this is done, I shall have available at least the scaffolding for a framework into which to fit this book's conclusions, conclusions which it will take so much later work to prove that an early start at clarifying their content is desirable.

The philosophical reader will perceive that in this chapter I am asking from him a suspension of theoretical disbelief. (I do not mean that I shall not help him to this suspension by arguing for what I posit. But these arguments will be deliberately incomplete, involving excessive appeal to intuition.) I say "theoretical" disbelief because, as these remarks have suggested, I suspect that even philosophers who think toothache involves perception of a tooth are disposed to believe, before theoretical difficulties enter, that the pain of toothache is both a conscious state and a part of what we are conscious *of*.

In pursuing the special objective of this chapter I shall proceed in the following way. I shall take feeling a toothache as my illustrative sensation. I shall try to make it plausible, to a first approximation, that feeling a toothache is an instance both of perceiving one's tooth and of being conscious of pain. On the basis of incomplete argumentation I shall then adopt the hypothesis that pain is not where it seems to be (in the tooth) but is, rather, interior to consciousness. Next I shall notice that this assumption makes it less easy than it at first seemed to be to understand how feeling a toothache can be a case of perceiving a tooth; for it will become less clear to us what genuine feature of a tooth one *can* perceive by means of the sense of pain.

Postponing the solution to this latest problem, I shall explore what it can mean that the pain we are conscious *of* belongs *to* this very consciousness. That inquiry will lead me to an examination of our sensuous mode of representing our tooth to ourselves when we feel a toothache. Then I shall be in a position to solve the problem of explaining how one can perceive by the sense of pain a genuine condition of one's tooth. In developing that explanation I shall need to distinguish the sensuous from the conceptual mode of representation involved in perceiving one's tooth through the sense of pain, and to say something about misperception and veridical perception.

2. Perceiving a Tooth through Feeling a Pain

A small girl with a newly loose tooth may be distracted from her usual concerns. For a time her attention is held by her tooth. More exactly, it is held by this new condition of her tooth, its being loose; when an object attracts our attention it does so in virtue of at least one of its features commanding our attention. The form that the girl's attention to her tooth takes is feeling it: her tooth's holding her attention consists in her attentively feeling her tooth. With her tongue she feels the tooth move, and she also feels this through the gum in which her tooth is embedded. In feeling the tooth move she feels with her tongue the shape of the tooth and its texutre—its smoothness or roughness, hardness, sharpness—and she feels its resistance and its yielding to the pressure of her tongue; and in her gum she feels the effect upon her gum of the tooth's movement. Her attention to the tooth takes the form of her attentively feeling, with her tongue and her gum, these features and actions of the tooth. She has a tactual form of awareness of some of her tooth's present features. It is not possible for one's sensory attention to be held by one's tooth (or by any physical object) and not be held by a specific feature of it.

Our sensory attention can be held by other features of a tooth than its being loose. For example, a tooth's aching may hold our attention. When my attention is held by my tooth's aching it is held by my tooth. When the child's tooth holds her attention through its motion, her attention takes the form of sensory awareness caused by the action of sensory receptors within the gum and the tongue. When my tooth holds my attention through its aching, my attention takes the form of sensory awareness caused by the action of sensory receptors located within the tooth itself. But one's attention can be held by one's tooth only in virtue of being held by some feature of the tooth. With a loose tooth, it is the motion of the tooth that strikes our attention, and other features, such as shape and texture, play their part in holding our attention.

To what feature of the tooth is attention given when the tooth holds our attention in virtue of its aching? Not to the tooth's shape or texture or motion, not to its color, its taste, smell or sound, not to its weight or pressure or action upon some other structure in the mouth, nor to anything perceived through perceiving any of these features. For no other sensory modality than the single one that mediates pain is involved. And it seems that the single feature of the tooth that holds our attention is the tooth's aching. Again the form of this attention is called "feeling": we feel the tooth by feeling it ache. The tooth's aching here plays the role that the tooth's moving plays in one's tactual awareness of a loose tooth.

I have described two forms of perceptual awareness of a tooth in the mouth.

Why say there are two forms of perceptual awareness here? Both are instances of feeling the tooth's presence in the mouth. Both are properly labeled "perceptual" in virtue of their comprising a knowledge gained through the sense organs of the presence in public space of a physical object that contributes to its own detection by its causal action upon these same organs. In the one instance, the motion of the loose tooth affects the sense receptors in the tongue and gum; in the other, the abnormal condition of the pulp of the tooth affects the sense receptors located within the tooth itself; both effects of the tooth on the sense receptors cause the person who has the interesting tooth to become aware of the presence in his mouth of a single physical object, his loose and moving tooth or his diseased and aching tooth. Why speak of two forms of sense-perceptual awareness rather than of one?

There is good reason for speaking of two forms. Feeling the loose tooth move is an exercise of the sense of touch: the receptor organs of the sense of touch are located within the tissue of various bodily structures and are responsive to mechanical pressure (from objects external to these structures) which causes deformation of tissue; and the action of these receptors causes sense perception of the pressing objects by causing perception of these objects' pressure. Feeling the abscessed tooth ache is an exercise of the sense of pain: the receptor organs of the sense of pain are also located within the tissue of various structures of the body, but are responsive not specifically to mechanical pressure and deformation of tissue but to damage or threat of damage to the tissue within which they are embedded; and the activation of these receptors causes sense perception of the bodily structures within which they are embedded by causing perception of the painful condition of these structures, e.g., of their aching. Hence we properly speak of two forms of perceptual awareness of objects before our sense organs.

Let us now begin to focus our attention upon perceiving a tooth through perceiving its aching, which we call "feeling a toothache." What is it about this experience that leads us, upon reflection, often to think of it as not an instance of perceiving the body? It is the fact that within this experience is an experience we think of as merely feeling pain. When we think of feeling a toothache as an instance of feeling pain, the considerations that lead us to think of feeling pain as not an instance of sense-perceiving anything may lead us to think of feeling toothache in the same way. Why does feeling pain not qualify as sense perception of pain?

One way to answer this question is the following. To perceive through the senses a state of an object is to gain knowledge of this state in virtue of the state's contribution to the object's acting causally upon one's sense organs. Rather, this is certainly true of perceiving those states which we think of ourselves as perceiving as directly as any we perceive before our sense organs, and it is that sort of perceived state which is relevant in thinking of pain as a possible object of perception by sense. Thus, if a tooth's motion is to count as a state of the tooth that we perceive in this relatively direct way, then the tooth's motion must cause us, through its action upon our sense organs, to feel its occurrence before those organs.

Suppose that what we feel is inseparable from our feeling. Then it seems certain that what we feel cannot be situated externally to our sense organs and hence cannot so act upon them as to cause us to feel itself; so we cannot be said to perceive it through our senses. But pain and our feeling are inseparable: if the pain exists then we must feel it, and if we seem to ourselves to feel it then the pain exists. Contrast in this respect the motion of the tooth: the tooth may be there and move without our feeling it to move or even to be there; and I may seem to feel a tooth there when none is, or a tooth may feel to me to be moving when it is not. The motion of the tooth is capable of acting upon the receptor organs of the tongue and causing me to perceive itself. So feeling the tooth move can be an instance of gaining through the senses knowledge of the tooth's motion. But my pain is inseparable from my feeling, so it cannot cause me to feel itself by acting upon my sense organs; this feeling, therefore, cannot be an instance of sense perception of the pain that is felt.

When, therefore, we think of feeling a toothache as an instance of feeling pain, we find ourselves thinking of it as not an instance of perceiving something through the senses. The mistake in this way of thinking of toothache should by now be evident. What I sense-perceive in feeling a toothache is not the pain but the tooth. It is because feeling a toothache is an instance of feeling my tooth's presence in my mouth that feeling a toothache is an instance of sense perception of my body, specifically of my tooth. In feeling my tooth move I perceive my tooth by perceiving a state of my tooth, its motion. In feeling a tooth ache I also perceive my tooth by perceiving a state of my tooth, its aching. Perhaps the word 'state' is being used too loosely. If an action of one thing upon another is not to be called a "state," then an aching is not a state of a tooth. For a tooth's aching is undoubtedly an action of the tooth upon the person who has it: it is a way in which the tooth affects this person. But this is a relational property of a tooth. If a person perceives by sense that one thing has a certain relationship to another thing, then he has perceived the first thing by perceiving a (relational) feature of it.

To be sure, we are not yet home free. The feature of a tooth which I have said that we perceive in feeling a toothache does offer difficulties. A tooth's aching is a feature of a tooth that depends for its occurrence upon feeling, in a way that a tooth's moving does not. Therefore an exact account of how this feature of a tooth can be perceived by the senses presents a challenge which a similar account of perceiving a tooth's motion does not present. I shall take up this challenge later in the chapter. For the present I shall rely upon the case that has been made, and upon the reader's good sense, to warrant adopting the working assumption that in (attentively) feeling a toothache we do commonly perceive by sense a particular tooth in our mouth.

Even before carefully stating—let alone trying to solve—the problem of specifying how we can perceive by sense a tooth's aching, I propose now explicitly to make an assumption which will have the effect of making that problem as difficult as it can be made. The assumption was implicit in the reasoning of four paragraphs back. The assumption is this: that the pain we feel in feeling a toothache is *both* an object of our attention—hence something we are conscious *of*—and a state of our consciousness (rather than of our tooth). Intuitive support for this assumption is to be found in remarks made four paragraphs back about the inseparability of the pain felt and the feeling, and in certain connections between feeling, attention, and consciousness. Let me explain.

Motion is separable from the feeling of it: one may have the feeling as of a motion when there is no motion to be felt; and a motion may be there to be felt, yet no one feels it. Pain, however, is not separable from the feeling of it. If one has a feeling as of a pain, then there is a pain and one feels it; if a pain exists at a time, then someone feels it at that time.

From this inseparability of pain and feeling I posit the following consequences, on the indicated grounds. Since the pain we feel is inseparable from our feeling it, it does not belong to the tooth which we also feel: it is not a feature or condition or activity of the tooth. This I assert on the ground that no condition of a tooth at a given moment can always depend for its being such a condition upon our feeling it at that moment. We should not count motion a state of a tooth if its being such a state at a given moment always depended upon our feeling the motion at that moment. We do not rule it out that a property of an object before our sense organs may depend for its being such a property upon its being felt in some particular circumstances, provided that it remains a property of the object on occasions when these circumstances happen not to be realized: being warm may be such a property. We do deny that a feature of a physical object before our sense organs can depend for its being such a feature, at any time whatever and under any circumstances whatever, upon its being felt at that time and in those circumstances. And I have assumed that a pain's existing at any time and in any circumstances does depend upon its being felt at that time in those circumstances.

I further assume as true the following conditional statement and, hence, infer the truth of its consequent from the truth of its antecedent. If pain and feeling are inseparable, then pain when it occurs qualifies the feeling: when we feel a pain we have a pained feeling. Therefore, if we feel a pain in feeling a tooth then in feeling our tooth we have a pained feeling of our tooth. But of course we do not have a "toothed feeling"—the tooth does not belong to the feeling. Nor does the motion belong to the feeling when we feel the motion of a tooth.

Let us now take notice of the connection between feeling and certain sensory forms of attention and of consciousness.

Suppose a loose tooth suddenly attracts my attention. What form does this attention take? In what does this attention consist? It consists in my suddenly becoming conscious of the motion of my tooth. What sort of consciousness is this? It is not merely mental consciousness: I do not suddenly begin merely to *think* of my tooth. It is sensory consciousness; specifically, it is feeling the motion of my tooth. Suddenly I feel my tooth move. My attention to my tooth takes the form of my feeling my tooth move. Attention to the motion of my tooth, sensory consciousness of this motion, (attentively) feeling my tooth move: these are the same state of affairs described in three different ways.

Suppose a tooth's aching suddenly commands my attention. What form does this attention take? In what does this attention consist? It consists *in part* in my attention's suddenly being held by a pain. And what form does this latter attention take? In what does it consist? My attention to my pain consists in my being conscious of the pain. What sort of consciousness is this? It is not merely mental consciousness. I do not suddenly begin merely to *think* of pain. It is sensory consciousness; specifically it is feeling the pain. Suddenly I feel a pain. My attention to my tooth's aching consists in part in my attention to a pain. My attention to this pain takes the form of my being conscious of it. My being conscious of this pain takes the form of my feeling it. Attention to my pain, sensory consciousness of this pain, (attentively) feeling the pain: these are the same state of affairs described in three ways.

I think that what I have just written of pain, attention, and feeling is true. Intuitively it appears to be evident. Yet because of difficulties to which assumption of its truth leads, it may be denied in some part. I do not wish to argue further for it here. I shall assume it is true, in order to follow out its implications.

From the inseparability of pain and our feeling I have just now drawn the conclusion that pain qualifies our feeling when we feel pain. If pain qualifies our feeling of it and if our feeling pain is identical with our being conscious of it and our attending to it, then pain qualifies our consciousness and our attention, when these are directed upon pain. If we are conscious in a sensory way of a tooth's aching, then, since this includes our being conscious of a pain, pain qualifies our consciousness of our tooth: our awareness of our tooth is a pained awareness. (Our attention to our tooth is a pained attention.) And these attributions are to be taken literally. A pain is a feature, a condition, a state of our consciousness. It is not a state of a tooth.

As an ·upshot of my assumptions and arguments I have now drawn this picture of feeling a toothache: It is an instance of sense perception of a tooth. It includes within itself sensory awareness of a pain. However, sensory awareness of pain is not an instance of sense perception of pain, since its being so would require what the pain is a state of to be capable of acting upon the sense organs so as to cause us to become aware of itself; and this consciousness cannot do. Unlike the motion we feel when we feel a tooth move, which of course is not a conscious state of ours, the pain we feel when we feel a tooth ache is a conscious state. In being conscious of an aching tooth we are conscious of a pain, and the pain we are conscious of is—at least partly constitutes—a state of our consciousness.

Since the pain we are aware of is not before the sense organs, indeed partly constitutes our conscious state, we are *directly* aware of it. Our awareness of pain is not mediated by awareness of something else. On the other hand, the tooth we are conscious of *is* (most of it) before the receptor organs by means of which we perceive it, since the latter are sensory nerve endings embedded within the tooth.

Since we perceive the tooth by perceiving its aching, it now becomes clear that we perceive the tooth in virtue of our sensory awareness of pain. We might have become conscious of this very pain without becoming conscious of a tooth's aching; but we cannot become in a sensory way conscious of a tooth's aching without becoming conscious of a pain; hence consciousness of the tooth is not necessary for sensory consciousness of the pain, but the latter is necessary for attentive perception of the tooth through the sense of pain. Furthermore, the tooth is before the sense organs, the pain is not, and in fact the pain partially constitutes our conscious state itself. We are, therefore, indirectly conscious of the tooth in virtue of our direct consciousness of pain. Direct awareness of pain mediates indirect awareness of a tooth. As I have described it, the structure of our sense perception of an aching tooth is indirectly realistic.

A few pages back I mentioned a difficulty which I proposed first to make as formidable as possible before facing up to it. I am still not ready to try to meet the difficulty, but it is time to put it more explicitly before us.

By contrast with the sense of touch, the content of perception affected through the sense of pain seems simple. When one feels a loose tooth the feature of the tooth that holds one's attention may be its motion, but its hardness, smoothness or roughness, resistance to pressure, shape, and perhaps other features of the tooth figure also among the qualities of which we may become tactually conscious. When, however, one feels a tooth aching no other feature of the tooth than its aching seems to present itself in a sensory form. If the tooth is to hold one's sensory attention some feature of the tooth must hold it. When the sense of pain is the sole vehicle of perception, it seems that reflection offers no choice of feature to specify as the one that holds our attention: this feature, it seems, can be nothing but the tooth's aching. Apparently we perceive by sense a tooth's aching condition. This, however, is none too easy a thing to do. It is the subjectivity of pain that gives trouble. It does so in two ways.

I can begin to elicit the first problem by asking what an aching in a tooth appears, to our sense of pain, to be.

Suppose one asked oneself what the movement of a loose tooth appears to the sense of touch (using the tongue) to be. One might answer that it appears to be a movement—what else? Perhaps the "what else?" could be answered thus: it appears to be a yielding by the tooth to the felt pressure of the tongue upon the tooth. A pressure on the tongue is felt, and one also feels a corresponding displacement of the source of the pressure, as one's tongue pushes the tooth. That's how the motion of the tooth is felt. But in this fact no problem presents itself to the account of this affair as perception of motion, since the physical motion of the tooth is in fact a displacement away from the tongue of a center of resistance to the pressure of the tongue. What here appears to be the case is the case. The tooth is as it feels to be. Appearances here present no obvious obstacle to this condition upon perception: that it must know how it is with the tooth. (We shall need to wait until Chapter Seven to discover whether there is a less-than-obvious obstacle.) What of the appearance that an aching in a tooth presents to the sense of pain?

To the only sense here involved, the aching condition of the tooth presents a very simple appearance. It presents itself as a pained condition of the tooth. The aching of the tooth presents itself to our sense as the pain of the tooth. Putting the matter the other way round: we feel pain as if it belongs to the tooth. There seems to be nothing more to the way in which the aching of the tooth sensibly appears to us than as a pain belonging to the tooth.

Partly through argument and partly by stipulation backed by intuition, it has been posited that pain does not belong to the tooth. If we perceive the aching condition of the tooth we do so by feeling a pain as if it were this aching condition of the tooth; yet the pain is no condition of the tooth. So what we feel as if it were the aching condition of the tooth cannot be that—provided that the aching condition *is* a condition of the tooth: what is not a condition of the tooth cannot be identical with what is one. Here, then, lies the first difficulty in conceiving our feeling a toothache as our sense-perceiving the tooth: if it is perception of the tooth, then it must involve perception of the aching condition of the tooth; but since the pain we feel as if it were the aching condition of the tooth is no condition of the tooth, any claim we make to be perceiving the aching condition of the tooth would seem to be mistaken. There is our first difficulty. Here is the second. To solve the first difficulty we need first to decide what an aching of a tooth really is, in order then to inquire whether or not we could know its presence on the basis of an admittedly deceptive appearance. I shall not just yet try to answer the question that follows upon settling what an aching really is. However, another difficulty arises when we analyze aching.

With the situation pictured as I have drawn it, it is clear that an aching condition of a tooth consists at least in part in the tooth's causing us to feel pain. (At least in part) that's what the aching of the tooth is. It seems to follow that if we are to perceive the aching of the tooth then we must perceive the tooth to be causing us to feel pain. For a tooth's causing something is a (relational) property of a tooth. And to perceive a property of a tooth (or of anything else) one must perceive *that* the tooth (or other thing) has the property. That's what perceiving a property of an object is. This brings us, at last, to the second difficulty.

Feeling a pain is being conscious of a pain. A tooth's causing us to feel a pain is, therefore, the same thing as a tooth's causing us to be conscious of a pain. Feeling a toothache can constitute (attentive) sense perception of a tooth only if it consists in being in a sensory way conscious of the aching condition of a tooth. Therefore feeling a toothache consists in attentively perceiving a tooth only if it consists in being conscious of the tooth's causing us to be conscious of pain. Even the simplest form of feeling a toothache will, therefore, include being conscious of being caused to be conscious of something. This is to say that even the simplest instance of feeling a toothache involves being conscious *of* being conscious of something. This seems implausible. Its implausibility constitutes the second obstacle I mentioned which stands in the way of our fully explaining how we can have a sense perception of the aching condition of a tooth. Unless we can meet this difficulty we cannot, it so far seems, hold the view that feeling a toothache is sense-perceiving a tooth. For the latter requires perceiving a feature of the tooth, and its aching condition seems to be the only feature that offers itself.

I shall return to these two difficulties. Until I do so I shall continue to assume that in feeling a toothache we do perceive our tooth and that, hence, we do succeed in sense-perceiving the aching condition of the tooth. I shall assume that the two difficulties can be overcome. However, I shall be in a better position to overcome them if I first explore more fully how to make coherent the indirectly realistic structure that my mix of assumptions and arguments has yielded as characterizing our sensory consciousness of a tooth as aching. In this exploration the assumption that the two difficulties just discussed can be solved amounts to the decision to treat the realistic component of this conscious structure as, for the moment, unproblematic. What we need to explore, then, is how to make coherent for ourselves the indirect aspect of this indirectly realistic structure. The indirection is constituted by the fact that we are conscious of the tooth only through the mediation of our more direct—indeed our absolutely direct—consciousness of pain. And the first puzzle sure to bother the philosopher here is what it can mean to say that a state of consciousness includes a consciousness of its own character.

3. How a Conscious State Can Be a Consciousness of Its Own Character

In feeling a toothache we are conscious of a pain. This pain is not, as it seems to us in feeling it, a condition of the tooth. It is a condition of our consciousness. In being conscious of a pain we are conscious of a condition or state of this very consciousness. The pain we are conscious of could also be said to be a quality of this consciousness: being in a certain condition or state is having a certain feature, and some features it is natural to speak of as "qualities." To be in a pained state of consciousness is to be in a conscious state that is specified by a pained quality. In what terms can we explain what it comes to for a pained condition of consciousness to obtain? One way to do this would be to explain the *function* of this condition within a larger conscious structure. This I shall do.

One function that a pained state of consciousness performs is being a motivator. In virtue of having a pained state of consciousness I am moved to do something that I believe will eliminate that state—for example, to go to a dentist. Its role in thus influencing one's behavior helps explain what it comes to for pain to constitute a conscious state. However, it is from pain's cognitive function that a more pertinent light can be expected.

Pain is normally felt in the context of feeling a hurting bodily part. In feeling a toothache we are conscious of pain as if it specifies a condition of a tooth, which it does not. We are thus conscious of a pained condition of our consciousness as if it were a pained condition of our tooth. How is this to be understood?

To be conscious in a sensory way of a tooth one must be in this way conscious of a feature of a tooth. To be conscious of a feature of a tooth is (among other things) to know that the tooth has this feature. To know that something a has the feature B, one must be in possession of the truth that a is B. To be in possession of the truth that a is B, one must do something like—or be in a state like—affirming that a is B. To do—or be in—this last, one must do something like attributing B to a. Hence to be in a sensory way conscious of a tooth one must do something like—or be in a state like—*attributing* a sensible feature to this tooth. I conclude that in feeling a toothache we must "do" something like this: *attribute* to the tooth a pained condition.

If I told him about it another person could become aware of my toothache. He too would then know that my tooth aches. Of him too we could then say that he makes something like an affirmation that my tooth aches and, hence, that he does something like attribute pain to my tooth or to me. But his awareness of my toothache is mental awareness of it, not sensory awareness; his affirmation is mental, not sensory; his attribution of the pain to my tooth or to me is a mental, not a sensuous attribution. On the other hand, my awareness of my tooth's aching is a sensory awareness: affirmation that the tooth aches is therefore a sensory affirmation, and my attribution of the pain to the tooth is (let us call it) a sensuous attribution.

I draw this conclusion: what it comes to for us to be conscious of a pained condition of our consciousness as if it were a pained condition of our tooth is for us *sensuously* to *attribute* to the tooth the pain that specifies our conscious state. In feeling a toothache the pained condition of our consciousness of the tooth *functions* as the content of our sensuous attribution of a pained condition to the tooth.

In functioning as the content of a sensuous attribution of a feature to a tooth, the pained quality represents its own character as the character of the tooth. The sufferer sensuously attributes to his tooth a character that is available for his attribution in virtue of being exemplified by his conscious state. One represents to oneself a condition of one's tooth by the method of exemplification.[1]

This method of representation is analogous to the method used by a painter who represents the red color of a brick house by exemplifying on his canvas the red that the painting pictorially attributes to the house. The color on the canvas represents itself as the color of a real house. So, too, the pain of our consciousness represents itself as the condition of a tooth.

How does attention figure in this account of feeling a toothache? What immediately holds our attention is the pain, which is a condition of our consciousness. But this pain to which we attend functions as the sensuous content of an attribution of itself *to* the tooth. Hence our attention reaches the tooth. This attention *to* is nothing but consciousness *of*. Hence also our consciousness, of which our pain is an interior "object" and thereby a condition, "reaches the tooth"—it is consciousness of the tooth. The attribution to a tooth of a sensuous condition of consciousness (pain) carries to the tooth the attention that is directed to this sensuous condition. We are directly conscious of the sensuous content of our attribution of a condition to the tooth and, thereby, indirectly conscious of the tooth.

Let us return to the contrast between the sensuous sort of attribution of pain to a tooth and the mental sort.

If a second person concludes from my remarks and other behavior that I have a toothache, then either in speech or in silent thought he may attribute pain to my tooth but will probably attribute it to me. His attribution is not sensuous. It is a conceptual attribution: in making it he exercises only his *concept* of pain. The content of his attribution is the content of a mere concept of pain. In applying his mere idea of pain to me he thus becomes only mentally aware of pain as if in me. The condition he has ascribed to me is indeed a sensuous condition of my consciousness: in thought he ascribes to me the same condition I feel. But only the thought of this condition figures in fixing the character of *his* conscious state, not the condition itself.

Now return to me, suffering a toothache. I too am attributing pain (to my tooth) . But for me the pain itself is sensuously present in the consciousness within which it is attributed. I am

1. Here I have been influenced by Nelson Goodman's account of reference by exemplification. See *Languages of Art* (Indianapolis: Hackett Publishing Company, 1976) , pp 52–67.

not applying to my tooth my concept of pain. This would be merely to think of my tooth as pained. Within my consciousness of my tooth I am representing the pain by exemplifying it there: pain itself is instantiated in a conscious state and thereby represents itself as the condition of my tooth. In this way I more than merely think of my tooth as if pained: I feel it so.

It may be useful to contrast the sufferer's sensuous ascription of pain to his tooth with his own mental ascription of the same. This can be done by applying to the present case another theory of perception and, thereby, also contrasting that theory with the present one. This contrast should favor the present account. However, one fruit of turning to this other theory will be the emergence of a new candidate for the genuine feature of the tooth which one perceives in feeling toothache. In the next section this candidate will be taken seriously.

In *A Materialist Theory of the Mind*, D. M. Armstrong characterizes sense perception of an object before the sense organs as nothing but gaining a belief about the object as a result of causal action by the object upon the sense organs. If this account is to apply to sensory consciousness, then the belief acquired must be a consciously held belief. Feeling a toothache comes out looking like this: by its action upon the sensory nerve endings within the tooth, the abnormal physical condition of the tooth—disease or damage—causes the tooth's owner to gain the belief that something is wrong with his tooth. This belief causes him distress, in this sense only: he feels an aversion to having the belief. So he tries to relieve himself of this belief by trying to eliminate its cause, the physical trouble ascribed to the tooth.

By this account the sufferer's perception of trouble in his tooth consists in (gaining) a consciously held belief that there is trouble in the tooth. But consciously believing that there is trouble in one's tooth is no more than consciously thinking that there is trouble in the tooth. Apart from its causal history, as a conscious state this belief is indistinguishable from the conscious state of the dentist who observes to himself that his patient has trouble in his tooth. Even if we add that the patient further believes that his belief about trouble in his tooth is in some rather direct way caused by the trouble itself, whereas the dentist has no such belief about the causation of his own belief about his patient's tooth, even so, the patient's conscious state is in the following respect exactly like the dentist's: both are merely *thinking* that there is trouble in a certain tooth. Both are applying to this tooth the mere idea of trouble. Both are *conceptually* attributing trouble to the tooth. Neither, therefore, has been described as feeling pain as if of the tooth. We shall have described the latter condition only if we characterize the patient, but not the dentist, as ascribing trouble to the tooth by *sensuously* attributing pain to it.

It is necessary to suppose that the content of the patient's attribution of trouble to his tooth is not merely the content of an *idea* of trouble (or even of pain) but is the condition, pain itself, actually characterizing his consciousness of his tooth, functioning there as a sensuous content of a sensuous attribution of trouble to a tooth. Now the patient but not the dentist *feels* the tooth, by *feeling* trouble in the tooth.

For the philosopher resisting indirect realism it is of no avail to try to locate the pain in the aversion we have to a belief that there is trouble in a tooth. Aversion to mere thoughts is not aversion to pain; even less is it pain itself. Aversion to (gaining) a mere belief about trouble (or even about pain) in one's tooth is nothing but aversion to the thought one is having about one's tooth—or at most it is aversion to gaining this thought because of the real trouble one is merely thinking of. The pain itself has dropped out of this account. As an account of toothache it therefore fails.

The importance for a theory of sense perception of the idea of *sensuous attribution* of a feature to an object before our sense organs cannot be exaggerated. After first making several assumptions, I have presented this notion as specifying the difference between one sort of sensory awareness of such an object and any merely mental awareness of the same object. It will be a principal thesis of this book that in this respect all other sensory modes of awareness of physical objects resemble the pained mode as here described.

4. The Feature of a Tooth which we
   Perceive in Feeling a Toothache

I have now to show that our sense perception of our tooth is realistic. To do this I must show that we perceive by the sense of pain a genuine feature of the tooth. Earlier I remarked that the only candidate for this feature which seems to suggest itself is the tooth's aching. And I remarked that this candidate suffers from the following two defects. First, it would seem that we perceive the aching condition of the tooth as if it is a pained condition of the tooth; but pain is not a condition of the tooth; so the pained condition cannot be the aching condition, if the latter *is* a condition of the tooth: it seems that we have failed to perceive a condition of the tooth. Second, since a tooth's aching consists in its causing us to feel pain, to perceive its aching is to perceive that it is causing us to be conscious of (to feel) pain. Hence (attentively) to perceive a tooth's aching is to be conscious of being conscious of something. And this requirement that even the simplest feeling a toothache should be an instance of iterated consciousness seems implausible.

The reason why a tooth's aching seemed to be the only feature of a tooth that we can perceive by the sense of pain was that such perception is mediated by direct awareness of pain, and it seemed that the only genuine feature of a tooth that pain might represent for us is a tooth's causing us pain, i.e., its aching.

However, the second problem just mentioned is so hard to solve that an alternative candidate for the perceived feature of the tooth would be welcome. I believe that there is another condition of the tooth that one can perceive through the mediation of one's awareness of pain: the condition I described in the previous section as something being wrong with the tooth, or trouble in the tooth. This feature was suggested by applying to toothache an account of perception as gaining mere belief about the cause of one's belief. Since pain drops out of the picture on that theory of perception, the awareness of a tooth described by the theory is not sensory awareness, not feeling the tooth. I shall try to show that trouble in the tooth is a condition of the tooth which we can perceive through the sense of pain—can *feel*.

Because it still seems true both that a tooth's aching is a condition of the tooth *and* that we have sensory awareness of this aching, it seems reasonable still to expect that one can explain how it is possible for us to sense-perceive a tooth's aching. I shall try to do this, but only after (and with some help from) showing that we can by feeling pain feel something wrong with the tooth.

I begin by developing more carefully the reason why one must, in one's account of our pain-perception of a tooth's condition, take seriously the causal relationship between that condition and our perception of it.

Before a person's tooth begins to ache he knows that his tooth exists where it exists. But he is not conscious of his tooth. He may, however, become conscious of his tooth merely by beginning to think of it. Perhaps he is looking at an old dentist's bill and is reminded of work the dentist did on this tooth. The knowledge he has of the existence in his mouth of this tooth is "activated," and he begins to think of the tooth: his new awareness of his tooth takes the form of his beginning to think of it. This is not sensory awareness of his tooth. It is mental awareness of it.

Now consider the pained mode of becoming aware of one's tooth. A person knows his tooth is in his mouth in a certain place, but he is not presently conscious of it. It begins to ache. He becomes conscious of pain that seems to him to belong to his tooth. The pain of which he is conscious as if of a condition of his tooth is in fact not a condition of the tooth. However, he already knows, before feeling pain, that his tooth does exist in this place. So we conclude that he has become conscious of his tooth. Furthermore, since he is conscious of his tooth in virtue of feeling pain as if of the tooth, we further conclude that he has sensory awareness of his tooth: he *feels* the tooth's presence in his mouth. So we imagine ourselves reasoning.

This will not do. If we describe a man as merely hallucinating a sensible feature of a tooth then we have not described him as achieving sense perception of his tooth. And the account just given describes no more than such a hallucination. Consider an analogous situation.

A man is sitting at his dining table going over bills. Fifteen minutes ago he turned on the air conditioner in the living room. His son, who likes his rooms cool, is sitting in the living room playing the guitar. The man knows his son would tell him if the air conditioner suddenly went off, which it has never done. So he knows the air conditioner is running. However he is not thinking of it, so he is not presently conscious of its running. Now he comes across the bill for electricity; this causes him to think of the presently running air conditioner (which he cannot hear and whose cooling effects he cannot yet feel in the dining room) : he becomes conscious of the air conditioner's presently running. His being conscious of its running takes the form of his thinking of its running. It is not sensory awareness, it is mental awareness of the machine.

Suppose instead that the man did not come across a bill that would make him think of the air conditioner but walked into the living room and began to hear the air conditioner operating. At this moment he becomes conscious of the air conditioner's running in the living room. Now his consciousness takes the form of his hearing the machine run—a sensory form of awareness.

Now suppose a third case. The air conditioner's operation is (to humans) entirely silent. Sitting in the dining room it is not possible for him to hear the machine running. He does not come across an electricity bill that starts him thinking of the air conditioner. But he does, as before, know, while sitting in the dining room, that the air conditioner is running, without being presently conscious of its running. Now he seems to hear a sound which seems to him to be the sound of the air conditioner. So he does now become conscious of the air conditioner's running in the living room. However, this apparent sound is purely hallucinatory, it exists only "in his mind."

I think this much is evident: in this third case no one would hold that the man *hears* the air conditioner running, since the machine runs without making a humanly audible sound. But, other than his hearing it, there is no form of sense perception of the air conditioner which we have reason to ascribe to him. Therefore we must conclude that his awareness of the machine is not sensory.

Suppose we allow that in this third case the man does become aware of the air conditioner's running. Our reason has to be that his seeming to hear the machine running is either an instance of or an occasion for his beginning to think of the air conditioner, like the occasion provided by his coming across an electricity bill: we view him as coming to think of a state of affairs he already knows to obtain but to which he had not before been giving thought. We remain firm in denying that he hears the machine running, hence in denying that he has sensory awareness of the machine.

The same principle must be applied to the person who seems to feel pain in his tooth although there is no pain there. If we limit ourselves to this aspect of the situation, treating his seeming to feel pain in his tooth as pure hallucination, then, although we may allow that he becomes conscious of something he already knew, the presence of his tooth in his mouth, we can do so only because we think of his seeming to feel a pain in his tooth as either an instance of or the occasion for his coming to think of the presence of a tooth he already knew to be there. We cannot on these grounds justify saying that he *feels* his tooth's presence in his mouth.

We nonetheless do believe that he does achieve sensory awareness of his tooth, that he feels its presence in his mouth. So it seems that our idea of the situation is not adequately expressed by an account in terms of purely hallucinatory awareness of pain as if in a tooth. It must be that the analogy provided by the man who seems to hear the operation of an actually silent machine is seriously imperfect. And of course we know that it is.

For there is no causal connection whatever between what the man seems to hear and what is happening in the air conditioner. Whereas we know that there is the closest causal connection between what the sufferer seems to feel in his tooth and the actual condition of his tooth. For the damaged or diseased condition of his tooth is the cause of his feeling pain as if in the tooth. So let us now take this causal relationship into account.

What causes the sufferer to feel pain as if in his tooth is this: the tooth's being diseased or damaged. The tooth's being diseased or damaged is an instance of there being something wrong with the tooth. Something's being wrong with the tooth can also correctly be said to cause the person who has this tooth to feel pain as if in it.

Furthermore, whenever a person feels pain as if in his tooth he feels something to be wrong with his tooth. For us, to feel pain as if in one's tooth is also (in part) to feel something to be wrong with one's tooth. And when this is felt it is generally the case that there is something wrong with one's tooth. There being something wrong with it is, then, the genuine condition of the tooth which one perceives when, suffering from toothache, this condition of the tooth, acting upon the sensory receptors embedded in the tooth, causes one to feel pain as if in the tooth and thereby to perceive something wrong with the tooth. Surely this awareness we have of trouble in our tooth is not a mere thought of trouble, a thought that is in a peculiar way caused by the trouble; it is sensory awareness, since (in addition to its peculiar causation by the trouble) it is an awareness that is partly constituted of *feeling* pain.

The pain does not belong to the tooth, something is wrong with the tooth, and what is wrong with the tooth does, by acting on the receptor organs of the sense of pain, cause the sufferer to feel the pain as if in the tooth and in feeling this to perceive something's being wrong with the tooth. In suffering toothache we perceive a tooth's presence in our mouth by perceiving that condition of the tooth which consists in something's being wrong with the tooth.

That conclusion solves our primary problem. We have found a condition of the tooth that we can perceive by the sense of pain.

In reaching this solution, however, I stopped trying to make out a tooth's aching as a feature of the tooth which we perceive in feeling toothache. Something's being wrong with the tooth replaced the tooth's aching as the genuine condition of the tooth which I undertook to show that we perceive by the sense of pain. However, I should still like to show that we can perceive the tooth's aching, now relying upon the fact that we perceive trouble in the tooth.

Before attempting this, I want to pause to make sure that—within the framework I have constructed—I have been justified in characterizing the direct object of our indirect awareness of the tooth—the pain—as a *representation* of the trouble in the tooth. Is it certain that the indirectly realistic account of a bodily sensation which I have now given is also a representational account?

Let us begin with another imperfect analogy: I turn the handle of the kitchen water faucet to the "off" position, and I see that a small stream of water continues to flow from the faucet. I push the handle hard, making it as tightly "off" as possible. The small stream of water continues to flow. I now see that there is something wrong with the (presently invisible) valve that controls the flow of water. I do not see what is wrong—perhaps a worn-out washer—but I do see that something is wrong with it. I see this by seeing the water flow in circumstances in which I know that the handle has been turned tight in the "off" position. In these circumstances, in seeing the water flow I perceive something's being wrong with the faucet valve.

However, it would certainly be an unnatural, forced way of speaking to describe this perceived stream of water flowing from the faucet as serving for me as a visual representation—as a picture—of the trouble in the faucet. I am perfectly conscious of the stream of water as one thing, the trouble in the valve as another; of the second as the cause, the first as its effect. I do not visually treat the character of the flowing water as specifying the character of the trouble in the valve: I do not perceive the valve to be either watery or flowing. Indeed it is natural and probably correct to say of me that from the flowing water I infer as a cause something wrong with the valve. The evidence, the stream of water, is certainly not functioning for me as a picture of the cause I infer from it, of the fault in the valve.

Now come back to the person suffering from a toothache. He perceives that something is wrong with his tooth. But does he perceptually attribute some specific condition to the tooth as the something that is wrong with it? Or is this trouble in the tooth quite indeterminably specified within his sense perception of the tooth, merely as "something wrong there"? And does he infer this something wrong in the tooth from the pain he feels, rather in the manner of the person who infers trouble in the faucet from seeing the water flow after the handle has been turned off?

The answer to these questions is given by the fact that the sufferer from toothache feels pain as if belonging to the tooth. The condition of the tooth which consists in there being something wrong with it he perceives as the condition, pain. A pained condition—this is what he sensuously attributes to the tooth as the trouble in it. Since, as a sufferer of a toothache, he involuntarily and sensuously attributes the pain itself to his tooth, it is evident that he does not infer the presence of this pain as if in his tooth—from what? There is not room here for an inference to the pain, which presents itself from the start as in the tooth.

Because we perceive the trouble in our tooth as having the form of pain, it is proper to speak of the pain belonging to our sensory consciousness as a representation for us of the something that is wrong with the tooth. The pain does represent for us this trouble. It is a sensuous representation of the trouble in the tooth.

Now, however, we have another problem. Since our representation of the trouble in the tooth is a misrepresentation, our perception of our tooth appears to be a misperception.

5. Sensory Illusion and Conceptual Accuracy:
   Conceptual Attribution in Feeling a Toothache

As the word 'misperceive' more than suggests, the fact that we misperceive an object does not entail that we fail to perceive it. On the contrary, it implies that we do perceive the misperceived object. So too with misrepresentation: a misrepresented object is a represented object. Hence, my affirming that our sensuous representation of trouble in the tooth misrepresents this trouble does not force me to withdraw the claim that feeling a toothache is realistic perception of a tooth. However, for this perception to be realistic, it is necessary that in feeling a toothache one perceive, as it is, a genuine feature of a physical tooth located in public space. Therefore, although I am not trying to *prove* indirect realism's truth for this case, to show how it *can* be true nonetheless requires explaining exactly how—on the present account—it happens that, in spite of a sensuous misrepresentation of the trouble in the tooth, we nonetheless do perceptually represent as it is a condition of the tooth. This explanation is my present task.

Suppose that by some sudden movement I rip the achilles tendon of my right foot, but I do not know that this is what has happened. I feel no pain, but immediately I notice that there are things I normally do with my foot that I cannot now do. I judge that something is wrong with my foot. The content of this judgment has two components, one functional, one structural. In judging that something is wrong with my foot I am judging that there is a new structural abnormality of some kind in my foot and that this has the effect of preventing certain actions normally possible for my foot. I do not know what the structural abnormality is, i.e., that it is a ripped achilles tendon. I do nonetheless get it right in judging that there is a structural abnormality, something that needs to be corrected (or to correct itself) if my foot is to regain its normal functions. Since, we may suppose, I have no sensory clues to the nature of the structural abnormality, this component of my judgment consists primarily in the exercise of concepts. Prominent is the concept, "structural abnormality."

In feeling a toothache I may, but need not, perceive a functional failure: the tooth may be as capable as ever of playing its part in chewing. Suppose I do not perceive such a failure. Nonetheless, because of the aversion I have to the pain I feel, I do judge that there is something wrong with the tooth. I judge that there is a structural abnormality. Pain itself does not have as part of its content "structural abnormality in a tooth"; but pain caused by trouble in a tooth does, in mature percipients, cause us to make a perceptual judgment having that content. I conclude that this perceptual judgment involves the exercise of concepts, prominently the concept having as its content something like "structural abnormality," and the concept of a tooth.

This is a perceptual judgment; the exercise of concepts is here part of the sense perception of the tooth. Otherwise the pain we feel we could not experience as if it were what is wrong with the tooth, since the pain does not contain within itself the content, "structural abnormality of a tooth."

Our perceptual objectification of the pain, whereby we "make" it into a representation of trouble in the tooth, is effected, I suggest, by a kind of "fusion" of a pain with a concept of a tooth and a concept of a structural abnormality in the tooth. We conceptualize this pain as belonging to a *tooth,* and we conceptualize the pain as a structural abnormality in the tooth. In saying this I do not mean to say that we form a concept *of* the pain. Rather that, by "mixing" with the pain a conceptual element, we make of the pain a sensuous component in a mongrel "sensuous-conceptual" representation of a structural abnormality in the tooth. In short, we impose upon the pain, considered as the sensuous matter or stuff of a representation of a state, a partially conceptual form, so that the fusion of sensuous and conceptual representation yields consciousness of the pain as if of a structural abnormality in a particular tooth in the mouth. The conceptual element in this perceptual representation of the tooth depicts things as they are. There is a tooth in that place in the mouth, and it does have a structural abnormality. So far this perceptual judgment is veridical in the same way that my merely mental judgment that my foot has a structural abnormality (when my achilles tendon is torn) is veridical. In the latter case, however, there is no affirmation of the specific character of the abnormality, hence there is no misrepresentation. In feeling a toothache I do represent for myself the specific character of the abnormality: as pain. To this extent I misrepresent—and misperceive—the condition of the tooth. This is the element of sensory illusion. Nonetheless, although I get something wrong I get as much right as I do in the merely mental judgment about my foot. In feeling a toothache I commit myself to more than I do in judging the condition of my foot. In that more that I sensuously affirm, I am mistaken. But being partly wrong does not keep me from being partly right. And being partly right is quite enough to qualify my experience as realistic perception of trouble in my tooth.

The concepts whose exercise I have just ascribed to the experience of feeling a toothache should not be identified with the capacity to use words or with something dependent upon that capacity. I do not wish to say that in feeling a toothache a person without language could not perceive this tooth. How are we to think of these concepts?

First a word about the imprecision of the verbal expression of such perceptual concepts. To say that the matter contributed by my pained consciousness to a representation of a tooth is given "objective form" by a concept, "structural abnormality," is merely to hint at something like the following. The concept of a material object, a tooth, is fused with the sensuous content, pain, the two linked together by either the conceptual or the sensuous content, "belonging to" or "of"; that character of pain which accounts for our aversion to feeling it is then sufficient for it to seem to constitute, to our perception, a defect, a bad condition *of the tooth*. To put it another way: there is a concept, "tooth," which needs joined with it only a sensuous representation of an aversive quality in order to become a representation of objective trouble in the tooth, a defect, a deficiency that belongs to the tooth, hence to become a representation of what I have called a "structural abnormality" in the tooth. What is this concept of a tooth which is independent of the use of words (or may be so) ? I take it that perceptual concepts of parts of our body are powers of representing such parts for the purposes of action alone. They are what make it possible for us to map out in advance strategies of action directed toward particular parts of our body. If a person with a damaged ankle can figure out in advance a noninstinctual plan of action for treating specifically his ankle, then he is, in making this plan, exercising a concept of his ankle. Of course for all we presently know a sensuous representation might serve a similar function. A careful treatment of the differences between these two modes of representation must await the final chapter of the book. For the moment I rely simply upon introspective assurance that pains merely as such do not include within their content such representational elements as "ankle," "tooth," "skin," and the like.

6. How We Can Sense-perceive a Tooth's Aching

I want now to give my solution to this question: How can we, by means of the sense of pain, perceive the aching of the tooth? It is no longer necessary to solve this problem in order to be assured that we do sense-perceive the tooth in feeling a tooth-ache. For I have provided another genuine condition of the tooth that we do perceive by the sense of pain: something's being wrong with the tooth. However, since I began this chapter by speaking of our perceiving the tooth by perceiving its aching and because it seems so natural to believe we do perceive the aching, I should like to be able to show that we can do this.

It will be remembered that there were two apparent obstacles to our sense-perceiving an aching of a tooth. One of them should now seem less troublesome, since it consists in the need to discover how we could represent a condition (the aching) of a tooth by misrepresenting it (as pain), and we have just seen how one instance of this sort of problem can be solved. The more acute difficulty, therefore, is the second one: since a tooth's aching consists in its causing us to feel pain, it seems that we need to be conscious of being conscious of pain in order to be conscious of a tooth's aching. This seems implausible for the simplest instance of feeling toothache. Let us seek a solution to this second difficulty.

Our problem is to explain how the causation of a certain effect can be perceived by sense. A tooth's aching consists in its causing its owner to feel pain. Our question is this: How can we sense-perceive the tooth's causing us to feel pain?

In being conscious of a tooth's causing a certain effect one must, as a starter, at least be conscious of a part of this effect. The whole effect is one's feeling pain. Is this effect divisible into the pain felt and the feeling of it? Existentially no: neither can occur without the other. But to say this is to say no more than that the pain felt and the feeling are existentially interdependent. This is not the same as to say that they are indistinguishable. Exactly how to understand this particular way of being distinguishable but inseparable I shall not try to explain until Chapter Eight. For now I assume it. But I remark that my having said that the pain qualifies or belongs to our consciousness (our feeling) does not commit me to the indistinguishability of the pain from the consciousness (the feeling). If the way in which the pain belongs to consciousness—specifies a conscious state—is by providing it with its interior object (without which it would not be a conscious state), then the pain may be distinguishable from the consciousness (the feeling) as two elements in a whole, where the whole may get its name from either element, and so either might be described as qualifying the other: the pain is conscious; the consciousness is of pain.

I therefore divide into two components the effect upon us of the diseased tooth: the pain we feel and the feeling of it. And I remark that whereas to be conscious of feeling pain is to be conscious of being conscious of something, to be conscious of pain (to feel it) is not (in the problem-making sense) to be conscious of being conscious of something. My solution is to suggest that in being conscious of pain (feeling it) we are conscious of a part of the effect caused by the tooth; that being conscious of part of an effect can serve for being conscious of the effect; and to suggest that when the way in which one is conscious of a whole effect is by being conscious of a part of it, certain objections to the idea that we are conscious of the whole effect lose their force. That is to say, I am suggesting that we are conscious of the whole effect, feeling pain, by being conscious of a part of this effect, pain itself; and that this way of being conscious of our feeling pain is acceptable as always present in feeling a toothache. Here I appeal to an analogy with vision.

One can see an apple when only a part of the apple is visible. It wouldn't be an apple we see if the apple didn't have insides. But we don't see the insides. In seeing a part we see the whole, but in seeing the whole we don't see other parts which are essential to the whole.

So too I suggest that in being conscious of pain we could be said to be conscious of the whole comprising the components, pain and feeling, but without being conscious of the component, feeling. The effect of the tooth upon us is our feeling pain. We are conscious of this effect in virtue of being conscious of the pain but without thereby being conscious of feeling, hence without being conscious of being conscious.

The question that remains to be answered is this: in order to be conscious of the tooth's causing us pain, what more than the pain must we be conscious of? Since I have argued that this mode of consciousness consists in a mode of representation of our tooth, the question can be given this form: in addition to being directly aware of the pain, what must we represent to ourselves in order to represent the tooth's causing this pain?

An answer to this question based on an accepted general theory of the perception of causation is not available. I shall therefore characterize in a certain way what we do represent to ourselves which might suffice for representation of the causation. Then I shall suggest that it does suffice.

I have so far ignored the fact that, in sensuously representing to ourselves the condition of our tooth as pain, we represent this condition as a kind of activity in the tooth. In perceiving a tooth's motion we represent to ourselves a kind of activity of the tooth, its moving. (Let us suppose this—I've done nothing to show that this perception involves representation.) In sensuously representing to ourselves the condition of our tooth as pain, we also feel this condition of the tooth as a kind of activity in the tooth, as something the tooth is doing. Without introspective inaccuracy we might have called this activity "paining." We didn't. We called it "aching." Earlier I suggested that pain represents trouble in the tooth by being fused with a concept of a structural abnormality in the tooth. Now I suggest that pain represents aching in the tooth by being integrated with a concept of causation by the tooth *of* the pain. This is somewhat analogous to our hearing a bell, say, as ringing: we hear the bell as *making* the sound we hear—we hear the bell as *sounding*. This requires the operation of a concept of causation within the auditory perception of the sound—indeed requires an integration of this concept with a sensuous representation of tonal quality and loudness. The "paining" we feel is analogous to the sounding we hear. Fused with the sensuous representation—the pain—is a concept of an activity of the tooth which consists in "making pain." We perceive the tooth as making a condition of itself, the pain. The pain itself we experience as a "paining," scarcely distinguishing the activity of the tooth from the product of this activity. Surely there is some misrepresentation here. Yet the tooth *is* causing the pain. This we get right.

We can see now that one cannot sharply distinguish our perceiving trouble in the tooth from our perceiving the aching of the tooth. To speak of the first is to emphasize our perception of a *defect* in the tooth; to speak of the second is to emphasize our perception of that *action* of this defect which leads us to perceive the defect *as* a defect.

We can also now see why we feel pain as if *in* the tooth. What we are correctly locating is both the damaged condition of the tooth and the initial phase of the action of this damage (upon the sensory receptors *in* the tooth). Both the damage and its action are in the tooth. But of course both the damage and its action are misrepresented, as "paining."

One problem remains. It is a requirement generated by our concept of the sense perception of a feature of a physical object, where this feature is perceived as directly as any feature of an object before our sense organs, that the feature itself should play a causal role in generating the perception of itself. However, here the feature perceived is already itself an instance of causation: the tooth's causing pain. Can this causation be a cause of our perceiving itself? I think it can.

Our merely feeling pain is not the same thing as our perceiving the tooth or perceiving the aching of the tooth. The latter requires that we conceptually attribute toothhood to the tooth and that we conceptually attribute causation to the tooth. It seems to me not implausible to suppose that the tooth's causing me to feel pain causes me on this occasion to attribute both toothhood and causation (of the pain) to the tooth. In that event the tooth's causing me to feel pain causes (brings into existence) the rest of that conscious state of which feeling pain is but one component, the state of perceptually attributing aching to the tooth. Thereby the tooth's aching—which is its causing me pain—causes me to perceive its aching.

7. Talking and Thinking of Aches versus Feeling Them

In my account of feeling toothache—and by implication of feeling all hurting bodily parts—I have said that there is always misperception. Perceptual error, if you like. Sensuously we ascribe to the tooth or other bodily part pain that does not belong to it.

To some readers it may seem to follow that always in *reporting* our perceptions of hurting bodily parts we make mistakes by *verbally* ascribing pains to these parts. Such an outcome of my view would count against the view's truth. Fortunately my account has no such implication.

When we *say* that a tooth aches I take it that we use the term 'aches' to refer to the kind of event I have said an aching is: the tooth's causing us to feel pain. So too if we *say* that some part of our body hurts we are saying that it causes us to feel pain. Indeed we are saying a little more: that the bodily part causes us to feel pain *as if* in *that* bodily part. Such a remark certainly does not mislocate the pain; it does not ascribe the pain to the bodily part. I see no reason to think that in our thought and talk we are not clear about what an aching or a hurting of a bodily part is. This means that we are more accurate in our thought of aches and hurts than in our sense perception of them. This should be no surprise. One of the primary functions of thought and talk is to improve upon our sense perceptions of things. (Consider physical theory.)

Sometimes in speech we even speak of pain itself as if we were ascribing it to a bodily part. Whereas a hurting or an aching does belong to a bodily part, as a relational feature of it, pain does not. When someone says something like, "There is a constant, throbbing pain in my right toe," I take it that he is engaging in a mere manner of speaking. When a physician asks, "Where is the pain?" I suppose him to mean, "Where do you feel the pain?" And I take the reply, "In my right toe," to mean, "I feel the pain as if in my right toe." So too I read the person who gives the unelicited report, "There is a constant, throbbing pain in my right toe," as saying, "I feel constantly a throbbing pain as if in my right toe." This implies that we are more accurate in our thinking about pain than in our feeling it. This should be no surprise. One of the primary functions of thought is to improve upon our sense impressions of things. And pain is a sense impression of a (hurting) bodily part. A little more surprising perhaps is the implication that we are sometimes more accurate in our thought than our words suggest. But this does not seem to me to be very surprising either, because not uncommon. A person engaged in an experiment on afterimages, who reports, "I see a black and white, striped, rectangular after-image, right there, on the wall," does not mean to assert that there is something on the wall which he sees to be of a certain character. He means to say that the way in which he has the afterimage is as if he were seeing a part of the wall to be of the described character. We use the shorter forms of speech because doing so is convenient.

Chapter Three   SMELL

1. The Argument of This Chapter

I begin with a characterization of odor which I retain throughout most of the chapter. In the last two sections I adopt another way of conceiving odor, and I formulate (and reformulate) the conclusions of the chapter in slightly modified language. The two conceptions of odor yield equivalent descriptions of the facts.

Treating odors as airborne substances, it becomes empirically evident that odors are smelled less indirectly than anything else before the nose. Since the direct realist must therefore hold that it is always some feature of an odor that we directly perceive whenever we smell anything before the nose, to test the truth of his thesis I need first to discover the nature of an odor's sensible character and then to ask whether such a character *can* be directly perceived by smell. Sections 3 and 4 are devoted to the first of these two inquiries. And in §5 I argue that the nature of an odor's sensible character (as settled in §4) is such that it cannot be directly perceived by smell. I conclude that indirect realism is true of smell.

That conclusion, however, is tentative, partly because the account of olfactory awareness it entails needs to be shown to be coherent and partly because an alternative account of odors' sensible characters may be proposed by the direct realist which would, if true, entail the truth of direct realism. So in §§6 and 7 I develop in detail the direct realist's account of odors' sensible characters. And in §8 this account is criticized and rejected. However, the argument of §8 can be developed more perspicuously in connection with heat and cold; so here I merely sketch the argument, postponing the full presentation to the next chapter. After introducing in §9 a new characterization of odor, in §10 I complete the indirectly realistic account of smell begun in §5.

2. The Nature of Odors, and Direct Realism's Thesis

One can find in a dictionary the following three definitions of the verb 'to smell': (1) to be or become aware of by means of the nose, (2) to inhale the odor of, (3) (intransitive) to give out an odor. I use the verb transitively in the first sense and intransitively in a richer sense than the third one. (2) is of interest as reflecting our experience of objects' odors as carried to us by the air we breathe. And (3) reflects our experience of odors as given off into the air by the objects that have them. It seems that a concept of odor that matches our sensory experience of odors and comports with some of our ways of talking of them could specify an odor as something that belongs to an odorous object, can detach itself from the object, enter the air, be carried by the air to our nose, be inhaled with the air, and be perceived through the sense of smell as belonging both to the air and to the object from which it has detached itself.

Since it is known from scientific research that what accounts for our smelling the odors of objects is molecules of these objects detaching themselves and moving as gaseous effluvia through the air and into our nose, where they interact, when we breathe, with the olfactory membrane of the nose, it is consonant with both our olfactory experience and the known facts to suppose that the odors we smell are these gases in the air we inhale.

Although we do commonly smell odors as given off by substances and inhaled by us, we do not through smell discover the nature of odors as streams of molecules. That the information we gather by smell is thus limited does not prevent us from perceiving by smell these streams of molecules. Water is another sort of system of molecules; we perceive it both by vision and by touch; but we do not through either sense discover water's molecular character. Of course, in order to become visually or tactually aware of a bit of water we must become thus aware of some property it has. So, too, we need to achieve olfactory awareness of some feature of an odorous gas in order to perceive the gas by smell. In attentive olfactory perception of a gas we may miss the gas's microstructure but we cannot miss all its properties without failing to smell the gas.

Since we are more directly aware of odors in the air than of anything else we smell before our nose, for direct realism to be true of smell our olfactory awareness of odorous gases must be absolutely direct. But since we are aware of a gas in virtue of being aware of some feature of it, direct realism must assert that we are directly aware of (an instance of) a feature of an odor in the air whenever through smell we become aware of the odor. Direct awareness of that feature is olfactory awareness of it that is not mediated by awareness of something *not* before the nose.

In evaluating direct realism concerning smell our task, then, is to discover whether each odor we notice has a feature of which we are directly aware. One way to put that question is thus: Is the feature of an odor that holds our attention when we smell the odor a feature that we *can* be directly aware of? To answer this question we need to understand the nature of the feature that holds our attention when we smell an odor. So we need to answer the following question: What, exactly, do we find out about an odor in attentively smelling it?

3. What We Discover about an Odor in Attentively Smelling It (I) : Criticism of J. J. Gibson's Answer

Few psychologists and even fewer philosophers have taken an interest in the sense of smell. And the number of those who have been interested to defend a directly realistic account of olfactory awareness is still smaller. This makes the chapter on taste and smell by the philosophically rather sophisticated psychologist of perception, James J. Gibson, in his book, *The Senses Considered as Perceptual Systems,*[1] the more interesting; for he attempts, throughout his book, to defend a directly realistic theory of sensory perception. His analysis of perception by smell is worth examining.

Gibson begins pretty nearly as I have done. The "main function," of smelling, he writes, "is the detection of things at a distance by means of their odors or, more exactly, their effluvia." Many of the objects of particular interest to animals are sources of odors specific to these objects. "Each animal is the source of an invisible cloud of diffusing vapor that seems to be specific not only to his type but also to him as an individual. The air is full of such overlapping clouds of emanation," or "field (s) of diffusing volatile material," of which he writes, "If it can be smelled it is an odor" (144). "The specificity of an odor to its source holds for plants as well an animals. The flowers of plants are especially odorous because their pollination requires the cooperation of insects, often bees, and these can be attracted by particular odors. The fruits of plants are also characterized by "essences". . . . So are plant products like resins and gums and spices. The state of a plant, like the state of an animal, is often

1. Boston: Houghton Mifflin, 1966. Parenthetical page references to Gibson are to this book.

characterized by a special emanation. Finally, some natural events are advertised by the fields of their volatile products. Burning yields smoke, and the oxidation of different things yields different smokes. Mineral springs and fumaroles, swamps and seashores, all have specific odors that are detectable from a distance when the wind is right" (145). And again, "The function of this perceptual system is, first, to evaluate and identify the source of the odor in the environment, and, second, to orient and control behavior . . . with respect to the source" (146).

But Gibson's emphasis upon the source of the odor and upon its practical meaning for the animal sniffing it leads him in a direction I believe to be mistaken. Perhaps his concern for a directly realistic theory plays a part, too, in fixing this direction. In any event, having, as I have done, identified odors with the gaseous emanations inhaled with the air, Gibson has to ask what it is that we find out in smelling these emanations. And he does not look with favor upon an answer involving qualities uniquely accessible to smell.

Under the heading "The Sensations of Smell," Gibson writes: "A man can attend to the subjective experience while smelling, instead of attending to the source, and then he has what can be justly called a sensation. An effort to find out by introspection what the elementary irreducible qualities of these sensations are has been made by a number of investigators . . . but they do not agree with one another. The qualities of smell are not like sweet, sour, salt, and bitter, or like red, yellow, green, and blue. . . . Henning's list of primary qualities . . . consists of *fruity, flowery, spicy, resinous, burning,* and *putrid.* . . . Note . . . that these words are names for classes of objects or events (fruits, flowers, spices, resins, fires, or decaying bodies), not classes of chemical substances. The supposed qualities seem to be perceptual, not sensory" (149).

By "perceptual qualities" Gibson here means perceptible, objective properties of the source of the odor, as distinguished from qualities uniquely accessible to a single sense, whose ontological status is (he believes) arguable, like sweet, sour, salty, and bitter, or red, yellow, green, and blue, which might turn out to be subjective qualities of mere "sensations." That Gibson tends to view qualities accessible to smell alone, if there are any, as subjective, is indicated by his speaking of them as possible qualities of sensations and as qualities to be found, if at all, by introspective attention to one's conscious state. His suggestion seems to be that no such qualities present themselves to normal, olfactory perception of the external world; such qualities do not hold our olfactory attention when this attention is directed to odorous objects before our nose. That Gibson expects the features that do hold our olfactory attention to be definable in terms of their practical relevance for the animal is indicated by other remarks:

"Organic odors contribute potential stimulus information about their sources but the whole range of this information is not perceived and responded to by any one species. The pickup of an odor depends on its relevance to the animal" (146). And the "information registered depends on the animal registering it. For a scavenging species, the odor of carrion is attractive; for others repulsive. Plants, foliage, flowers, and fruit are objectively specified by odors but are differently attractive to different animals depending on the biochemical constitution of the animal in question, that is, on his diet.

"What the individual picks up in smelling is primarily what the source affords—the 'invitation quality' or 'demand quality' of the stimulus (Lewin, 1935). The quality cannot be explained as a cluster of associations to a bare sensation. It must be conceived as a kind of information—the quality of being edible or inedible, ripe or unripe, mate or stranger, own species or foreign species, young or adult, prey or predator, alive or dead, safe or dangerous. The individual distinguishes the important differences. . . . The same is true of man. He smells what interests him" (147).

After devoting some space to the failure, so far, of attempts to analyze odors in terms of the chemical structure of the molecules responsible for our smelling the odors, and suggesting an "ecological chemistry" of values as more fruitful, Gibson writes:

The chemistry of nutritive value is like the chemistry of pigment color: neither is now understood. But it is conceivable, strange to say, that the nose and the eye understand them, when the chemist does not. Consider ripe and unripe fruit, which primates needed to distinguish when their perceptual systems were developing. Ripeness is characterized by a type of odor tending to be "fruity" and a type of color tending to be red rather than green. The chemical causes of ripening and redness are enormously complex. But the nose and eye of the arboreal animal may have evolved to pick up just this complex information by way of the essential oils we call "fruity" and the class of absorption spectra we call "reddish." What is complex for chemistry and physics may prove to be simple for the nose and eyes" (151).

But what is this *simple* ripeness that Gibson seems to want to say we smell to belong to the fruit that is before our nose? In the apple, one would think, the ripeness *is* the very complex microstructure that Gibson has put aside as the subject matter of the chemist. This ripeness in an apple has, however, a practical consequence for the percipient primate: it means that the apple is edible. This relational feature of the apple suggests itself as what Gibson must settle upon as the relatively simple feature we smell the apple to have in smelling its odor. Its relative simplicity arises not from the fact that eating and digesting an apple is simpler than the chemical constitution of ripeness in the apple, but from the fact that the practical information, "edible," is a rather simple kind of recipe for action. Although there are clear indications elsewhere in the text that Gibson wants to hold that the perceptual identification of objects must precede the appreciation of what to do about the identified objects, in this paragraph the only way to coherence is to surrender that doctrine. Is this account just sketched on Gibson's behalf a possible sketch of the truth? I do not think so.

(In the discussion that follows read the perceptual meaning of 'ripe' as "edible" whenever this helps Gibson.)

Suppose I look at a shiny red apple, see that it is shiny and red, and thus perceive with my eyes that it is ripe. But I am too far away to smell its odor, which I have forgotten. Now I walk close to the apple and smell its odor. What new information do I get? On Gibson's account, it seems, I get none. I merely perceive again (this time with the nose) that the apple is ripe. But certainly he is wrong. When I walk up to the apple and smell it I rediscover its odor, which I had forgotten. So smelling a ripe fruit's odor cannot be merely perceiving with the nose that the fruit is of a certain kind and is ripe.

It seems that Gibson's account of smelling an odor must be false. When we smell it with attention we find out about the gas in the air more than the fact that it is the effluvium of a ripe (or edible) apple. But this last statement is no sooner made than Gibson is provided with an answer to my rebuttal. Some new information I get when I move up to the apple and smell it is now apparent: that there is before me an apple with the effluvium characteristic of a ripe apple. Before that I had known only that there was before me an apple with the color of a ripe apple.

Fair enough. I myself already asserted that in smelling objects we are ordinarily conscious of the presence of something or other in the air before our nose. And vision does not ordinarily inform us about the contents of the air. Moreover I said that we are aware that this something or other in the air is coming to us from the object we smell. If for the moment we use the word 'effluvium' to mean no more than "something in the air that comes from an object," then in smelling an apple I do often become conscious of the presence of the effluvium of a ripe apple, and this is more than I described myself as discovering about the apple by vision alone.

Let us, then, start again. I see a ripe round red apple and I see that it is red and I see that it is round, and I thereby see that it is a ripe apple. But I cannot smell it yet. I am too far away. What's more, I have forgotten the odor of ripe apples. I have even forgotten whether or not they have odors. Near the apple and sniffing it is a friend whom I trust completely, and with good reason. She tells me it does have an odor. I know what an odor is, that it is an effluvium given off by an object into the air and whose presence in the air is detectable by using the nose and sniffing. So now I know that the apple I see to be ripe has an odor, that is to say, I know that it gives off an effluvium into the air which can be detected by the nose. Moreover, and finally, my friend tells me that its odor is the characteristic odor of ripe red apples.

Have I anything to learn about the apple by moving up to it and sniffing it? On Gibson's account the answer is "no". But this is clearly mistaken. For I have forgotten what a ripe apple's odor is. And this I discover by going up now and smelling the apple. Gibson's account must be false. There is something more that I learn about the odor of a thing by smelling it than that it is the effluvium in the air, detectable by the nose, which is characteristic of objects of a certain kind. And the more that I learn is what the odor is. That is to say, the additional information I get by smelling the odor is what we commonly specify as "finding out what the odor is."

But what, exactly, is this peculiar knowledge, of what the odor is, knowledge of? It is evident that when we speak of its acquisition as "finding out what the odor is" we do not at all mean to speak of finding out the constitution of the emanation, as a chemist or other physical scientist might explain it to us, since smell never enables us to do this.

It is very natural at this point to have the thought that what we mean by "knowing what the odor is" is knowing what the odor is like. And since 'like' means "resembles," this insight may seem to provide an answer to the question: What, exactly, is this peculiar knowledge *of?* It is, one may think, knowledge of what the odor resembles. We can be more disposed to this answer when we realize that one sort of information that it really can be helpful to give a person who has forgotten the odor of a kind of object concerns what the odor resembles: "It is exactly like the odor of smoke," may put him in the position of knowing what a particular odor is without smelling it.

This is a wrong hunch. Finding out what the odor is is finding out what it is like. And being told what an odor resembles may inform us what an odor is like. Nevertheless, finding out what an odor is like is not finding out what an odor resembles. The word 'like' in this context does not mean "resembles." For I may have a vivid experience of a peculiar and memorable odor. Others may have had the same. We may agree that this odor resembles no other odor we happen to know. But we also agree that each of us, by contrast with those who have not smelled this odor, knows what this odor is like. The reason that telling us what an odor resembles may give us knowledge of what the odor is like is that we may have smelled the odor it resembles and may remember this odor. But if we have not smelled the second odor or we do not remember it, then knowing that the first odor resembles the second does not tell us what the first odor is like. What, then, do we know about an odor in knowing what it is like?

4. What We Discover about an Odor in Attentively
    Smelling It (II) : Its Olfactory Sensible Character

What we find out when by smelling it we find out what an odor is like is its olfactually sensible character. The reason that someone's telling us what an odor resembles can help us know what it is like is that it resembles other odors in virtue of having the same, or a very similar, sensible character; and if we remember the sensible character of an odor it exactly resembles, this makes us conscious of the sensible character of the odor we are curious about, conscious of it in the way we are when we recall a sensible character from having smelled it before. So too, when we recognize an odor we are smelling, as, say, the odor of smoke, when no cues are given to us by any other sense, how we tell that this is the odor of smoke is by remembering that the sensible character we are now conscious of in virtue of breathing in the smoke is the sensible character we have earlier been conscious of when we knew we were smelling smoke.

When we are walking outdoors and are suddenly struck by an odor in the air, and for the first few moments have not so much as an intimation what it is the odor of, what strikes and holds our attention is not, primarily, that there is something or other in the air or that we are detecting by breathing something or other in the air, or that we are in this way detecting something we realize is an emanation of the sort detectable by the nose and called "an odor." These elements are, it may be, a part of the perceived framework of what it is that strikes our attention, but by themselves they are quite incapable of holding even the smallest degree of our olfactory attention to a mere odor. For this attention to be held it is necessary that the olfactually sensible character of the odorous emanation hold it.

Knowing what the odor of an object is is knowing what the odor is like. We can know what an odor is like only by smelling it (or by knowing that it resembles an odor we have smelled). But knowing what an odor is like is knowing its olfactually sensible character. Hence we can know this sensible character of an odorous gas only by smelling it.

If the sensible character of a gas is a property whose nature is in principle specifiable without making reference to how the gas smells, it seems impossible that knowing what that sensible character is would require smelling it. If the nature of the feature we smell were olfaction-independent, then our means of knowing what this feature is would not be limited to our smelling it.

Certainly there are physical features of things around us which we can *perceive* only through the mediation of a single sense (whenever we do not perceive the feature in virtue of first noticing some other feature of something before our sense organs). Intensity of heat is an example. But since intensity of heat is in principle describable without reference to how it feels, knowing its nature ought to be possible for us by conceptual understanding alone, just as the visually sensible feature, being square, can be conceptually grasped without knowing how it looks. And indeed, knowing what the property, intensity of heat, is, is perfectly possible for someone who has never felt it. He need only master the science of heat, which he can do without feeling heat.

But no merely scientific understanding of some physical feature of an odorous emanation the likes of which one has never smelled can constitute knowing the sensible character others discover in smelling this odor. One has to smell the odor, and be in this way conscious of it, to know what the odor's sensible character is.

For lack of another plausible explanation of it, this fact about odors makes credible the hypothesis that the peculiar, sensible character of each distinct odor is in some way internally related to a particular sort of olfactory experience. For one form this relation might take we are already prepared, from the preceding chapter: each odor's sensible character may consist in that odor's disposition, when sniffed, to smell a certain way to us. An odor's sensible character may be somewhat like the sort of thing that an itch would be if we counted the itch as existing when, because our attention is directed elsewhere, we do not feel it.

There is other evidence that how an odor smells to us figures in the nature of the odor's sensible character.

To speak of a feature of a substance or object as sensible is not by itself to ensure that the nature of this feature involves its appearance to sense. The shapes of moderate-sized surfaces are sensible features of the surfaces, but it does not follow from this fact that how a square surface looks figures in what it is for a surface to be square. A person could understand perfectly what being square is without knowing how a square surface looks. And a creature who knew of squareness *only* how squares look— he could distinguish what we call square things from others by their look but knew *nothing else* of what it is to be square— would be so ignorant of the nature of squareness that he could not correctly be said to see that a surface is square. But to see a feature of an object is to see *that* the object has the feature. So such a creature cannot see the square shape of a surface even though he knows the looks of square surfaces. We might say that for him the look of a certain shape is sensible but the shape itself is not a sensible feature.

Now consider how we speak and think of the (olfactually) sensible character of an odor. Recall the person who sees that an apple before him is red and hence that it is ripe but has forgotten the odor of ripe apples, and who goes up to the apple to find out what its odor is by smelling it. We make no distinction between his finding out what the odor is *like,* what the sensible character of the odor *is,* and how the odor (and the apple) *smells.* Indeed we do not in any way distinguish in thought or speech between the nature of an odor's sensible character and the odor's smelling a certain way to us. Unlike a surface's visible shape, an odor's olfactually sensible character is conceived by us to be identical with the odor's characteristically appearing a certain way to the sense of smell. In our concept of the sensible character of an odor no provision is made for the nature of that character being something more or other than the odor's smelling to us a certain way. An odor's sensible character *is* its smelling to us a certain way.

This conclusion about the nature of an odor's sensible character is reinforced by noticing that it explains the fact that one can know what an odor is only by smelling it. What marks a vaporous effluvium as an odor is its olfactually sensible character. By itself this fact would not entail that in order to know what the odor is one must smell that character; perhaps the nature of the character could be conceptually understood. But once we realize that the odor's sensible character is nothing but its characteristically smelling a certain way when sniffed, no puzzle remains: now we understand why we treat only those who smell the odor as knowing what the odor's sensible character is (and hence knowing what that gas is *as* an odor). For we have no notion of any other way to understand how something smells than by smelling it (or smelling something like it). And one cannot know what disposition a disposition to smell a certain way *is* without knowing what that particular way of smelling is.

Some adjudication is now needed of certain opposing "claims" presented, on the one hand, by olfactory perception and, on the other, by our way of thinking of what we perceive by smell.

Were olfactory perception to articulate in words what it takes itself to perceive in the way of an odor's sensible character it would perhaps not say anything about the odor *smelling* a certain way; it would merely report that way, as a quality, say, "sweet". *That* this quality is a way of *smelling* does not immediately engage our olfactory attention; the sensuous quality does.

On the other hand, as just remarked, conceptually we specify the nature of the sensible character of the odorous effluvium in this way: "characteristically smelling sweet," and we imply that 'sweet' *here* signifies nothing but a way of smelling to us.

Olfactory perception itself, imagined as articulating its immediate content, declares the sensuous, olfactory quality—which is how the odor smells to us—to *be* the character of the odorous effluvium. But in thinking of what we perceive we do not so conceive the sensuous quality; we say it is *merely* a way of smelling to us and that the character of the odorous effluvium revealed to smell is this: "characteristically smelling to us a certain, sensuous way when sniffed."

Since what is in question is how we shall think of olfactory perception, I give priority to how we do think of it (although I shall, in §§6 and 7, provide an extended opportunity for a spokesman for olfactory perception's "view" of its own achievement to state a directly realistic version of its case). We affirm that we do perceive by smell a genuine character of the odorous effluvium as stable as the effluvium itself, and we call this its "sweet" character—unhappily (for philosophers) here using 'sweet' in a second sense. But the odor's sweet character we conceive to be its characteristically smelling a certain way. I won't here continue to call the way of smelling "sweet," for fear of suggesting an infinite regress: call it *"thus."* According to our conception of what we smell, then, what is perceived by smell that does characterize the odorous gas is a disposition in the gas to smell *thus.* Although this disposition is all that olfactory perception in fact discovers in the way of a stable feature of the effluvium in the air, what it "thinks" it discovers of that sort is the basis in the gas of this disposition—it takes the sensuous, olfactory quality *thus* to be an inherent feature of the gas that accounts for what it takes to be the gas's revealing itself as (and not *merely* smelling) *thus.*

I draw the tentative conclusion that the sensible character of an odor—as stable as the gas itself—which we discover in smelling the odor is the odor's disposition to smell *thus* when it is sniffed. I treat this conclusion as tentative for two reasons: first, more needs to be said to clarify how we can plausibly be said to smell such a disposition although olfactory perception itself, if articulate, would perhaps not express its content in that manner. I have given an initial explanation, but more needs to be said. I shall return to this task in §10. Second, after drawing out (in the next section) the bearing of this conclusion upon the point of dispute between direct and indirect realism, I shall want to offer the direct realist the opportunity to present an alternative account of the sensible character of an odorous effluvium. Until this alternative account of what we perceive by smell has been evaluated, my present conclusion needs to be considered tentative.

There is another matter upon which some light is thrown by the conclusion that an odor's sensible character is its disposition to smell a certain way to us. Some readers may have suspected that I have relied upon an unacknowledged introduction of a special sense of 'know'—know by acquaintance—in appealing to our incapacity to know an odor's sensible character except through smelling it, and that my argument was thereby weakened. Although it is true that the sort of knowing what a sensible feature is which occurs when we can know it only by smelling it is special, and properly called "knowledge by acquaintance," this is not, we can now see, because a special sense of the word 'know' is being used. If the feature consists in a disposition in a gaseous substance to smell a certain way, then we cannot conceive any way in which a person could understand what that feature is which did not include as a necessary step his undergoing the way of smelling to which the feature is a disposition. This necessity arises not from our using a special sense of the word 'know' (or 'understand') but from the special nature of the feature whose nature one is said to know.[2]

5. First Argument for Indirect Realism

The foundation has now been laid for an argument for indirect realism in regard to smell.

Direct realism can be true of smell only if we have direct, olfactory awareness of whatever it is before our nose that we perceive less indirectly than anything else out there. Among the substances before our nose, those of which we are olfactually least indirectly aware are the gaseous effluvia of odorous objects—the objects' odors. Direct realism can be true of smell only if we have direct awareness of these odorous gases, i.e., only if our awareness of them need not be mediated through our being directly aware of something *not* before the nose.

To be olfactually aware of the gas one must be thus aware of some feature of the gas. Olfactually to be directly aware of the gas one must, therefore, be directly aware of an instance of some feature of the gas, an instance that is before the nose, where the gas is. We have already discovered something important about the nature of that feature. For we have discovered that what holds our attention when we become olfactually conscious

2. I have discussed elsewhere another conceivable way of knowing such features. But this way is "conceivable" only on the assumption not only of the truth of materialism but also of a complete theory of sensations as brain states, which does not presently exist. See "Matter, Sensation and Understanding," *American Philosophical Quarterly*, VIII, 1 (January 1971) : 1–12.

of an odorous gas is the gas's sensible character, and that this character *is* the gas's disposition to smell to us a certain way. This is an objective feature of the gas, as stable as the gas itself. We are more directly aware of an instance of this feature than of anything else *before* our nose. Therefore, if direct realism is to be true of smell, then our olfactory awareness of an odor's disposition to smell a certain way to us must be absolutely direct. If it should turn out that we can be olfactually aware of this disposition of the gas only in virtue of being aware of something else that is *not* before the nose, then direct realism will be false of smell, and indirect realism true of it.

A gas's smelling to me a certain way on an occasion consists in the gas's causing me to have a certain sort of olfactory experience. The disposition a gas has to smell a certain way to us is therefore a disposition whose manifestation consists in the gas's causing one of us, on a particular occasion, to have a certain kind of olfactory experience. Therefore, in becoming through smell conscious of the sensible character of an odor we become conscious of the odor's disposition commonly to cause in us a certain sort of olfactory experience. The only way one can through *smell* become conscious of a particular instance of this disposition is by becoming olfactually conscious of a particular manifestation to oneself of this disposition: one must become olfactually aware of an odor's causing in oneself, on a particular occasion, a certain sort of olfactory experience. One might become (mentally) aware of an odor's disposition by inferring it from something one sees happening with another person, or by being told of it; but this would not be *smelling* the odor's presence before one's nose.

For me attentively to smell an odor, then, the odorous gas must so act on the olfactory membrane of my nose as to cause me to become olfactually aware of its presently causing in me a certain sort of olfactory experience. How am I to become olfactually aware of the latter causal action upon myself? Surely I can do so only through becoming olfactually aware of the effect (upon myself) that is caused: I have no way of becoming aware through smell alone of a gas's causing in me a certain effect unless I am aware of the effect. I have no olfactory way of directly inspecting the causation itself, apart from its effect. But the effect is a certain sort of olfactory experience I undergo. I must, then, become conscious *of* this experience. This experience must have a peculiar character, since the only thing that distinguishes one odor from another is the difference in what its sensible character *is* a disposition *to*. To become aware of a particular odor, then,

I must become aware of the peculiar character of the experience it causes me to undergo.

To summarize: an odor's sensible character is its disposition to smell a certain way to us. Its smelling a certain way to us is its causing us to undergo a certain sort of olfactory experience. For me to become olfactually aware of the disposition I must become thus aware of its manifestation; this manifestation consists in the odor's causing in me a certain sort of experience; to become olfactually aware of this causation I must become thus aware of the effect that is caused; the effect is an experience having a character that marks it as the peculiar manifestation of *this* odor's disposition. It is necessary, therefore, for me to become conscious *of* the experience I am undergoing, and more specifically, for me to become conscious of a peculiar character of this experience, if I am to become olfactually conscious of the sensible character of the odor responsible for the experience.

But the experience of mine which the odorous gas causes and *of* which I must be conscious in order to be conscious of the gas's disposition to cause this experience, this experience of mine is *not* before my nose. My awareness of its peculiar character is, therefore, direct awareness. So I can become *olfactually* aware of an odor's disposition to smell to me a certain way—I can attentively *smell* its sensible character—only in virtue of becoming directly aware of something *not* before my nose. The odor itself, however, is a gas before my nose. I am, therefore, always indirectly aware of an odor when I become aware of it by smelling it. Since of things other than odors of which I become aware through smell I am even more indirectly aware than I am of odors, of everything before my nose of which I become olfactually aware I am always indirectly aware. When with attention I smell objects and events and their effluvia before my nose, my perception of all of them is indirect. At least the weaker form of indirect realism is true of the sense of smell.

To reach that conclusion is not enough. More needs to be said about how olfactory awareness specifies for itself the peculiar character of each odor's disposition. To say more of this I shall need to give a fuller account of the peculiar character belonging to the "olfactory experience" that a particular odor's disposition is a disposition to cause and of the role this character plays in our awareness of the odor's disposition. I shall also need to determine in what sense we can be said to perceive *as* a disposition the odor's disposition to smell a certain way.

Before completing that story, however, it is necessary to question, on the direct realist's behalf, a crucial premise of the last stage of my argument, the assertion—itself defended by argument—that the sensible character of an odor *is* its disposition to smell a certain way.

But before questioning that proposition let me say a word about why I do not think it necessary in this chapter to discuss carefully an alternative account of olfactory perception which might be given by an "adverbalist" who means to avoid the indirectly realistic conclusion I have reached. (I shall examine this account of perception in Chapter Six, since adverbalists have dealt chiefly with vision.)

An adverbalist might say that our perceiving an odor consists in nothing but the odor's smelling a certain way to us and that this last consists in nothing but the odor's causing us to sense in a certain way, e.g., causing us to "sense muskily" when we smell a musky odor. And, he might say, to sense muskily is not to become aware *of* anything: it is merely a certain manner of sensing.

To this short way with indirect realism my reply is also short. I am not speaking of "perceiving an odor" in that sense of 'perceive'. I am trying to understand *attentive* perception of an odor, hence being aware—being conscious—of an odor. If you are describing a state that involves no awareness of anything, your account cannot conflict with an account of olfactory awareness.

Thereupon an adverbalist may be expected to provide the following account of our becoming olfactually *conscious* of, say, a musky odor: it is sensing muskily, together with consciously believing that the odor is causing one to thus sense. Of this account I first remark that the (conscious) belief that the odor is causing one to "sense muskily" includes the (conscious) belief that one is thus sensing. On this account, therefore, one is conscious *of* one's own sensing *thus,* hence conscious of an event (or state) that is not before one's nose. And one's awareness of the odor before one's nose is mediated and in part constituted by one's awareness of one's own sensing *thus:* the adverbalist's account of olfactory awareness of odors is also indirectly realistic.

I therefore believe that all that keeps the argument I have given for indirect realism from being conclusive (apart from the need to complete coherently the picture of indirect perception I have so far only sketched) is the possibility that a different account from the one I have given of the nature of an odor's sensible character may be true, and may entail the truth of direct realism. I think there is only one such account possible which would entail direct realism's truth and which has some initial plausibility, and I believe that this account is false. The next two sections present the direct realist's position. In §8 I criticize it.

6. Direct Realism's Thesis (II) : An Odor's Sensible Character Is a Molecular Causal Property

The direct realist may not accept my argument for indirect realism. He may deny that the sensible character of an odor is its disposition to smell a certain way. Perhaps he will make an analogy with the visible features of surfaces. If one thought of these features merely as visible, one might find oneself saying of a surface's being square that this consists in its disposition to look square to us. Indeed a square surface (of adequate size) does have a disposition to look square. As it happens, however, how it looks in this respect is how it is. The visible feature (shape) of the surface does not *consist* in its commonly (from a certain vantage point) looking square. Its visible character coincides with how it *is,* apart from looking any way. How it looks is square, and its vision-independent character is the same— square.

"So it is," the direct realist now claims, "with smell. Your argument for indirect realism fails."

"First we notice," he continues, "that, even on your indirectly realistic account, what marks off one odor's sensible character from another's is *how* (on an occasion) it smells to us. For you make out every odor's sensible character to be a disposition to smell a certain way; so one odor's sensible character is distinguished from another's only by how it smells to us when its disposition manifests itself. Our capacity to perceive a particular odor must, therefore, depend upon our capacity to become olfactually aware of a peculiar way of smelling to us on an occasion. Therefore this way of smelling to us must itself be an olfactually sensible quality.

"Now," says the direct realist, "although you did not spell this out, the olfactually sensible quality that constitutes how the odor smells to us on an occasion—what you sometimes speak of as *thus*—will turn out, on your view, to characterize the percipient's consciousness: his olfactory attention to the odor's disposition will be directly held by a quality instantiated *within* his consciousness. That's how your idea of direct awareness of "the peculiar character of an olfactory experience" will be developed.

"But in reasoning in this way," the direct realist contends, "it is as if you had argued that visible squareness *is* the disposition to look square; visual attention to this disposition presupposes visual attention to its manifestation; this disposition's sensible manifestation is within the percipient's visual consciousness; therefore visual attention to the surface's square shape is mediated by direct attention to the "square look" characterizing the percipient's visual consciousness.

"However," the direct realist argues, "the facts about visible shape are not as your argument about odors would suggest. In fact, how the surface looks is how it *is* (square) : so attention to how it looks on an occasion is nothing but *visual* attention to a visible but *physical* feature (the square shape) of the surface, a feature whose nature could be specified without reference to the surface's looking any way to us. Of course you have shown that you understand these facts about shape. Where you go wrong is in failing to see that odors are in this respect like shapes."

"How an odor smells to a normal perceiver is how it *is*," concludes the direct realist. "Attention to how it smells is of course attention to an olfactually sensible quality, but this quality belongs to the odorous vapor independently of its smelling any way to anyone. Being musky—the nondispositional musky that corresponds to your '*thus*' that expresses how a musky odor smells—this is as physical a feature of a gas as being square is of a surface, and it happens to be sensible only to smell, as being square is sensible only to vision."

In making his analogy with vision the direct realist seems to ignore the fact that we discover shapes not only by vision but, and this more authoritatively, by measurement. However, we can imagine the following reply by him to our assertion that odors' sensible characters can be known only through smell:

"This is a *mere* belief, which nearly everyone holds, but a mistaken one, grounded in ignorance. Once the physical nature of odors' sensible characters is fully and widely understood—which will require further results from the chemistry and physics of odors—you will all give up this belief." In this I believe he is mistaken.

As to the direct realist's observation that on my account of smell the direct object of olfactory awareness will turn out, when I fill in the picture, to be an odorous quality instantiated within that very awareness, I entirely agree with him. We distinguish each odor by noticing the manifestation of its disposition to affect our experience in a certain way, we notice this manifestation by noticing the effect on our experience, and I shall assert that this effect consists in our conscious state's becoming in part constituted by an instance of a particular sensuous quality. So I shall conclude that the instance of this sensuous, olfactory quality which partially constitutes our conscious state is the direct object of our olfactory attention.

The direct realist and I are therefore in agreement that the direct object of olfactory awareness is not a disposition to smell *thus* but a nondispositional, odorous quality, the quality I have expressed as *thus,* which is *how* the odor smells. I hold that this nondispositional quality constitutes the peculiar, sensuous character of an olfactory experience and belongs to our olfactory consciousness itself; he holds that it is nothing less than a physical feature of the odorous gas, a feature to whose nature it no more pertains to be smelled than it pertains to the nature of the square shape of a surface (which happens to be visible) that it be seen—and he further holds that this olfactually sensible but physical feature *is* the sensible character of the gas. Whereas I shall hold that the olfactually sensible character of the gas is its disposition to cause our conscious state to acquire the nondispositional, sensuous quality to which we directly attend in smelling the gas. This disagreement leads to a difference in vocabulary.

The direct realist can call the nondispositional, odorous quality of which we are directly aware a sens*ible* quality because according to him it is a physical feature of the vaporous effluvium before our nose, hence it can play a causal role within the effluvium's interaction with our olfactory membrane, and so can be a proper object of olfactory sense perception. Since I hold that this nondispositional quality inheres in consciousness, I shall not call it "sensible," which might seem to imply that it belongs to an object we can perceive in virtue of the object's causal action upon our sense organs. So I call the quality "sensuous" whenever I speak in my own voice. However, in developing the direct realist's position I shall describe as "sensible" the nondispositional quality I believe to be only sens*uous* but he believes to be sens*ible*.

Another terminological matter. In saying that the direct realist and I are in agreement that the object of *direct* olfactory awareness is (an instance of) a "nondispositional" feature, I use the word 'nondispositional' in a narrow sense: the word here rules out as the feature's nature only a disposition to smell a certain way. Since the direct realist holds that the nondispositional quality we directly smell is in fact a physical feature of the odorous gas, this "nondispositional" feature might, on his account, turn out to be a physical disposition, i.e., a disposition physically to affect other physical systems in certain ways. The word 'occurrent' is sometimes used in place of 'nondispositional' when the latter is used in this special sense.

If perceptual realism of any kind, direct or indirect, is true of smell, then the olfactually sensible characters of odors in the air are objective features (which may be relational features) of these gases. We perceive instances of these characters more directly than we perceive any other instance of a feature of something before the nose. However, if the nature of an odor's sensible character can be specified only by reference to an effect of the odor upon the experience of those who smell it, so that the sensible character consists in a disposition of the odor to smell a certain way, then, for the reasons I have given, I hold that we can perceive this sensible character only indirectly, hence only in virtue of being directly aware of something *not* before the sense organs. *Direct* realism, therefore, can be true of smell only if the nature of an odor's sensible character can in principle be specified without reference to the odor's effect upon the olfactory experience of those who may smell it. My task now is to assume for the direct realist the burden of proof of the thesis that the nature of an odor's sensible character can in principle be specified in an olfaction-independent manner.

The direct realist must now *identify* the olfactually sensible character of an odorous gas *with* the physical feature of the gas that is responsible for the gas's causing us to discern by smell that very sensible character. This he must do for the following reasons. What qualifies as the sensible character whose nature he must describe as olfaction-independent is the character we perceive by smell. So in picking out this sensible character the direct realist must, in the first instance, pick it out *as* the character we discern by smell. However, as I have argued, at least prima facie this quality we smell is olfaction-*de*pendent. So the direct realist must find a feature of the odorous gas which is specified both in a manner that will assure its olfaction-independence and in a way that will seem to assure the feature's being the very one we discern by smell. I know of only one way to do this: first, assure the feature's olfaction-independence by specifying it in terms of some causal role that its possession by the gas enables the gas to play in interacting with other *physical* systems. Second, in order to assure that the feature selected is the one we discern by smell, pick, as the causal power of the gas which possession of this feature explains, the following: the power of the gas to so affect the olfactory membrane of the nose as to elicit from us an olfactory perception of the very feature of the gas that gives the gas that power. These two steps yield this result: the olfactually sensible character of the gas *is* the physical feature of the gas which enables the gas to cause us to perceive that sensible character.

Here the analogy with vision, to which the direct realist initially appealed, may be helpful. The feature of the surface we are looking at which accounts for the surface's power to cause us to see the surface's square shape *is* the surface's square shape. That how the surface looks to us—the shape it looks to be—is how it *is* is (in one way) explained by the fact that it is this very square shape of the surface which enables the surface to cause us to see its shape to be square. The direct realist must now argue that an odor's sensible character resembles in this way a surface's visible shape.

Of course the causation we are here speaking of is only partial causation. The square shape of the surface we are viewing head on is the feature of the surface which is causally relevant in explaining the *surface's* contribution to our coming to perceive the *square* shape of the surface. There is a long chain of further causal factors that must operate after the shape of the surface has done its part, if we are to perceive the surface's shape. So, too, the direct realist holds that the sensible character of an odorous gas that we discern by smell is identical with that physical property of the gas which accounts for the *gas's* part in causing us (by its action on the nose) to discern by smell that very sensible character. Of course many other causal factors must operate within the olfactory membrane and the peripheral and central nervous system if, in virtue of its having a certain physical property, the gas is to succeed in causing us to perceive this property.

The direct realist's task, then, is this. He must discover what the scientist provides in the way of an explanation of an odorous gas's part in causing us to smell its peculiar, sensible character, looking for a property of the gas that carries the burden of this explanation. Next he must make it plausible to us that the gas's sensible character, which we know through smell, is indeed identical with this causally efficacious, physical property of the gas.

Now we may well believe, in advance of specific inquiry, that the causal property of the gas which will turn up explaining what we smell will be a molecular property, since the gas consists of loosely aggregated molecules streaming through the air. And since the olfactually sensible character of the gas is an observable feature of the gas, whereas molecules cannot be perceived by sense, we may believe that the direct realist is bound to fail in his project of equating a sensible feature with a molecular one.

But this is surely premature. The intensity of heat of a gas is an observable feature of the gas. We can even feel it. Yet it is said to be identical with a molecular feature of the gas, with the mean kinetic energy of the gas's molecules. There is no short way to dismiss the solution to his problem which the direct realist is now proposing to articulate in more detail. And since, if I am right, this is the only solution that offers any hope to the direct realist, I propose to take the long way and to lay out with some care the account he must offer of the nature of the olfactually sensible characters of odors.

7. Direct Realism Made Precise: A Chemical
    Account of Odorous Qualities

On the direct realist's behalf we need now to get some idea of the present state of the scientific attempt to explain, by reference to a physical property of the gas, our perception of a gas's sensible character.

There has not been much interest in the psychology of smell. Scientists seeking a theory of smell are largely engaged in seeking the properties of odorous gases to which we are responding in distinguishing the gases by smell. But this is exactly the research our present inquiry requires. If each of the odorous gases we smell as if having the same odorous quality, say musky, has a common physical property whose possession enables the gas to cause us to smell the gas as having this musky quality, then this common physical property of the gases is the property the direct realist will affirm to be identical with the musky quality we smell.

Since what acts upon the olfactory membrane of the nose when we inhale an odor are molecules comprising a gas, the property that explains the gas's role in causing us to smell its sensible character must be a property of these molecules. Although scientists seeking a theory of smell have not yet fully discovered what it is about the gases that smell the same to us which enables us olfactually to distinguish them from other odorous gases, the work done is sufficient to reveal a range of answers within which the truth is probably to be found. This should suffice for our purpose. The attempt to discover the properties of molecules to which the olfactory membrane is differentially responsive divides itself into three interacting projects: identifying like-smelling classes of odorous gases; seeking the common property of the molecules of the gases in each such set which functions as the basis of our olfactory discrimination of these gases; and exploring the responsive capabilities of the olfactory membrane in the nose, both for a source of hypotheses about the common property of the molecules and as a check on such hypotheses when these are independenly developed.

The set of gases that will be counted as the same odor is selected on the evidence that every gas in the set smells the same to human percipients, that is to say, appears to them to have the same odorous quality. The number of kinds of odorous qualities perceived is very large. In the interest of system and from hope of analogy with taste, where molecular properties are also in question and where four primary qualities seem to serve as the elements of which all gustatory qualities are composed, students of smell have hoped to find a group of primary olfactory qualities. As Gibson remarked, no consensus has been reached about a list of primary olfactory qualities, although probably some qualities have appeared on each list proposed. Of course, agreement on a list of primary qualities is unnecessary so long as there are some qualities commonly smelled as belonging to identifiable gases, so that determination of the basis, in molecular properties of these gases, of our olfactory discrimination of these qualities can be made. Certainly there are such olfactually sensible qualities, and a great deal of research has been done in the effort to locate the properties of gases' molecules that account for our smelling the same quality in response to each member of the class of gases we count as the same odor.

One somewhat surprising negative proposition has emerged from this research: it appears that the kind of property of molecules initially expected to account for our smelling a common quality, the chemical structure of the gases' molecules, is not going to be sufficient to account for our olfactory discriminations. Gases whose molecules have radically different chemical structures may smell the same, and gases whose molecules' structures are so similar they are optical isomers—differing in structure only as the right hand from the left hand—may (exceptionally) smell different from one another. This is not to say that affinities of chemical structure will turn out to play no role in determining smell; but it does appear that they cannot be the whole story. It will be useful to consider the work of a scientist who concluded that chemical structure is largely irrelevant to the smell of gases—except for the distinct olfactory sensory system called the "trigeminal" system, mediating our smelling of pungency and putridness—and then go on to take note of how his conclusions have been qualified by the work of others.

In order to arrive at a list of primary olfactory qualities, John E. Amoore in 1952 began to pore through a voluminous mass of publications in organic chemistry, collecting the most frequently occurring names of odorous qualities, working on the assumption that the primary olfactory qualities would be most distinctly perceived and hence most consistently and most frequently named the same. He came up with this list: camphoraceous, musky, floral, pepperminty, ethereal (ether-ish), pungent, putrid. He also made a list of the substances most consistently smelled as having each one of these seven qualities. Turning away right off from the search for similarities of chemical structure among these substances smelling the same, he took up a suggestion of R. W. Moncrief that all the molecules composing the gaseous substances smelling the same have a similar shape and size, which permits them to fit into one set of receptor-cell sites with a matching shape. He applied to olfactory perception a geometric—or stereochemical—theory of chemical interaction which had proved fruitful in biological applications to the interaction of enzymes with their substrates, to the process whereby certain acids govern the synthesis of proteins and to other processes in living organisms.

Starting with over a hundred compounds he had found described as having a camphoraceous odor, Amoore devised a test for the hypothesis that however different in chemical composition these compounds' molecules were, the molecules would all reveal a common shape and size that would permit them to fit into a common receptor site in the olfactory membrane. By then the chemical tools were at hand to construct a physical model, 100 million times actual size, of any molecule whose formula was known. This he did for each of the substances smelling camphoraceous. And he found that all the molecules had roughly the same shape: spherical. When the molecular dimensions for these substances were calculated, all turned out to have approximately the same diameter: about 70 millionths of a millimeter. He concluded that the receptor site for what he called "camphoraceous molecules" was a spherical bowl about 70 millionths of a millimeter in diameter. Those of the molecules studied which were not rigid bowls were slightly flexible "and could easily shape themselves to the bowl," he judged. Amoore's own language in summarizing the results for the other allegedly primary olfactory qualities is worth reading.[3]

> When other models were built, shapes and sizes of the molecules representing the other primary odors were found. . . . The musky odor is accounted for by molecules with the shape of a disk about 10 angstroms in diameter. The pleasant floral odor is caused by molecules that have the shape of a disk with a flexible tail attached—a shape somewhat like a kite. The cool pepperminty odor is produced by molecules with the shape of a wedge, and with an electrically polarized group of atoms capable of forming a hydrogen bond, near the point of the wedge. The ethereal odor is due to rod-shaped or other thin molecules. In each of these cases the receptor site in the nerve endings presumably has a shape and size corresponding to those of the molecule.
>
> The pungent and putrid odors seem to be exceptions to the Lucretian scheme of shape-matching. The molecules responsible for these odors are of indifferent shapes and sizes; what matters in their case is the electric charge of the molecule. The pungent class of odors is produced by compounds whose molecules, because of a deficiency of electrons, have a positive charge and strong affinity for electrons; they are called electrophillic. Putrid odors, on the other hand, are caused by molecules that have an excess of electrons and are called nucleophillic, because they are strongly attracted by the nuclei of adjacent atoms.[4]

Amoore, with his collaborators, went on to seek and in his view to find empirical confirmation of his theory from other facts either independently discovered by others or predicted and

3. It will be evident from a moment's thought that the fact that Amoore says "primary odors" where I have said "primary olfactory qualities" does not mean that Amoore intends by his phrase to refer to primary, odorous gases, since this would, in the context, make no sense. It is clear that he is using the word 'odor' to refer to a single, sensible character each gas in a set of gases appears to smell to have. This suggests that my own (and Gibson's) use of the word 'odor' is not quite satisfactory. I shall reconsider the definition of 'odor' in §9 of this chapter.

4. Richard Helm and Whitman Richards, eds., *Perception: Mechanism and Models* (San Francisco: W. H. Freeman, 1971), pp. 70–1. Reprinted from John E. Amoore, James W. Johnson, Jr., and Martin Rubin, "The Stereochemical Theory of Odor," *Scientific American* (February 1964) : 67–74.

confirmed by himself. His theory, however, is too simple, and has not been accepted by other scientific workers—indeed Amoore himself has more recently admitted this was only a beginning, and only part of the story. Nevertheless the kind of answer that is to be expected is, for our purposes, well indicated by Amoore's theory, especially if we treat as having a more general application his account of the pungent and putrid qualities, an account which is wholly in terms of chemical structure, and his account of the pepperminty quality, which mixes size and shape with considerations concerning the character and position and consequent potential role at the olfactory receptor site of the functional group in a carbon compound.

Most investigators do appear today to agree that molecular shape and size play a part in determining perceived odorous quality, but believe that chemical composition and structure, including the character and position within carbon compounds of functional groups, also play an important part. Some theorists work back to the molecular properties from a theory that the activation of olfactory receptors is by selective puncturing of cell membranes by the odorant molecules; this entails some importance for size and shape as well as chemical constitution of the odorant molecule. One theory, motivated originally by the presence of pigmentation in the olfactory membrane, which suggests a selective reception of electromagnetic vibrations, has attempted to locate the cause of our smelling odorous qualities in the characteristic infra-red vibration—or more specifically, the characteristic Raman shift within the infra-red spectrum—of odorant molecules; but this theory seems at best to have a chance of contributing one factor to several that play a role in determining the peculiar quality we smell as belonging to a gas.

For our purpose, then, which is the determination of the likelihood that the nondispositional qualities we become directly aware of through smell belong to the gases we smell, the gamut of possibilities indicated by Amoore's theory is quite adequate: size, shape, empirical and structural chemical formula, including the position and character of the functional group within the molecule; these give a highly likely picture of the complex properties of the molecules of a gas which the direct realist must identify with the olfactually sensible quality of the gas.

Indeed, little harm is done, in the context of assessing the probability of truth of direct realism in regard to smell, if we use for this purpose the simplest form of Amoore's theory and assume that it is a particular (size and) shape of the odorant molecule that provokes our olfactory awareness of a particular quality. So far as the general physical facts go, it might have been true. And for our purpose, of deciding what it is that is veridically perceived about what, the physical character of molecular shape and size is on a par with the chemical constitution and structure of molecules, the chief difference—complexity—being one that makes the selection of size and shape favorable to the direct realist: because of visual and tactual (and perhaps thermal and aural) perception of size and shape, it sounds slightly less implausible to suppose that we detect by smell shape and size (of molecules) than to suppose that in smelling, say, that an odor is musky we perceive that the aggregate of atoms that composes the molecule of the gas inhaled has "a rigid, closely packed structure of a certain size and a well accessible, weakly basic functional group."[5]

Therefore, in order to simplify both images and sentences, I shall, in the discussion that follows, treat molecular shape as a stand-in for the complex pattern of molecular properties that probably elicits our olfactory awareness of a single odorous quality. I shall proceed as if it is highly probable that the characteristic shape of the molecules of like-smelling emanations of odorous substances is the property of these gases which elicits, in attentive perceivers, olfactory awareness of a single, odorous quality.

Let us now remind ourselves of the direct realist's position.

He admits that if the sweetness of an odorous gas were nothing but the disposition of the gas to affect our olfactory experience in a certain way then direct realism would fail: we could not be directly aware of such a disposition. But he denies that the odor's sensible character *is* a (mere) disposition. The odor does have a disposition to smell a certain way, but it has this disposition because it *is* the way it smells. Its olfactually sensible character—for example, its sweetness—is an olfaction-independent, physical feature of the gas—in fact *is* a certain shape of its molecules—and it is this feature's revealing itself to us, in virtue of its causal role in the gas's interaction with our olfactory membrane, which *is* the gas's smelling to us a certain way, i.e., *is* its smelling to us to have that very feature. The sweet-

5. M. G. J. Beets, "Olfactory Response and Molecular Structure," in Lloyd M. Beidler, ed., *Handbook of Sensory Physiology*, vol. IV, Chemical Senses 1, Olfaction (New York: Springer-Verlag 1971), p. 295.

ness of the gas, therefore, is a "nondispositional," physical feature of the gas which, like the square shape of a surface that looks square to us, reveals itself to us when the gas smells a certain way to us.

The square shape of a surface does dispose a surface to look square to us, but the shape's nature does not consist in this disposition. So too, says the direct realist, the sweetness of a gas does dispose the gas to smell sweet to us, but its nature does not consist in this disposition. The nature of the sweetness of the gas can be specified in purely physical terms, without reference to how a sweet gas smells to anyone, just as the nature of the squareness of a surface can be specified in purely physical terms, without reference to how it looks to anyone. In the sense of the term 'nondispositional' explained earlier, an odor's sensible character is a nondispositional, physical feature of the odor, the very feature that enables the gas to cause us to become conscious of an instance of this feature before the nose. Since, as we are now supposing, the feature that plays this role for sweet-smelling odors is a certain shape of the odors' molecules, the direct realist holds that the nondispositional, sweet quality that directly holds our attention when we smell the sweet air near a candy factory *is* a certain shape of the molecules emanating from the factory.

It will be recalled, too, that in my initial comments on the direct realist's proposal of his alternative account of the sensible character of an odor, I agreed with him that there *is* a nondispositional quality that most directly engages our attention when we perceive by smell the sensible character of an odor. It is, I held, by recognizing this quality that we discern the peculiar disposition to smell a certain way which marks off one odor from another. I held that we can olfactually perceive that disposition only through perceiving its manifestation, which consists in its causing in us an olfactory experience having a certain quality, and that we can perceive this causation only through awareness of its effect, hence only through awareness of the peculiar quality of the olfactory experience we undergo, which *is* that effect. Consequently I acknowledged that on my view the olfactory quality that directly engages our attention constitutes the peculiar character of the olfactory experience caused by a particular odor. So I called this quality a "sensuous" quality rather than a "sensible" one, to mark the fact that it is *not* instantiated before the nose.

Our present task, then, is to decide whether or not the nondispositional quality of which we are directly conscious in smelling an odor *can* be a certain shape of the molecules composing the odor, as the direct realist holds. If it cannot, then direct realism fails for smell, and the account I have given of this quality—and of the sensible character of the odor—will emerge as the credible one.

8. Second Argument for Indirect Realism: Odorous Qualities Not Identical with Molecular Structures

Mr. Amoore did not find the sweet odorous quality to be a primary quality. So presumably the stereochemical mark of gases having this odor would have turned out, had he investigated them, to be (allegedly) a certain mixture of two or more shapes of molecules, or something of the sort. Let us suppose the case to be simpler, and imagine being sweet to be a primary olfactory quality; and let us suppose that among odorous gases all that smell sweet, and only these, have S-shaped molecules. Now suppose that Amoore did what the passage quoted from him shows he would not do, he asserted that the sweet quality we become conscious of in attentively smelling the airborne effluvium from a candy factory *is identical with* the S-shape of the molecules composing the gas. We are to imagine Amoore saying to us, "The sweetness we become olfactually conscious of *is* the S-shapedness of the molecules." This is direct realism concerning our olfactory consciousness of sweet odors.

Our first reaction is to say that this is nonsense. Remember that it is properties, not entities, not concrete particulars, that are being identified. And sensory awareness of a property consists in sensory awareness *that* something or other has this property. The proposal at hand, then, seems to entail that attentively to smell that a gas is sweet is to become olfactually aware that the molecules of the gas have an S-shape. And we all know that we never become aware *that* molecules in the air have certain shapes, in becoming olfactually aware merely of the sweetness of airborne effluvia. The proposal to identify being sweet with (molecules') being S-shaped seems to be sheer nonsense.

However there is a weakness in this attack upon the direct realist's proposed identity. The attack seems to rely upon the premise that if a property specified by 'P' is identical with a property specified by 'Q', then to become perceptually conscious that something is P entails becoming perceptually conscious that this thing is Q. But consider this example, from an essay by Robert L. Causey,[6] where it is put to quite different uses: the property, being black, is identical with the property, being the color of any opaque object that reflects no visible radiation when illuminated; but a person who becomes visually aware that an object before his eyes is black need not thereby become aware that this object has the color of all opaque things that reflect no visible radiation when illuminated.

It may be objected to the use of this example that the more plausible premise of the critic of direct realism is this one: where 'P' and 'Q' are different specifications of the *nature* of a single property, then to become perceptually aware that something is P is to become perceptually aware that this thing is Q. But the longer specification of the property, being black, just cited, does not specify the nature of this sensible quality; so our counterexample fails.

Let us, then, try another example (also adapted from Causey's essay) with which to defend direct realism against its critic by attacking that revised premise of the critic's argument. The new premise of the critic's argument seems appropriate, since both 'sweet' and 'S-shaped' would normally be taken to specify the nature of the property each signifies; and the critic of the direct realist's identification of sweetness with molecular S-shapedness would now contend that if sweetness *is* S-shapedness then olfactory awareness that the air is sweet should entail olfactory awareness that some of the air's molecules are S-shaped, since both "being sweet" and "being molecularly S-shaped" are meant to specify the nature of the property each signifies.

A counterexample to that criticism of the direct realist is the following: in becoming tactually conscious of the pressure of a strong wind on my face I become conscious of the force exerted by the wind on each perceptible unit-area of my face that I feel the wind blow upon; but this pressure, we are told, is identical with the statistically averaged transfer of momentum from each molecule of air to my face. Both of these descriptions of the property, pressure, can plausibly be construed to specify the nature of pressure. Yet in becoming tactually aware that the force per unit area is of a certain (tactually specified) magnitude, I do not become tactually aware that the average transfer of momentum from a molecule of air to my face is of a certain

6. "Attribute-identities in Microreductions," *Journal of Philosophy*, LXIX, 14 (Aug. 3, 1972) : 407–422.

magnitude; I do not even become aware that the air is composed of molecules.

Hence even though "being P" specifies the nature of the same property that "being Q" also specifies the nature of, being perceptually aware that something is P does not entail being perceptually aware that this thing (or anything) is Q. So the fact that we can be olfactually aware that something is sweet without being aware that this thing's molecules are S-shaped does not entail that its being sweet is not the same property as its molecules' being S-shaped. The direct realist's suggestion that these apparently different properties are really the same property cannot be so easily refuted.

Nevertheless the incredulity of most of us in regard to the suggested identity of nondispositional sweetness with molecular S-shapedness is not appreciably lessened by attention to the example of pressure. We do not believe that that sweetness *is* S-shapedness—the required reduction of occurrent sweetness to molecular S-shapedness can be carried out. Why is this?

The answer is to be found in the conditions that are met by the microreduction of pressure to average molecular transfer of momentum and in the fact that these conditions cannot be met by the suggested reduction of occurrent sweetness to molecular S-shapedness. A full appreciation of the character of these conditions is not easily achieved. I shall not attempt to achieve it until the next chapter, on the sensory perception of temperature, where I shall take advantage of the fact that the purported direct object of thermosensory perception—intensity of heat (temperature) —figures centrally in the most celebratedly microreduced physical discipline, macroscopic thermodynamics. For very good reasons no comparable physics of olfactually sensible properties of physical systems exists. So the material is not at hand for developing now a full appreciation of the problem of microreduction in connection with sensible odorous qualities. And justice cannot be done to our example, to pressure itself— which does have, of course, a sophisticated physical treatment— until we come to the chapter on the sense of touch, where pressure will emerge as the direct realist's candidate for the property whose instance before the skin we directly feel.

For now, in regard to odors, I can give only a sketch, presented somewhat dogmatically, of what those conditions are which alone would make both intelligible and plausible to us the microreduction necessary to justify the identification of occurrent sweetness with molecular S-shapedness, and of the reasons there are for believing that these conditions cannot be met; my remarks about pressure—and temperature—will consist in part of promissory notes to be paid off in the chapters on thermal and tactual feeling.

The concept of pressure has an exact analysis, as the amount of force exerted by one body upon a unit area of another body in contact with the first. If the second body is free to move, it will receive an acceleration which is a function of—among other things—the pressure exerted by the first body. One way to explain the acceleration received by the second body is to construe it as the sum of the accelerations caused by the parts of the first body. If the first body is a gas and the second a container with a freely moving piston as one of its walls, such an explanation can be effected by analyzing the total force exerted by the gas against the piston as an aggregate of the forces exerted by each of the moving molecules of the gas, as the molecules strike the piston. This entails construing the pressure of the gas as the average momentum transferred from each moving molecule of the gas to the piston.

This microreduction of macroscopic pressure of a gas to a statistical property of the molecules composing the gas pre-supposes, for its intelligibility, that we begin with an analysis of our concept of macroscopic pressure, and that the content of this analysis coheres with the content of our microstructural analysis: understanding the concept of a force exerted per unit area by a large body entails appreciating the naturalness of this force's being analyzed as some sort of function of forces exerted by very small parts of this large body. Exactly what function of exactly what parts only theoretical inquiry and empirical testing can tell us. This microreduction also presupposes, for its plausi-bility, that there should be well-known physical laws specifying the functional interrelations of observable pressure and other well-defined physical quantities, and that these empirical laws should be explained by the new statistical-mechanical laws in which the microstructural analysis of pressure figures. For example, the empirical laws relating the observable properties, pressure, volume, and temperature of gases, would need to be explained in this way. However, this requires the microreduc-tion of temperature as well (to mean kinetic energy of mole-cules, as it turns out) ; microreduction of pressure alone is in-sufficient. And of course this explanation of macroscopic by microstructural laws also presupposes that the gas itself is iden-tified with an aggregate of molecules in motion (and hence that the volume of the gas is identified with the volume occupied by the moving molecules) .

Both the intelligibility and the plausibility of the claim that the observable temperature of a gas is identical with the mean kinetic energy of the unobservable molecules composing the gas presupposes a similar set of conditions: an initial analysis of the concept of observable temperature which coheres with (but does not entail) the microstructural analysis; (discovering this initial analysis will take some labor in the next chapter) ; a set of empirical laws specifying functional interrelationships of observable temperature with other well-defined physical quantities, such as pressure, volume, entropy; and an explanation, provided by the statistical-mechanical, microstructural laws, of why these macroscopic, physical laws hold. When all these conditions are realized, but not before, the initially strange identification of easily observable temperature with molecular properties that certainly are not initially discoverable by observation becomes perspicuously intelligible as well as plausible to us, whereas, as a merely asserted identity of an observable with an apparently unobservable property, it would be scarcely intelligible to us, and certainly not rationally acceptable.

Now let us return to the identity suggested by the direct realist, between the nondispositional, odorous quality, sweet, and the S-shape of the molecules of the gas that smells sweet. Why is it that we cannot expect that the strangeness of this proposal will give way to a perspicuous intelligibility (and a plausibility) of the sort we find with both pressure and temperature when these latter macroscopic properties are identified with molecular properties? The reason is that the conditions just sketched are none of them realizable in connection with the proposed microreduction of odorous qualities. First, the concept of the nondispositional, odorous quality, sweet, has, almost certainly, no analysis at all; hence there is no way the proposed microreduction of this quality to the S-shape of molecules can be found to cohere with this concept of sweetness. Second, there are no physical laws articulating functional interrelationships between a nondispositional, sensible sweetness of gases and other well-defined physical properties of substances with which gases interact. And the whole history of science works against the presumption that any such laws are forthcoming: no one expects physicists to begin to undertake an empirical investigation of the causal role played among physical systems by a nondispositional, sensible sweetness belonging to gases.

Consequently the identification of occurrent sweetness with S-shapedness cannot gain either intelligibility or plausibility in virtue of the explanations that theoretical laws concerning molecular S-shapedness will offer of nonexistent (and nonforthcoming) empirical laws exhibiting the causal role of nondispositional, sensible sweetness of gases before our nose. For these reasons the initial and apparent unintelligibility and implausibility of the proposed identification of odorous quality with molecular shape has to be judged to be final and genuine. But molecular shape is not to be distinguished, in regard to this outcome, from the more complex pattern of physical and chemical properties of molecules which may be expected to constitute the true causal ground (in the odor) of our sensory experience of odorous qualities.

The direct realist's only hope, that the nondispositional, odorous qualities we become directly conscious of in smelling odors should turn out to be olfaction-independent, physical properties of the odors' molecules, is doomed to be disappointed.

We may therefore return with warranted confidence to my earlier account of the sensible character of an odor as the odor's disposition to smell a certain way to us. And we may accept the argument I based upon that account, which, in brief, went as follows (with an addition—concerning sensuous quality—that emerged from the direct realist's correct anticipation of how my account will be completed in §10) .

Since we can be olfactually conscious of an odor's disposition to smell a certain way to us only through being thus conscious of the manifestation of this disposition, and since this manifestation consists in the odor's causing us to undergo an experience having a peculiar sensuous quality, and since we can become olfactually conscious of this causal action of the odor only through becoming thus conscious of its effect, hence conscious of the peculiar sensuous quality of our olfactory experience, whose instance is *not* before our nose; since all this, we are directly conscious of the sensuous quality of our olfactory experience whenever we attentively smell an odor, only indirectly conscious of the disposition in the odor to cause in us this olfactory experience. So we are indirectly conscious of the gas's sensible character and hence of the gas (the odor) before our nose. Indirect realism is true of smell.

9. What We Discover about an Odor in Attentively
    Smelling It (III) : The Odor's Nature

If a gas can have an odor then an odor is not itself a gas. Gases can have odors. So odors are not gases.

If gases have odors then surely these odors are the olfactually sensible characters of the gases.

But if odorous objects emit odors and we inhale these odors, then odors are not sensible characters, for sensible characters can neither be emitted by objects nor inhaled by us. And odorous objects do emit odors; we do inhale them. So odors are not sensible characters.

If the sensible characters of gases are not the odors we smell, then surely the gases themselves must be the odors.

Odors are gases. Odors are not gases, they are the sensible characters of gases. Odors are sensible characters. Odors are not sensible characters, they are the gases that have these characters.

From this dialectic I draw this conclusion: the word 'odor' is sometimes used to speak of an odorous effluvium of an object or process, and it is sometimes used to speak of the olfactually sensible character shared by an odorous object and its effluvium.

Until now I have spoken of odors as the gases given off by odorous objects. This has been useful so long as we have been trying to settle the issue between direct and indirect realism. For it helped put the focus on the substance the direct realist must choose as his candidate for direct object of olfactory perception, the gas emitted by the odorous object. Now that we have resolved that issue in favor of indirect realism it will be convenient to take up the other meaning of the word 'odor' and use the word to refer to the sensible character shared by the object and its emanation—indeed, to let the emanation recede into the background of our discussion. This last is possible because in smelling things up close we often scarcely notice or don't notice at all that there is an emanation, but experience the sensible character we smell as belonging to the odorous object itself. Even when we forget the emanation, in smelling an object up close, the case can still be made for saying it is the emanation we smell more directly than the object emitting it. Since, however, everything before the nose is perceived indirectly, we can stop caring about the relatively more or less directness with which we perceive what is before the nose, and give our attention to the content and structure of our olfactory consciousness. In doing this it will be simpler to speak of the sensible character of the odorous object and drop the object's molecular emanation from our discussion.

This policy causes no difficulty for the dispositional conception of an olfactually sensible character. By this conception a sensible character is a disposition to smell a certain way; and the odorous object has exactly the same disposition to smell a certain way as its odorous emanation has: how the object smells to us is how its effluvium smells to us, and the object's disposition to smell this way is a function of the effluvium's.

When I bring a bar of soap up to my nose and smell its odor, I do not have the experience as of perceiving some transient condition, state, process, or action of the bar of soap, or observing some change in its condition. Smelling the odor of a piece of soap is not an experience like seeing the shrinking of a deflating balloon or hearing the wailing of a siren or feeling rain strike your face. It is more like seeing the color or feeling the smoothness of the soap. The odor is perceived as a relatively enduring feature of the soap, like its color and smoothness. And no doubt the odor is as stable a feature of the bar of soap as its color, perhaps more stable than its texture. The odor of the bar of soap is its olfactually sensible character; that sensible character is the soap's disposition to smell to us a certain way; and the disposition is relatively stable.

We are now in a position to give a fifth rendering of our answer to the question, "What is it that we find out about an object in becoming conscious through smell of its odor?" Transposing our earlier answers to this question into our new language, in which an odor is no longer an object's molecular effluvium but its olfactually sensible character, our earlier answers read like this: we find out what the object's odor is; we find out what the object's odor is like; we discover the object's olfactually sensible character; we find out that the object smells a certain way. Now we can say straight out: we discover the nature of the object's odor. For the odor of the object is its olfactually sensible character, this character has for its nature its being a disposition of the object to smell a certain way, and it is this disposition we discover when we smell with attention the object's odor. We become conscious of the object's smelling a certain way to us now, and we presume that it would go on smelling this same way if we went on smelling it. This presumption is counted as knowledge by our epistemic community; so we are justified in describing our attentively smelling an object's presence as

involving our becoming olfactually conscious of the object's more
or less stable disposition to smell to us the way it is now smelling.
My inquiry here reaches a fork in the road. One turn would
take me the way of epistemology, asking what entitles us to
treat as knowledge our perceptual presumption that the present
way of smelling manifests a constant disposition in the object.
Since being conscious of an object's disposition is a certain form
of knowing that it has this disposition, that question needs to
be answered if, as a student of smell, one is to be fully justified
in affirming that we are olfactually conscious of the object's disposition to smell a certain way (which *is* its sensible character).
Nevertheless I shall not take the epistemological turn, here or
in other chapters. Instead I shall assume that any answer to the
epistemological question which would deny me the right to
affirm that when we attentively smell an object's presence we become aware of a sensible character of the object has misconstrued
the word 'know'—and I set aside as a project distinguishable from
my present project the attempt to specify the epistemic foundation of that right.

The other turn in the road, the one I shall follow, is not as
easily named as the epistemological turn. In another context of
inquiry, where the vehicle of knowledge under discussion is linguistic—perhaps sentences—rather than, as here, sensory states,
one could contrast with the epistemological turn the turn to
theory of meaning. The present inquiry is closer to the theory of
meaning than to the theory of knowledge. It is even closer to the
theory of belief and hence also to the theory of concepts. My
interest is in how we apprehend the world, not with the reasons
for saying that in apprehending it we *know* it. Yet that remark
can be misleading, since a part of the reason we have for saying
we know the world is our belief that our apprehension of it is
often correct, that we often get things as they are; and I *am* interested in asking: Given that we know it, in what way does a
particular, sensory form of consciousness of the world enable us,
in being thus conscious, to grasp things as they are, or cause us
to fail to do so?

My persistent concern is with the structure and content of our
sensory consciousness of the world. In regard to smell we have
still a little way to travel down this path of inquiry. For there
is something puzzling in the notion that we smell an object's
disposition to smell a certain way. Indeed there is something
puzzling in the notion that an object's (olfactually) sensible
character *is* a mere disposition to smell a certain way. Even when

convinced of the truth of these theses one is uncomfortable with them. It is possible to rid ourselves of this discomfort only by describing more carefully our manner of becoming conscious by smell of a mere disposition to smell a certain way.

10. The Structure and Content of Sensory Consciousness of Odors

An object's disposition to smell a certain way can hold our olfactory attention only in virtue of the disposition's manifestation doing so. This manifestation consists in the object's smelling that way on some occasion. This in turn consists in the object's causing one (by emitting an effluvium that acts upon one's olfactory membrane) to undergo an olfactory experience having a certain character. One can attentively perceive the object's causing this effect upon one only if the effect itself holds one's olfactory attention. But this effect is an experience of ours that has a certain character; it is *not* before the nose. Therefore our olfactory attention to the disposition of the object before our nose (and so to the object) is mediated by our attention to the character of an experience of our own. But olfactory attention is olfactory awareness. So our olfactory awareness of the object's disposition (and so of the object) is mediated by our *direct* awareness of the character of an experience of our own. All this I have already established.

How is it possible for direct awareness of the character of an "olfactory experience" to mediate sensory awareness of an object's mere disposition to smell a certain way? This question can be answered only through replacing the vague notion of "an olfactory experience," having a certain character, with something more precise. We can make a start at doing this by answering another question: Why do we tend to think that we don't perceive a disposition in the object but smell a quality? Surely the answer is because it *is* a nondispositional, olfactory quality that most directly holds our attention. In smelling an odorous object we perceive its odorous disposition *as* a determinate quality, for example, as *sweet*. (The italics distinguish this quality from the dispositional sweetness belonging to the odorous object.) How do we do this?

We have explored the direct realist's answer to a connected question and found it mistaken: that the nondispositional, olfactory quality belongs to the odorous object or its effluvium, to something before the nose. We do not perceive the object's disposition *as* a quality by perceiving the causal ground, in the object, of this disposition, that is, by perceiving an olfaction-independent, physical property of the object which *is* the quality we perceive the disposition *as*. We do not do that.

On the other hand we are directly aware of the character of an experience of our own which manifests for us the sensible character (the *peculiar* disposition) of the odorous object. One idea will ground the answer to all three of our questions: that the "character of our experience" of which we are directly aware is the sensuous quality, say *sweet,* which we perceive the object's disposition *as*. Let me explain.

Suppose that when we smell an odorous substance, the character of our conscious state is partly constituted by its instantiating an olfactory sensuous quality, say *sweet*. Now we remind ourselves that in perceiving the object's dispositional sweetness—smelling it to be sweet—we perceive *that* it is sweet; and we further remind ourselves that it is reasonable to believe that perceiving that a thing is sweet requires something in the way of a perceptual affirmation that the thing is sweet. But perceptually affirming this last requires that within perception we olfactually *attribute* dispositional sweetness to the object before our nose.

But if the olfactory perceiver attributed dispositional sweetness to the object by applying to it a mere concept of that disposition, then he would be merely *thinking* that the object is sweet. This he is not doing; he is smelling it to be sweet. So he must attribute its disposition to the object by means of something other than a concept. What else has the perceiver "at hand" with which to effect this attribution? He has, by our present supposition, the nondispositional, sensuous quality *sweet* instantiated within (partially constituting) his olfactory state of consciousness.

Let the structure of olfactory consciousness be as follows. It is direct consciousness *of* its own sensuous character *(sweet)*, and it is an attribution of this very character to the object before the nose, for example, to a chocolate bar. The sensuous quality, *sweet,* functions as the content of an olfactually sensuous attribution of itself to the candy bar. Sensuously to attribute (olfactory) *sweet* to a candy bar is to smell the candy bar as if having this quality.

Not every question is yet answered. We have not discovered what makes of this perceiving the object if sensuously *sweet* a perception of the object's disposition to smell *sweet*. No olfactory representation of the disposition *as* a disposition has yet emerged.

Since to perceive a feature is to perceive that something has this feature, to perceive a disposition is to perceive that something has this disposition. How does our sensuous attribution of non-dispositional *sweet* figure as olfactual attribution of dispositional sweetness?

Well, it cannot quite do that. But it can figure in that attribution, in this way: in addition to sensuously attributing *sweet,* the perceiver conceptually ascribes to the thus attributed *sweet* the power to reveal itself to his olfactory inspection. If the sensuously attributed *sweet,* as olfactually affirmed *of* the candy bar, is augmented by a conceptually ascribed power to reveal itself to the perceiver, then in smelling the candy bar he has affirmed of it the disposition to smell *sweet* to him. To be sure, olfactually he has misrepresented the basis, in the candy bar, of this disposition. He has nonetheless got the disposition right. To this extent his perception is realistic.

With this last piece of the puzzle filled in, we can now understand why we are inclined to disbelieve that one smells the olfactually sensible-character of an object *as* a disposition: one olfactually ascribes to the object before one's nose something equivalent to a disposition but not in those terms (*and* in affirming the ground of this disposition one thus ascribes *more* than a disposition to the object, thereby also *mis*perceiving the object).

It is plausible to suppose that mature perceivers do, in attentively smelling an object's odor, ascribe to this odor the power to do what it then seems to them to be doing: reveal its nature to them. Since this supposition is all we need in order to complete the answer to all our questions and because I know of no other account that will do the job so plausibly, I conclude that we are warranted in believing that the sense of smell is in fact structured in the way I have just supposed.

It remains to remark that I have now completed the argument for the representative version of indirect realism in regard to smell. For surely one is entitled to say, on the present account, that what we are directly conscious of, the instance of a sensuous quality, e.g., *sweet,* which figures within our consciousness of the candy bar as the content of our sensuous attribution of itself to the candy bar, *represents* for us the sensible character of this sweet food.

Chapter Four   FEELING
                          HEAT AND COLD

We feel with our skin the cold of a winter wind, the coolness
of an iron railing in summer shade, the heat of a nearby fire,
the warmth of the sun. When it is attentive, this feeling the heat
and cold of things before our skin I speak of as thermosensory
perception, thermal perception, or thermoperception.

Everything we thermally perceive before our skin we perceive
to be there by feeling the presence before our skin of some degree
of heat or cold. But in this mode of sensory perception we do
not tell that the heat or cold is there by perceiving that something else is before our sensory organs—as we do, for example,
when we tell how hot the roast in the oven is by looking at the
thermometer inserted into it: among the things *before* our skin
that we thermally feel, it is heat and cold that we feel most directly. Therefore, if this heat and cold before our skin is nonetheless to be indirectly felt by us, then in feeling it before our
skin we need to be still more directly conscious of something not
before our skin: the indirect realist says, "And so we are." The
direct realist believes we are not.

Several facts about perception of heat and cold conspire to
make it strategic ground for the conflict between direct and indirect perceptual realism. First, the independent physical reality
of what we most directly feel among the things before our skin
is vividly evident, since, when intense enough, heat and cold
will burn or freeze our skin, even kill us. Second, the characteristic content of thermal awareness is simpler than that of visual,
tactual, and auditory awareness. So the character of what most
directly holds our thermal attention—whether before the skin
or not—is exceptionally distinct. Third, by contrast with taste
and smell, whose content is comparably simple, the character of
what we most directly thermoperceive among the things before
our sense organs, intensity of heat, has been for several centuries
the subject matter—under the name 'temperature'—of one of the
fundamental branches of physics, thermodynamics.

Fourth, thermodynamics has undergone an exceptionally thor-
oughgoing microreduction, to statistical mechanics, with the consequence that the nature of intensity of heat (temperature) has
gone through interesting stages of specification by the physicists,
from the more or less operational and observational, through

the theoretical but macroscopic, to the theoretical and micro-structural; and philosophers have given fruitful attention to these stages. In short, the relative lucidity, simplicity, and immediacy of our thermosensory apprehension of temperature meets a lucidity, complexity, and development in our scientific comprehension of the same property; for the philosopher concerned to know exactly what it is that we most directly perceive through our senses, this confrontation generates a tension whose clarity is not matched in any other sensory modality.

The indirect realist is presented with an opportunity and the direct realist with a challenge whose elements appear to be especially perspicuous: the sharp contrast between, on the one hand, the apparently simple character of what we thermally feel to be before our skin, and, on the other, the complex nature of what we scientifically know to be there strongly suggests that our thermosensory attention is given to a complex property of things before our skin in virtue of its being more directly held by a simple quality of something not before our skin.

Because I want to do justice to both the opportunity and the challenge, the argument of this chapter will be lengthy. Roughly speaking, in §§1 to 6 an argument for indirect realism will be developed which relies upon an extended comparison between thermometer observation of temperature (intensity of heat) and feeling temperature, and upon the discrepancy between the theoretically specified nature of temperature and what can be discovered about temperature either by thermometer observation alone or by merely feeling it. In §§7 and 8, the thermoperceptual indirect realism just defended will be clarified. Then the challenge offered to the direct realist will be taken up, on his behalf, and the rest of the chapter, §§9 to 13, will be devoted to an exposition and criticism of four arguments for direct realism which try to overturn the case made for indirect realism. All four arguments attempt to exploit in some way the microreduction of thermodynamically specified temperature (of gases) to mean kinetic molecular energy by extending this microreduction of thermometer-observed temperature to include *directly* felt, thermal qualities, which these arguments for direct realism construe as temperatures. Incursions into the territories of both physics and the philosophy of science become necessary, and lengthen the argument.

1. Before Our Skin the Most Direct Object of Thermal Consciousness Is the Temperature of Our Skin

When we feel the heat or cold of an object in contact with our skin, the sense of touch cooperates with our thermal sense in rendering for us the body of what is laid against us. Here the heat we feel comes to our skin through conduction from an adjacent object. When, however, the heat we feel comes to our skin chiefly by radiation, as when we discover by thermal feeling alone that wood is burning in the fireplace, that the nearby radiator is turned on, or, moving outdoors, that the sun is shining, then no other sense plays a present part in forming our awareness of these objects and happenings before our skin (although, of course, earlier experience through other senses contributes something). With the full-bodied object of the sense of touch absent, in these purely thermal perceptions of things before our skin the objects that are hot or cold recede, and the degrees of heat and cold themselves occupy the foreground of our attention. However, for this more purely thermal awareness, the bodies outside us, which only touch can fully vivify for feeling, are commonly replaced by something closer to us: our own skin. For it does seem that we commonly feel the sun's warmth, for example, by feeling our skin warm up—and we feel the heat from the radiator and the fireplace in the same way. Very often, then, if not always, we feel the heat and cold of things that are not in contact with us by feeling the heat or cold of our own skin.

Having noticed this fact, when one returns to think of thermally feeling things we are also touching, one may suspect that here also we feel more directly the heat and cold of our own skin and, through feeling *it,* feel the heat and cold in the object touching our skin. Certainly the sensory mechanism, except for the method of transmitting heat from object to skin, is the same: the object before the skin warms (or cools) the skin, and the thermosensory receptor organs located within the skin respond to this change in the temperature of the surrounding skin; whether the heat comes to the skin (or leaves it) by conduction from (or to) an adjacent object, or is transmitted by radiation from (or to) a more remote object, the final stage of the process of sensory stimulation is the same. Furthermore, we certainly do often become thermally conscious of what we recognize as our skin's warmth or coolness when we feel the temperature of an object we are touching. Can we say that we feel our own skin's temperature even when, from preoccupation with objects pressing upon us, we fail to recognize the heat and cold as our skin's?

Consider an analogy. Suppose I am watching a woman in a soundproof studio sing but I do not realize there is a glass partition between her and me, nor that there is a loudspeaker in the room I'm in, relaying her voice to me. Assuming fidelity of reproduction, her voice holds my attention; but I am aurally conscious of the sound she makes in virtue of being aurally conscious of the sound the speaker makes. Although on another occasion I might realize this, I do not now recognize the process of mediation for what it is. So too we may be thermally conscious of the heat and cold in things before the skin through being thermally conscious always of the heat and cold in our skin itself, sometimes recognizing the latter for what it is, sometimes not. I see no good reason not to say that we always become thermally conscious of the heat or cold of our own skin in becoming thermally conscious of the heat or cold in things before our skin. And there are gains from this analysis, two of which deserve immediate notice.

We feel iron as colder than wood at the same temperature because iron is a better conductor of heat than wood is, so it cools our skin faster. This misperception of the temperature differences between objects that differ in their conductivity has made some philosophers question the realism of thermal perception: it seems that we do not get temperatures as they are. But if we feel our skin's temperature more directly, then we do get this right; for our skin *is* cooler sooner when we feel an iron railing than when we feel a wooden railing at the same temperature.

There is a "physiological zero" for thermal perception of our skin temperature, a temperature range within which we do not feel our skin's temperature because it is then the normal temperature of our skin. We therefore do not thermally feel objects in thermal contact with our skin when their temperature falls within this range. More interesting, objects before our skin whose temperature is below this physiological zero we feel as cool or cold, whereas objects whose temperatures are above our physiological zero we feel as warm or hot. And the felt difference between hot and cold is as qualitative a difference as the experienced difference between the sound of a trumpet and the color scarlet. This division of temperatures as they are felt into two qualitatively different continua, when compared with the single continuum of quantities of mean molecular kinetic energy believed to constitute the objective progression of temperatures in the objects before our skin, gives rise to two arguments, one against perceptual realism in regard to thermoperception, the other against direct realism alone. But both arguments are called in question by considering thermal perception's most direct object before the thermal receptor organs to be the temperature of the skin itself.

Consider first the argument against thermoperception realism.

In the objects before the skin there is a single temperature progression constituted of amounts of molecular kinetic energy. But thermally we feel two distinct progressions, the cold and the hot, ascending in opposite directions from a common center, the physiological zero. Since this duality corresponds to no thermal reality before the skin, we fail, thermoperceptually, to get things as they are. Thus the argument against thermoperceptual realism.

And the answer. When we observe temperatures on the Fahrenheit scale we also observe two progressions, the plus and the minus, ascending in opposite directions from a common center, zero degrees Fahrenheit. We do this by observing a Fahrenheit thermometer, more directly, and the intensities of heat in the objects to which the thermometer is applied, less directly. You will not complain that because we observe two progressions, whereas the molecules' kinetic energy has only one, therefore we are not making observations of thermal facts as they are. Nor does the fact that Fahrenheit zero does not correspond to absolute zero elicit this complaint. Similarly, in thermoperception we feel the temperatures of our skin more directly, the temperatures of objects before our skin less directly. And corresponding to the plus and the minus and zero on the Fahrenheit scale, our skin provides a scale comprising the hot and the cold and physiological zero, by means of which we thermoperceptually measure the temperatures of objects and happenings before our skin. The grounds offered for repudiating thermal perceptions of temperature serve equally to repudiate thermometer observations of temperature. Since you accept the thermometer observations, you must renounce your argument against accepting thermal perceptions.

Next, the argument against *direct* thermoperceptual realism.

Granting that the hot-cold scale can be used to represent the temperatures of the objects before our skin, nevertheless this representation does consist of two qualitatively different sorts of thermal quantities, heat and cold, whereas the objects before our skin have only one sort of thermal quantity, called "intensity of heat," which is actually quantity of molecular kinetic energy. More specifically, our thermal perception of ascending degrees of cold must be perception of something not belonging to objects before the skin, since in fact there is no qualitatively distinct, ascending progression of thermal intensities characterizing that ordering of objects before the skin which we thermally feel as more and more cold; rather there is a single descending progression of quantities of molecular kinetic energy (intensities of heat), continuous in character and direction with the temperatures of objects we thermoperceive on the hot side, but lower than those in quantity of molecular kinetic energy. Since, then, the degrees of cold we feel are not before the skin, they must constitute direct objects of thermal perception which are behind the skin and which are, therefore, in all probability, subjective, phenomenal objects representing for us the physical heat before the skin.

And the answer: it is true that there is something we thermoperceive more directly than the things before our skin. But this something is not a subjective, phenomenal object; it is our skin itself. Among the things before our thermosensory receptor organs, "organs" located within the skin, we most directly thermoperceive the temperatures of our skin itself. But the intensities of heat of the skin are quite as physical and as subject to the laws of thermodynamics as are the intensities of heat of objects outside (before) the skin. There is nothing merely subjective or phenomenal about the intensities of heat of our skin.

As to the qualitative break between the hot and the cold: the physiological zero is a physical dividing line that segregates thermal receptor organs in the skin into two sets, those which respond positively to temperatures above the zero range and are inhibited by temperatures below it (hot receptors), and those which are inhibited by temperatures above the zero line and respond positively to those below it (cold receptors); and being a temperature-above-physiological-zero is as qualitatively different from being a temperature-below-physiological-zero as any qualitative difference. We can, if we like, think of ourselves as thermally feeling the above-physiological-zero-ness and the below-physiological-zero-ness of the intensities of heat in our skin, first, and through this thermoperception feeling the same dimensions of the intensities of heat in objects before our skin. Why isn't being-a-skin-temperature-above-physiological-zero as qualitatively different from being-a-skin-temperature-below-physiological-zero as being scarlet is qualitatively different from being the sound of a trumpet?

That I conclude this rebuttal of the argument given against direct realism with a rhetorical question I intend as an indication that I am not convinced that the direct realist has an adequate answer to his opponent. However, the argument for indirect realism based on the qualitative difference between hot and cold I prefer not to adopt myself, so I shall leave it and its putative rebuttal in this sketchy form, confronting each other. And from now on I shall suppose that we do thermally feel the intensities of heat of objects before our skin always through feeling (more directly) the intensities of heat of our skin itself.

Now a word about what I shall count as "before the skin." It is so natural to consider the skin as the organ of thermal feeling that I wish to continue doing so. It is also convenient for me to speak, with regard to each of the senses, of things perceived before the sense organs and of things of which we have sensory awareness which are not before the sense organs. For this is a useful way to picture the dividing line between the sorts of things the direct realist contends comprise the most direct objects of sensory awareness (things before the sense organs) and those to which the indirect realist assigns this place (things not before the sense organs).

However, with regard to thermal perception we have now discovered that these two inclinations are incompatible (without some verbal juggling). For the physical condition that we most directly feel before the thermal receptor organs is the intensity of heat of the skin itself, which is, of course, not before (all of) the skin; for our purposes, therefore, the thermal receptor organ turns out to be, strictly speaking, not the (whole) skin but the system of thermosensory nerve endings within the skin. But in order to continue the natural habit of thinking of the skin as what we feel heat and cold with and to speak in the indicated way of things before and not before the thermal receptor organ, I shall make this verbal adjustment: I shall treat the part of the skin whose intensity of heat the thermal receptors within the skin are responding to, in initiating our thermal perceptions, as before the part of the skin comprising these thermal receptors (nerve endings) embedded within the skin. And I shall describe this intensity of heat of part of the skin as simply "before the skin," but meaning, before the other part of the skin, the part constituted by the thermal receptors embedded within the skin. In this way I can include the intensity of heat of the skin, which is a physical property of a physical object before out thermal receptor organs, as among the set of things we perceive "before the skin."

2. The Key Question: How Can We Become Thermally
   Conscious of Temperature without Perceiving Its Nature?

What causes us to feel the intensities of heat of bodies before
our skin is, nearly enough, those very intensities of heat themselves. When it is measured by a thermometer, intensity of heat
is called "temperature." According to the most common interpretation of their work, the theoretical physicists of heat have
discovered that the temperature of a body *is* the mean kinetic
energy of the body's constituent molecules—if the "body" is a
gas. If it is a solid its molecules do not move freely through
space but vibrate in position, and the body's temperature is
therefore constituted by both its kinetic and its potential molecular energy. For our purposes nothing important is lost and
economy is gained if we treat the formulation for gases as if it
covered the general case and so speak only of kinetic energy,
dropping reference to the potential energy of molecular vibrational motion in solids.

Since the intensity of heat we feel in a body before our skin is
the mean quantity of kinetic energy of the body's constituent
molecules, one is tempted to say that in feeling the body's intensity of heat we feel its molecules' mean kinetic energy. But
it is attentive, thermal perception that interests us here. And
what we attentively feel we are conscious of. So when we attentively feel a given intensity of heat before our skin we are
thermally conscious of this intensity of heat. A body's intensity
of heat is a property of this body. To be aware of one of a body's
properties is to be aware *that* something or other has this property—one may be ignorant of exactly what has the property but
one is aware that something or other has *it*. Hence to be thermally conscious of a certain intensity of heat is, at a minimum, to
be thermally aware *that* something or other has this intensity of
heat. But the property, intensity of heat, is the property, mean
molecular kinetic energy. To succumb to the temptation to say
we feel the molecular energy is, therefore, to seem to assert that
in attentively feeling a body's intensity of heat we become thermally aware *that* something has a certain mean kinetic energy
of its constituent molecules.

Yet we all know that in merely feeling heat or cold no discoveries about molecules are made. We are confronted, therefore,
with the fundamental question of this chapter: how is it possible
for us to become thermally aware *that* something before our skin
has a certain intensity of heat without becoming conscious of
the nature of this property? More specifically, what content does

our thermal awareness that something before our skin has a certain intensity of heat have if this awareness fails, as it does, to encompass the nature of intensity of heat? Since our thermo-sensory consciousness of things' temperatures fails to include within its content something equivalent to the idea, "so much mean molecular kinetic energy," how does it specify the temperatures it apprehends?

This puzzle about thermoperception can be expressed in another way. To perceive with attention a property of an object before our sense organs is to be conscious in a sensory way of the instantiation of this property in something or other before our sense organs. To be thus thermally conscious of a property's instantiation is to know that something or other has this property. This knowledge is doubly special: it is sensory knowledge, and it is consciously held knowledge. To feel with attention how hot an object before our skin is involves, therefore, our possessing conscious thermosensory knowledge that the object is just so hot. But the physicists have told us—on one common interpretation of their conclusions—that the object's intensity of heat *is* its constituent molecules' mean kinetic energy. So we have gained conscious knowledge that something or other before our skin has a specific property; this property's nature consists in being a certain mean kinetic energy of an object's constituent molecules. Yet we gain this knowledge without gaining the knowledge that anything whatever has any degree of mean kinetic molecular energy. In what form then, do we possess this knowledge?

For the general problem of how to know that an object has a property P whose nature is given by the specification 'N' but not know that P has the nature N, we might expect the solution to be: by knowing that the object has a property which one ascribes to the object under a description 'D' (which might be 'P'), which does specify the property P, and which is not synonymous with the specification 'N' of this property's nature. Here is an imaginary example in which the knowledge is gained by observation and hence is of the sort that most interests us here.

Suppose we somehow know that fireflies light up only when flying in a certain direction (upward, downward, to the left, to the right) but we do not know which direction this is, because for some reason we can observe fireflies only from a considerable distance; at this distance we cannot discern their bodies, and their lighting up is so brief that our seeing the light does not reveal to us the direction of flight. And let us say that what constitutes the nature of fireflies' flight when lighting up is the specific direction of this flight.

Let us now introduce a new phrase, 'star flight', and give it this meaning: "flight of fireflies in the direction, whatever it is, in which they always fly whenever they light up." We shall be able to make accurate observations and reports of fireflies engaged in star flight, since we need only see them light up in order to see that they are engaged in star flight. Let us now suppose that, unknown to us, the nature of star flight is upward flight. Then we are able to observe that fireflies are engaged in star flight, but we are not able to observe that fireflies are engaged in upward flight—yet being engaged in upward flight is what being engaged in star flight consists in. This is to say that we are able to observe that fireflies have the property, being engaged in star flight; this property has the nature, being engaged in upward flight; but we do not observe that fireflies are engaged in upward flight. The way we accomplish this is by observing fireflies under the description 'star flight', which, in virtue of its meaning, ascribes to fireflies, when applied to them, a property with an easily observed mark—the fireflies' lighting up—but, also in virtue of its meaning, leaves unspecified the nature of this property (the specific direction of flight) .

If we were to invoke the same sort of analysis for thermal perception our account would have to take something like this form: we feel objects before our skin under a description D, which in fact specifies the property, intensity of heat, a property whose nature is described by the term 'mean molecular kinetic energy', but this latter characterization we are not, as mere thermal percipients, in a position to apply to objects before our skin.

But what would it mean to say that we feel the intensity of heat of objects before our skin "under a description"? And what is the description? Or should we expect that it will turn out that we thermally feel the intensity of heat of objects before our skin under something analogous to a description? And what kind of thing is this?

I believe that in order to understand how we can become thermally aware of the temperature of objects before our skin without awareness of the nature of temperature we shall indeed have to turn to the idea of thermally feeling the temperatures of these objects under something analogous to a description. However, since proving this thesis will also prove indirect realism, I wish to proceed carefully. We shall be better prepared for the argument if we work out first the solution of a similar puzzle that arises in connection with the observation of things' temperatures by the use of thermometers in the context of the scientific study of heat. I shall therefore postpone attacking the thermoperceptual puzzle until I have presented and solved the thermometer-observation puzzle.

Before turning to consider the puzzle about thermometer observation it is necessary to introduce a qualification of a fundamental assumption with which I shall work throughout most of this chapter, indeed, until the last section, §13. I shall assume that the microtheory of thermal phenomena, the statistical-mechanical molecular (and atomic) analysis of them, provides the framework within which the nature of the property, intensity of heat (temperature), can be correctly specified, so that the idea of mean kinetic energy of molecules is a satisfactory approximation of the sort of analysis this property would get were its nature to be perfectly specified. This assumption can be questioned.

It can be questioned either by denying that the microreduction of thermodynamics affirms an identity of macroscopic and microstructural properties or by questioning the success of the microreduction itself. On either basis of criticism, my assumption may be replaced by an account of temperature's nature which relies entirely upon so-called "phenomenological" thermodynamics as the framework within which this nature is to be specified. Contemporary thermodynamics is a sophisticated, physical discipline, and it is not possible for me to anticipate the particular form this articulation of the nature of temperature by a critic of my assumption might take. Surely the operational conception of temperature, shortly to be sketched, is much too naive and impoverished a concept for the contemporary thermodynamicist to fall back upon.

Why, then, do I proceed upon the assumption that the microtheory of temperature specifies the nature of this property? First, because it does seem that this is today the most common assumption of physicists and philosophers of science. But, second, the fundamental difficulty generated for the direct realist by this assumption will remain—as I show in §13—even when my assumption is replaced by the assumption that the nature of temperature is to be specified within the framework of thermodynamics and hence by a macroscopic rather than microstructural analysis. For the difficulty for direct realism arises from the fact that the nature of intensity of heat cannot be discovered through attentively feeling its presence before the skin. This is the source of the problem for the direct realist. And as I shall point out in §13, this difficulty would remain even should we conclude that the nature of temperature is to be specified thermodynamically (macroscopically) rather than statistical-mechanically (microstructurally). If one takes an operational approach to specifying the nature of temperature on the basis of thermodynamics, it will turn out that the nature of temperature cannot be discovered by thermoperception; and if one provides a theoretical specification of the nature of temperature by appealing to thermodynamic theory alone, it will also turn out that the nature of temperature cannot be discovered through thermoperception. This judgment I shall defend in §13.

In the meantime, the problem for direct realism generated by the fact that we can thermally feel temperature without perceiving the nature of temperature can be more distinctly and vividly laid out by proceeding upon the assumption that temperature's nature is in principle specifiable microstructurally. And this assumption does appear to be the one most commonly held at this time by physicists and philosophers of physics.

Even the preliminary puzzle to which I am about to turn, concerning the observation of temperatures with thermometers, even this puzzle would remain if instead of the microstructural analysis any purely thermodynamical specification of the nature of temperature were adopted other than the operational conception (and a contemporary philosopher of physics will not adopt the latter). For by merely making observations by means of thermometers one cannot discover the nature of temperature even as thermodynamically (but not merely operationally) defined, since such a definition presupposes a sophisticated, thermodynamical analysis, virtually a theory, which mere observation with thermometers is quite incapable of yielding. Therefore it would still remain a puzzle how we can observe by thermometers a property (temperature) whose nature is not revealed to us by means of this observation. And this is all the puzzle needed to provide the analogy wanted with the puzzle about thermally feeling intensities of heat.

One further cautionary note is needed. Throughout this chapter I often speak of what we thermally feel, when attentive, as "temperature." Of course this word is more properly used to specify intensity of heat *as* measured by a thermometer. It would be somewhat better English, therefore, to speak always of what we feel as "intensity of heat"; to save words, space, and time, I shall not always do this. I shall use the word 'temperature' at will to refer to intensity of heat both as measured by a thermometer and as felt by us—and of course as belonging to physical systems when altogether unobserved by anyone.

I turn now to an explanation of the preliminary puzzle.

3. An Analogous Question: How Can We with Thermometers Observe Temperature without Observing Its Nature?

The science of heat was pursued for more than two centuries before the kinetic, statistical-mechanical theory of heat received a formulation making it capable of playing an important role in the analysis of thermal phenomena. Thermodynamics, the science of heat, became an important, in some respects fundamental branch of physics without essential use of a theory of heat as molecules of matter in patterns of motion obeying certain statistical and mechanical laws. Even today thermodynamics can be presented as a rigorous and powerful physical discipline in which no appeal is made to the microstructure of matter. This independence of the macroscopic analysis of thermal phenomena from any microtheory of those phenomena has as an upshot the puzzle of present interest to us: how was it possible for scientists to observe *that* a system had a certain temperature without knowing the nature of that property they were observing the system to have?

Our puzzle can be sharpened for us if we begin by exhibiting one account of the concept of temperature—the operationalist analysis—which is partly motivated by the desire to show that in observing temperature experimentalists *are* discovering the nature of temperature. First a word about some of the concepts with which thermodynamicists operate.

The Boyle-Charles law, stating the functional interdependence of the volume, pressure, and temperature of gases; the law of conservation of energy, which is the First Law of Thermodynamics; the Second Law of Thermodynamics, stating that entropy increases in all actual transfers of energy, hence that the energy available for work is always decreasing (the universe is "running down") —these thermodynamic laws all have as their subject matter quantities either easily observed or simply constructed from easily observed ones: pressure, volume, and temperature obviously fall in the easily observed category; density, quantity of heat, energy, and entropy fall in the second category. Density is the ratio of mass to volume; quantity of heat in a substance (or process involving the substance) is a simple construction from the amount of work it takes to raise by one degree the temperature of a unit mass of the substance; the quantity of energy involved in a process is measured in various easy ways taken over from mechanics—for example, by measuring the quantity of work done; and the entropy of a process is the ratio of the quantity of heat transferred to the temperature at which it is transferred. Macroscopic heat itself is today thermodynamically conceived simply as any quantity of energy transferred as a result of a difference of temperature between two regions in thermal contact with each other. This last, contemporary definition points up the fact that the basic, peculiarly thermal quantity of thermodynamics is temperature—intensity of heat, whose simple measure has always been a thermometer reading.

It is perhaps no accident that Percy Bridgman, the creator of operationalism, a philosophy of science that construes concepts of physical properties as concepts of the operations, with their minimally construed results, whereby we determine the presence of the properties, was by profession an experimental thermodynamicist. Operationalists have held that in the pursuit of the empirical laws of macroscopic thermodynamics one makes essential use of a concept of temperature which embraces no more than this content: the result of applying a thermometer to a physical system *is* the temperature of this system. The operationalist argues that nothing figures essentially in one's working concept of temperature beyond the experimental operations of perfecting and using thermometers, and the numerical values of the readings on these thermometers. One may wish to acknowledge that a body has a temperature when no thermometer is being applied to it. Then one adds to the concept of temperature a counterfactual component: if no thermometer is being applied then the temperature at a time is the reading one would have got if one had applied a thermometer at this time. This counterfactual component can be verbally centered on the body that has the temperature by calling the conditional fact it states a "disposition" of this body.

Stopping short, here, of articulating the operational presuppositions of a physical system's being a thermometer relative to another system, at its largest the operational definition of temperature would look like this: the temperature of a physical system S_1, at a given time, is a relationship between S_1 and another physical system S_2, where S_2 comprises a thermometer in thermal equilibrium at this time with S_1, whereby S_1 yields up a reading on S_2; or, in the absence of such an actual relationship, the temperature of S_1 is its disposition to yield such a reading in case a thermometer were applied at this time to S_1.

On this analysis the idea of "yielding up" a reading on a thermometer is an idea of the merest conjunction of events; there is not so much as an allusion to what causally accounts for a body's yielding up a reading when a thermometer is applied to it. And this, the operationalist holds, is fair enough: in empirical thermodynamics he finds that ideas about the causal explanation for one body yielding up a reading on another body (the thermometer) play no essential part in the scientists' work, if such ideas occur at all. Where they exist such ideas are merely private speculations in the minds of investigators whose professional interest in temperature does not extend beyond uniform and precise determination of its numerical value and discovery of its lawful covariations with other observable quantities and with quantities easily constructed from these.

Of course, the thermodynamicist will want to understand the presuppositions of his use of thermometers; but this can be achieved well enough by reflection upon the evolution of this use and without going beyond the invocation of other purely operational concepts, of pressure, volume, density, thermal equilibrium, heat sources, and—but only for getting off the ground— felt changes in intensity of heat. Once the concept of temperature (and the use of thermometers) is on its operational feet, no further use is found in scientific investigations for thermally *feeling* intensity of heat. The inception of the scientific study of heat is marked by the independence of this study from any reliance upon what we thermally feel and hence an absence of interest in the sensible qualities warm, hot, cool, cold, which figure in thermal feeling. As to the appeal to ideal gases and perfectly reversible heat engines, which figures in Kelvin's development of a scale of absolute temperature, this is to be analyzed in terms of the utilization of certain limits which certain measures upon actual gases approach as the gases approach minimal density and of other limits approached by certain measures on heat engines as these engines approach their maximum efficiency.

Suppose we now turn our thought to thermodynamics after the time when the mathematical physicists, Maxwell, Boltzmann, Gibbs, *et al.*, have invented and perfected the statistical-mechanical, kinetic theory of heat, and the proposal has been made to affirm the identity of the temperature of a physical system with the mean kinetic energy of the unobservable molecules that in the aggregate constitute this physical system. It turns out that, if taken as a definition, the operational conception of temperature blocks, upon reflection, acceptance of this proposal.

We cannot consistently accept as a definition of the property, temperature, that the temperature of a body is the relationship this body has to a thermometer, a relationship that consists in the thermometer's showing a reading when in thermal contact with the body, and also accept as a specification of the nature of this temperature that it is the mean kinetic energy of the molecules of the body to which the thermometer is applied. For the state of affairs that consists in a body's having a certain mean kinetic energy of its constituent molecules at a given time is not the same state of affairs as that constituted by this same body's being in thermal contact with a thermometer and the thermometer's showing a reading. The second state of affairs consists, characteristically, in a relationship between the hot body and another body, the thermometer. The first state of affairs involves the hot body alone and no relationship with another body. Having a temperature according to the operational conception cannot be the same thing as having a temperature according to the statistical-mechanical conception. The two conceptions are not two specifications of a single property. If the operational conception of temperature does correctly specify the property experimental thermodynamicists were observing in observing temperature, then we cannot accept the statistical-mechanical conception of the mean kinetic energy of molecules as specifying the nature of temperature.

From one perspective, the suggested conclusion, that the property the microtheory of heat defines cannot be the property that the experimentalists were so easily observing, is not surprising: the mean kinetic energy of molecules is not, we want to say, speaking from this perspective, an observable property of physical systems. If it were, then Boyle and Charles and Carnot and Fourier and Kelvin and the rest would have discovered that this is what temperature is by merely making observations. There would have been no need to wait for the invention, the elaborate mathematical-theoretical work of Maxwell, Boltzmann, Gibbs, *et al.*, in order to make the discovery that mean kinetic molecular energy is so closely associated with temperature. Since for more than two centuries observations in the form of increasingly precise measurements of temperature were made without yielding any information about molecular kinetic energy, it is evident, we are disposed to say, that the property observed was not mean kinetic energy of molecules. Small wonder, then, that the operational conception of temperature serves to demonstrate the impossibility of temperature's identity with mean molecular kinetic energy.

And yet—when we allow what I shall venture to call our "physical intuitions" to move us, we find it very nearly irresistible to say that of course the kinetic theory shows us what temperature really is; of course it shows us the real nature of intensity of heat, to wit, that it is mean kinetic energy of the molecules of the body with a given temperature. In this frame of mind, our puzzle is presented for us: How might it be possible that the property experimental thermodynamicists were observing objects to have but without gaining any information about molecular energies was all along this very property, mean kinetic energy of molecules? What must the content of the observation of an object's temperature have been in order that this temperature should have been a property whose nature its observers remained ignorant of even as they made more and more precise determinations of its degree? Is there a way that the operationalist analysis of the experimentalists' conception of temperature can be corrected so as to give us a conception at once consistent with temperature's turning out to be the mean kinetic energy of molecules and consonant with the interpretations physicists with no workable microtheory made of their observations with thermometers?

In looking for an affirmative answer to this question, we may be helped by returning for a moment to an aspect of the operationalist's analysis of the conception of temperature which I left in the background while explaining the inconsistency between this analysis and the microtheoretical analysis. On the operational account, when a body has no thermometer applied to it at a certain time its temperature at this time is its disposition to yield a specific reading in case a thermometer were applied at this time to it. And one way to see that this conception of temperature cannot be a conception of the property, mean kinetic energy of molecules, is to appreciate that the latter property is what it is about the hot body that causally accounts for the reading you get when you do apply a thermometer, whereas the mere disposition to yield a reading is not the sort of thing to which a role is assigned as causing the reading you get when you apply a thermometer. Indeed, the operationalist would never permit use of the term 'disposition' if he thought it would be used to speak of a causal agent. For him, to ascribe to a body a disposition to yield a certain reading is merely to state the fact that if you applied a thermometer to this body you would get a reading. But this fact certainly plays no causal role in producing the reading we get.

So the operationalist's idea of a disposition to yield a reading is not an idea of the sort of thing that can play a part in causally accounting for the occurrence of the readings we get. The specific mean kinetic energy of the hot body's molecules, on the other hand, does provide a causal explanation of the fact that we get a specific reading when we apply a thermometer to the hot body. If the mean kinetic energy of molecules causally explains the body's yielding up a thermometer reading, whereas the operationally conceived disposition to yield a reading is not the right sort of thing to be the cause of anything, then the mean kinetic molecular energy of a body at a given time is not identical with the body's disposition at this time to yield a reading—and, once again, the operational conception of temperature cannot be a conception of the property whose nature consists in being the mean kinetic energy of many molecules.

4. Answer to the Question about Thermometer Observation of Temperature

The inconsistency between an operational analysis of the description under which the experimentalists observed temperature and the later microtheoretical conception of temperature suggests a correction in the operational analysis. I suggest that we suppose that from early on, through the use of thermometers, the scientific students of thermal phenomena observed temperature under this description: the property of the physical system to which the thermometer is applied, whatever the property's (presently unknown) nature may be, which causally accounts for the part that physical system plays in producing the reading we are now getting on the thermometer. This analysis of the experimentalists' conception of temperature instantly removes the mystery about how earlier thermodynamicists made precise observations of a property whose nature was inaccessible to their observation. For nothing can be more intelligible to us than that a property observed as "that property, whatever its nature, which causally accounts for its possessor's producing *this* observed effect" should have a nature not discoverable by more careful observation but capable of being discovered through theoretical explanation of the empirical laws its observation had founded. The puzzle is solved.

A few words are needed about how a system of molecules' mean kinetic energy can causally account for the production of a certain effect. Let us suppose that a thermometer that has been registering the temperature of the air in a refrigerator is removed and hung in the kitchen, to record the temperature of the kitchen air. Since the kinetic energy of a molecule of air is one-half the product of the molecule's mass and its squared velocity, if its mass remains constant the molecule's kinetic energy is a function of its velocity. So the average kinetic energy of all the molecules of a body of air is a function of the average velocity of all these molecules. The kitchen air being hotter than the air in the refrigerator, its molecules are moving much faster. So when these molecules hit the thermometer they cause the thermometer's molecules to begin to vibrate faster than they had in the refrigerator. Moving faster, the vibrating molecules of mercury in the thermometer travel farther before they begin their return journey. Hence the average boundaries of the volume of mercury increase wherever they are free to do so: the mercury expands. Once thermal equilibrium is attained between the mercury and the kitchen air, the expansion stops. And there we have a thermometer reading which has been produced by the kitchen air.

What is it about the kitchen air that causally accounts for its producing this expansion? One could say that it is how fast its molecules are moving. Or one could say that it is the mean kinetic energy of these molecules, which is a function of velocity and mass. The first answer is appropriate as responsive to an interest in the simplest difference between the refrigerator air and the kitchen air which could be assigned responsibility for the change in the thermometer reading, as the thermometer is moved from the refrigerator into the kitchen. The second answer, however, by including the role of the air molecules' masses, seems to capture all the aspects of the air that play a part in making the mercury expand. It is certainly plausible that the mean kinetic energy of the molecules of the kitchen air should turn out to answer to the original description under which the temperature of the kitchen air was, if I am right, taken in: "that property of the kitchen air, whatever its presently unknown nature, which causally accounts for the kitchen air's producing *this* reading on the thermometer."

Is there evidence that earlier thermodynamicists did conceive temperature in this way? If it exists anywhere it should exist in studies of the conduction of heat and in the theory of heat engines. For in both of these subjects the dynamic role of temperature is in the foreground. And both were carried to a sophisticated development well before the statistical-mechanical theory's effective existence.

In the years 1807–1819, Joseph Fourier published papers in which he perfected the mathematical theory of the conduction of heat, culminating in his work, *The Analytical Theory of Heat*.[1] Although Fourier believed in the caloric theory of heat, which speculated that heat is a material substance transported in conduction, and although he engaged in occasional speculations on these lines in his book, the primary work of the book is wholly independent of microtheoretical assumptions, and is so understood by Fourier:

> The chief results of our theory are the differential equations of the movement of heat in solid and liquid bodies, and the general equation which relates to the surface. The truth of these equations is not founded on any physical explanation of the effects of heat. In whatever manner we please to imagine the nature of this element, whether we regard it as a distinct material thing which passes from one part of space to another, or whether we make heat consist simply in the transfer of motion, we shall always arrive at the same equations, since the hypothesis which we form must represent the general and simple facts from which the mathematical laws are derived (*ibid.*, p. 464).

This I read as Fourier's version of the clause, 'whatever the nature of the property may turn out to be', within the description under which he made his thermometer observations and formulated his empirical laws concerning temperature.

Fourier's fundamental "principle of the communication of heat," in which we should find the causal role of temperature suggesting itself, he formulates verbally in this way:

> The quantity of heat communicated by the point n to the point m depends on the duration of the instant, on the very small distance between these points, on the actual temperature of each point, and on the nature of the solid substance. . . . Now experiments have disclosed in this respect, a general result: it consists in this, that all the other circumstances being the same, the quantity of heat which one of

1. New York: Dover Publications, 1955.

the molecules receives from the other is proportional to the difference of temperature of the two molecules (*ibid.*, p. 43).

When, as here, the area of the conductor and the distance the heat is conducted are treated as extremely small, the "other circumstances" pertain to the nature of the conducting solid and constitute its "heat capacity" and its "thermal conductivity". It is reasonably clear that the temperature difference emerges as the one dynamic factor that might be construed as driving the heat from the point of higher temperature to the point of lower temperature. But without knowledge of the nature of heat, nothing useful could be said about how differences of intensity of heat account for the direction of movement of heat. Nevertheless Fourier has, as remarked, his moments of speculation. The passage that follows can be read as an indication that Fourier did conceive temperature as a property causally responsible for certain observable, mechanical effects—but we must take his earlier disclaimer concerning the microstructure of heat as still operative, so far as the particular sort of cause he here speculatively posits that temperature is:

> Heat is the origin of all elasticity; it is the repulsive force which preserves the form of solid masses and volume of liquids. In solid masses, neighboring molecules would yield to their mutual attraction if its effect were not destroyed by the heat which separates them.
> This elastic force is greater as the temperature is higher; which is the reason why bodies dilate and contract when their temperature is raised (*ibid.*, p. 40).

This remark is very close to explicit statement of a belief that the higher temperature *is* the greater "elastic force", is, that is to say, the intensity of the "repulsive force" which constitutes, according to this speculation, the dynamic aspect of heat. For it is impossible to make sense of Fourier's speaking of "the reason why bodies dilate" when their temperature is increased if all he understands by the temperature of a body is a disposition in the body to dilate (and contract) under certain conditions. The natural reading of Fourier's last sentence is as saying that the reason why bodies contract and dilate when their temperatures go up or down is that their temperatures going up or down *is* the increase or decrease in the "elastic force" exerted internally by the heat in the bodies. That Fourier did not take temperatures to be constituted by their thermometer measures, which are "dilatations" and contractions of thermometric substances, i.e., thermometer readings, is further indicated by the following remark, which has to be understood in the light of the fact that his book *is* very largely devoted to calculating temperatures:

> The solar heat . . . which penetrates the interior of the globe, distributes itself therein according to a regular law which does not depend on the laws of motion, and cannot be determined by the principles of mechanics. The dilatations which the repulsive force of heat produces, observation of which serves to measure temperatures, are, in truth, mechanical effects; but it is not these dilatations which we calculate, when we investigate the laws of propagation of heat (*ibid.*, p. 23) .

That Fourier's "principle of the communication of heat" naturally lends itself to thinking of temperature as a causal factor in driving heat shows up in the analogies often made in those more recent discussions of his principle which are still conducted at the macroscopic level and without reference to the microstructure of heat. Consider the following example from a textbook in heat engineering, which begins its discussion by attributing the fundamental equation to Fourier, and proceeds in this vein:[2]

> The flow of heat between two points in a body of homogeneous material is analogous to the flow of electricity in a conductor. In each case the quantity flowing per unit time is proportional to the following quantities:
>
> 1. The conductivity of the material . . .
> 2. The area of the conductor perpendicular to the path of flow.
> 3. The potential gradient in the case of electric flow and the temperature gradient in the case of heat flow.

Just as it is natural to think of an electrical potential difference as constituting a kind of force, an "electromotive force" or "electrical pressure" driving an electric current through a wire,

2. A. I. Brown and S. Marco, *Introduction to Heat Transfer* (New York: McGraw-Hill, 1942) , p. 8.

so Fourier's macrotheory of heat conduction makes it natural to think of a temperature difference as constituting a kind of thermal potential constituting a "thermomotive force" or "thermal pressure" driving the heat through a conductor. And indeed more recent writers, laying out systematically the basic principles of macroscopic thermodynamics without reference to the kinetic theory of heat, will be found defining temperature as the property that determines the tendency of heat to flow from one point to another. As an example, the author of the article on thermodynamics in the 15th edition (1974) of the *Encyclopædia Britannica* first observes that the condition of thermal equilibrium between two systems, which coincides with the condition of equality of temperature, is marked by equality between the ratio of rate of change of entropy of each system to rate of change of energy of the system, as the two undergo changes which are equal and opposite (under certain further conditions). This ratio, he remarks, "may be thought of as a potential that governs the tendency of energy to pass from one system to another. . . . Conversely the reciprocal quantity may be thought of as an 'escaping tendency'." The reciprocal quantity which the author speaks of is, of course, the ratio of the rate of total energy change in the system to the rate of change of its entropy. The author proceeds:

> The potential that governs the flow of energy is called the temperature. A scale of temperature may be defined in terms of any function of [either ratio just mentioned above] that continuously increases or decreases with either. The scale commonly used in thermodynamics is the Kelvin scale of temperature. It is denoted by K and defined as [the ratio of the rate of total energy change in the system to the rate of change of its entropy], so that T becomes a measure of the escaping tendency of energy (Volume 18, p. 295).

To conclude my mustering of a small quantity of evidence for my suggestion that temperature was—and is—conceived within macroscopic thermodynamics by reference to a causal role it plays, I turn to a single sentence of Kelvin's, written in the course of articulating a rigorous definition of a temperature scale independent of the physical properties of actual thermometers. This work of Kelvin's, in which he completed the macrotheory of the heat engine begun by Carnot and applied this theory, along with ideas about ideal gases, to the working out of his scale of absolute temperature, was completed before the effective existence of a statistical-mechanical analysis of heat. The single, key sentence of Kelvin's is this one:[3]

> The characteristic property of the scale which I now propose is that all degrees have the same value, that is, that a unit of heat descending from a body at the temperature T of this scale to a body B at the same (T-1) would give out the same mechanical effect, whatever be the number T.

Kelvin is defining a unit of temperature by reference to the power of producing work which is possessed by a fall in one unit of temperature in a heat engine receiving heat at the higher temperature and discharging heat at the (one degree) lower temperature. Here the causal role of temperature seems again to come into the foreground. And power of producing work, what is more, is energy. It seems that already temperature is being conceived as an intensity of some form of energy. That Kelvin suspected this form of energy was kinetic is true, for he believed the caloric theory of heat to be mistaken, and was helped to discover that Carnot had made an error in his theory of the heat engine by noticing that Carnot had relied upon the caloric theory. But Kelvin's new definition of a scale of absolute temperature relied upon no microtheory of the constitution of heat. Yet the way had by now been paved, by both Fourier and Kelvin, to treating the forthcoming, statistical-mechanical theory as a theory of the nature of heat and, hence, to finding it intelligible that the property (temperature) that is causally responsible for both the flow of heat and the work done in a heat engine is the "thermal potential" which is constituted, in its nature, by a difference in the mean kinetic energies of the molecules of two thermally communicating physical systems.

I do not contend that no early thermodynamicists conceived temperature in the operationalist fashion. This positivistic attitude is economical: do not burden yourself with conceptual material that is playing no essential role in your investigations. And no doubt some scientists took up this posture; perhaps most fell into it at some time. Nevertheless I think the evidence supports the idea that those who were especially interested in what made thermodynamics thermo*dynamics* were, unavoidably, sensitive to the causal role of temperature and were laying the groundwork, both by the dynamic laws they were discovering and by

---

3. *Mathematical and Physical Papers*, vol. 1 (Cambridge, 1882), p. 240.

the conception under which they tended to observe temperature, for the forthcoming, mathematical explorations of the microstructure of thermal phenomena. In the light of the evidence and of the later developments, it seems reasonable to construe the working conception of temperature deployed by these latter physicists when making temperature observations—and to reconstruct that of the more positivistic group—in this way: the property of a body, whatever the intrinsic nature of this property, which causally accounts for the body's role in producing *this* reading on *this* thermometer applied to *that* body.

Our puzzle concerning the content of scientific observation of temperature by the use of a thermometer is solved. Scientific thermometer observation of temperature has within it, as it were, a blank space left to be filled in by microtheoretical inquiry, in which the nature of the property can be explicitly specified. In the meantime one may be observing the property that has this nature but in entire ignorance of the fact that it has it. The observable property, temperature, may have the nature, mean kinetic energy of molecules, not discoverable by observation, and no puzzle is left as to how this is possible.

And we are now free to consider the equation,

$$\text{Mean kinetic energy of molecules} = \tfrac{1}{2}m\bar{v}^2 = kT$$

where m is the mass of a molecule, $\bar{v}^2$ is the square of the mean velocity of the molecules, T is absolute temperature in degrees Kelvin, and k is Boltzmann's constant, whose units are ergs per degree, as simply providing the conversion factor k, whereby the "historically accidental" unit for measuring temperature, degrees Kelvin, is converted into the "true unit", ergs, which shows on its face the real nature of temperature, energy—whose kinetic form is given by the left-hand side of the equation.

Another "historical accident" provides us with the puzzle that is here our chief concern, the evolutionary "accident" that, quite outside contexts of scientific inquiry and without the use of instruments, we feel—hence, when attentive, we become thermally conscious of—the very same property that is observed by thermometers and whose nature is mean kinetic energy of molecules, and we thus thermally perceive that objects have this property without perceiving that these objects have a certain mean molecular kinetic energy. The puzzle is to discover what the content of this thermal perception must be in order for that achievement to be possible. And I am suggesting that solving, as I hope I have just done, the analogous puzzle for thermometer observations of temperature will help us to solve our thermo-perceptual puzzle.

5. Further Specification of the Key Question about Feeling Temperature

We have discovered how it is possible to become observationally conscious of temperature while gaining no awareness of mean molecular kinetic energy: one looks at an object—a thermometer—characteristically quite distinct from the object whose temperature one is interested in observing, and one sees a property quite distinct from the temperature one is engaged in observing. We look at the point of coincidence, say, between a numeral on a sealed glass tube and the top of a red, mercury column inside the tube. This is the property of the thermometer which we observe. And we conceive this thermometer reading as the effect of the operation of another property of another object that is in thermal contact with the mercury column. We then construe the numeral at which the column of mercury in the thermometer ends as a representation, within a scale, of the magnitude of that other property of the object in thermal contact with the thermometer, "the property, whatever its nature, which is causally responsible for that object's role in producing *this* reading on the thermometer." The property thus observed as the cause of something seen is the observed temperature of the object to which the thermometer is applied.

As it turns out, from statistical-mechanical, microtheoretical developments, the nature of this property is that it is the mean kinetic energy of the molecules composing the object whose temperature has been observed. And it is in virtue of the quantity of the mean kinetic energy of the object's molecules being what it is that the object plays the causal role it plays—in conjunction with properties of the thermometer—in bringing about the expansion of the thermometer's mercury. So all along it was indeed the property whose nature consists in being the mean kinetic energy of an aggregate of molecules which experimental thermodynamicists were becoming observationally conscious of, without becoming conscious of this nature that it had.

There we have a model of the kind of work we have to do in order to explain to ourselves how it is possible that we can attentively feel an object to have this same intensity of heat and, thereby, become thermally conscious of this property's belonging to something before our skin, without becoming conscious of the property's nature. If I can produce as coherent and complete an account of the content of thermosensory awareness of temperature as the account just given of the content of thermometer-observational awareness of temperature, then I shall be satisfied, and otherwise not.

It will help us to sharpen the focus of the distinctively thermoperceptual puzzle if we set before ourselves an aspect of the thermometer observation of temperature whose presence was quite indispensable to the solution proposed to the puzzle about this sort of observation's content, but which cannot be ascribed to the thermal feeling of temperature and which, therefore, cannot be used to help us with the solution to our thermoperceptual puzzle.

I have so far taken insufficient notice of the fact that thermometer observations of temperature are not only observations of the property, temperature, nor even only observations of the property, such and such degree of temperature; they are observations of the instantiation in a particular physical system of the property, such and such a degree of temperature; we may call this, for short, observation of an *instance* of the property, temperature. A part of the problem, therefore, of discovering the description under which thermometer observations of temperature are made was to find a description that uniquely identified a particular instance of the property, temperature. How does the description we came up with accomplish the identification of the instance of temperature? It does it by specifying the instance of temperature as that instance which is causally responsible for *that* (observed) body's role in producing *this* (observed) thermometer's reading.

The aspect of this mechanism of identifying the instance of temperature to which I want now to draw attention is this: the instance of temperature is observationally identified through the more direct (visual) observation of the instantiation of another property, the property, such and such a thermometer reading, which stands in a special relationship with (here, that of being the causal effect of) the observed instance of temperature. We visually observe the instance of temperature through more directly observing with our eyes one of its effects, an instance of another property of something before our eyes, a particular reading of a particular thermometer.

This feature of thermometer observation does not carry over to the thermoperceptual situation. As I have earlier remarked, one thing that distinguishes becoming thermally conscious of temperature from observing temperature with a thermometer is that in attentively feeling temperature there is no other property of something before our sensory organs through the perception of which we tell that the temperature is there. Among the properties of things before our skin which we thermally perceive, it is temperature that we most directly perceive. It follows that it *cannot* be the case that, when attentive, the way we become thermally conscious of temperatures before our skin without becoming conscious of the nature of temperature is thus: by thermally perceiving these temperatures under a description (or analogue of one) which relates them to another property of something before our skin which we perceive more directly than the temperatures. Our thermoperceptual puzzle promises, therefore, to be a tougher nut to crack than our thermometer-observation puzzle turned out to be.

Another, added difficulty that awaits us in searching for the content of thermal awareness of temperature arises not so much from a difference between it and observation by thermometer as from the rather relaxed standard we were able to adopt in counting the job of analyzing the content of thermometer observations as completed. We were able to relax our standard in this connection not because thermometer observations are not examples of the primary subject matter of this book, sensory perception, but because they are instances of visual perception, whereas the concern of this chapter is thermal perception. If our present concern had been to articulate adequately the content of a visual perception, we could not have stopped as we did with so little clarity attempted concerning that part of the content of the visual perception which I introduced with the words 'this thermometer reading', or 'this coincidence between the numerical marking on the glass tube and the end of the mercury column'. For as it stands, this account might be taken to specify a content that is entirely conceptual, even verbal. Certainly I have supposed the thermodynamicists to be exercising concepts in making their observations: the concept of an instance of one property's playing a causal role in producing an instance of another property is one, the concept of a thermometer is another. Nor should I wish to put any limit on how sophisticated the concepts may be which contribute to the content of a scientific observation—perhaps the statistical-mechanical theory of heat itself, once it has been assimilated by experimentalists, could enter into this content and make even an observation of mean kinetic energy of molecules possible.

However, there is a limit on how much of an observation's content can be conceptual: it cannot be entirely conceptual. For if it were it would be nothing but the *thought* that there is a certain degree of temperature instantiated in a certain nearby physical system. And no one believes that observation of a temperature by a thermometer is nothing but coming to *think* that some substance nearby has a property causally responsible for a reading merely thought to be showing on a nearby thermometer merely thought to be nearby. No doubt the place where the distinctively sensory content enters into thermometer observations is in the visual perception of the reading on the thermometer. This we could pass over in the present context, since we are not trying at the moment to see all the way through vision. But we are trying to do this for thermal perception. So a preliminary appreciation of what this undertaking entails is wanted.

We give our thermoperceptual attention to a certain intensity of heat of an object before our skin, hence in feeling it we are conscious of this intensity of heat before our skin. Yet we do not thereby become conscious of the nature of this property of the body before our skin. Neither do we thermoperceptually take in this property under a description that relates the property to another property of something before our skin which is observed more directly by us. How is it, then, that the reader of the first sentence of this paragraph commonly has the impression, despite his already knowing what is said in the next two sentences, that the content of thermal awareness of intensity of heat has been quite adequately described by the clause 'in feeling it we become conscious of the intensity of heat before our skin'? Because when it is said that we become thermally aware that an object has a certain intensity of heat, it is rather as if it had been said that our thermal awareness has for its content the proposition, "The heat of this body is very intense"; and this is rather as if one had said that our thermosensory awareness takes hold of the world before our thermal sense organs entirely by means of the words, 'Heat here, very intense', or at least entirely by means of the concepts these words express.

In describing a certain form of consciousness by reference to its content one characteristically expresses its content in a sentence; one's readers appreciate this content themselves in this sentential form, and, as it were, hold it before their minds conceptually. Unless some correction is provided, something to counter this tendency, both the reader and the writer tend to find themselves thinking of this form of awareness as if it were like the form of awareness we have, as writers and readers of its characterization, and hence find ourselves thinking of it as if it were linguistically grounded, conceptual awareness of the content, "heat here, very intense." But this is to think of attentive, thermal perception as if feeling heat were merely thinking the thought, "Heat here, very intense."

6. First Argument for Indirect Thermoperceptual Realism

If attentively to feel a body's temperature is not to become conscious of the nature of this temperature, as belonging to the body; nor merely to apply to the hot body some concept of temperature, in response to stimulation from the heat in that body; nor to apprehend the body's temperature under a description that identifies this property as the one related in a special way to another, more directly perceived property instantiated before the skin—then exactly what is the content of our thermal perception of a body's temperature? I shall argue that direct realism cannot offer a plausible answer to this question, but indirect, representational realism can.

We imagine that a person lies in a quiet place in the sun, her thoughts on distant matters, her eyes closed, aware of no sights or sounds or smells. But the sun is warm and her thought lapses as she becomes conscious, not of the sun heating her but of her forehead warming up. She allows her thought to lapse and her attention to focus upon the pleasant growing warmth of her forehead. Even the idea of her forehead recedes, and she is conscious almost solely of its warmth, feeling the warmth as suffusing a bodily region, thinking of almost nothing.

Now we remind ourselves of the direct realist's position in regard to this person's experience: what she is directly conscious of, he holds, is the physical property, such and such intensity of heat, belonging to the portion of the skin of her forehead that is before the thermal receptor organs located within that skin. But our earlier discussion makes it evident that the direct realist needs to give us more information about how this physical property, intensity of heat (temperature) of her forehead, presents itself to the woman's thermal perception.

It will not suffice for him merely to use the phrase, 'intensity of heat', in specifying the content of her thermal awareness. For he surely does not mean to say that her feeling with attention the warmth of her forehead comprises her relating to intensity of heat in the way we readers do when we read his description of the content of her thermal awareness as "an instance of intensity of heat." He does not want to say that her feeling her forehead warming up consists in nothing but her deploying in some interior way a linguistic skill dependent upon her mastery of words used to speak of temperature. Under what aspect, then, does this instance of temperature present itself to her consciousness? In what guise does she appreciate it? How shall we analyze the form in which she takes it in? Here our earlier examination of the nature of temperature and of its observation by means of thermometers helps to specify the problem.

We know this woman is not, for example, thermally conscious of her forehead's temperature as a property with the particular nature that it in fact has: she is not thermally conscious of the increasing temperature of her forehead as the increasing mean kinetic energy of the molecules of the skin of her forehead. Although a person looking at a thermometer is not, either, normally conscious of the nature of temperature, he is conscious of it under the description, "the property, whatever its nature, belonging to *that* body, which is causally responsible for *this* that I see, this visible position of the mercury in the tube before my eyes." But the woman lying in the sun and merely feeling the temperature of her forehead, by means of the thermosensory receptors located within the skin of her forehead, has no such device available to her, on the direct realist's view of her situation. For whereas the person observing the temperature of a roast in the oven by looking at the thermometer inserted into the roast tells what the temperature of the roast is by giving his attention more directly to a property other than this roast's temperature, namely to one of the latter's effects, to the reading he sees on the thermometer, and thereby achieves indirect attention to the temperature of the roast, as the cause of what he sees, the direct realist holds that the person lying in the sun does not give her attention to the temperature of her forehead through giving her attention to any other property than this very instance of temperature itself. There is no instance of any other property, either before her sense organs (as I too have claimed) or not before them, he holds, which commands her attention more directly than the temperature itself.

What, then, on the direct realist's view, is the woman conscious of the temperature of her forehead *as?* She is not conscious of it as what it is, the mean kinetic energy of her forehead's molecules. She is not conscious of it in terms of one sort of thing it does, bring about some effect that she notices, for she does not attend to it through the noticing of anything else, according to the direct realist; for this reason neither can she be conscious of the temperature through more direct awareness of some other property with which it is merely associated—or resembles, or to which it has any other relation. It is difficult to think of plausible things a direct realist might say. His most hopeful course may appear to him to be to appeal to behavioral dispositions.

The direct realist may say that in feeling her forehead warm up the woman acquires the power to discriminate through her behavior the temperature of her forehead from other properties of her forehead and to discriminate between this instance of temperature and others involving other objects, times, places. If what is wanted is that the behavior she acquires the power to perform be not only a function of temperature but constitute some mode of "aiming" at temperature, then the direct realist may cite her new power to aim, in her behavior, at changing the present temperature of her forehead. And if it is objected that a present power—or even a present disposition—to behave in a way tending to change temperature is not the same thing as a present awareness of the temperature, and this no matter how complexly purposive the behavior may be, then the direct realist may reply that her thermal awareness of the temperature of her forehead is achieved through the person's more direct awareness of her new power of undertaking to change (what is in fact) the temperature of her forehead, or her awareness of a new disposition she has to do this.

What the direct realist has now proposed is that the description under which the person lying in the sun thermally feels the temperature of her forehead is this one: "that property of my forehead (whatever its nature), an increase (or reduction) in the quantity of which would be the effect of the behavior to (for) which *this* disposition (power) in me is a disposition (power)." Since the property that answers to this description is, we may suppose, the present temperature of her forehead, the woman is conscious of her forehead's temperature under a description that does succeed in identifying it uniquely. But how are we to understand the reference to "*this* disposition"? In its context the phrase '*this* disposition' (or 'this power') serves to indicate that the woman's new disposition (power) to undertake to change the temperature of her forehead is the direct object of her thermal awareness. She is directly conscious of a disposition in herself to behave in a certain way, and it is through her direct awareness of this disposition in herself that she is indirectly conscious of that which would in fact be altered by her behavior (her forehead's temperature) if this behavior were to occur. But of course this disposition in her is not something before her skin or other sense organs. Through her more direct awareness of this condition of herself that is not before her sense organs she is conscious of her forehead's temperature.

The direct realist has abandoned his position. The direct object of our thermal awareness is not before the thermosensory receptors in the skin. But if the direct realist is going to abandon his direct realism, he has no longer a motive to resist letting the object of our thermal attention that is not before the sense organs be described in terms that answer more closely to our experience. For our experience informs us that it is not a new disposition or power to behave that holds our attention when all we are undergoing is feeling our forehead warming up; it is, rather, the determinate quality, warmth.

One might suppose that the direct realist had reached the end of his invention. Not quite so. He may now adopt a position that is suggested by—is perhaps the same as—the line D. M. Armstrong has taken in regard to the perception of pain and of color.

Applied to feeling heat and cold it goes like this. Within thermoperception we neither identify temperature through something like a description, as "the property that . . . ", nor become conscious of its nature. Rather we become thermally conscious only that there is *some* property instantiated in a certain object or region. Thermal awareness selects an instance of temperature only in association with the "stage setting", to adapt a term of Wittgenstein's. This is to say that both the behavior and the language that manifest this thermal awareness can converge upon a single instance of temperature because our thermoperceptual response, for all its vagueness in content, is in fact a systematic function of that temperature; so our words can be applied to objects as a systematic function of temperature difference between these objects, and our behavior can be adaptive to instances of temperature itself. Nevertheless our thermal awareness captures the temperature of things before our skin only as, "some property or other, here." Thermal awareness of temperature takes the basic form, "there is something here," and all further identification of temperature is accomplished in virtue of interaction between an instance of temperature, receptor organs, behavior, and language.

The thermal awareness of the person lying in the sun, her thought lapsed, her attention held by the warmth of her forehead, has nothing more specific in the way of content than the quite indeterminate content: "something or other, here."

It is evident that this account is false. The woman lying in the sun attentively feeling the warmth of her forehead is not merely aware that "something or other is here." Her attention is held by a determinate quality, "warmth" we call it, although she uses no word in merely feeling with attention its presence.

We can become conscious of a property of physical objects under such a wholly indeterminate specification as "something or other there now," only by *thinking* the general proposition, "Something or other is there now," through the exercise of concepts expressed by the words 'something or other' (or synonyms of these words), an exercise that presupposes mastery of words like 'something or other'. But feeling warmth is not merely thinking of warmth.

Sensory awareness of an object before our sense organs always realizes a determinate delineation of a character purporting to belong to a thing or region before the sense organs. This determinate character always figures as at least at part of what holds our attention. But the direct realist has nothing left to propose as the delineation some property before the skin receives in serving as direct object of our thermal attention.

The indirect realist, on the other hand, is not restrained by the principle that what we are directly conscious of is before the skin. So he does have a proposal: a delineation of temperature for thermal awareness is provided by the sensuous, thermal qualities *cool, cold, warm, hot,* which are instantiated, not before the thermosensory organs in the skin, but "behind" them, in fact *within* thermal consciousness. Within thermal consciousness a sensuous thermal quality—say, *cool*—always serves as the internal, direct object of our thermal attention to a given intensity of heat before the skin; and that quality there holds this attention by serving as the sensuous content of our involuntary, thermoperceptual *attribution* of a temperature to something before the skin. The woman lying in the sun feels the temperature of her forehead as this: *warm.* (By italicizing the quality-name in this context I mean to signify the presence within her conscious state of the sensuous quality-instance.) The indirect realist concludes that he can offer a solution to the puzzle the direct realist cannot solve and, therefore, that he has the truth of the matter. This is the author's solution.

Let me summarize the reasoning that yields this climax to this portion of our story.

First, that in attentive, thermal feeling we become conscious of a thing's temperature entails that this temperature receives some delineation for thermal awareness. Second, in attentively feeling a thing's temperature we do not become thermally conscious of the nature of this temperature, since in its nature it is mean kinetic molecular energy. Third, thermoperceptually we do not specify a thing's temperature under a description couched entirely in verbal or conceptual terms, nor, fourth, do we specify it in an entirely general and indeterminate fashion (as "some property or other"), since the latter form of specification must be an example of the former method, and a purely conceptual specification of temperature constitutes merely thinking of a thing's temperature, which is not feeling it. Fifth, the just preceding point takes the positive form that temperature must be delineated for thermal feeling in some manner other than by purely conceptual specification.

Sixth, thermoperception cannot resemble thermometer observation of temperature this far: that temperature turns out to be thermoperceptually specified as the property related to another property which is instantiated before the sense organs and more directly perceived. The reason is that in thermal perception instances of temperature are perceived more directly than any other properties of things *before* the sense organs. We do not feel intensity of heat by more directly perceiving another property of something before the sense organs.

Seventh, if we maintain the restrictions imposed by direct realism upon our analysis of thermoperception, namely, that no instance of a property instantiated *not* before the sense organs shall be the direct object of our thermal awareness of a temperature before these organs, then when due consideration is given to the first six points, we are left with no way in which to conceive the specific guise under which a thing's temperature receives its delineation for thermal consciousness, hence with no way in which to understand how one can, in attentive, thermal feeling, become conscious of a thing's temperature.

Eighth, we are therefore driven to drop the direct realist's restriction, and to look for a solution under the assumption that our thermal awareness of a thing's temperature is at least partially constituted of a more direct, thermal awareness of a property instantiated "behind" the skin.

Ninth, because the property-instance *behind* the skin functions as what we thermally feel the temperature of something *before* the skin as being, it is most plausibly conceived as belonging to thermal consciousness itself and as there providing for the latter the *sensuous content* of its *attribution* of a temperature. In fact there is not a single property that plays this role but a spectrum of properties, the sensuous, thermal qualities, *cool, cold, warm, hot.* The way we make sense of the idea that these qualities belong to thermal consciousness itself is by thinking of the role they play there. They function there as the sensuous contents of our sensuous attributions of specific intensities of heat or cold to things before our skin, with the effect that what we thermally feel the nature of a temperature to be is this: *cool*, or *warm* (and so on).

In speaking of the necessity that temperature should have some *delineation* for thermal awareness I have chosen the word 'delineation' as neutral in meaning between, on the one hand, the idea of the indirect realist (hence my idea) that temperature has a representation within thermal awareness in the form of some analogue of a concept—for which the phrase '*specified* by thermal awareness' would be more apt—and, on the other hand, the direct realist's original working idea: that temperature is simply revealed to thermosensory awareness without mediation through any representation of itself within this awareness—for which the phrase '*presented* to thermal awareness' would be more apt. I have been saying that the direct realist is required to explain to us in exactly what form temperature reveals or presents itself to thermal awareness. And this he is unable to do.

On the indirectly realistic view now taking shape, the delineation temperature has for thermal awareness consists in a *specification of* temperature *by* thermal awareness, in the form of an *attribution* (to something before the skin) of a property whose character is specified in virtue of this attribution's sensuous content consisting of an instance of a sensuous quality *within* thermal consciousness itself. Here we discover a distinguishing mark of sensory awareness generally: in sensory awareness some properties ascribed to objects before the sense organs are represented by the method of exemplification, whereas characteristically (in conceptual thinking, at least, as distinguished from thinking with mental images) in mental awareness this method of representation by exemplification is not used. If one makes a watercolor painting of a red brick house one may use the red color of one's paper to represent itself as belonging to the brick house: the color instantiated in the paper represents its own nature as instantiated in the brick house. So too, I have argued, within thermal consciousness the sensuous quality *cool* actually instantiated there represents its own nature as instantiated in some object before the skin. A similar procedure has already revealed itself in bodily feeling and in the sense of smell.

Let us now look more closely at two aspects of the function within thermal awareness which I have assigned to the sensuous thermal qualities belonging to this awareness.

7.   Sensuous Attribution of Thermal Qualities

I have ascribed to the sensuous thermal qualities belonging to thermal consciousness a twofold function. First, an instance of one of these qualities figures as what we are directly conscious of and directly attend to whenever we attentively feel a temperature before the skin. Second, instances of thermal qualities serve as the sensuous contents of our thermoperceptual attributions of heat and cold to things before our skins.

The case for assigning the first of these two functions should be obvious. For without serving the first function, thermal qualities could not contribute to the solution of our thermoperceptual puzzle, which requires an account of the delineation that things' temperatures receive for thermal awareness. This delineation the attentive thermal percipient must be conscious *of*. And the sensuous thermal qualities provide the delineation. So it must be *of* them that we are directly conscious. If I said merely that thermal awareness is *warm* or *cool,* this alone would go no way to establish that we become conscious of each temperature *as* this: *warm,* or *cool,* and so on. To say that we are *cool-ly* or *warm-ly* conscious of temperature does not say that the character we thermally feel a thing's temperature as being is *warm* or *cool*. We can feel a temperature as cool only in virtue of being conscious *of* the quality *cool* in being conscious of the temperature of something before the skin. By the same reasoning, how our attention is held by the temperature of something before the skin is at least partially explained if we know that it is directly held by the sensuous quality *cool;* but this attention is not even partially explained if we are told only that one attends in a *cool* manner to the temperatures of things before the skin.

Having granted this much, it is easy to see how one can be led, as I have been, to complete the solution of the puzzle by affirming that what it comes to for our direct awareness of the sensuous quality *cool* to be awareness of a temperature before the skin is this: the quality *cool* provides the sensuous content of a sensuous attribution of a temperature to something before our skin. But the question arises: Might we be thermally conscious of temperature through being directly conscious of thermal qualities which partly constitute our conscious states but do *not* function there as the contents of perceptual *attributions* of temperature? There is a way this can be answered affirmatively with initial plausibility, and a motivation for this answer is found in our earlier discussion of the need, in solving our thermoperceptual puzzle, to explain the mechanism of perceptual reference to instances of temperature before the skin. I shall now consider this answer; but first its motivation.

It will be recalled that the solution to the problem of reference for thermometer observation of temperature explained the observational mechanism of reference to an instance of temperature before the eyes in this way: temperature was specified under a description that identified it as the property that is causally responsible for *this* (seen) thermometer reading. We appealed to the visual perception of the thermometer reading to help identify the observed temperature-instance as the one that is connected (causally) to a particular instance of a thermometer reading. Now we are engaged in trying to see all the way through thermal perception as we were not there trying to do for visual perception. So we need to understand the mechanism of reference to a temperature-instance in so far as the latter's presence before the skin is *felt*. We decide to try out for the moment a solution that follows very closely in its structure the solution just recalled for the thermometer-observational puzzle. However, as we shall shortly discover, it will not be possible to adhere for very long to the idea that the thermal qualities do *not* function within thermal consciousness as contents of sensuous attributions of temperatures.

Outdoors on a winter day you feel with your hand the iron railing you have grasped. How you feel the cold of the railing, we shall now suppose, is by thermoperceptually attributing to the railing a property-instance which you identify thus: "that in the railing which causes me to feel *this*"—where I use the word 'this' (but you do not) to refer to an instance of the sensuous quality *cold,* occurring within your thermal consciousness and functioning there as the direct object of your attention. According to this story, you thermally perceive the temperature of the iron railing under the quasi-description, "that property of the railing which causes me to be thermally conscious of *this* (sensuous quality *cold*)". And the quality *cold* belongs to your thermal consciousness itself, comprising its sensuous content. However, this quality-instance has now *not* been described as providing the content for a sensuous attribution of itself to something before the skin (or anywhere else).

If this were the way it happened, would you thereby have succeeded in thermoperceptually attributing to the iron railing before your skin the temperature of the iron railing? Yes you would have. For it is in fact the temperature of the iron railing, indeed the mean energy of the random, vibrational motion of the atoms of the iron railing which causes you to come to have the sensuous quality *cold* as the direct object of your thermal awareness. You have therefore thermally felt the very property Kelvin observed with his thermometer and provided an absolute measure for and Boltzmann and others characterized as to its intrinsic nature. You have come into conscious, thermosensory possession of enough truth about an instance of temperature before your skin so that, if whatever else needed to make this truth also knowledge is present you will have conscious, thermoperceptual knowledge of the temperature of the iron railing. Will have, that is, if this is the true story.

However, this is not to say that in perceiving in that manner, you would be free of error. To get some insight into this matter, we may ask whether or not there is an analogue in thermal perception of the clause earlier attributed to thermometer observation of a thing's temperature, the clause, "whatever its nature may be," which we supposed attached to the description under which thermodynamicists using thermometers made their observations of temperatures. We can think of that clause as indicating a suspension of judgment as to the nature of the property they were observing. Is our thermoperceptual judgment also not committed as to the nature of the feature of the iron railing that we believe causes us to feel the sensuous quality *cold?*

I'm afraid I have to say that it is evident that our thermoperceptual judgment is committed on this subject. And it gets the nature wrong. We take the property of the iron railing that we believe causes us to become thermally conscious of the sensuous quality *cold* to have exactly the nature that the sensuous quality *cold* manifests. In our thermal awareness of temperatures before our skin, the sensuous quality *cold,* which is in fact not instantiated before the skin, represents for us its own nature as belonging to the iron railing. It is this sensuous quality's nature that we thermoperceptually attribute to the iron railing as the nature of the property of the railing which we believe to be the one causally responsible for our becoming thermally conscious of this very property-nature. Assuming, that is, that we do within thermoperception make this causal judgment, as our present hypothetical account does assume, it is evident that the story will have to be completed in this way.

The facts of thermal perception makes it impossible, after all, to deny to the sensuous, thermal qualities the role of contents of sensuous attributions by us of temperatures to things before the skin.

The sensuous quality *cold* functions, even on the present, partly hypothetical account, as the most vivid (the sensuous) part of the content of our thermoperceptual attribution to the iron railing of a feature we presume accounts for our thermally feeling this very sensuous quality, *cold*. On the present hypothesis it is as if our most primitive sort of causal inference goes on the principle that like causes like, as if within thermal perception of temperature we reason thus: "something belonging to the iron railing that is identical in nature with *this* (that I feel) causes me to be thus thermally conscious of (this same) *this*." And of course we should be as wrong in this as Fourier was when, in developing his theory of heat conduction, he revealed that he believed that the heat whose laws of conduction he was giving a correct account of was, as regards its nature, a fluid substance transported from place to place.

Despite having some false beliefs about the nature of the heat that is conducted, Fourier managed to get hold of a good deal of truth about heat. So too, we may say in defense of the present hypothesis, do we in our thermal perception get hold of an important truth about the iron railing. The iron railing does have a single feature that is causally responsible for our feeling what we thermally feel. And this is in fact roughly the same feature the wind has, just as we believe, that causes us to feel, when the winter wind blows upon our face, the very same sensuous quality. It is also, as we also believe, the same property which, in a certain degree, causes water to freeze. And so on. Our thermoperceptual truth is in some respects not as interesting as Fourier's mathematical truth (though in some respects more interesting to us), but our error is certainly no more grievous than his was. However, in its full complexity this present account of thermoperception is, on my part, hypothetical. Is it too complex?

I have already remarked that although we began by trying to develop an account of attentive, thermal feeling in which the sensuous, thermal qualities are not required to function as contents of sensuous attributions of temperature, the facts of thermal feeling forced us to give up this attempt. The question now arises whether or not the rather complex "description" under which, in making this attempt, we supposed temperature to be thermally felt is something we should retain in our final analysis of thermal feeling.

I think that the particular complexity we came up with is, if it can be avoided, more than we want to accept. We made out the simplest and most primitive instance of feeling heat before the skin to contain a causal judgment. Unless this seems inescapable—or at least supported by introspection—it is undesirable. Also this simplest sort of thermal feeling was made out to include cognizance of a part of itself, conceived as an effect of the affirmed cause (temperature) : we were said to feel temperature as the cause of our feeling a sensuous, thermal quality that we feel more directly than the temperature. Certainly it is desirable to avoid assuming that the most primitive thermal perception makes a reference to a part of itself conceived as a part of itself—again, unless this is either evidently how thermal experience goes or it is for some other reason unavoidable. But this self-referential character of thermal feeling does not suggest itself to introspection and cannot be verified by introspection: thermal feeling does not seem to us to have this self-referential content. So we need to ask now whether a simpler story may be accurate.

The simplification of our story that suggests itself as eliminating the causal judgment and the self-referential content of thermal perception and as answering more nearly to what our thermosensory experience seems to us to hold, is this: within our thermal perception we sensuously attribute to something before our skin a feature whose nature is specified solely by the thermal quality we are feeling. In the place of the complex analogue of a description—too close an analogue—which I have just been considering, there occurs nothing but the simple, thermal quality functioning as the content of a sensuous attribution (to something before the skin) of a feature whose nature is specified, within this attribution, by this very thermal quality itself. This is our way of thermoperceptually attributing intensities of heat to things before the skin, hence it is our way of attentively feeling these temperatures.

Now the minimal content of thermal consciousness takes the form, "This is *thus,*" in the simplest case, where '*thus*' is my verbal indicator of what in the thermal percipient is the sensuous content of his perception, say, the sensuous quality *warm;* and where 'this' is my verbal indicator of the percipient's thermoperceptual (and possibly conceptual) specification of some item, perhaps determinate (the radiator, the fire), perhaps rather indeterminate (a region), which he perceives to have the property whose nature is specified for the thermopercipient by the sensuous quality *warm* (or *cool,* and so on). But this simplification in our analysis of thermal awareness exacts a price, which we must now contrive to pay. In the end we shall not find the thermal quality to be the sole content of thermoperceptual attribution of temperature.

8. Thermoperception's Mechanism of Reference

The mechanism of reference to an instance of temperature before the skin is no longer evident. On the more complex, hypothetical account, an instance of temperature was successfully identified within thermoperception by being conceived therein as the cause of what we feel. But what is it, in our simpler picture of the content of thermal perception, that singles out intensity of heat as the felt property, and singles out, moreover, a particular instance of it before the skin? The obvious answer is, "Nothing at all." It is as if we had a picture of a property, but the picture does not in the least resemble the property, and there is nothing else that makes the picture a picture *of* that property.

We must assign the identifying mechanism to the behavioral (and causal) context. The answer that William James gave in 1895 to the question, How does our thought of the tigers in India manage to be *of them?* is the answer for thermoperception as well: our behavior singles out the intended object and feature of an object, discriminates it. This context of behavior within which human thermal awareness functions, when understood to include the causal action of temperatures acting as stimuli to our thermosensory system, provides the mechanism of identification by the thermopercipient of a particular instance of temperature before the skin.

When we think of this referring to a temperature-instance as something the thermal percipient *does* it is appropriate to think of the context provided by his behavioral powers and dispositions as the context that contributes the mechanism of reference. (It is doubtless also this context that imports into the thermosensory experience the "feeling of being referential"; it is, if you will, a posture of the body that imbues thermal awareness with its felt, interior character as of an outward "gaze" upon the world.)

When, however, we think of the temperature before the sense organs as arousing in us a thermosensory *impression* of itself, then it is appropriate to emphasize the causal relationship extending from the instance of temperature before the skin to the thermal perception as figuring prominently in the context that makes the perception an impression of a particular instance of temperature. That it is this instance of temperature before the skin which causes the thermoperceptual reaction helps to make this thermal perception a sensory *impression of* this instance of temperature.

Of course a moment's reflection will assure the reader that the causal and behavioral contexts are in fact a single context: for behavior to be responsive to and thereby discriminatory of temperature, temperature must, as stimulus, causally determine behavior.

Nevertheless what nature temperature presents itself to our thermal attention as having—which is to say, what thermal awareness sensuously attributes (to something before the skin) as the nature of temperature—is determined by the nature of the sensuous quality instantiated within thermal consciousness. For this quality functions as the sensuous content of our sensuous attribution of intensity of heat to the object before our skin; hence it functions as that through attention to which our attention is given to the intensity of heat before the skin. It is the fact that in going through this sensuous representation of temperature's nature, our attention actually reaches an instance of temperature before our skin which is accounted for by the causal and behavioral context of this attention. What we feel the temperature *as* is determined by the felt character of the sensuous quality; that it is a temperature we feel is determined by our discriminatory, behavioral response to a temperature-instance before the skin.

I have now to retract my statement that sensuous, thermal qualities provide the entire content of our thermoperceptual representation of the nature of temperature, hence that its nature is altogether *mis*represented within our thermal perception of it. It is likely that concepts also have a role in mature thermal perception. Indeed, as will shortly appear, emphasis on behavioral reference to temperature supports the idea of a partially conceptual content for thermal feeling, since conceptual specification is a form of behavioral specification.

Insofar as temperature is perceived as having certain causal powers—and probably in the thermal perception of an experienced percipient this occurs—so far, at least, mere concepts must be thought to function within thermal perception. And if the notion of a property's nature, as perceptually ascribed, is understood to include the property's ascribed causal powers, then the nature of the temperature that is thermoperceptually attributed to things before the skin by experienced percipients can be said to be partly specified by those concepts of the causal powers of temperature which are exercised within mature thermal perception.

The idea of the cold of the iron railing as a property that enables the railing to make the flesh of my hand also become (physically) cold when I grasp the railing, and the idea of cold as a property which when present in a certain degree enables the air to freeze things; the idea of heat as a property whose possession by an object makes other nearby things hot too, if intense enough burns things, or boils them or melts them; these are concepts of temperature's causal powers which perhaps operate within the mature thermal perception of temperatures. Even the idea of heat and cold as causing us to feel their presence may enter into our mature, thermal experience of temperature. To the extent that such concepts of the causal powers of temperature are exercised within thermal perception, to this extent the behavioral dispositions that I have treated as if providing for thermal awareness only a mechanism of reference to temperature-instances must be supposed to contribute something to the content of our experience-seasoned thermoperceptual attribution of temperature to things before our skin, hence to help constitute what experienced percipients perceive temperature *as*. For the exercise of perceptual concepts must be analyzed behavioristically—but of this I postpone discussion until Chapter 8.

Now it is time to return to the direct realist. We shall discover that our indirectly realistic solution to the thermoperceptual puzzle has stimulated him to a new proposal.

9. The Statistical-Mechanical Microreduction Defense of Direct Realism: The Identity Interpretation

The direct realist now acknowledges the truth of one conclusion of the argument just given for indirect realism: a determinate quality is the direct object of our attentive thermal perception. *It* most directly holds our thermal attention. However, he now proposes to take advantage of the fact that some observable properties that do not appear to the observer to be nonetheless are microstructural properties, and, most notably, of the fact that thermometer-observed temperature *is* mean kinetic energy of molecules. He now proposes that we consider the thermal quality one directly feels in thermal perception to be a temperature *and hence identical with* mean molecular kinetic energy. Since the nature of the latter property is analyzable without reference to any effects it may have upon our thermal sensory experience, the nature of the thermal quality we directly feel is so analyzable as well, because the so-called "two" properties are actually one.

According to the direct realist, the statistical-mechanical kinetic theory's reduction of thermometer-observed temperature to the energy of motion of molecules is to be construed as having accomplished as well the reduction of the thermal qualities we *directly feel* to (the same kinetic energy of) molecular motion. The thermal quality of which we become directly conscious in attentively feeling the cold iron railing before our hands *is* a certain mean vibrational energy of the railing's atoms, although we, like the thermodynamicists of old when making their thermometer observations of temperatures, are unable to perceive that this is so. This is the direct realist's new defense of his position. This defense requires a careful examination. The rest of this chapter will provide one.

10. Refutation of First (Identity) Microreduction Defense of Direct Realism

In reflecting upon this proposal of the direct realist it is well to remind ourselves that it goes beyond anything asserted by the microreduction of thermodynamics. What is identified with mean molecular kinetic energy when the thermodynamics of dilute gases is reduced to their statistical mechanics is thermodynamic temperature. And thermodynamic temperature is not specified by reference to thermosensory perception—far from it. The mark of the inception of the scientific study of heat is the ending of any role whatever for what we thermally feel in determining the physical quantities, such as temperature and quantity of heat, which are being experimentally investigated and whose lawful covariations are being discovered. Thermodynamically determined temperature is temperature as visually observed, and this indirectly, through directly observing thermometer readings by looking at them. The thermal qualities as directly felt are nowhere to be found in the picture explicitly drawn by thermodynamicists actually plying their trade.

The proposal that the thermal qualities we directly feel are to be identified with microstructural quantities goes beyond any propositions found or presupposed in the microreduction of thermodynamics. Yet the thesis looks to this microreduction for its sole support. The only standards we can properly use in evaluating the support to be found there are those which have figured in evaluating the identities explicitly asserted in the scientific microreduction of thermodynamics. These standards are associated with the explanatory value of the microreduction. It is necessary, therefore, to understand the explanatory achievement of the microreduction.

Here is a thermodynamic situation analogous to the thermo-perceptual situation to which the direct realist's thesis pertains. We remove a mercury-in-glass thermometer from a refrigerator whose temperature the thermometer presently records, and we station this thermometer in the kitchen air. The mercury rises in the glass tube, and we read off from the thermometer the higher temperature of the kitchen air. We have observed the temperature of the air as the property of the kitchen air causally responsible for that action of the air on the thermometer which makes the mercury in the glass tube expand and hence rise in the tube, yielding a higher reading for the kitchen air than for the refrigerator air. Nothing is said, known, or presumed about the nature of this property. Now, as theoreticians, we assert that this property is the mean kinetic energy of the randomly and rapidly moving molecules that constitute the air. And we demonstrate that, if this identity is accepted, then how the temperature of the air causes the mercury in the thermometer to expand can be understood as an extremely high probability which is itself entailed as a statistical-mechanical necessity.

Leaving out the statistical content and describing the mechanism very informally, the picture looks like this: the molecules of the kitchen air are moving much faster than those of the air in the refrigerator; hence their mean kinetic energy is much higher than the mean vibrational energy of the molecules of mercury, since the latter initially still reflects that of the refrigerator air's molecules, and some of this greater energy of the kitchen-air molecules is transferred, upon impact, to the slower-moving molecules of the thermometer glass and transmitted to the molecules of the mercury within the glass; this causes the mercury's molecules to vibrate farther from their center of motion before returning; this *is* an increase in the volume of the mercury, hence *is* its expansion, hence *is* its rise in the glass tube (whose expansiveness is less).

When we remind ourselves of our pre-theoretical, observational specification of the temperature of the kitchen air as the property (of unknown nature) belonging to the air and responsible for the air's causal role in making the thermometer mercury rise, we find that our now making the theoretical assumption that this temperature is in its nature the mean kinetic energy of the air's molecules effects a great increment in the intelligibility for us of the warmer air's mode of operating upon the cooler thermometer. The assumption that observed temperature has this microstructural nature makes intelligible to us how it plays the causal role we observed it as playing. And we therefore find the asserted identity between the air's observed temperature and its molecular kinetic energy—originally so puzzling—now perspicuously intelligible to us. If the direct realist's thesis is to get support from the kinetic theory of gases, the identity he proposes must become comparably perspicuous for us for similar reasons. We shall want, then, to compare once again thermometer observation of temperature and feeling temperature. But first more discussion is needed of the form of intelligibility that accrues to the theoretical identification of thermodynamic temperature with molecular kinetic energy.

It might appear from the brief account just given that only two factors contribute to this intelligibility: that temperature is pre-theoretically observed as a presumed cause of an observed effect, and that the identification of macro- with micro-property succeeds in explaining how this causation works. But there is a third factor: the so-called "presumed cause" just mentioned is but one instance of the operation of one of the fundamental laws of thermodynamics, the Boyle-Charles law (strictly speaking, this is true only for gas thermometers) ; and the asserted identity has the effect of explaining for us the whole range of phenomena coming under this law as well as those coming under other known laws, for example, the second law of thermodynamics. It is this comprehensive, explanatory success which makes the asserted identity between observed temperature and molecular kinetic energy become for us so perspicuously intelligible. Let me spell this out a little.

The Boyle-Charles law asserts, in part, that the volume of a dilute gas increases and decreases in direct proportion to increase and decrease in the gas's temperature, provided the pressure is held constant. If the mercury thermometer we just imagined in a kitchen were replaced by a constant-pressure gas thermometer, then its increase in volume would reflect its own increase in temperature in consequence of coming into thermal equilibrium with the initially warmer kitchen air; so the asserted identity between temperature and mean molecular kinetic energy serves to explain for us this part of the Boyle-Charles law. This law also asserts that the pressure of a gas varies in direct proportion to variation in temperature, provided the volume is held constant. Why this is so is also made intelligible to us by the assumption of the same identity, in the following, again very informally presented way. The macroscopic property, the pressure of a gas upon its container walls, is the force exerted by the gas upon a unit area of the container wall. Why does this force per unit area exerted by the gas upon the container walls increase in direct proportion to the gas's increase in temperature? Because an increase in temperature *is* an increase in mean kinetic energy of molecules. Assuming identical masses for all the gas's molecules, this means that these molecules are traveling on the average faster. Therefore, if the volume of the container is held constant, the gas molecules will strike the sides of the container more frequently and with more speed. Hence the average impact of the molecules on the walls will be greater; that is to say, the average momentum transferred from the molecules to the container walls per unit time and area will be greater. Here another identification of macroscopic with microstructural property is made, and we assert that this *is* an increase in the pressure of the gas.

Because we have empirically specified temperature as the property of which pressure is a function (when volume is constant) and because we have identified macroscopic pressure with microstructural mean transfer of molecular momentum to container walls, identifying temperature with mean kinetic molecular energy makes intelligible to us—as an instance of statistical-mechanical necessity—why temperature plays the role in relation to pressure which the Boyle-Charles law assigns to it. Because that identification of temperature with molecular kinetic energy accomplishes this explanation, the identity becomes for us perspicuously intelligible.

One more illustration. Thermometer observations exemplify not only the operation of the Boyle-Charles law (a constant-volume gas thermometer would exemplify operation of the aspect of the law we have just examined), they also fall under the Second Law of Thermodynamics, one very simple statement of which is this: within a closed system heat flows spontaneously only from a region of higher temperature to a region of lower temperature. The warmer kitchen air raises the cooler mercury column because heat flows from the air to the mercury. If the mercury thermometer were put back into the refrigerator heat would flow away from it to the refrigerator air, and the mercury would contract.

Within macroscopic thermodynamics there is no explanation of the second law. This law does not, for example, follow from the law of conservation of energy, the First Law of Thermodynamics: considering only what the law of conservation permits, heat might be transferred spontaneously from a colder to a hotter body, provided that the amount of heat gained by the hot body were equal to the amount lost by the cold body. Again we find that identification of temperature with energy of molecular motion makes possible an increment in the intelligibility of an empirical law and thereby becomes itself perspicuously intelligible. And again I give the barest sketch of how this works.

When a volume of hot gas is joined with an equal volume of cold gas, initially there are many more fast-moving molecules in the hot region than in the cold and many more slow-moving molecules in the cold region than in the hot. If heat flowed from the cold region to the hot region, then the distribution of molecular speeds in the new volume of hot and cold gas would become even more ordered, with still more high speeds in the one region, more low speeds in the other, since the hot region would become hotter and the cold region colder. That outcome is like this one: on a billiard table with many billiard balls, half blue and half red, all moving, there is a partition in the middle of the table and most of the blue balls on one side, most of the red on the other; when the partition is removed all the blue balls end up on one side of the table and all the red balls on the other side.

Why are both of these outcomes improbable? Because the number of ways in which it is possible for the molecular speeds (or colored balls) to distribute themselves throughout the entire region in a random and hence disordered way is much greater than the number of ways in which they can line up with most of the fast molecules (or blue balls) in one region and most of the slower molecules (or red balls) in another region. And the larger the number of items in the collection the greater is this difference between the number of ways of making the disordered and the ordered distribution. With a drop of water comprising something of the order of magnitude of 2×10^{22} molecules, this difference is enormous. And this difference between the number of ways open to the molecules to fall into two regions ordered as fast and slow, and the number of ways open to them to distribute themselves randomly with regard to speed throughout the whole water drop, this difference corresponds to the difference between the probabilities of each of these two distributions occurring. The probability that the distribution will be random turns out to be so large that this distribution of speeds is unlikely to differ from equal numbers of fast and slow molecules in both regions of the water drop by more than one part in one hundred million. The probability amounts, therefore, to a virtual certainty that the faster molecules will transfer energy to the slower molecules until both regions of the gas have molecules moving with the same average speed. But if we identify macroscopic temperature with mean kinetic molecular energy, then we have just said that the spontaneous flow of heat will always be from the region of higher temperature to the region of lower temperature. And this is what the Second Law of Thermodynamics asserts.

Once again, affirming the identity of observed temperature with mean molecular kinetic energy becomes intelligible to us in virtue of our coming to understand through this identification why temperature (here a temperature difference) plays the part it plays in the physical world according to a well-established empirical law of macroscopic thermodynamics: the overwhelming probability that it will play this part becomes a matter of statistical-mechanical necessity. And also once again: if the direct realist's contention that the thermal qualities we directly feel are identical with quantities of molecular energy of motion of physical systems before the skin is to get support from the source he looks to, the reduction of thermodynamics to statistical mechanics, then this identity that he proposes must become perspicuously intelligible to us for similar reasons. For otherwise its initial unintelligibility to us will be decisive against it. Let us, then, turn back to the direct realist's thesis and to the similarities and differences between thermometer observation of temperature and feeling temperature.

The direct realist has acknowledged that in attentively feeling our skin warming under the influence of the sun's rays we do not become thermally conscious of the mean vibrational energy of the molecules of our skin *as that*—we do not become thermally conscious of the nature of the temperature of our skin, just as in observing with a thermometer the temperature of the kitchen air one does not become observationally conscious of the nature of the temperature of the air.

The direct realist also now affirms that in both instances we become conscious of a determinate sensible character of something before our sense organs: in the thermometer observation this is a visibly sensible character constituting the configuration made by one end of the mercury column and an adjacent numeral, a visible configuration which I call, for short, the thermometer reading. And it is through our visual perception of this visibly sensible character of the thermometer, the reading on it, that we observe, more indirectly, the temperature of the air, by conceiving this temperature as that property of the air which accounts for the air's causing the thermometer to show this reading. In the thermal feeling of temperature, the determinate sensible character we directly feel, which occupies a position analogous to that of the thermal reading, is the thermal quality "warmth." (I use quotation marks so as to leave it open whether this is a physical feature of an object before the skin, as the direct realist holds, or a sensuous quality of thermal awareness.) And just as we become observationally conscious of the property that is (unknown to us) the mean molecular kinetic energy of the kitchen air's molecules, through looking attentively at the thermometer reading, so too we become thermoperceptually conscious of the property that is (unknown to us) the mean kinetic-potential energy of the vibrating molecules of our skin, through directly feeling the quality "warmth."

Of course the way this is done in thermometer observation is, as we have earlier discovered, not in virtue of an identity between the thermometer reading and the temperature of the air; it is through the application to the observation of the thermometer reading of this "description": "that property of the air, whatever its nature, which is causally responsible for the air's part in making *this* thermometer reading." Now, however, the direct realist asserts that in the thermoperceptual situation the way our directly feeling the quality "warmth" manages to constitute our thermal awareness of the temperature of the skin is in virtue of this directly felt quality's *being* the temperature of our skin and, hence, *being* the skin's mean energy of molecular vibration.

A thermoperceptual situation so analyzed leaves us with an alleged identity between a directly felt, thermal quality and a quantity of molecular kinetic energy, which is, so far, opaque to our understanding. This purported identity is not, at least not yet, intelligible to us. The elements in the thermometer-observational situation which contribute to the intelligibility of the initially surprising identity discovered there are altogether missing from the thermoperceptual situation as now analyzed by the direct realist. The conception through which one attributes temperature to an object when using a thermometer enables us, through its content, to understand, upon reflection, how this temperature one has ascribed to an object can be a form of molecular energy: in thermometer observation one attributes temperature to an object as the unanalyzed cause of something else which one more directly perceives (sees) ; this fact makes it intelligible to us that the theoretical analysis of this cause—hence of observationally ascribed temperature's nature—should turn out to have a microstructural content, when, *in addition,* such an analysis yields for us an understanding of how this cause (the very temperature we observationally attributed) operates in producing what we see (the thermometer reading) .

On the other hand, within the thermoperceptual situation, when a person attentively feels that an object has a certain temperature, the delineation which temperature receives is provided entirely by the directly felt, thermal qualities, one by one. And the property of which one is directly conscious in merely feeling an object to be cool—the thermal quality "coolness"—is an apparently different property from the property specified in kinetic theory as the mean molecular energy of vibration of the constituent molecules of the same object before the skin. Therefore the assertion that the thermoperceptually attributed property *is* the other—that the directly felt quality "coolness" *is* a certain mean molecular kinetic-potential energy—is, so far, unintelligible to us, incoherent, mere nonsense. Unless the direct realist can contribute something more to the analysis of the thermoperceptual situation, something that will function to give to the purported identity of directly felt quality and molecular energy of motion the kind of intelligibility—and plausibility—which the identity he relies upon for support has—the identity of thermometer-observed temperature and mean molecular kinetic energy—we shall have to reject his present thesis as patently false.

But where can the direct realist turn for such help? He must discover a way in which tempertaure is specified within thermal perception which coheres with the nature of temperature as a form of molecular energy and coheres with the identity of each directly felt, thermal quality with a temperature having this nature; and he must show us how this identity becomes perspicuously intelligible in virtue of what it helps to explain about some part these directly felt qualities play in the physical world before our sensory organs. This project, obviously, divides itself into two tasks: finding within thermoperception a suitable specification of temperature, for one, and, the other, finding a role these directly felt qualities play in the physical world before our skin which can be explained by the identification of these qualities with mean kinetic molecular energy. But the microreduction of thermometer-observed temperature to molecular kinetic energy explains a role of thermometer-observed temperature in the physical world, a role which is described by the empirical laws of thermodynamics: the Boyle-Charles law and the Second Law of Thermodynamics, for example. What scientific laws have we whose upshot is a description of the role played by directly felt, thermal qualities in the world before our skin? None. These qualities were left behind the moment the investigation of heat became scientific, since this moment is marked by the substitution of thermometer observation of temperature for feeling it.

As to the other task, finding a description under which temperature is specified within thermal perception which prepares the way for the identification of the felt thermal qualities with mean energies of molecular motion: we solved the analogous problem for thermometer observation of temperature by pointing out that the most directly observed property before the sense organs, the thermometer reading, could not be identified with temperature if the microreduction of temperature is understood to assert an identity between temperature and mean kinetic molecular energy; and we then came up with this conception, under which temperature as observed by thermometers is ascribed to bodies: that property of the object to which the thermometer is applied which is causally responsible for the object's role in producing *this* reading. What we observe, but only indirectly, by thermometer is what plays those various interesting roles in the physical world before our sense organs which the empirical laws of thermodynamics identify but do not explain. So the way is open for a microreduction of thermometer-observed temperature to be intelligible to us.

But what comparably facilitating conception or description, or analogue of a conception or description, can the direct realist discover as plausibly the description under which we attentively *feel* things to have a certain temperature? For the reason already given, he has nowhere to turn, because the analogue of a description under which an object is attentively felt by us to have, say, a temperature in the cool range is nothing but the thermal quality "coolness" itself. Not the word 'cool' nor the concept this word expresses, but the quality itself constitutes this analogue of a description under which the temperature is attentively felt to belong to an object. But this gets the direct realist nowhere along his way. For there is nothing whatever about the simple, directly felt quality "coolness" which helps us to understand how this quality can be identical with mean kinetic energy of the skin's molecules.

Only if there were, waiting to be explained by assertion of this identity, laws of thermodynamics that specify the causal or other functional role, in the physical world before our skin, of directly felt "coolness" could the direct realist have so much as an intimation of a plausible—even an intelligible—story to tell. But thermodynamics offers to the direct realist no such laws. Nor does any other physical science. Nor have we any reason to believe such laws will ever be forthcoming.

11. Refutation of Second (Identity) Microreduction Defense of Direct Realism

We may now imagine the direct realist to reply to the argument just concluded by trying to apply to thermal perception the account I offered of thermometer observation of temperature, an account whose purpose was to accommodate the theoretical identification of observable temperature with molecular energy of motion. The direct realist now proposes that we attentively *feel* temperature under this description: "that property of (say) this iron railing before my skin which causally accounts for my feeling *this*"—where the directly felt, thermal quality "coldness" takes the place of the word 'this'. He may first point out that the temperature of the iron railing does answer to this description. But since he now holds that the directly felt, thermal quality *is* this temperature, he must hold that the physical feature of the railing which causes me to feel *this* is—*this* itself, that is to say, is the directly felt, thermal quality. *It* is the property of the iron railing (or of my skin) which causes me to become thermally conscious of itself.

Now, he argues, since the property of the object which explains why I feel what I feel is the mean kinetic energy of the object's molecules, asserting this to be identical with the directly felt, thermal quality explains how the directly felt, thermal quality causes me to feel itself as a feature of the object before my skin. This, he suggests, is the very sort of explanation of a causal role possessed by the directly felt quality which, he now concedes, is needed in order to make the identity, through affirming which this explanation is achieved, both perspicuously intelligible and plausible to us. So we can now accept the identity of the thermal qualities we directly feel with various quantities of mean kinetic energy of the molecules of the portion of the skin before the thermosensory receptor organs located within the skin.

This will not do. The "explanation" of why one feels a thermal quality which is provided by identifying this quality with the mean energy of vibration of the molecules of my skin is not the sort of explanation that is needed in order to make this identity intelligible to us. It is not at all like the explanation of why the kitchen air causes the mercury in the tube to rise or the explanation of why the pressure of a gas rises when, the volume being held constant, the temperature is increased; these explanations are effected by affirming the identity of temperature and mean kinetic molecular energy (and by jointly affirming the identities of the macroscopic properties, pressure and volume, with certain microstructural, molecular properties), and the success of these explanations makes intelligible to us the affirmed identity of macroscopic with microstructural temperature. Once the several identities are affirmed, these explanations make the overwhelming probability of the pressure rising or the volume increasing, given an increase in temperature, a matter of statistical-mechanical necessity. And the initially puzzling identity is thereby made both intelligible and probable. But how does the explanation to which the direct realist now appeals work?

Well, we first discover this correlation: whenever the mean speed of vibration (and associated kinetic-potential energy) of the molecules of one's skin reaches a certain figure, one directly feels a certain thermal quality; call it "C." We accept, furthermore, that this correlation involves a causal influence of the molecular velocities upon what one thermally feels. But how this causation works is altogether inscrutable to us; why it happens this way we have no idea. Then this answer is provided to us: "Because the molecules of your skin gaining that much energy of vibrational motion *is* your skin's having the thermal quality C. So naturally C is what you feel! What could be more intelligible? It's not a case of statistical-mechanical necessity, but that isn't the only sort of intelligibility an explanation can yield. And doesn't this explanatory success, in turn, make the affirmation of identity between the directly felt quality C and mean molecular kinetic energy of the skin perspicuously intelligible?"

Not at all. The explanatory success is entirely illusory. What had to be explained was how the molecules in my skin moving at a certain speed cause me to feel the sensible quality C. To "know" that molecular motion of this speed (or its associated energy) *is* the directly felt quality C helps me not at all to understand how its being this quality causes me to feel the quality it is. We know that the skin affects my consciousness by affecting first the thermosensory organs located in my skin. So, understanding how the molecular motion causes me to feel C must involve understanding how it works upon the thermosensory organs to accomplish this result. But it is no help for this project to be told that the molecular motion *is* the directly felt quality C that I feel. For this makes the mystery of how the skin's molecular motion works on the thermosensory receptor organs in the skin even greater, not less: how can the directly felt quality C work on these receptor organs? We have no inkling of an answer to these questions. Surely this path is a dead end for the direct realist.

Impatiently the direct realist now points out to me that I have misunderstood him. I have supposed that it is the molecular motion's operation that gets explained by the sensible quality, when in fact it is the other way around. We start out "knowing" that the directly felt quality C, belonging to the skin, causes us to be conscious of itself, somehow, but exactly how it does this we do not understand. Then we affirm that this quality is identical with the mean kinetic-potential molecular energy of the skin. And we can understand (in principle) how this energy can affect the thermosensory receptors in the skin and, hence, how it can cause us to become conscious of the thermal quality C, which is to say, of itself. Since how the thermal quality C makes us thermally conscious of itself is thus explained for us by affirming the identity of this quality with the molecular motion's energy, this identity thereby becomes for us both perspicuously intelligible and plausible.

But if this is what the direct realist means, then my response can only be to remark that it is simply false that how the thermal quality C (supposed to belong to the skin) makes me conscious of itself is explained by identifying this quality with the skin's energy of molecular motion. Although at the moment we do not know, doubtless we shall before long know how the thermal energy of the skin affects the thermosensory receptors in the skin and causes them to discharge. But this knowledge will surely constitute no explanation for us of why it is we directly feel the specific, thermal quality C rather than, say, the very different, thermal quality H. Nor have we at this time any clear idea what such an explanation would look like if, say, the causal process were followed further into the nervous system, even to the cortical center of the brain where "thermal sensory impulses" terminate.

We can, however, say this: if somewhere along this chain in the nervous system an explanation is achieved that does make it clear to us why we directly feel the specific quality C, just as it earlier was made clear to us why an increase in temperature caused the volume or the pressure of a thermometer to increase, then we shall have good reason for, at most, identifying the directly felt quality C with whatever property of the nervous system (doubtless central rather than peripheral) it is whose description effects this explanation for us. But there will be no reason to work all the way back to the remote place on the causal chain at which the skin's energy of molecular motion initiated this process, and affirm the identity of this molecular energy with the thermal quality C, for this identification accomplishes nothing in the way of explaining to us why we directly feel the thermal quality we feel. Surely this path is as unpromising for the direct realist as the path I first thought he meant to follow.

12. Refutation of Third Microreduction Defense of Direct Realism: The Elimination Interpretation

Although I find the direct realist's stock of possible rebuttals almost depleted, it is not quite used up. For there are two other interpretations of a microreduction of observed, macroscopic properties which he might invoke to replace the interpretation I have given. I have treated the properties of empirical thermodynamics such as temperature and pressure, which get reduced to statistical microstructural properties such as mean kinetic energy of molecules and the like, as asserted, by this microreduction, to be identical with the properties they are reduced to. But two other interpretations of this reduction are possible: elimination of the macroscopic properties; and mere correlation between the macroscopic and the microstructural properties. So it is necessary to inquire how the direct realist's proposal to construe the directly felt, thermal qualities as themselves reduced to microstructural properties fares under these two interpretations of this reduction. Let us first consider the elimination interpretation.

On this view we no longer suppose that observable temperature has been shown to be identical with mean molecular kinetic energy. Rather, we judge the original thermodynamic conception of temperature to be scientifically inadequate in a way that requires its repudiation, as not specifying an actual property of physical systems.

More generally, the macroscopic properties figuring in the thermodynamic laws, such as pressure, temperature, entropy, are abolished from our representation of the physical world before the sense organs, and the thermodynamic laws in which these properties' behavior is described are rejected. In place of the laws of macroscopic thermodynamics there now appear the laws of statistical mechanics and the kinetic theory of heat, and in place of the old macroscopic properties there now appear the microstructural properties. There is no thermodynamic temperature to be identified with mean molecular kinetic energy. Our belief that macroscopic properties are instantiated in physical systems was merely a way station along the road to a more accurate belief that replaces the original one. According to the new belief, there may well be an observable temperature, but if so it is newly observable, microstructural temperature only, that is, observable mean molecular kinetic energy; proper observation now requires additional steps of calculation, yielding observed ergs instead of degrees Kelvin, and presupposing, within observation, use of the complex, statistical-mechanical microtheory.

Furthermore, the direct realist now argues, the directly felt, thermal qualities have also been reduced by this microreduction. They too, therefore, have been eliminated from our representation of the physical world before our sense organs. They were never there to be felt. Of what, then, are we thermally conscious? Mean kinetic energy of molecules.

But of course the scientific observations of this molecular quantity which are now imagined to be possible involve new calculations, the use of a complex microtheory within observation, and an observable temperature expressed in ergs instead of degrees Kelvin. And these scientific observations of the new temperature still include as a more directly observed property the visibly sensible configuration comprising a thermometer reading. What corresponds to these new calculations and to the more directly observed thermometer reading, according to this account of thermal feeling? There is no answer. The direct realist has merely returned himself to the point where he had admitted the need for a new start, and repudiated the new start.

For remember that we have supposed the direct realist to acknowledge that there is a determinate, thermal quality of which we always become directly conscious in attentively feeling temperatures; this he did when faced with refutation, otherwise, of his direct realism. He further asserted that this directly felt quality is instantiated before the thermosensory organs in the skin, hence characterizes the portion of the skin that is before the thermal receptor organs within the skin. In order to make out his claim that this thermal quality is independent in its nature and existence from human thermosensory consciousness, he argued that it is to be understood as reduced to mean molecular kinetic energy of the skin. But now he defeats himself by proposing that this reduction constitutes elimination of felt, thermal qualities. For this leaves him with a dilemma. Either he construes this elimination as abolishing the thermal qualities from the physical world only and takes them to be instantiated, instead, within the thermal percipient's consciousness or else he takes them to be banished from the universe altogether.

If he supposes that the directly felt, thermal qualities are instantiated within thermal consciousness, then, since he began the present phase of his defense of direct realism by affirming them to be the direct objects of thermal awareness, he will have made them into *internal* direct objects of thermal awareness, and renounced his direct realism. If, however, he makes the other choice, and construes them as eliminated from the entire universe—following the interpretation made of the reduction of thermodynamic temperature—then there never was a thermal quality for anyone to be directly conscious of in feeling a temperature. And now the direct realist has rejected the starting point of this phase of the discussion. And our original argument which persuaded him to make this new start regains its cogency. For now he holds that there is nothing to function as a delineation of temperature for our thermal awareness but the property's own nature, mean kinetic energy of molecules, and this with no thermometer reading to mediate observation and no microtheory employed to mediate calculation of ergs. No ground has been gained, nothing important enough has changed; our earlier argument against the direct realist, before he admitted determinate qualities as direct objects of thermal feeling, again becomes operative, and effective.

13. Refutation of Fourth Microreduction Defense of Direct Realism: The Correlation Interpretation

The direct realist has one last chance. He can drop both the identity and the elimination interpretations of the microreduction of thermodynamics to statistical mechanics and adopt instead the covariation, or correlation interpretation, and then apply this to his thesis that the directly felt, thermal qualities are instances of physical temperature before the skin. It remains for me to show that this last effort to avoid indirect realism must also fail.

We now construe the relationship of thermodynamic temperature to molecular energy in this way: the mean kinetic energy of the molecules is one property of a physical system, not to be identified with the system's temperature; its temperature is another, entirely distinct and macroscopic property of this physical system, a quantity specified within thermodynamics: thermodynamic temperature; and this macroscopic, thermodynamic temperature varies in direct proportion to variation in the microstructural quantity, mean molecular kinetic energy. There is no identity between macroscopic temperature and molecular kinetic energy; but neither is the reality of the macroscopic property specified by thermodynamics denied—on the contrary, the thermodynamic specification of temperature is affirmed as revealing the whole nature of temperature, and temperature turns out to be merely systematically correlated with the very different property, mean molecular kinetic energy.

One way to illustrate this covariation interpretation of the now merely so-called "microreduction" of thermodynamics to statistical mechanics is to construe it as a framework within which to accept the operational specification of the nature of temperature, a mode of specification which I earlier argued is inconsistent with an interpretation of the microreduction as establishing an identity of macroscopic with microstructural temperature. Although an operational conception of temperature is unlikely to be adopted by either a contemporary thermodynamicist or philosopher of physics, I shall first employ this conception as an illustration and argue that, on this version of the covariation interpretation of the microreduction, direct realism still fails. Then I shall briefly show that my argument against thermoperceptual direct realism would not be weakened by using other modes of thermodynamic specification of the nature of temperature in working out the covariation idea.

Now we imagine temperature to be conceived as comprising a disjunctive property; the components of the disjunction are the manifestations of each of the thermometric properties of physical systems—the set of thermometer readings. If we use a constant-volume gas thermometer, the temperature of a gas *is* the manifestation of the pressure of the gas; with a constant-pressure gas thermometer, the temperature of a gas *is* the manifestation of the volume of the gas; and with an electrical resistance thermometer the temperature of a solid *is* the manifestation of the solid body's electrical resistance. In each instance the "manifestation" of the thermometric property will be some form of thermometer reading, for example, a needle pointing at a numeral. (For absolute temperature, which is what actually figures in the microreduction, it will be necessary to use certain limits which are approached as constant-volume and constant-pressure gas thermometers are made to approximate more and more to perfect or ideal gases.)

Now we understand the direct realist as adding to this picture this thesis: that the thermal qualities we directly feel are each of them also manifestations of a thermometric property of what we thermoperceive before the receptor organs in the skin; hence these directly felt, thermal qualities constitute "thermometer readings," as it were, and are therefore actual temperatures of the skin (and of the objects before the skin which we thermally feel and which are in thermal equilibrium with the skin).

For simplicity's sake, let us suppose that the direct realist limits himself to asserting this thesis only for the object most directly perceived before the thermosensory organs, the skin itself. Then on this view the directly felt, thermal qualities are physical properties of the skin, each instance of a thermal quality constituting a manifestation of an instance of some thermometric, physical property of the skin (such as pressure or volume or electrical resistance). The thermal qualities we directly feel are the skin's own thermometer readings, reflecting in their variation the variation of some property of the skin which itself varies as a function of variation in the mean energy of random, vibrational motion of the skin's molecules.

This is perhaps an interesting conception. But the aspect of it we need immediately to appreciate is the fact that this interpretation of the relationship between thermodynamic temperature and molecular energy, when extended to encompass as well the alleged microreduction of directly felt, thermal qualities to physical temperatures, has the consequence that once again the direct realist is affirming an identity between the directly felt, thermal quality and a physical property of the skin, as he did when he used the identity interpretation of the microreduction. The only way, therefore, that the task of the direct realist, in its crucial moment, now differs from the task he needed to accomplish but could not when working from the identity interpretation of the microreduction, is this: it is now not explicitly required that the physical property of the skin with which the directly felt, thermal qualities are said to be identical be a microstructural property of the skin.

Indeed, since the physical property of the skin with which a thermal quality is identified is alleged to be thermally perceived by us in a way that makes it function as an analogue of a thermometer reading, one might well suppose that the physical property of the skin will need to be a macroscopic, not a microstructural property. Certainly we should assume this, since only on that assumption do we have a situation to examine that is new, in any way that might hinder our earlier argument against the direct realist's thesis, when he used the identity interpretation, from being applied to this, the covariation interpretation of the reduction. For it should be evident that, if we supposed that the physical property of the skin which is taken to *be* the directly felt, thermal quality was a microstructural property (for example the electrical resistance of the skin, conceived microstructurally, as, say, a property of atoms and their electrons), then the situation would be enough like the attempted identification of directly felt, thermal qualities with molecular kinetic energies to require no new argument in rebuttal.

So let us now suppose that the quasi-thermometer readings within the skin with which the directly felt, thermal qualities are identified are constituted of instances of one or more macroproperties of the skin, properties we should think of as observable in some easy way. I say one or more, because the difference between the hot and the cold sides of the thermosensory scale suggests that we might expect two properties to figure as thermosensory "thermometer readings". What properties of the skin might play this role? I have no idea. But for our purposes it does not matter whether or not we get the most plausible candidate, provided we choose the right kind of property. We may, then, imagine that in response, say, to changes in the electrical resistance of the skin, itself a thermometric property for the skin, varying in direct proportion to changes in the mean speed of the skin's molecular vibrational motion, the skin undergoes some deformation comparable to a needle moving its position; and some set of deformations of the skin is identical with the set of thermal qualities that we directly feel in attentively feeling our skin's temperature.

In its simplest form, then, the direct realist's thesis now says that, in becoming thermally conscious of the sensible quality "cool," we are becoming directly conscious of a change of shape in our skin. The directly felt quality "cool" and the skin's deviation in a certain way from its shape at physiological zero are the same property. The directly felt quality "warm" and the skin's deviation in some different way from its shape at physiological zero are the same property. It will save words and not affect the cogency of the argument if we simplify still further and speak of change of shape simply as shape: the skin's having the directly felt, thermal quality "cool" is identical with the skin's having a certain shape. The directly felt quality "warm" *is* another skin shape, and so on. Even more bluntly put, this thesis entails statements of this sort: "Directly felt warmth is rectangularity; directly felt coolness is triangularity."

I shall take advantage of having been rather expansive in my critical discussion of the direct realist's thesis under the first (identity) interpretation of the microreduction of temperature and of the alleged microreduction of directly felt, thermal qualities, and be brief in criticizing this present version of the thesis. In another context, if someone said that the "warm" quality we directly feel is in fact rectangularity, we should think he was making a joke, speaking figuratively as in a poem or in the argot of some youth ("to be cool is not to be square") , or uttering nonsense. The only thing that could make it possible for a philosopher to say something of this kind in the present context and hope not to be thought to be doing any of those things would be his reliance upon the extraordinary success of the microreduction of thermodynamics in making us feel at home with certain initially strange-seeming identities of properties, for example, of thermometer-observable temperature and apparently nonobservable mean kinetic molecular energy. But relying upon this comfort that we have acquired from the scientific examples, in proposing his present thesis, is either disingenuous in the direct realist or confused. For there is no help to be had for him from this quarter. Turning to it leaves his thesis standing unsupported by a redeeming context and, therefore—since neither a poem, street slang, nor a joke—sheer nonsense.

For how is a directly felt quality conceived or described (or "conceived" or "described") within thermal perception in such a way as to facilitate our understanding how the directly felt quality "cool" can be identical with a triangular configuration of the skin?

Since the only analogue of a description under which we directly feel the quality "cool" is the quality "cool" itself, which does not in the required way cohere with a shape of the skin, there is no analogue of a conception or description under which we feel this quality which the direct realist can cite as a help in understanding how this quality can *be* a triangular shape of the skin.

And what thermodynamic laws describe the role that the directly felt quality "cool" plays in the physical world before our thermosensory receptor organs? And what explanation of this role is provided by the assumption that this directly felt quality is identical with a triangular shape of the skin, which would help make intelligible to us the assertion of this otherwise inscrutable identity? As we have remarked earlier, there are no such thermodynamic laws concerning directly felt, thermal qualities of objects before our sense organs; and there are therefore no such explanations—and there is every reason to think there never will be any of these things. The direct realist's thesis has to be rejected as apparent nonsense unredeemed by the only kind of support that could redeem it, hence rejected as genuine nonsense.

To be sure, the particular version of the covariation interpretation of the relationship between thermodynamics and statistical mechanics which I have given may not be very close to the version we should expect from a contemporary philosopher of physics serious about the project. Operationalism has few if any supporters today among philosophers of science. An approach to an interpretation of this relationship through careful construction of a definition of temperature based upon the most sophisticated contemporary statements of thermodynamics would have a very different look, indeed, from an operational specification of temperature by reference to thermometer readings. The reader may here recall the passage quoted from a recent *Encyclopædia Brittanica* article (above, p. 119), in which thermodynamic temperature is defined as the ratio of the rate of total energy change in a system to the rate of change of its entropy, as one example of an alternative definition to the operational conception I worked with just above.

Whatever articulation of a concept of temperature might emerge from such work in contemporary thermodynamics, I think the argument just sketched succeeds in giving conclusive reason for believing that the temperature-property so specified will not provide the direct realist with a viable candidate for identification, in its various degrees, with directly felt, thermal qualities. For we can be confident that this concept of temperature will be too complex and sophisticated for the assertion of identity between a particular degree of the quantity thus specified and a directly felt, thermal quality—in its simplicity— to be initially intelligible to use, let alone credible.

We should therefore require, for the intelligibility and credibility of such an identity, an account of the description (or analogue of a description) of temperature under which temperature is felt and which coheres (in a way the simple thermal quality does not do) both with temperature's having the complex nature thermodynamics specifies for it and with the directly felt, thermal quality's having this same nature (which it must have if it is to be identical with temperature). However, since the only analogue of a description under which temperature is thermally perceived is one or another directly felt, thermal quality, no one of which will cohere with the anticipated, thermodynamic specification of temperature's nature in a way that will help make intelligible to us how this directly felt quality can itself be identical with a property having the complex nature of thermodynamic temperature, this requirement cannot be met.

Its not being met provides all the more reason why we should therefore also require, for the intelligibility and plausibility of the asserted identity between directly felt, thermal quality and degree of thermodynamic temperature, a set of thermodynamical laws expressing causal or functional relationships between directly felt, thermal qualities of physical systems before the sense organs and other physical quantities characterizing such systems; and we have all the more need to find these relationships explained for us by the assumption of an identity between the thermal qualities we directly feel and the range of thermodynamic temperatures, so that this inscrutable identity might somehow, despite failure of fulfillment of the first requirement, become intelligible (and credible) to us in virtue of the work it does in helping us to understand why the laws it explains hold.

However, as before, no such thermodynamical laws governing the behavior in the physical world before our sense organs of the thermal qualities we directly feel are forthcoming; so the conditions required even for intelligibility—not to mention credibility—of the assertion of identity between the thermal qualities we directly feel and degrees of thermodynamic temperature cannot be realized. Interpreting the relationship between thermodynamics and statistical mechanics as involving only correlation between thermodynamic temperature and statistical-mechanical quantities like mean molecular kinetic energy provides no help whatever to the thermoperceptual direct realist.

The first two-thirds of this chapter mounted an extended argument for an indirectly realistic, representational account of thermal awareness of heat and cold. Section 6 brought that to its climax. Sections 7 and 8 provided details of the indirect realism that solved the thermoperceptual puzzle. And in §§10 to 13 I have examined four distinct forms of this rebuttal. Each has been found unacceptable. The plausible replies of the direct realist to the original argument for indirect realism have been canvassed and all have failed. I conclude that the original argument was cogent and that the indirectly realistic account of thermal awareness of heat and cold offered in §§6 to 8 is the correct account. Our thermal awareness of heat and cold before our skin is always mediated by direct awareness of instances of sensuous thermal qualities belonging to (and partly constituting) our conscious states themselves.

Chapter Five HEARING

Colors are perceived neither as substances nor as ingredients of events: most of the colors we see are colors of the surfaces of objects, and we experience and think of these colors as sensible characters the surfaces have. An odor is sometimes perceived, and thought of, in much the same way, as a sensible character belonging to an object we are smelling. As we observed earlier, however, an odor is also sometimes experienced and thought of as a rather ethereal substance carried in the air, inhaled in breathing, sometimes deposited on objects as a material trace (the scent) of whatever has made contact with these objects, and as having a sensible, odorous character rather than being such a character. Whenever it happens, our experiencing odors as carried through the air is immediate, because we detect odors by sniffing them, by breathing them in. Of course we are helped in this experience by the fact that an odor, like a sound, often comes to us without our seeing or otherwise knowing for certain what its source is and by the further fact that we often do know that the source is at a considerable distance from us. Despite this similarity in our cognitive relation to the sources of both sounds and odors, because sounds are not sniffed or inhaled as odors are our experience of sounds as carried through the air is less immediate than is our similar experience of odors. It is more nearly inferential.

1. The Sounds We Hear Are Trains of Airwaves

Sooner or later nearly everyone has the experience of a sound "carrying" more easily (because farther) over the surface of a still lake than down a city street. Or one has the experience of seeing a distant object make a puff of smoke or a splash in the water, and some seconds later hearing the sound of the rifle shot or of the splash; we then form the thought and have the experience of a sound as occupying some time in traveling from where the distant, visible object is making the sound to where one stands and hears it. Such experiences, as well as many in which the time that sounds take to travel to our ears is not discernible to us, illustrate another difference between our experience of sounds and of odors: very often we see the thing that makes the sound making it, whereas we never see (or otherwise discern) the object that gives off an odor actually giving it off. Often seeing the sounds we hear being made at various distances from us, frequently by seeing objects strike other objects but always by seeing at least something move in some way, helps us to form the idea that sound, after being made at some distance from us, has to travel through the air to where we are listening, before we can hear it. That sounds are perceptibly weakened by distance (and by intervening barriers) suggests the same thought to us. This idea that a sound travels from its source to us is expressed, especially when we are puzzled about exactly where the sound's source is located, in our often speaking of a sound as coming from a certain region rather than as located in this region. "Where is that sound (noise) coming from?" is probably a more common form of question than "Where is that sound (noise) ?"

To be contrasted with this experience and with this thought of a sound as traveling through the air from its source to us is our hearing (and our consequent thinking of) a telephone's ringing in the office down the hall, the dishes rattling in the kitchen, a squeak in one's car as in the right rear wheel, and the back-firing of someone else's truck as on the street in front of the house, the roaring of the wind as outside the window at the corner of the house, the creaking of a floorboard as in the next room, the loud screeching of automobile tires as having occurred a block down the road, and so on. The more or less onomato-poetic verbal nouns we often use to speak of these sounds—a screeching, a squeaking, a rattling, a creaking—signify both a physical process that is making the sound and the sound that is being made. And we both hear and think of the sound belonging to this process as located exactly where the process occurs in which the sound is made.

What is more, the sound contributes to the sensible character of this process: to our auditory perception the sound "inheres in" the sound-making process—in the ringing or the squeaking—quite as closely as, to our comparable olfactory perception (or our experience of colors) the odor of a bar of soap we hold to our nose and sniff (or its color we see) inheres in the bar of soap, as part of the soap's sensible character. But because we do not see odorous objects giving off their odors, when we sniff them at close range we do not, at least ordinarily, experience odorous objects as "making odors," whereas even at the moment in which we perceive a phone's ringing as having for its sensible quality a certain sound, we yet hear the phone to be making the very sound which its ringing has as its sensible character: our wide audiovisual experience of sounds being made (and our practical experience of making them ourselves) is carried with us into auditory experiences in which we believe that the sound we are hearing is being made even when we cannot see how (or even that) this is being done. In any event, these sounds, perceived as ingredient in such recognized sound-making processes as ringings and backfirings, are experienced, characteristically, not as traveling through space but as being located where the processes in which they are being made are located, hence commonly as located at some distance from us. Strangely enough, even the crack of the distant rifle shot, whose puff of smoke is seen first, may also be heard as located way off where the firing is occurring.

Is our way of experiencing and thinking of sounds self-contradictory? Can sounds both be located at their sources when we hear them and travel to us before we can hear them? Can they, as well, both be things that are made at a distance and travel to us but also comprise the audible characters of the distant processes wherein the sounds are made?

The most convincing, simple inference that yields for us the thought that a sound travels is presumably this: "I saw the explosion some seconds before I heard it. So apparently the sound of the explosion takes some time to travel from the explosion to me, before I can hear it." But is this thought consistent with that other idea of a sound, grounded in that other content of our experience of sound, the idea of a sound as located at its distant source at the very instant one hears it? Does the sound first travel to me and then travel (very quickly) back again to its source? No one thinks this. Then how can it be at the source when I hear it, if it has first to travel from the source to me in order for me to hear it? Our common conception of a sound seems to contain a contradiction.

Also, if a sound is the sort of thing that travels through the air to a listener, then, upon reflection, one would think it has to be either a bit of stuff, like a molecule given off by an odorous object, or some sort of physical disturbance in the air or in space, perhaps some sort of wave. But if this is true, then how can a sound comprise the aurally perceptible character of a wailing or a howling or a roaring that is occurring away off at a distance from the listener?

I turn to the solution of this second puzzle first. In view of the strength of our disposition to think of a sound as the sort of thing that can be made by a vibrating physical object and can travel through space and because of the scientific evidence, shortly to be considered, which supports this belief, it would be helpful if there were a plausible way to construe such utterances as we are disposed to make in which we seem to speak of sounds as if they were audibly sensible qualities of sound-making objects and their actions in a way that makes out this apparent intent of our words to be only apparent. A plausible way to interpret this way of speaking of sounds is easy to provide. These utterances of ours contain an ellipsis; what we mean in saying, "It was a loud, deep bellow," and in saying, "This bell has a nice, mellow sound," or "What a loud bell!" is this: "The sound he made in bellowing was loud and deep," and, "This bell (ordinarily) makes a nice, mellow sound," or "What a loud sound this bell makes!" The appearance of inconsistency in our choice of a category under which to subsume sounds is removed: instead of being sometimes conceived as traveling things produced by vibrating physical objects and being at other times conceived as sensible characters which some physical objects and their actions have, sounds are always conceived, on this interpretation of our discourse about them, as things that have sensible characters, never as sensible characters that things have. The audibly sensible qualities we hear are not themselves sounds and do not belong to sound-making objects or to the actions of these objects; they are audibly sensible qualities of the sounds some vibrating objects produce.

If we seem also sometimes not merely to speak of but even to perceive with our ears audibly sensible qualities as belonging to sound-making objects or to the actions of such objects, this is to be counted a kind of aural-perceptual ellipsis, or illusion, and these sensible qualities are to be thought of as more properly ascribed to the sounds made by such physical objects in action.

Of course no harm is done if we now allow to bells and hammerings and the cracking of a branch a kind of honorary or derivative possession of audibly sensible qualities: the bell, the hammering, the cracking may be loud or piercing or sharp in the sense that each of these produces a sound that has one or more of these audibly sensible qualities. Indeed some sound-making processes—bellowings, ringings, and squeakings, for example—may properly be conceived as including within themselves the sounds that are made, process and product composing a conceptually unified whole. Then the process may be thought of as acquiring for itself an audibly sensible quality in virtue of its product's having this quality. A sound with its audibly sensible quality is conceived as an ingredient (the product) of a sound-making process, of a squeaking, for example; so the process, the squeaking, possesses the quality possessed by one of its ingredients. This possession is not honorary but literal. On the other hand, the action of the sound-making object, taken alone, can have an audibly sensible quality only in the honorary sense, as being the cause of a sound that has this quality.

So little strain is put upon the beliefs we already hold about sounds and so much is gained in coherence by this interpretation of both our auditory experience and our speaking and thinking of sounds that I shall adopt it forthwith. Sounds are things that physical objects make by striking other objects and by vibrating, and they are things that it makes sense to think of as traveling through space. The aurally sensible qualities we hear are not themselves sounds, nor are they qualities of the physical objects and actions that produce sounds; they are qualities of the sounds themselves (and hence of any sound-making process conceived as including within itself the sound made). To hear an audibly sensible quality is to hear a quality that belongs to the sort of thing—a sound—that can be produced by a vibrating physical object and that possibly travels through space. One apparent inconsistency in our common conception of sounds is, then, only apparent.

What of the other apparent contradiction within our common conception of sounds—our thinking of sounds as both traveling from their sources to us before we can hear them and as located at their distant sources when we hear them? The findings of physics inform us that there is something that is produced by the vibration of a sound-making object, is first located in the neighborhood of this object, and then travels through space to our ear, where it causes us, by virtue of its action upon our ear, to hear the sound we hear. So physics can be said to provide independent corroboration of at least part of the apparent information conveyed to us in auditory experience—provided that this something which physics' findings specify *is* the sound we hear. And why should it not be? Certainly it will reveal to physical inquiry properties it does not reveal to auditory perception. But we shall surely no longer expect that the most direct object of sensory perception that is located before the operative sense organs must reveal all its properties to sensory perception.

What physics discovers is this: that a wave of pressure in the air is generated by the distant sounding object's vibration and is transmitted through the air to our eardrum, which it sets to vibrating, whereupon neural impulses are started up in the auditory nerve and transmitted to the auditory cortex of the brain, whose action in turn either directly causes or, if materialism is true, constitutes our auditory experience. If there is a physical something before our ears which is the sound we hear, the only plausible candidate for this role is the wave of pressure in the air—commonly called a "soundwave"—which is generated by a sounding object's vibration and which beats upon our ear and elicits from us the reaction comprising our auditory sensory impression. For there is nothing else we know of from physical inquiry which is generated by the sounding object, exists first in the neighborhood of the object, then travels to our ears, and causes us to hear itself. In the interest of believing our ears, therefore, we should adopt the hypothesis that these waves of air pressure are the sounds we hear and relinquish this hypothesis only if, under close critical scrutiny, it causes more trouble than it removes. Does this hypothesis, as a start, resolve the apparent inconsistency of our believing sounds to be, at the moment of our hearing them, both in our neighborhood and in the neighborhood of the distant sounding object?

The hypothesis identifies a sound either with a single soundwave or, in case one soundwave striking the eardrum is not enough, the shortest sequence of soundwaves that, by beating upon our eardrums, is sufficient to cause us to hear such a sound. It is true that soundwaves are to be found both in the neighborhood of the distant sounding object and in the neighborhood of our ears: a given wave of air pressure begins out there and travels through the air to our ears. But the waves that cause me to hear what I hear at a given moment are certainly not the waves that are at this same moment just leaving the distant object; they are the waves that have already traveled from the object to my ear and have just finished striking my eardrum. Assuming that the airwave that I hear at a certain moment is the one that caused me to hear itself by acting upon my ear a few milliseconds before I heard it, only airwaves that have reached my ear can be the sounds I hear. The airwaves just departing from the distant sounding object are left without a role as heard sounds, and so we are left with no way of consistently believing that the sounds we hear are both out where the sounding object is and here where our ears are.

Our hypothesis, then, needs revision. A natural revision to try is this: the sound we hear is identical with the train of airwaves that stretches from the distant sounding object to our ear. At what moment? At the moment at which we hear the sound, or at the moment (a few milliseconds earlier) at which the airwaves that cause us to hear themselves are striking our ear? Let us stick to the rule that what we most directly perceive that is before our sensory organs must play a role in causing us to perceive itself. The train of airwaves to be identified with the sound I hear is the one whose near end caused me to hear this train of airwaves. So the relevant train of airwaves is the one that stretches from the sounding object to my ear at the moment in which the airwaves that cause me to hear a given sound are striking at my eardrum. Why not say that this train of airwaves is the sound I hear? It has one end at the distant sounding object and one end at my ear; so the sound I hear is both in my neighborhood and in the neighborhood of the sounding object. The appearance of inconsistency is removed from our common conception and experience of sounds.

It may be objected that the soundwaves comprising the more distant portions of the train of soundwaves have no part in causing us to hear the sound we are hearing and therefore should not be included within the sound we are said to be hearing. To this the reply must be that when I see a house by looking at its exterior front wall neither the rear wall nor the interior floor of the house plays a part in causing me to see the house of which each is a part. It is no part of our criterion in deciding what object before our sensory organs it is that we perceive with these organs that every part of such an object must play a part in causing us to have our sensory perception. The far end of the train of airwaves is no worse off in this respect than the interior floor and rear wall of the building I see by looking at its front side. And if the building I am looking at happens to reach through to the next street, then what I see is located at the moment I see it both on the street where I am standing and on the next street over. Somewhat analogously, if the train of airwaves stretching from the sounding object to my ear is the sound I am hearing, then the sound I am hearing is located both here where I am and out there where the sounding object is.

But will the sound I hear, on this hypothesis, have traveled from the sounding object to my ear before I hear it, as our common conception of sounds requires? By way of objection to our hypothesis it may be said that obviously the entire sound (the train of airwaves) has not traveled to my ear before I hear it, since part of it is stretched out from my ear to the sounding object.

If a person stands three feet from a closed door and another person opens it outward from the other side, the first person may be struck by the free-swinging end of the door, so the door has moved three feet from its closed position to the person it strikes. However, the hinged end of the door has moved scarcely at all in the direction of the person who is struck by the door. Somewhat analogously, we may say that the train of waves has moved from the sounding object to the listening person's ear before he hears the sound, because a part of the train of waves has traversed this distance, although another part has scarcely moved at all toward the person, and still other parts have moved intermediate distances along the path from sounding object to listener.

The hypothesis that the sound we hear is identical with the train of airwaves stretching from sounding object to the listener's ears at the moment part of this train strikes the ear turns out to be quite fruitful. It transforms the apparent contradiction within our common experience and thought of sounds into a harmless conjunction of consistent predictions: the sound we hear is in two places at once because it stretches from the sounding object to the listener's ear; and it travels through space from its source to the listener while remaining more or less fixed near its source, because one end of the sound travels this distance before the other end has got (very far) under way.

I have already remarked that it constitutes no obstacle to the sounds we hear being trains of airwaves that these sounds turn out to have properties we do not discern in hearing the sounds, for example, that the sounds comprise waves of condensation and rarefaction of the air. No one wants to say that because we do not discover by mere sense perception that the water we see and feel comprises hydrogen and oxygen, therefore this water is not H_2O. Similarly in the fact that we do not discover from hearing alone that sounds are waves of pressure in the air there is no reason to be found for denying that sounds are just that. On the other hand, since there is an initial presumption in favor of the truth of the delivery of our auditory perceptions, it does count against the hypothesis that sounds are trains of airwaves if the assumption of its truth entails that some of what our auditory experience leads us to believe about sounds turns out to be false. And this does happen: by the time the airwaves that cause us to hear a very brief sound strike the eardrum there will be no train of audible airwaves stretching back to the source of this sound; also, in the very last moment of their striking our eardrum so as to cause us to hear them, sounds of longer duration will fail to have a train of audible airwaves stretching back to the sounding object. At both of these moments if we have the impression or the thought that the sound we hear is located at its source we shall be mistaken. I suggest that we nonetheless accept this consequence of our hypothesis, on the ground that we thereby ascribe to ourselves far less illusory auditory experience than we should need to if we rejected this hypothesis.

The fact that the train of airwaves identified with the sound we hear has to be temporally located a few milliseconds before we hear it may suggest that there is systematic illusion here too, since we do form the impression that the sound is occurring at the moment at which we hear it. But the milliseconds' delay between airwave striking our ear and our hearing the sound as if occurring when we hear it is a smaller interval of time than we can in general discriminate. An "error" on this scale scarcely deserves the name. (Of course the time it takes sound to travel from its source to us is sometimes noticeable, but this interval is not relevant to the present objection, since the train of airwaves that constitutes the sound we are hearing is the train that stretches back to the source after the front end of the train has reached the eardrum and set it to vibrating.)

There are questions that arise concerning the duration and the individuation of sounds to which it is not easy to provide answers entailed by common conventions or by beliefs clearly shared. Exactly how it may be best to revise our hypothesis so as to bring the conception of sounds it specifies into the closest possible agreement with our common conception is therefore not easy to know. For the purpose of our inquiry it is not necessary to make our hypothesis fully determinate in regard to matters left indeterminate both in everyday thinking about sounds and in scientific thinking about soundwaves. Suppose there is an explosion that is heard in all directions as far away as five miles. Do the persons a mile to the west of the explosion hear the same sound (and not merely the same explosion) as those a mile to the east? Perhaps most of us would say they do or say things that seem to imply that they do. If this judgment is to be taken seriously then it is clear that the idea of a train of airwaves will have to be somewhat complex, since we shall need to treat as a single train airwaves moving out in all directions at once from the sound-making process.

And do persons five miles from the explosion hear the same sound as those located one mile from it? If the explosion is audible to each person who hears it for only a part of a second, then a person one mile from the explosion will have ceased to hear the sound approximately twenty seconds before a person located five miles from the explosion begins to hear it. (Air-borne soundwaves travel approximately a fifth of a mile in a second.) If we are to say that both sets of persons hear the same sound, then the sound must be said to last not for only a part of a second, as it appears to those who hear it to do, but for about twenty-five seconds, the period of time during which it is traveling to the most distant point at which it is audible. (I assume that an airwave ceases to be the front end of a sound as soon as it ceases to be audible.) The auditory impression that everyone who hears the explosion will have, that the sound lasts for only one second, will be egregiously mistaken. If we want to say that persons placed five miles from the explosion hear the same sound as those one mile from it, we shall simply have to accept the idea that we are mistaken in thinking we can tell by listening how long a sounds lasts. Of course for most occasions on which we have an interest in noticing how long a sound lasts we are chiefly interested in how long the sound-making object persists in its sound-making action. (How long did the telephone ring? How long did the dog continue to whine?) And about this our auditory perception informs us correctly.

Giving our attention thus briefly to questions about the duration of sounds does bring to us one needed revision in our hypothesis. When a sound persists for some time it cannot comprise a single train of airwaves. One train is replaced by another as the individual airwaves continue to flow out from the source and on to the listener, replacing those which were there a moment before. So it is not a single train of airwaves that constitutes a sound but a succession or sequence of trains of airwaves stretching from the listener's ear back to the sound-making object throughout the duration of the sound. However, for simplicity in expression I shall treat a sequence of trains of airwaves as if they constitute a single train.

Beyond this I shall not attempt to go in revising or making more determinate the hypothesis in order to provide answers to questions concerning the duration and individuation of sounds. These questions are generated not specifically by the hypothesis but by reflection upon our experience and talk of sounds. And the interests of the present inquiry do not require of us that we should labor over the choice of criteria for deciding upon the most useful answers to these questions. But a word about the effect of certain decisions. If we decide that we want to count everyone who hears the same explosion as hearing the same sound, then the perceptual error that now gets charged to hearing—for taking the sound to have a much shorter duration than it actually has—is surely an artifact of this decision. If we had wanted to make out hearing to be more accurate, then we could, quite consistently with the physical facts of the situation, have decided to count people at different distances who hear the explosion at different times as hearing different sounds, deciding to "carve" the spreading trains of airwaves into distinct sounds on a different principle. A perceptual error arising from such a decision should not be very seriously charged against the sense of hearing.

One other problem suggested by these latest reflections deserves notice. I spoke of the velocity of "air-borne soundwaves". This reminds us that the waves of pressure that comprise the sounds we hear, if sounds are soundwaves, are often partly constituted of waves moving through other media than air, and may be wholly so constituted. This means that we have no good reason for making airwaves the sole constituents of sounds. And this in turn means that to be accurate we should either need to specify each sound in terms of the different sorts of soundwaves —airwaves, water waves, wood waves, glass waves, and so on— which make it up, or else work out a more abstract characterization of the kind of physical process, the kind of moving disturbance in some medium or other, which every different sort of soundwave exemplifies. Again for simplicity of exposition, and from limitation of my own powers, I shall not attempt to make this sort of correction, and shall continue to use, as the by now evidently very rough approximation to the hypothesis physics suggests for us, the identification of sounds with trains of airwaves.

2. Direct Realism's Thesis: Loudness and Tone Are Airwaves' Intensity and Frequency

It is time now to turn to the issues that divide the direct and the indirect realist.

When we listen attentively, our hearing the sound we hear consists in our becoming aurally conscious of this sound. But the sound is a train of waves of pressure in the air. So it is waves of air pressure of whose presence before our ears we become conscious in hearing the sound to which we listen with attention. Yet everyone knows that in merely hearing it before our ears we do not commonly become conscious of a wave of air pressure *as* a wave of air pressure. If we did we should not have to wait for the physicist to tell us that this is what the sound we hear is; we should discover this by merely listening with attention and perceiving the sound to be a wave of air pressure.

Since the soundwaves' being waves of pressure in the air, indeed their even being waves of any kind, is not what it is about them that attracts or holds our attention when we listen to them, it is necessary to ask what feature they have that does hold our auditory attention. For it is not possible for this attention to be held by a train of soundwaves before our ear and not to be held by some feature of these waves.

Of course, if the attention that we give to sounds when we listen attentively to them were always mediated by an attention given more directly to something else, then the property of soundwaves that holds our attention might be a relational, perhaps a causal property. And indeed this does appear to characterize our auditory relationship to sounding objects: what it is about the bell that holds my attention, insofar as its ringing holds my auditory attention, is its making a sound (of a certain kind). But this shows that it is not of the bell itself that I am directly conscious in hearing it ring: my attention to the bell's making a sound of a certain kind is held by virtue of the sound the bell makes holding my auditory attention more directly. My auditory awareness of the bell is in part constituted of my more direct auditory awareness of the sound which the bell produces in the air that stretches between it and me. But we know of nothing else out there before our ears by virtue of our hearing which we tell that the sound is before our ears; the sound itself is the most direct object of our auditory attention among the particulars before our ears which succeed in holding our attention.

So if the direct realist is right in believing that there is nothing that is not before our ears to which our attention is still more immediately directed, then one should not expect the property of a soundwave which attracts and holds our attention to consist of a causal relationship in which the soundwave stands to something this wave brings about. Our attention to a sound is not held more directly by something before our ears which this sound produces; and it is not, if the direct realist is right, held more directly by something not before the ears which the sound produces, for example, by an auditory impression or "sensation" in us. And there is no other sort of merely relational property of sounds which we might suspect of being the property that attracts our attention—except sounds' locations. But the location of a sound can hold our attention only if another one of its properties holds it: a sound cannot attract our auditory attention merely in virtue of its interesting location. The sound we hear is a train of soundwaves, waves of pressure in the air. So if the direct realist is right, what holds our attention most directly when it is held by what we hear are certain nonrelational ("intrinsic") features of the waves of air pressure striking our eardrum.

Whatever these features are they must correspond to what we all doubtless understood just now when I said that what it is about a bell that holds my attention insofar as its ringing holds my auditory attention is its making a sound of a certain kind: if the sound had no character that held my attention, the sound itself would not hold it, and neither, therefore, would the bell's ringing. What we are now in a position to appreciate is that in order for direct realism to contain the truth about our auditory awareness of sounds, the characteristics of sounds of which we are most directly conscious in hearing sounds include intrinsic features of the waves of air pressure that compose these sounds. It is time to try to determine whether or not this requirement direct realism imposes upon auditory perception is in fact met.

It is easy to doubt that the traditional ways we have for specifying the properties that most directly hold our attention in listening to sounds do justice to our experience of sounds. But I think we can let the test of time these labels have passed suffice to warrant our treating them as adequate to our purposes. We are said to notice sounds by noticing their loudness, their pitch, their brightness, their timbre, their volume, their density, their rhythm, their melodic organization, their location. To simplify discussion I shall subsume pitch, timbre, brightness, and melody under the single rubric "tonal quality"—for short, "tone"—and I shall ignore volume, density, rhythm, and location, on the presumption that one's auditory attention could not be held by any of these traits of sounds without being held by something in the way of loudness and tonal quality, whereas the converse of this presumption seems probably false.

If direct realism is to be true of hearing it appears to be necessary to suppose that the loudness and tonal qualities of the sounds we hear are identical with two purely physical properties of the airwaves that constitute these sounds. For it seems reasonable to believe that sounds can hold our attention only by virtue of their loudness and tonal quality holding our attention, that we do not hear loudness or tonal quality by virtue of becoming more directly aware of some other property of sounds, and therefore to believe that what it is before our ears of which we are most directly conscious in hearing sounds is the loudness and tonal quality of these sounds. This in turn leads the direct realist to believe that these two properties belong to soundwaves independently of these waves' effect upon our auditory experience. For if loudness and tonal quality of sounds were properly defined as mere dispositions in the sounds to cause in us certain auditory impressions, then there would seem to be very great difficulty in understanding how our auditory attention could be held by loudness and tone except in virtue of being held by these properties' manifesting this disposition. The manifestation of the disposition consists in a sound's causing in us an auditory impression of itself. But we could notice this causation only by noticing its effect. So our attention would need to be held by the auditory impression the soundwaves cause in us, which is *not* before our ears.

Direct realism, therefore, seems to require that the loudness and the tonal quality of a sound each be identical with some purely physical property of the wave train that constitutes the sound, a physical property which is in principle specifiable without reference to the effect these air-waves have upon auditory experience.

What are the natural candidates for these two physical properties of airwaves? Roughly speaking, for loudness, intensity of pressure in the airwaves, for tonal quality, frequency of vibration of these waves of air pressure. If direct realism is true, then in becoming aurally conscious of sounds it appears that we must become directly conscious of the intensity and the frequency of the waves of air pressure which strike our ear and comprise the sounds we hear. Our auditory awareness of intensity of air pressure and of frequency of vibration of the air must not be mediated by a more direct awareness of any other property of anything.

I have just now oversimplified the facts in a way that needs to be remarked, although I think that once the needed correction is noted the distortion can be left standing without harm. Tonal quality is a function not of frequency alone but of frequency and intensity of soundwaves. The heard pitch of pure tones of high frequency increases as the intensity of the soundwaves increases, increasing the more sharply the higher the frequency of the soundwaves; and the heard pitch of pure tones of low frequency decreases as the intensity of the soundwaves striking the eardrum increases, decreasing the more rapidly the lower the frequency (there are further complications as the frequency descends below 100 cycles per second). So vibration frequency alone is not a viable candidate for identity with tonal quality. Furthermore, loudness of pure tones is not a function of intensity of soundwaves alone, but of intensity and frequency: the lower the frequency the more intensity is required in soundwaves in order to achieve a given level of loudness. So intensity of pressure alone is not a viable candidate for identification with loudness of sounds.

The proper course for the direct realist to follow in the light of these facts seems fairly clear. He should suppose that when we aurally respond to a train of soundwaves by hearing a certain pitch, what we are perceiving in the soundwave is not its frequency, simply, but a more complex attribute of the soundwave comprising a function of frequency and intensity. What we have separated in our scientific conceptualization of soundwaves is not separated in concrete fact: the magnitude of the air pressure characterizing a given soundwave and the frequency of recurrence of this pressure are not separable in nature; you cannot have a pressure with no frequency or a frequency with no pressure. If auditory perception joins these two aspects of a train of airwaves more closely than our conceptual mode of apprehending the soundwave does, this gives us no reason to suppose that anything other than purely physical attributes of the soundwave, in their concrete interconnection, are being aurally perceived. The peculiar function of frequency and intensity to which the ear responds in a systematic way may not be of much interest to the physicist analyzing airwaves for their own sake; and it may be more trouble than it is worth for a psychologist to figure out exactly what the function is, rather than develop a graph and make some generalizations from the graph. But the presumption may reasonably be made, and in any event certainly should be allowed to the direct realist, that such a function exists. We might then give a new name to this imagined property, calling it, say, "frequinteny," and suppose that what accounts for our hearing the pitch of sounds is actually the frequinteny of the soundwaves. Hence, the direct realist might conclude, the tone we hear *is* the frequinteny of the soundwaves we hear. More complex forms of tonal quality (timbre, for example, and melody) will perhaps be more complex functions of frequinteny itself.

Since we know that intensity of soundwaves has a larger weight in determining our auditory perception of loudness, we could call the presumed function of intensity and frequency of soundwaves which accounts for our hearing loudness, "intenfrequity," and the direct realist could affirm—with how much safety it remains to be seen—that the loudness of a sound *is* its intenfrequity: that what we perceive about soundwaves in hearing their loudness is their intenfrequity. Both frequinteny and intenfrequity are purely physical attributes of soundwaves: once each property has been picked out as the property that elicits a particular auditory response in us, it can then be fully specified in purely physical terms, without reference being made to the auditory responses to which we have appealed only as a guide to the identification of the eliciting property. Particular instances of frequinteny and intenfrequity of soundwaves are, therefore, for the direct realist, appropriate candidates for the position of direct objects of our auditory awareness of sounds. Having said as much, I shall continue to simplify my discussion by speaking of simple intensity and of simple frequency as if each were the plausible candidate for identity with, respectively, loudness and tone of sounds.

Let us now put before ourselves a *directly realistic* account of our attentive, auditory perception of a telephone.

Suppose that I am sitting in a dark room and that, whether or not I know that there is a telephone in this room, I am not at that moment conscious of its presence—my thought is directed elsewhere, and I can't see the telephone. Suddenly the telephone's presence in the room attracts my auditory attention: suddenly, therefore, I become aurally conscious of its presence in the room. The telephone attracts my auditory attention—it makes me aurally conscious of itself—by virtue of something it does, its ringing, attracting my attention and making me conscious of *it*. Suddenly the phone rings; and this ringing of the telephone attracts my auditory attention in virtue of something that is produced by the telephone's vibration attracting this attention: the sound in the air which the telephone's vibrations create attracts my attention. This sound is a train of airwaves stretching from the telephone to my ears. So the telephone's ringing attracts my auditory attention in virtue of the train of waves of pressure which the telephone's vibrations produce in the air attracting this attention: I become aurally conscious of this train of airwaves which stretches from the telephone to my ears. This train of airwaves—the sound that the telephone makes —in turn attracts my auditory attention in virtue of some of its properties doing so.

The most obvious of these properties are the loudness and tone (and "rhythm") of the train of airwaves: in the direct realist's view it is instances of these properties which directly attract and hold my aural attention and hence it is of them that I am directly conscious. My auditory awareness of instances of the loudness and tone of the airwaves mediates my auditory awareness of the presence in the room of the telephone itself, which may appear to me to be itself loud and to have a certain tonal quality.

However, the direct realist continues, let us not analyze this loudness and tone of the train of airwaves generated by the telephone's vibrating action as a disposition in this train to cause in us certain auditory impressions. For with this analysis we should probably have to concede that a listener's auditory attention could be held only by this disposition's actually manifesting itself. And the listener's auditory attention being held by the manifestation of such a disposition of the airwaves to affect him with an auditory impression must consist in his attention being held by some aspect of his own auditory impression. But a sense impression is not before the sense organs. So direct realism would probably turn out to be false of hearing if loudness of sounds consisted in sounds' disposition to sound loud.

The direct realist therefore proposes that the airwaves' loudness should be defined not as a disposition in the airwaves to affect our experience in a certain way, but as the intensity of pressure of the airwaves. Similarly, according to direct realism we should try to avoid assuming that the tonal quality of the sound made by the vibrating bell in the telephone is a disposition of the airwaves to cause in the listener a certain (tonal) sensory impression; rather the tone that holds the listener's attention *is* the frequency of vibration of the train of airwaves he hears. Both intensity of air pressure and frequency of passage of waves of air pressure are purely physical properties of the soundwaves: no reference is needed, in defining them, to their affecting in some way the auditory experience of sentient beings.

To be aurally aware *of* a certain loudness is to be aurally aware *that* something or other is loud. Yet in being aware that a sound is loud we do not commonly become aware that it has a certain intensity of air pressure. So the direct realist has upon his hands the task of explaining how it is possible for a sound's loudness to be its intensity of air pressure and yet for our aural awareness *that* the sound is loud not to be an aural awareness *that* the sound has a certain intensity of air pressure.

Similarly, to be aurally aware of a certain tonal quality is to be aurally aware that a certain sound has this very tone. And the direct realist asserts that for sounds to have a tonal quality is for them to have a certain frequency of vibration in the air. So the direct realist has also upon his hands the task of explain-

ing how it is possible for a sound's tone to be its frequency of
vibration of the air and yet for our aural awareness *that* the
sound has this tone not to be an aural awareness *that* the sound
has a certain frequency of vibration.

3. Criticism Of Direct Realism (I) : Disposition versus
   Structural Properties of Sounds

We discovered in the last chapter that it is possible for a property F to be identical with a property G and yet for us to observe
that something is F without observing that anything is G. The
fact, therefore, that in becoming aurally aware that a sound is
loud and of a certain tone we do not become aware that the
intensity and frequency of soundwaves are of some magnitude
does not provide a proof that intensity of soundwaves is not identical with loudness nor frequency identical with tone.

What is needed now is an investigation into our concepts of
loudness and tones of sounds. For convenience's sake I shall focus
upon loudness. The inquiry could be conducted along exactly
the same lines in speaking of tonal quality or pitch.

What I wish to discover is whether or not it is consistent with
our concept of loudness of sounds that loudness should be, as
the direct realist maintains, identical with intensity of air pressure of soundwaves. I shall argue in two stages for a negative answer to this question, the first stage in this section, the second
stage in the next. I shall then return in §7 to buttress this position with certain empirical facts about how we hear sounds of
very low frequency. In the present section, containing the first
stage of my argument, I try to exhibit as intuitively plausible
the conception of loudness as a disposition in a sound to sound
loud to normal, attentive listeners. Then I consider an argument
for direct realism's thesis, that loudness is intensity of pressure,
which accepts it as a premise that loudness is a disposition in a
sound to sound loud, but contends that this disposition is identical with its own structural underpinning in the loud soundwave's
theoretically comprehended nature. The primary task of this
section will be to show that this latter contention is mistaken.

Let us being by making a contrast between what we should
say about two imagined worlds different from ours in a similar
way, the one thermally different, the other acoustically different
from our own.

Suppose there is a world that is thermally different from ours
in the following way: the caloric theory of heat, or something

like it, is true in that world, and this means that the property
of bodies which is causally responsible for their yielding the
thermometer readings they yield is not the kinetic energy of the
bodies' molecules but some structural feature of a caloric fluid.
In a gross way, however, thermosensory experience and thermometer observations in that world resemble our own. Suppose
that in that world what thermometers measure is also called
"temperature" and that the original observational conception
of temperature held by early thermodynamicists in that world
was the same as ours, i.e., the conception of the property, whatever its presently unknown nature, which is causally responsible
for the observed thermometer readings. Informed of the facts
in that world, we should probably say that what thermometers
measure is a different property there than it is here. For here it
is mean kinetic energy of molecules and there it is a certain non-
kinetic, structural feature of a substance, caloric fluid, which
does not exist here. What the property called "temperature"
turns out to be in each world depends upon the theory of the
structure of matter which best explains that world's thermometer
observations and thermodynamic laws.

Now imagine a world acoustically different from ours in this
way: if we went to that world and investigated the properties of
soundwaves that we heard as very loud we should find that they
had a lower intensity of air pressure than the sounds we heard
as not loud. In fact the louder a sound sounded to us there the
lower the intensity of pressure of the airwaves would be discovered to be. In that world sounds cease to be audible when
the pressure of airwaves becomes very intense. On the other hand,
sounds become so loud to our sense of hearing as to become
painful to us, as the intensity of air pressure in the soundwaves
becomes extremely low. In other words, the feature of airwaves
which is causally responsible for our auditory impressions of
increasing loudness is not increasing pressure of the airwaves
but decreasing pressure, a very different feature. We said of our
alternative thermal world that because the property that explains thermometer observations is a different property there
from the property that does this in our world, the property
observed by thermometers there and called "temperature" is a
different property from our own temperature. Should we also
say of the alternative acoustic world that since the property that
explains hearing loudness of sounds is a different property there
than it is here, the inverse of intensity of air pressure of soundwaves, therefore what we call "loudness" in that world is a different property from loudness in our own world?

Of course before we investigated the physical features of soundwaves in that world we should say that sounds there have the same property they have here, the property loudness. But before we discovered in the alternative thermal world that heat was caloric fluid we might also have said that "temperature" there is the same property as temperature here. The question is whether or not we should do in our different acoustic world as we should in our alternative thermal world, and, after we had discovered the difference in the causal origin of our observational impressions, conclude that what is heard as loudness there is a different property of sounds than here, just as what thermometers measure is a different property in that other thermal world than it is here.

I find that the answer to this question is not so simple as I should have liked it to be. But I think that it will be helpful to appreciate the reasons for a certain indecision we may experience in trying to answer this question.

In one frame of mind one wants to say that sounds in the alternative acoustic world would have at least one property that is exactly the same as a property they have here, namely loudness. For the criterion we use in identifying this property is how sounds *sound* to us. If to normal listeners in normal circumstances sounds appear to have the usual variations in loudness that they have here, then they do have these variations: loudness in sounds *is* sounds' tendency, in appropriate circumstances, to present to normal listeners a certain (loud) aural appearance. That louder sounds in that world are not airwaves with more intense pressure does not change what loudness is there; it changes only the causal explanation of loudness in sounds.

However, if we explore a little what we mean by speaking of intensity of pressure as offering a causal explanation of loudness in our world we may be given pause. Once we assume that loudness consists in the disposition of soundwaves to sound loud to normal listeners situated near the source of the sound, although it is then natural to speak of the soundwaves' intensity of pressure as the cause of this loudness, on second thought we may be inclined to say that the intensity of pressure does not *cause* the disposition-to-sound-loud to exist, it causes, rather, in the appropriate circumstances, a listener actually to hear the soundwave as loud; and this is to say that it causes the manifestation of that disposition of the soundwave which constitutes the wave's loudness. It may now occur to us that for a structural property or a state of something to be the cause, not of a disposition of this thing, but of the manifestation of this disposition, is not clearly a sufficient reason—if it is any reason at all—for our concluding that the structural property is distinct from the disposition; the connection between the two is too intimate.

Indeed this connection may now seem so intimate that further reflection may make it seem plausible that a structural property and the disposition whose manifestation it causes ought to be conceived as identical. A succinct and lucid argument for this view is given by Max Deutscher:

> Consider the brittleness of a given object at a given time. For X to be brittle at t, it is not sufficient merely for the hypothetical "if X is struck even lightly at t, X shatters" to be true. Consider a hardened steel casing, which shattered though it was struck only lightly. It was tough but happened to contain dynamite and a detonator. The casing was not fragile at t, although the hypothetical was true at t. The steel casing is not fragile, in that it is not a part of its nature that it shatters when struck. The dynamite is not part of the casing. Call the whole thing a bomb and you might say that the bomb is fragile, though this is scarcely the *apt* term, but you cannot say that the casing is brittle. It would be very different indeed if putting dynamite inside a tough steel casing made the casing brittle. Thus, for an object to be brittle is for it to be of a nature which results in its shattering when struck. Now, if for a thing to be brittle is for it to have a nature which results in its breaking when struck, and if our scientific theories are correct, the particular type of bonding between its constituent molecules constitutes its brittleness. Nevertheless "X is brittle" neither entails nor is entailed by "the molecules of X are bonded in such-and-such a way."[1]

Insofar as we find Deutscher's argument persuasive we find ourselves now inclined to reverse our original judgment and conclude that "loudness" of sounds in our alternative acoustic world is a different property from loudness here. For the nature from which sounds' sounding loud results would be a different property there (inverse of pressure intensity) than here (intensity). And the loudness of the sounds we hear in our own world would be nothing more (or less) than these sounds' intensity of pressure, *which is exactly what the direct realist requires.*

1. "Mental and Physical Properties," in C. F. Presley, ed., *The Identity Theory of Mind* (University of Queensland Press, 1967), p. 74.

But how good is Deutscher's argument? Not good enough, I think. And I believe his conclusion is mistaken. The topic is rather elusive, but for our purposes not unimportant. Its elusiveness arises partly from the difficulty in knowing exactly what settles the question, what property, exactly, do we mean to speak of when we speak of a dispositional property? And this difficulty, in turn, depends in part on both the vagueness of the very idea of a dispositional property and on the great variety of terms that can plausibly be construed as specifying dispositional properties. For example, when one considers how plausible it is to construe every concept of a physical property as making allusion to causal powers accruing to whatever has the property, one realizes that some show of probability can be adduced for analyzing any physical property as dispositional. We shall do well, therefore, to take seriously the actual example used by Deutscher, brittleness, which is a paradigm of what is ordinarily thought by philosophers to be a dispositional property and which, therefore, ought to bear important resemblances to another such paradigm, loudness of sounds, and which furthermore is a subject of considerable practical interest to engineers and of theoretical interest to solid-state physicists. Since Deutscher's argument appeals to physicists' theories in connection with brittleness, as the direct realist's argument appeals to the same in connection with loudness, the actual practice of the scientists interested in investigating brittleness should be illuminating for us. In fact this practice does not support Deutscher.

Deutscher concludes concerning any brittle material that the "particular type of bonding between its constituent molecules constitutes its brittleness." He bases this conclusion partly on the premise that the bonding constitutes the "nature" from which the material's shattering when struck results. To a very rough approximation (shortly to be specified), let us for the moment grant this premise. If physicists' practice can be used as a guide, Deutscher goes wrong in concluding, from the fact that a substance is considered brittle only if its shattering when struck is a result of its nature, that therefore its being brittle *is* its having this nature. Physicists engaged in explaining brittleness do not find this a natural or useful approach. Their practice reveals that they do not conceive the brittleness of an object as that structural feature of the object possession of which "results in its shattering when struck," as Deutscher suggests they should do; on the contrary, they use the words 'brittle' and 'brittleness' entirely for the purpose of directing our attention to the peculiar behavior of certain sorts of material, as if they think of brittleness in this way: for a certain sort of substance to be brittle is for substances of this sort characteristically to shatter when struck. Since this behavior is characteristic of a sort of substance, it follows as a matter of course that its cause is to be sought in the nature of the substance. (But one does not identify a cause with its effect.)

The primary use of the adjective 'brittle' among physicists developing the explanation of brittleness is in the context, 'brittle behavior'. And the specific reference of the phrase 'brittle behavior' is to brittle fracture. Brittle fracture is defined as "fracture which occurs at or below the elastic limit of a material,"[2] which means that brittle-fracturing substances "show little or no permanent deformation prior to fracture." Brittle behavior, which is to say, brittle fracturing, is contrasted with ductile fracturing, in which there is considerable, permanent deformation before fracture. Describing brittleness a little more colorfully, Eisenstadt goes on: "The small elongation prior to fracture means that the material gives no indication of impending fracture, and brittle fracture usually occurs rapidly. It is often accompanied by a loud noise which has been known to send designers back to the drawing board."

For accuracy's sake I should here remark that it is not Deutscher's "shattering," but breaking, which defines brittle behavior for engineers and physicists: a tendency to shatter (into many pieces) is of specal interest in a material because it means that although, like all brittle materials, not much energy is absorbed by such a substance before breaking, more is absorbed *in* breaking than by other brittle materials, a feature which is useful in manufacturing such products as bullet-proof vests and safety windows for automobiles.

Philosophers really should take note of the fact that the dispositional nature of brittleness is largely irrelevant for physicists and ignored by them. Brittleness is, to be sure, speaking technically, from a logician's point of view, a dispositional property; but physicists think of it as a way certain materials behave— brittle materials are sorts of material instances of which *do* break with little prior plastic deformation. After all, they are doing it all the time! Consequently when solid-state physicists undertake to explain brittleness they are trying to explain a characteristic pattern of behavior of certain materials. That this

2. Melvin M. Eisenstadt, *Introduction to Mechanical Properties of Materials* (New York: Macmillan, 1971), p. 203. All quotations from Eisenstadt are from the same page of this book.

characteristic behavior of some materials is (of course) a result
of the nature of these materials shows up not so much in the
physicists' use of the word 'brittle' as in where they look for the
explanation of this brittle behavior—into the structural features
of the material, specifically into microstructural features. In
reading physicists' explanations of brittleness one can never
doubt that the brittleness being explained is a form of behavior
(a way of breaking) and that the explaining cause they have
located is conceived by them to be—and is in fact—quite distinct
from the brittleness it explains.

Here one should also notice, and not only for the sake of accuracy, that the explanation of brittleness in materials is not given,
as Deutscher supposes, by their "particular type of bonding":
when the fracture strength of a brittle material is deduced theoretically from its bonding strength, "[e]xperiment shows that
the actual fracture strength of real bodies falls short of the com-
puted value of the cohesive strength by as much as three orders
of magnitude. . . . Such a large discrepancy cannot be explained
by chance variation. Griffith postulated that it must have a deep-
seated cause in some inherent defects of structure, or structural
imperfections."[3] The cause of brittle fracture which A. A. Griffith proposed[4] and which is, according to Eisenstadt, "generally
accepted as valid," is the presence of minute cracks in the brittle
material.

Two qoutations concerning this explanation will illustrate
the use I have ascribed to interested scientists of the words 'brittle' and 'brittleness'. First Rosenthal: "Surface energy plays an
important [causal] role in the phenomenon of brittle fracture,
considered in this chapter. The direct cause of brittleness, however, is ascribed to the presence of minute cracks in solids, as will
be explained" (op. cit., p. 123). Notice here, especially, the identification of brittleness with brittle behavior. The structural
feature, here the minute cracks, cannot be identical with the
brittleness, which is the breaking of the material, since the cracks
are the causes of this brittleness, of this breaking. And now
Eisenstadt: "The mechanism which causes brittle failure has
been explained by Griffith, who postulated that brittle fracture
was due to the presence of small cracks in the solid. According
to his theory, at sufficiently high stresses these cracks would

3. Daniel Rosenthal, *Introduction to Properties of Materials* (Princeton,
N.J.: Van Nostrand, 1964), p. 124.

4. "The Phenomenon of Rupture and Flow in Solids," *Philosophical
Transactions of the Royal Society* (London 1920): A221, 163.

propagate through the material, resulting in failure." Eisenstadt continues, "In this section we shall consider changes in the stress on a material due to the presence of cracks. This information will then be combined with the surface energy concept to explain brittle fracture."

We can think of explanation by appeal to the surface-energy concept to which both Rosenthal and Eisenstadt refer as equivalent to explanation by reference to type of molecular bonding, of which surface energy is a function; but this explanation is so radically incomplete that there is, as we just saw, a tendency to specify as the cause of the brittleness not the molecular bonding but the minute cracks in the solid. We see, then, that if brittleness is to be identified with the "nature" of the material from which the breaking results, it must be identified with both the molecular bond (or surface energy) and the minute cracks in the material; but we also see that for the practicing scientists to do this would be for them to identify a cause with its effect! And this they do not seem disposed to do. The fact is that the term 'brittleness' is used to refer to a form of behavior (brittle breaking) which is characteristic of some materials and not of others (not of the ductile materials) and which offers a phenomenon to be theoretically explained by discovering a complex pattern of microstructural features of the brittle materials. If, as certainly seems unlikely from the present evidence, the term 'brittleness' came to be used for the cause of this brittle behavior, then some other term would need to be invented to specify the phenomenon being explained, the former brittleness (brittle breaking).

Because of the fact already remarked that almost any physical property can be conceived as a dispositional property, we can be fairly certain that what marks off those properties we find ourselves conceiving as peculiarly dispositional is that the term used to speak of this property characteristically serves to focus our attention upon the manifestation of the so-called "disposition," a manifestation which is, of course, commonly some pattern of behavior, although also frequently behavior involving in essential ways objects other than that to which the disposition is assigned. Since the very criterion of a dispositional property is the importance, in our conception of the property, of the manifestation of the disposition, hence ordinarily of ways of behaving and interacting with other objects on the part of the object with the disposition, the likelihood is very small that it will turn out to be correct to identify an object's dispositional property with that structural feature of the object which functions as the cause of the object's manifestation of its disposition. The disposition is too nearly identified with its manifestation for this to be a natural proceeding.

Starting from that observation, it seems reasonable to conjecture that the likelihood of its being proper to identify a dispositional property with a structural property that causes the disposition's manifestation is diminished the more need there is for explanation of the causal connection believed to exist between structural feature and manifestation of disposition; the more complex or lengthy or varied in nature the chain of events appears to be that extends from the structural feature to the manifestation of the disposition; the greater the practical interest we have in the manifestation by itself, so that a concept of a property serving primarily to direct attention to this manifestation is of practical value to us; and the more complex the disposition's manifestation itself is. Brittleness scores rather high on several of these tests. So it is not surprising that Deutscher is wrong in thinking that brittleness is identified by the experts with what serves causally to explain the pattern of behavior (kind of fracturing) to which the term 'brittle' primarily serves to direct our attention.

I think it is evident that the dispositional property, loudness of sounds, also scores high on these tests: its resistance to being identified with the structural causes of some airwaves' sounding loud rather than soft is, if possible, even higher than the similar resistance offered by brittleness to identification with the causes of some materials breaking in a brittle rather than a ductile manner. One reason for this greater resistance is the fact that the causal chain from structural feature to manifestation of disposition is lengthier and of a more varied composition for loud sounds than for brittle materials. After all, it is the brittle object itself which breaks. But the manifestation of a train of soundwaves' loudness is ultimately found in an extraordinarily complex response on the part of something quite distinct from the soundwave, a listening, sentient organism. Loud sounds are trains of air pressure which, as a result of their nature and of the nature of attentive listeners, characteristically sound loud to these nearby, attentive listeners. This means that they cause in such listeners a sensory impression of loudness. This manifestation of loudness requires a long and complex causal chain stretching way beyond the initial action of the vibrating air. The eardrum must vibrate, auditory nerve endings must thereby be activated (how, exactly?), neural impulses must be conveyed along a complex path to the cortex of the brain, and things must happen in the cortex (what, exactly?), before the disposition to sound loud, which *is* the loudness, is manifested. The idea of "reducing" so extended a process of manifestation of loudness to the simple structural condition, intensity of pressure, which initiates this manifestation, strikes me as so impractical that the possibility of its being seriously undertaken is negligible. This seems the more reasonable when we consider the practical interest nearly all of us have in the manifestation of loudness, in soundwaves' sounding loud to us. This interest makes it only the more likely that we should judge that, when the subject is loudness, to speak only of intensity of pressure of airwaves is to change the subject—it is more like speaking of the cause of loudness than of loudness itself.

Nevertheless some element of possible truth can be conceded to Deutscher's account of the relation between a dispositional property and its structural underpinning. We can concede to Deutscher that it is somewhat plausible to insist that the structural underpinning of a dispositional property be included as a part of the nature of the latter property. Thus while insisting that for a material to be brittle is for it characteristically to break (when submitted to certain stresses) at or before the material's plastic limit, we can concede that it belongs to brittleness that this happens in consequence of both the material's molecular bonding and its possessing certain sorts of minute cracks. This, we can grant, has a certain plausibility on the ground that something of this kind may be presupposed in thinking always of *sorts* of material as brittle in behavior.

In regard to sounds what we are conceding to Deutscher and thereby, to the direct realist, is that for a soundwave to be loud is for it not only (but above all) to sound loud to an attentive listener, when one is available, but also (less importantly) for its so sounding to a listener to be a consequence, roughly, of its intensity of pressure, the greater the pressure, roughly speaking, the louder its sounding (although noting as important that its so sounding is also a consequence of the nature of the listeners). We may therefore concede to the direct realist—at least not insist on denying—that a part of what it is for a sound to be loud is for its intensity of pressure to be, roughly speaking, responsible for how loud it sounds to listeners. Loud-sounding sounds in the alternative, acoustic world imagined earlier in this section can, therefore, if one likes, be said to be not exactly loud. Nonetheless, and most important for our purposes, in this world and in any world it is an indispensable part of what it is for a particular sound to be loud that that sort of sound characteristically will sound loud to a qualified and attentive listener located nearby.

4. Criticism of Direct Realism (II) : Measuring Loudness Contrasted with Measuring Temperature

That loudness will not reduce to pressure of airwaves can be made more certain for us by comparing the measurement of loudness with the measurement of temperature. In developing scales for measuring temperature no need has been felt to justify the choice of units and of zero points by considering how what they single out for our attention registers upon our thermoperceptual sensibility. The choice of units and zero points is made on the basis of physical considerations alone, considerations concerning either the empirically ascertained role of temperature among physical phenomena generally, or the theoretically determined nature of temperature; such facts as the boiling point of water, the freezing point of water, the amount of work done by a drop in intensity of heat between heat source and heat receiver in a perfectly efficient heat engine, the point at which random molecular motion is reduced to zero, and the like, are the relevant considerations in choosing temperature scales. No consideration whatever is needed of how well our thermoperceptual judgments coordinate themselves with these systems of measurement. The measurement of temperature can be—and is—carried out entirely by means of instruments never in any sense "calibrated" with the deliverances of our thermal sensibility. The reason for this is that the very idea of temperature was from quite early on preempted for measurements made by thermometers of a quantity whose interest for inquirers was, if you will, purely physical. The interest in temperature, the very property intended by the term, was marked by the coincidence between birth of a science of heat and separation of temperature's specification from any appeal to thermal perception.

On the other hand, no one has ever proposed that it makes sense to attempt to effect a similar separation of the measurement of loudness of sounds from all dependence upon how sounds register upon our sense of hearing. On the contrary, the system for measuring sounds that has been adopted, the decibel scale, although directly a measurement of relative intensity of pressure of airwaves (or of quantity of energy of airwaves), has been tailored to represent a useful indication of how loud sounds *sound* to us. The loudness of sounds is measured by a certain ratio between the pressure intensity of the sound to be measured and a reference intensity. This reference intensity is now standardized at .0002 dynes/square centimeter, which is approximately the absolute threshold pressure for audibility of sounds at a frequency of 1000 cycles per second. And the unit adopted for representing this ratio of the measured sound's pressure to that of the reference pressure, the decibel, is approximately equal to the amount of difference in intensity of two wave trains which accounts for a just noticeable difference in how loud each wave train sounds to a normal listener.

Decibel measurements of soundwaves' loudness, therefore, although explicitly measurements of pressure ratios among trains of airwaves, have been deliberately constructed so as to give us a useful indication of how much louder a measured sound sounds to us than a just barely audible sound sounds to us. It is hard to imagine better evidence that we treat intensity as only a part of loudness and that we consider the sounding loud, in appropriate circumstances, as the other part, than the evidence provided by this difference between our way of constructing a scale for measuring loudness and our method in devising scales for measuring temperature.

It seems safe to conclude that the loudness of a sound is the tendency of the sound, in virtue of its intensity of energy, to cause in normal listeners, whenever they are nearby, a particular sort of auditory impression, and to conclude that this property is not identical with the property, intensity of energy.

5. Defense of Indirect Realism

After giving so much attention to the nature of the loudness we hear, it is necessary to remind ourselves of the precise point of disagreement between the direct and indirect realist. Leaving aside, for the present, tonal quality, it is agreed between them that what holds our auditory attention more directly than anything else *before* our ears is instances of loudness of trains of airwaves. It is (now) further agreed between them that included in what this loudness *is* is the intensity of pressure of these airwaves. On the basis of this latter agreement the indirect realist may even acknowledge, without surrendering his indirect realism, that we become in a certain way aurally conscious of intensity of pressure, in becoming aurally conscious of loudness. He may not acknowledge this because he may think it is false; but to acknowledge it would not be to surrender his indirect realism. For the difference between the direct and indirect realist could then be recognized as precisely this: that the direct realist believes that there is nothing of which we are more directly conscious in hearing sounds than of their intensity of pressure or energy, whereas the indirect realist holds that *if* we can be said to be aurally conscious of intensity of pressure in airwaves this can be only in virtue of our being still more directly conscious of something *not* before our ears, of a sensuous quality of our auditory awareness, a quality that functions as the internal and direct object of our indirect awareness of airwaves.

It is time now to present the case for a representational and indirect form of perceptual realism as the truth about hearing. (To simplify discussion I shall for the present continue to focus on loudness and to leave the tonal quality of sounds largely out of the picture. Exactly analogous reasoning will apply to tones.)

When trains of waves of pressure in the air attract and hold our auditory attention, so that we become aurally conscious of their presence before our ears, they do so in virtue of their loudness attracting and holding our attention, and we become aurally conscious of them by becoming aurally conscious of how loud they are. This loudness, I have argued, is not simply the intensity (or intenfrequity) of the pressure waves, considered by itself, without reference to its effects. It is the causal power that a given intensity of pressure has, by virtue of how it affects the eardrums of an attentive listener, to make a particular wave of pressure sound *thus*, or *so*, to him. To give to the direct realist as much as we reasonably can, then, is to affirm that for an attentive listener to become aurally conscious of the loudness of sounds is for him to become conscious of the loudness of waves of air pressure before his ears and to acknowledge that this last consists in the listener's becoming aurally conscious of the causal power of these waves' intensity to make the waves sound to him *thus,* or *so.*

But the supposition that we become aurally conscious of this causal power as a mere power, and not as a power presently being exercised, is too implausible to need rebuttal. (If this were true then we could attentively *hear* how loud a sound is without noticing how loud it presently sounds.) Attentively to hear this causal power in the waves of pressure striking our ears is to become aurally conscious of these waves presently exercising this power.

What is it about these waves exercising the causal power their intensity has to make them sound *thus* or sound *so* to us which attracts and holds our auditory attention? The exercising of this power in the airwaves consists in the intensity of these waves causing in us an auditory impression of the waves as *thus* or as *so*. But what part of this causal process is it that most directly attracts and holds our auditory attention? In hearing a sound we do not ordinarily become conscious of the airwaves *as* striking our eardrum, nor of our eardrum *as* vibrating, nor of the afferent neurons of the auditory nerve *as* firing in response to this vibration. But even if we did, we should not thereby have become conscious of the airwaves causing in us an auditory impression. We can become aurally conscious of the pressure waves' causing in us an impression of them only by becoming aurally conscious of the effect thus caused, conscious, that is, of this auditory impression itself. But an auditory impression is not *before* the ears or other sense organs. Of *it,* therefore, we are *directly* conscious: when attentive we perceive the pressure waves' loudness in virtue of being *directly* aware of our auditory impression of the waves. We are, therefore, always *in*directly aware of sounds' loudness when we give our auditory attention to it. But a similar argument goes through, by similar steps, for hearing the tones of sounds: our auditory awareness of tones is mediated by our direct awareness of auditory impressions of tone. Since *before* our ears it is the loudness and tone of soundwaves which we hear most directly, but these are heard only *in*directly, indirect realism is true of the sense of hearing.

Now let me examine more carefully the content and structure of our indirect, auditory awareness of the soundwaves before our ears.

What is it about an auditory impression of soundwaves as *thus* which attracts and holds our attention? Certainly not the fact that the impression is an impression, nor the fact that it is an impression of waves of pressure. It is the impression's being of something as *thus* which attracts and holds our attention. This *thus* is how the pressure waves sound insofar as they sound loud; it is what they are like; it is the content of the auditory sense impression. This is what it is about our auditory impression which directly holds our attention when we hear a sound.

Why have I written that how a loud airwave sounds is *thus* rather than writing that how it sounds is loud? And why should I have written that how a sound of a certain tonal quality sounds is *so*, not that it sounds to be of a certain tone? The issues are the same for loudness and tone, but the vocabulary and grammar of loudness are simpler, so let us focus on loudness.

I have argued that the loudness of a sound is its disposition to sound loud (in virtue of its intensity of pressure). And this disposition to sound loud is the sound's tendency to cause in us an auditory impression of the sound as loud. However, when I turn to closer analysis of such an auditory impression and hence of how a loud soundwave sounds, if I continue to speak of how a loud sound sounds as "loud" I open the way to nonsense. For if we treat 'loud' as having the same meaning in the verbal phrase 'sound loud' as it has in the noun phrase 'loud sound', then when we substitute the analysis of the second-mentioned 'loud' for the first-mentioned occurrence we get this result: our auditory impression of a sound as loud is an impression of the sound as disposed to cause in us an auditory impression of the sound as—disposed to cause in us an auditory impression of the sound as—disposed to cause in us an auditory impression of the sound as . . . *ad infinitum*. But this is absurd.

Loud sounds are those which cause in us an auditory impression of them as *thus*—where '*thus*' signifies the peculiarly auditory quality that serves for us as the mark of a sound's loudness. The word *thus* signifies a continuum of qualities marking off the various degrees of loudness, but I shall ignore this complication. Indeed it may be that for every distinct tonal quality the *"thus"* of loudness is also distinct. I shall also ignore this possible complication and write as if a single auditory quality marks off all loud sounds. This quality, then, directly holds our auditory attention when a loud sound holds it. Another quality, signified by '*so*', directly holds our attention insofar as the loud (or soft) sound we hear is of a certain tone, i.e., is disposed to sound to be of a certain tone, i.e., is disposed to sound to us *so*.

To summarize, the situation looks like this: some waves of pressure in the air attract our auditory attention; those which do, do so in virtue of their loudness (and tone) attracting our attention; their loudness (tone) is their causal power, in virtue of their intensity (frequency), to make themselves sound loud (of a certain tone) to us; but this causal power can attract our auditory attention only insofar as this power's being exercised attracts this attention; the exercise of the power of the waves' intensity to make the waves sound loud to us consists in the waves' intensity causing in us an auditory impression of the waves as *thus*; the pressure waves' causing this effect in us attracts our auditory attention in virtue of the effect itself attracting our attention; since that effect is an auditory impression in us, it is this auditory sense impression that most directly attracts our auditory attention; what it is about an auditory impression that attracts our attention is its being of something as *thus* or as *so; thus* and *so* are auditory qualities; what most directly attracts (and holds) our auditory attention, therefore, is our auditory sense impression, in its character as being *of* something before our ears *as* having the (auditory) quality *thus* or *so.*

Our having the auditory impression of the airwaves before our ears as *thus* or as *so* can plausibly be analyzed only as our in some sensory manner taking the waves to be *thus* or taking them to be *so;* and this can in turn intelligibly be analyzed only as our in some manner aurally *attributing* to (what are in fact) waves of pressure the quality *thus* or *so.* For our forming the conscious, auditory impression that something before our ears is *so* constitutes our consciously taking in the apparent information that this something is *so.* And consciously taking in information—whether "good" information or misinformation—concerning a putative property of an object or process before our senses yields nothing that can immediately function in us as information, hence isn't consciously acquiring information, unless there occurs in us some formulation of this information which can guide us in our action. But the natural form for formulation by us of consciously held information concerning a property of something is our attributing this property to the thing.

I conclude that what directly holds our auditory attention to sounds is the auditory quality *thus* or *so* insofar as this quality figures as what our auditory impression is an *attribution* of (to something before our ears) . This idea can also be expressed in this way: in attentively hearing sounds we are directly aware of the auditory quality *thus* or *so* in its role as the content of our involuntary, aural-perceptual attribution of itself to soundwaves before our ears.

This latest formulation leads to the following realization: to give our auditory attention to the content of our involuntary, perceptual attribution of an auditory quality to something before our ears is to give our attention to this something that is before our ears. For our attending to the content of our own "act" of attribution amounts to nothing less than our entering whole-heartedly into our own involuntary, aural-perceptual attribution of an auditory quality to something before our ears;

and this entails our giving our auditory attention to this something before our ears.

Suppose that the content of our auditory attribution to the soundwaves of the auditory quality *thus* figured within this attribution only as the content of a concept. Then we should be ascribing the auditory quality *thus* by applying to the soundwaves only our concept of this quality. And this is to say that our auditory awareness of the airwaves before our ears would consist in our merely *thinking* of the waves as having the quality *thus*. But hearing sounds to be loud is not merely thinking that they are. Therefore the content of our involuntary attribution of the auditory quality *thus* to the soundwaves is not a purely conceptual attribution of *thus* to the soundwaves.

What else might it be? The only plausible alternative is that it should be a *sensuous* attribution of an auditory quality. If the sensuous quality *thus* inheres in our auditory consciousness, if it is a quality of this consciousness, and if it functions therein as a representation of itself as belonging to something before our ears (representing itself by the method of exemplification), then, and so far as I can comprehend only then, our attribution of this quality to the waves of pressure before our ears will consist, not in our merely thinking that something out there has the quality, but in our hearing something as having it. We shall have heard a loud sound.

Since the sensuous quality that most directly holds our auditory attention belongs to our aural awareness itself, instances of this quality exist where this awareness exists, which is certainly not before our ears. What we are most directly conscious of in attentively hearing sound is a sensuous quality-instance constituting part of the character of our aurally conscious state.

In the most inclusive sense of the term 'impression', our auditory impression of a sound can be taken to include everything that the mature and attentive listener to sounds characteristically and involuntarily attributes to the sounds, insofar as he attentively hears them. This would, of course, include all the other attributes of sound which we hear in attentively listening: tonal quality and location, for example.

It may also include our attributing to the sounds the power to cause in us an impression of themselves, i.e., our attributing to them the causal power to make us aware of them as if having the quality *so* or *thus*. Insofar as attentive, mature listeners do aurally attribute to sounds this causal power, do they ascribe this power to the intensity of the pressure waves, or do they leave the "nature" of the waves which accounts for this power indeterminate? Or is a third possibility realized?

In merely hearing sounds we do not perceive them to be waves of pressure in the air; hence we do not aurally perceive as the foundation of their causal power to make us aware of them as *thus* their having a certain intensity of pressure; nor do we, in merely hearing them, substitute for intensity of pressure the perhaps more recondite notion of intensity of energy. Neither, however, do we leave indeterminate the "nature" we perceive as if making us aware of the waves as *so* or as *thus*. It is, rather, to the auditory quality *thus* or *so* itself (which we involuntarily attribute to the soundwaves) that we ascribe the causal power in question. The "nature" that we aurally perceive the pressure waves as having, in virtue of which (as we perceive it) they have the power of making us conscious of their (apparently) being *so* or being *thus* is the very quality *so* or *thus* which we hear them as having. Within our auditory perception this sensuous quality figures for us as the apparent foundation in the sound of the sound's power to make us aurally conscious of the sound's (apparently) having this very quality.

Finally, notice that it is because of the fact just remarked that the word 'loud' can seem, before reflection, to be an adequate word to use in describing what it is that our auditory impression is an impression of the soundwaves *as:* because within auditory perception, loudness, even as a property of the sound in which is grounded its causal power to make us aware of itself, is perceived as the sensuous quality *thus;* within mature, attentive auditory perception of loudness this sensuous quality seems to us to have the role which in fact belongs to the intensity of soundwaves' pressure.

6. An Objection to the Defense of Indirect Realism

From someone sympathetic to direct realism I can imagine the following objection having been voiced earlier:

"Your argument depends upon your analyzing sounding loud as sounding *so*, where *so* is a peculiar, auditory quality not equivalent to the content of our linguistically articulated concept of loudness. And your argument for thus construing the phrase 'sounding loud' is that, otherwise, for something to sound loud consists in its sounding as if it has a disposition to sound as if it has a disposition to sound as if . . , *ad infinitum,* which, you point out, is absurd; and I agree with you that this is absurd and that this would be the logical consequence of substituting for the word 'loud' in the phrase 'sounding loud' the definition of 'loud', i.e., 'the disposition of soundwaves (in virtue of their intensity) to sound loud'.

"But notice that the solution you propose, to replace 'loud' in 'sounding loud' with *so* or *thus,* amounts to construing the word 'loud' in this particular context as specifying only a part of what, on your own analysis, loudness is: the part comprising a certain, auditory quality figuring as the auditory 'appearance' of a loud sound. On your own analysis the other part of loudness is the causal power of the intensity of the pressure waves to yield to normal, attentive listeners this peculiar, auditory appearance.

"Now consider this implication of your own procedure: if it is satisfactory for a part only of what loudness is to figure as what the 'loud' of 'sound loud' is about, then another part of loudness is acceptable in this role without objection arising from its being only a part of loudness and not the whole of it. There *is* another part of the whole state of affairs comprising a sound's being loud which may constitute what is picked out by the word 'loud' in the phrase 'sounding loud'; and if this alternative interpretation of 'sounding loud' is accepted, we do not reach indirect realism as our conclusion about the sense of hearing. This other element in a sound's being loud which I have in mind is the intensity of pressure of the soundwaves.

"Let us admit that your case is strong for saying that the objective property of sounds, loudness, is the disposition of the soundwaves, in virtue of their intensity of pressure, to sound loud. But suppose we take the phrase 'sound loud', in this definition, to mean 'sound to be of a certain intensity of pressure.' Then the rest of your argument will fail.

"For what will most directly attract our auditory attention 'about the auditory impression' will be, by your own reasoning, what the auditory impression is an impression *of* the pressure waves *as.* And now this is construed to be a certain intensity of pressure. An intensity of pressure is obviously not a property of the auditory impression (impressions have no air pressure) ; intensity of pressure is something 'about the auditory impression' only in the sense that it is what this impression is an impression of the pressure waves as having. So the conclusion we shall have reached is that what most directly holds our auditory attention is the intensity of waves of pressure in the air and, hence, that what we are most directly conscious of in hearing loudness is this same intensity of pressure. This is precisely the thesis of direct realism."

7. Reply: On Hearing Only Certain Sounds as if Feeling Them by Touch

The most obvious reply to this objection is that if intensity of pressure really did constitute the content of our auditory impression of the airwaves as loud, then in attentively listening to sounds we should be getting the information that they are waves of pressure. But this we do not normally discover from attentively listening to sounds. It is possible to develop this reply in less abstract terms, and to extend both objection and reply to encompass tonal quality, by giving our attention to some facts unearthed by the Hungarian scientist, George von Bekesy, a winner of a Nobel prize for his research on hearing.

It is an interesting fact and for our purposes a useful one that the situation imagined in the objection just articulated does occur under special conditions of auditory stimulation. Bekesy has shown that soundwaves vibrating at frequencies substantially below 20 cycles per second (cps) are aurally perceived as what they are, pulses of pressure vibrating at regular frequencies. He writes.

> For frequencies above 20 cps the sensation in the region of the threshold was always one of pure tone. When the frequency was reduced to 10 cps, however, the threshold stimulus in uniaural listening gave sensations of touch referred to the ear rather than sounds. In order to determine whether these touch sensations were mediated by the pressure nerves of the ear or by the auditory nerve, the phenomenon of directional hearing was utilized. When two exactly symmetrical points on the skin of the head, as for example two points at the entrance to the external meatus, were stimulated simultaneously, it was difficult to fuse them into one. Instead, they were separately localized at the two ears. On the other hand, two auditory sensations were automatically fused into a single impression . . . which was localized in the mid-line of the head. . . . It is clear that at very low frequencies there is a close similarity between auditory and tactual senations.[5]

5. *Experiments in Hearing* (New York: McGraw-Hill, 1960), pp. 258–9.

In the next-to-the-last sentence quoted from him, what Bekesy means by "auditory sensations" is impressions of pressure *as* pressure, which resemble ordinary tactual impressions but are mediated by the organ of hearing. As Bekesy's account continues, his language becomes somewhat confusing. It will perhaps be reassuring to read an account of these results from S. S. Stevens and Hallowell Davis' book, *Hearing: Its Psychology and Physiology*.[6]

> . . . it is at 18 cycles, according to Bekesy, that we pass suddenly from the perception of a succession of discrete impulses to a single fused sensation which possesses a truly tonal quality. Hence, 18 cycles may be called the fusion frequency of pitch perception. What, then, we may ask, is the nature of the sensation at frequencies below the fusion frequency? In this region the observer listening monaurally has the impression that alternating pressure gives rise directly to a tactual sensation. That this is not tactual in the ordinary sense, Bekesy demonstrates by showing that, under equal binaural stimulation, a tone of 10 cycles gives rise to an auditory sensation which is localized in the middle of the head, and which can be shifted from side to side by altering the intensity of the sound in one ear. . . . This cannot be done when tactual pressures are applied to the external ear.

Again I think it is quite clear that what Stevens and Davis mean by the "auditory sensation which is localized in the middle of the head" is an *auditory* impression as of *pressure* in the middle of the head, an impression which to the subject who has it seems to be an ordinary, tactual impression of pressure. We can describe what happens in this region of auditory stimulation in the following way. When audible soundwaves of quite low frequency are raised in frequency to 18 cps we suddenly become conscious of tonal quality and of loudness. At lower frequencies, for example at 10 cps, we are not conscious of anything that we should spontaneously call "a sound", since we hear neither tonal quality nor loudness; however, we do become conscious of pulses of pressure in one ear, if either one ear alone is stimulated or one ear has a more intense auditory stimulus than the other ear; and if both ears are stimulated by equally intense soundwaves at 10 cps, then we become conscious of pulses of pressure which

6. New York: John Wiley, 1938; pp. 45–46.

seem to us to be located in the middle of our head. In each case I should have said: we become conscious of pulses of pressure *as that*. The experience is for us as if we are not hearing sounds but *feeling* pressures vibrating at regular frequencies. The organs of touch, however, are not being used; the organ of hearing is. So we are not feeling these pressures, we are hearing them—or so we shall speak if we take the utilized organ as determining the correct sensory verb. The more intense the soundwaves' pressure is, the more intense the pressure we become aurally conscious of, *as* pressure; the higher the frequency of vibration of the soundwaves—if only it is below 18 cps—the more rapid the vibration we become aurally conscious of *as* a vibration.

Now I return to my critic. In brief, his objection was that if in attentive listening we become aurally conscious of loudness as intensity of pressure, then our auditory attention's being most directly held by what our auditory impression is an impression of the soundwaves *as* constitutes its being held not by a quality of the impression, but by an intensity of pressure which can only belong to the airwaves before our ears; hence we shall be most directly conscious of the airwaves before our ears rather than of our own auditory impression.

The first thing that Bekesy's work clearly shows is that the direct realist's idea, the idea of our becoming aurally conscious of soundwaves as waves of pressure, our becoming aurally conscious of their intensity of pressure as intensity of pressure, and our becoming aurally conscious of their frequency of vibration as frequency of vibration, is not only an intelligible idea, but an idea that is actually realized.

However, the second thing Bekesy has shown us is this: the very fact that we recognize this form of auditory consciousness to be a rare case, a case which is discovered to be restricted to the situation in which the frequency of vibration is below 18 cps, demonstrates that the auditory consciousness of soundwaves that characterizes most of our attentive hearing of sounds is not structured in this way. Beginning at 18 cps, where still some "roughness" remains, and unambiguously at 20 cps and higher, we cease to become conscious of any frequency of vibration, as that, and become conscious of tonal qualities; moving up from this same frequency we cease to become conscious of pressure, as that, and become instead conscious of a distinctively auditory quality, "loudness", i.e., *thus*. Below 18 cps, therefore, I can agree that we should have to argue from at least some of the direct realist's premises which contradict my own. But this is the exceptional case, and by the very fact of its being the exception, the ordinary case is shown to be not in accordance with the direct realist's premises.[7]

The third thing of interest to us which Bekesy's work reveals is this. In the objection I attributed to the direct realist, I imagined that he acknowledged the strength of the case for analyzing loudness as a disposition of the soundwaves, in virtue of their intensity, to sound loud to us. I did this because the case is so strong. But I think it has now become clear that if our attentive hearing of most sounds were structured as our hearing sounds below 18 cps is structured, we should not have a conception of the loudness of sounds as a disposition to sound loud. Nor should we have a conception of the tonal quality of sounds as a disposition of soundwaves, in virtue of their frequency of vibration, to sound to us as if having a certain tone. For in that event the sense of hearing would have been "on all fours" with the sense of touch. And we should have described what holds our attention most directly, among the things we perceive before our ears, not as "sounds", but as pulses of pressure, of varying intensities, arriving in regular frequencies of vibration.

We should have had no more reason to think or speak of what intensity of pressure is aurally perceived as, or of what vibration frequencies are perceived as— as something other than intensity of pressure and frequency of vibration itself—than we have in regard to the sense of touch. What we report as the feature of things before our skin which we most directly perceive by the sense of touch is not conceived by us as a disposition in the object to arouse in us a certain tactual impression; it is not conceived by us as a property to be defined by reference to how it feels to us; it is conceived by us as nothing less and nothing more than the intensity of pressure itself—or the rate of vibration itself— which is exerted—or which beats—against our skin; this is what we reflectively pick out as the property of which we become tactually most directly conscious among those before our skin which we feel by touch.

---

7. The exceptional case, just because it is so much like the situation of the sense of touch, which is especially difficult for the indirect realist, I shall not undertake to discuss in this chapter on hearing; I intend my discussion of the sense of touch, two chapters hence, to encompass it. At present it is necessary only to remark that for pressure to be the most directly perceived property among the properties *before* our sense organs which are perceived does not in itself entail that pressure is not indirectly perceived: it will remain to inquire whether something not before our sense organs mediates, as most direct object of our sensory attention, our tactual perception of pressure.

I think, therefore, that we can be certain that if our sense of hearing had been, throughout the range of its normal stimuli, structured as it now is only in response to frequencies of air vibration below 18 cps, then we should not have conceived loudness as a disposition to sound loud (hence should not have had a concept of loudness, as distinct from intensity of pressure); nor should we have conceived pitch as a disposition of sounds to sound as if of a certain tonal quality (hence should not have had a concept of tonal quality as something distinct from frequency). But we do have such conceptions of loudness and of tonal quality. Therefore we can be sure that in our normal auditory experience of sounds we form auditory impressions of sounds neither as having a certain intensity of pressure nor as having a certain frequency of vibration.

8. Hearing the Mockingbird's Song: Sensuous Representation by Exemplification

When at the midnight hour of a summer evening a mockingbird suddenly wakes from his sleep outside my open window and begins to sing, and I am first startled and then charmed to a rapt attention to this solitary sound, a part of what happens, if the argument of this chapter has succeeded in reaching the truth, is this. What it is about the mockingbird that first attracts and then holds my auditory attention is something he is doing: it is his singing that I become aurally conscious of. He holds my attention, therefore, in virtue of the sounds he makes holding my attention. These sounds are trains of waves of pressure in the air between him and me, waves which strike upon my eardrum. There is nothing else before my ears by my hearing which I tell that the sounds are there; it is the sounds that I hear more directly than anything else before my ears.

What it is about these sounds that attracts and holds my auditory attention is their loudness and tonal quality, and patterns these fall into. These properties of the sounds are dispositions in the waves of pressure to sound *thus* or *so* to me, in virtue of their intensity or frequency. These dispositions can hold my auditory attention only insofar as their present manifestation does so. But this manifestation consists in the soundwaves' sounding to me *thus* and *so;* it is the airwaves' sounding to me *thus* and *so* that attracts and holds my auditory attention. But their sounding this way to me consists in their causing in me, by virtue of their intensity and frequency, an auditory impression of them as *thus* and so *so*. What it is about the waves of pressure causing in me this effect which most directly holds my attention is the effect itself that is so caused; and this effect is my auditory impression. So what *directly* holds my auditory attention is an auditory impression I have of the waves of pressure as *thus* and as *so*. What it is about this auditory impression that holds my attention is the impression's being of something as *thus* and as *so*. And what this comes to is this: that my auditory attention is held by the sensuous qualities *thus* and *so,* but by these qualities functioning as the content of my own involuntary, aural-perceptual attribution of these very qualities to the waves of pressure before my ears.

However, if this attribution were merely conceptual on my part, I should be merely *thinking* of these auditory qualities as belonging to something before my ears. And this I am not doing. Therefore the sensuous quality I attribute figures not as the content of a concept but as the sensuous content of a sensuous representation of itself, wherein it represents itself as belonging to something before my ears and thus functions as the sensuous content of my sensuous attribution of itself to the soundwaves. This sensuous mode of representation distinguishes itself from the merely conceptual mode only in virtue of the sensuous, auditory quality's actually belonging to my aural consciousness, and therein representing itself, by the mode of exemplification, as belonging to something before my ears.

Singing alone in the night, the mockingbird has endowed my sensory consciousness with aural qualities. My manner of receiving this gift is to try to give it back in the very act of accepting it: I bestow upon his singing—by sensuously ascribing to it—the very qualities he has caused, by shaking the night air with waves that move my eardrums, to become a part of the character of my own conscious state. What he has given to me I am equipped to accept only by sensuously attributing it back to him as the quality of his song. This sensuous quality comprises a peculiar vividness shared between us: it is the instrument of my attending to him, it is his presence to me; it is the content of my consciousness of him, it is his appearing to me. It is how he sounds to me against the quiet of the night.

Chapter Six   VISION

We see objects: trees, books, rocks; we see happenings: flashes
of lightning, races, snow flurries; and we see things not naturally classified as either objects or events: the rainbow, the sky,
shadows, reflections of trees in lakes.

In saying that a person saw a tree or a flash of lightning, the
speaker ascribes to the seen particular (or specifies it by means
of) certain properties, those which make it a tree or a flash of
lightning. But he does not imply by what he says that the person
who saw that particular saw *that* it, or any of its component
particulars, had those features: the viewer may have seen the
tree, for instance, as a dark mass of nondescript nature.

Instead of saying that a person saw a particular, we sometimes
say that he saw a feature of a particular: he saw the color of
the dress, the shape of the bird, how fast a man was running. We
also speak of seeing a feature but without specifying the particular it belongs to: "I saw a color today I had never seen before;" "In the course of a day one sees many shapes that have
no names." In speaking thus we presume that a visible feature
always belongs to some particular and that in virtue of seeing a
feature one sees the particular that has it.

To simplify diction I shall speak of physical objects as representative of the several sorts of particulars we see.

To see a feature of an object is to see *that* the object has this
feature; hence seeing the feature is gaining by vision the knowledge that the object has this feature. We should normally take
the statement that a person saw that an object was red, round,
and moving to imply that the person became visually *conscious*
of the color, the shape, and the motion of the object—hence became conscious of the object before his eyes. Any cases we
recognize of gaining *unconscious* visual knowledge would be
exceptions to this rule, which we should in common speech an-
notate as peculiar.

1. Direct and Indirect Realism Pertain to Visual Awareness, Not to "Simple Seeing"

During the last two or three decades a number of capable
philosophers have found what they thought good reasons for

holding that merely seeing an object does not entail seeing that the object has some property. Indeed, they have argued, merely seeing an object does not require that one become in any way conscious of it. I shall call this (alleged) kind of seeing "simple seeing." According to these philosophers, simply seeing the large, brown dog, twenty yards before one, does not involve noticing the dog, gaining any knowledge of the dog, forming any belief about the dog, or even so much as acquiring an impression *that* "something or other" exists or has a certain feature or location. In simply seeing an object one is conscious of nothing whatever.

Some philosophers who have argued for simple seeing have offered little positive characterization of it. Others have described simple seeing, with two results of interest here: first, they believe that their description entails direct realism in regard to vision by entailing the falsehood of indirect realism. Second, "simple seeing" turns out, they believe, to be one of the key components of seeing *that* an object has a certain property, hence one of the key components of visual knowledge and, presumably, of visual awareness of objects. This conception of simple seeing will therefore repay examination.

According to this conception, simply seeing an object consists in the object's looking to one some way different from its surroundings. Looking, in turn, acquires a special characterization.

Preeminent among ways of looking, because it is both a necessary and a sufficient condition for the occurrence of any sort of seeing, is an object's looking a certain color to someone. For this reason, and because of the comparative simplicity of this way of looking, I shall develop the idea of simple seeing as it is exemplified by an object's looking a certain color to us.

Because simply seeing an object does not involve becoming aware of either the object or a feature of the object, looking blue—which is what a blue object's being simply seen consists of—is not a matter of causing in the viewer an impression *that* the object is blue. Rather, the object by emitting or reflecting light to the eyes causes a person to sense in a "blue" way—to "blue-sense." And the blue (or "blue") of blue-sensing isn't related to sensing in a way analogous to the way a football is related to kicking: the blue quality is not an object *of* our sensing, it is our *manner* of sensing. We sense blue-ly.

Blue-sensing is said to be a kind of sensing in the way waltz-dancing is a kind of dancing. The word 'blue' specifies the kind of sensing that is happening in the way the word 'waltz' specifies the kind of dancing that may be happening, without naming an "object" to which the sensing is related. To dance a waltz is not to dance some object but to dance some way. So, also, to sense blue is not to become aware of blue, it is not to become aware of anything; it is to have a peculiar "blue" kind of sensing happen to one.

This conception of seeing is thought by some philosophers to entail direct realism because it is thought to entail the falsehood of indirect realism: since seeing a thing involves, on this conception, no awareness of anything, it cannot involve awareness of something not before the eyes; so indirect realism is false. Therefore direct realism must be true.

This reasoning is confused. For direct realism holds that *when* we become visually conscious of objects before our eyes we need not become conscious of something not before our eyes. Direct realism is a thesis about our visual awareness of things. Since the account of simple seeing is not an account of awareness, the regular occurrence of simple seeing could not prove the truth of direct realism.

Neither could the common occurrence of simple seeing entail the falsehood of indirect realism. Indirect realism is also a thesis about visual awareness of objects: it holds that *when* we become visually conscious of objects before our eyes, we always become visually conscious of these things in part through becoming conscious of something that is not before our eyes. In simple seeing we are conscious of nothing. Therefore the regular occurrence of simple seeing could not falsify indirect realism.

Insofar as one simply sees an object the object does not hold one's attention and one gains no knowledge of it. However, when one becomes visually aware of an object the object holds one's attention and one gains knowledge of some feature of the object. Both direct and indirect realism give accounts of the structure of that visual awareness of objects which is achieved in *attentively* looking at objects. They are accounts of consciously held, visual knowledge of objects. Indirect realism holds that when an object before our eyes holds our visual attention we are visually conscious of some feature of this object and that always this awareness of the object occurs in virtue of—and in part consists in—our (direct) awareness of something *not* before our eyes. Attention to a feature of something before the eyes is always mediated by attention to something not before the eyes. Direct realism holds that no such mediation is needed and that none regularly occurs.

2. The Chisholm-Dretske Account
of Visual Consciousness of Color

Some of the philosophers interested in simple seeing are also interested in giving an account of visual knowledge. To these, this question presents itself: What role does simply seeing an object play in seeing that the object has a certain character? Simply seeing a blue surface consists in the blue surface, by reflecting light to the eyes, causing the percipient to sense blue-ly. What more is needed in order that a percipient see *that* the surface is blue? Because seeing *that* a surface is blue commonly consists in becoming visually conscious of the surface's blue color, an answer to that question may have consequences for perceptual realism.

We can now bypass the question, whether or not there is a common way of speaking of seeing objects that answers to the concept of simple seeing. For now simple seeing's interest coincides with the interest that objects' looking certain ways has for any account of visual awareness.

The two philosophers interested in simple seeing who have developed the most complete and persuasive accounts of visual knowledge are Roderick Chisholm and Fred Dretske. Their two accounts are in certain respects so similar as to constitute for our purposes one account, which I call the "C-D" account.

The analyses offered by both Chisholm and Dretske of a person's seeing that an object O has a property P—seeing that O is P—agree in imposing these four conditions: (1) O is P, (2) O looks some way to the person, (3) the person believes that O would not in the present circumstances look the way it does look to him if it were not P, (4) the person believes that O is P.

Chisholm and Dretske also agree in construing O's looking some way to someone as entailing no awareness, belief, knowledge, or assumption on the person's part about O or about anything whatever; nor does it entail having the impression *that* the object has some character; in short, they agree in describing O's looking some way to a person as I have described simple seeing, with this difference between them: Chisholm does and Dretske does not adopt the "sensing P-ly" way of speaking of "being looked to P." I shall, however, ignore this difference, and treat Chisholm's idea of sensing (with respect to an object) as a version of their common conception of simple seeing, or being looked to (by an object).

It is also true that Dretske does not (as Chisholm does) have occasion to speak of a percipient's "being looked to" but limits himself to speaking of an object's looking some way to someone. The reason for this is that Dretske limits himself to consideration of visual knowledge that is incremental relative to "protoknowledge" already held concerning the O that is seen to be P. One could expect that if Dretske did analyze seeing (merely) "that something is before my eyes" he would offer as the belief in condition #3 above: "I should not be looked-to in the way I am unless there were something before my eyes."

The final difference between Chisholm and Dretske is important in distinguishing their theories of (visual) *knowledge,* but of no importance for our purposes, so I shall henceforward ignore it: Dretske imposes and Chisholm does not impose this requirement upon seeing that O is P: that in the present circumstances O would not look the way it does unless it were P. (According to Dretske, this assures the percipient a conclusive reason, in how O looks, for believing that O is P, which Dretske believes and Chisholm does not believe is necessary to knowing that O is P.)

Dretske asserts and Chisholm does not explicitly assert but, one surmises, would accept the further requirement that condition #4's obtaining must be caused by conditions #2 and #3 obtaining: the person who sees that O is P must hold the belief that O is P as a causal result of both O's looking the way it does to him and his believing that O would not look that way unless it were P.

I shall limit my consideration of this (the "C-D") account of visual awareness of objects to the simplest sort of instance: seeing that an object, say a surface, is a certain color, say blue. No doubt it is somethimes possible to see that an object is blue when it looks red—but this is abnormal. Normally when we see that a surface is blue it also looks blue to us. In this common situation, then (if we ignore the additional condition Dretske imposes in order to ensure possession of a conclusive reason for believing the surface is blue) Chisholm and Dretske seem to agree in holding that a person S's being visually conscious of the blue color of the surface before his eyes involves these essential elements: the surface looks blue to S, S believes that the surface looks blue to him, S believes that the surface would not look blue to him if it were not blue; because of all this, S believes the surface to be blue. (And, as I began by saying, it is blue.)

Both Chisholm and Dretske show an interest in avoiding an account of vision that entails that we are directly conscious of a subjective, "being looked to," so that we are only indirectly conscious of the object before our eyes. And each seems to believe that his account of visual awareness succeeds in avoiding this upshot.

Yet if one were to judge by the general form of their account one ought to be surprised that either philosopher could believe he had escaped this entailment. For each clearly states that in order for a person to see that a surface is blue he must believe that the surface would not (now) look blue to him if it were not in fact blue. So it is clearly entailed that whenever a surface's looking blue to him leads him to see that it is blue, a percipient believes that the surface is now looking blue to him. Indeed it is (in part) because he believes that the surface is now looking blue to him that he comes to believe that it is blue. For O to look blue to S is for O to cause S to be looked-to blue. So it is reasonable to suppose that in believing that O looks blue to him S believes that he is looked-to blue (that he senses blue-ly). So his believing that he is now being looked-to blue is the partial cause of his believing that the surface before his eyes is blue. But just as one supposes that the percipient's believing that the surface before his eyes is blue constitutes his being conscious of the color of the surface, so, too, it is natural to assume that his believing that he is being looked-to blue constitutes his being conscious of his being looked-to blue.

This account, then, is naturally understood as saying that in part because we are aware of our own sensing blue-ly, we become aware of the surface before our eyes as blue. And this amounts to saying that our being conscious of the blue color of the surface before our eyes is mediated by our being conscious of our own sensing blue-ly, which is, of course, not before our eyes. This surely sounds like indirect realism. It does not quite explicitly answer to my characterization of indirect realism, because it does not positively assert that our visual awareness of the blue color of a surface before our eyes is partly constituted of our awareness of our own sensing blue-ly; yet this does seem implied. Surely on this interpretation of their account of visual awareness Chisholm and Dretske have come so near to indirect realism that the claim to have devised a means of escaping from it is more than misleading.

Although neither Chisholm nor Dretske seems to be aware of the possibility that he may be unintentionally giving us a variant of indirect realism, each does make remarks, apparently aimed only at assuring phenomenological credibility to his account, but which could be read as raising a barrier to the interpretation I have just given, with its unwanted, indirectly realistic upshot. For each wishes to make clear that he does not mean to suggest

that in seeing the blue color of a surface we *infer* that the surface
is blue, infer it from our belief that the object looks blue to us
together with our belief that if the object weren't really blue
it wouldn't under the present circumstances look blue. Seeing
that the surface is blue is not reasoning to the conclusion that
it is blue from the premises believed about its looking blue to us.

In the course of making this point, both Chisholm and
Dretske say things that seem to have the force that percipients
do not *consciously* believe what they believe about their being
presently looked-to blue; so these remarks could be taken as
denying that in seeing that a surface is blue we must be conscious
of our being looked-to blue. I say that these remarks at best
seem to have this force, because both Chisholm's and Dretske's
explicit denials of conscious status pertain to the complex belief,
"If the surface were not blue, it would not look blue"; one is left
uncertain whether or not the simpler belief, "It looks blue to
me," and the still simpler belief, "I am looked-to blue," are also
to be understood as not consciously held.

Dretske calls the complex belief that, under present conditions, the surface would not look blue to me unless it were blue,
a "background belief", of which he says this: " . . . there is no
question of this belief operating as a conscious intermediate
link between" the surface's looking blue to me and my forming
the belief that it is blue; our "arrival at this state of confidence
about the character of" the surface, i.e., our coming to believe
that it is blue, "manifests" the background belief that the surface
would not look blue unless it were blue; and this is all the
"manifestation" this belief ordinarily gets, i.e., it does not itself
normally enter into consciousness.[1] Dretske's readers will find it
natural to suppose that since the other quasi-premise, of which
the belief that the surface is blue is a "manifestation," is the belief that the surface is in fact looking blue to me now, this latter
belief is also to be considered not consciously held. But Dretske
does not here explicitly say this.

Speaking of (roughly) this same hypothetical belief about
one's own being appeared-to (or sensing), Chisholm writes of
the person perceiving, with any of his senses: "he accepts—or
assumes—certain propositions about sensing, or 'being appeared
to'." If, for example, he perceptually takes something to be a
row of trees, then "he assumes, with respect to one of the ways
he is sensing, that, if he were not sensing in that way, he would

1. Fred I. Dretske, *Seeing and Knowing* (Chicago: University of Chicago
Press, 1969) , p. 110. All quotations from Dretske are from this book.

not be perceiving a tree." Elsewhere Chisholm puts this idea this way: "If our perceiver takes something to be a cat, then he believes that a cat is one of the causes of the way he is appeared to."[2] Chisholm continues, "In saying that he assumes or accepts these propositions, I do not mean that they are the object of deliberate or conscious inference. . . . I mean merely that, if he were to learn that they are false, he would be surprised and would set out, deliberately and consciously, to revise his store of beliefs" (159–160).

Again one cannot be certain that the author means to say that the simple belief about one's sensing, for example, "I am sensing blue," which, it is implied, we have and which functions as one of the quasi-premises for the quasi-conclusion that the surface is blue, is also only unconsciously present in the percipient. But again it would be natural to read the author as meaning to say that. And of course it is this belief—that one is being looked-to blue, that one is sensing blue-ly—as contained in the belief that the surface is looking blue to one, which I had begun by suggesting that the reader, unless warned against it, would naturally suppose to constitute awareness of our being looked to blue, with the consequence that our visual awareness of the blue color of the surface before our eyes is mediated by a more direct awareness of our own "blue" sensing, which is *not* before our eyes. The remarks I have just been quoting from Chisholm and Dretske, although not quite explicitly hitting this target, can naturally be read as providing just the warning the reader needs, and thereby excluding this indirectly realistic interpretation of the theory.

We needn't rest with this evidence. Both Chisholm and Dretske make other remarks that seem to be unambiguous on this subject. The only uncertainty they leave in the reader's mind is this: in view of the rest of the theory, it is difficult to believe that either Chisholm or Dretske fully appreciates the internal strain his fully accepting these remarks introduces into his analysis.

In quite a different context of discussion—before beginning his discussion of "seeing that", while still discussing simple seeing, and as part of an attack upon indirect realism and its notion of a subjective thing of which we are directly aware—and hence at a moment when he might not have had present to his mind

2. Roderick M. Chisholm, *Perceiving: A Philosophical Study* (Ithaca, N.Y.: Cornell University Press, 1957), p. 77. All quotations from Chisholm are from this book.

his own requirement that in all instances of seeing properties of objects we must have a belief about how the object looks to us, Dretske says this: "The fact that the coffee pot's looking some way to S does not sound like the sort of thing of which S can be aware (it certainly is not colored or shaped like a coffee pot) should not disturb us; for there is nothing which should lead us to believe that being *directly aware* of this sort of thing is anything like being aware of something" (75). If we speak of ourselves as being "directly aware" of how some object before our eyes looks to us, then, according to Dretske, we have introduced so abnormal an object of this purported awareness (by contrast with the coffee pot itself, or its color or shape) that "the meaning of the term 'aware' has been so shifted that the phrase 'S is directly aware of A' is but an alternative way of describing the state of affairs which I have expressed by saying that D looks some way to S" (75). And of course Dretske has described D's looking some way to S—which is the same as S's simply seeing D—as involving no awareness on S's part of anything whatever.

Why this denial by Dretske of even the possibility of being aware of how things look to us is surprising, in him, is that, since we can, indeed must, by Dretske's own account, have a belief about how an object looks to us every time we see a feature of an object (see that an object is of a certain character), one would think that Dretske would have to admit that it is possible for this belief of ours to become conscious, hence possible for us to become aware of how the object looks to us. Surely Dretske needs to admit this. Dretske seems not to have brought into a single picture these two elements in his account of visual perception.

Chisholm too makes a similar statement on the same subject, which is for a similar reason surprising: "Ordinarily," he writes, "a perceiver may not notice the way in which the object of his perception happens to be appearing" (160). This might mean that although the visual perceiver does commonly form a belief about how the object is looking (since we do commonly see some properties of objects, and this requires, on Chisholm's account, that we form a belief about how the object is looking), this belief does not commonly reach the level of consciousness. However, Chisholm goes on: "to say of a man that he *does not notice* the way he is appeared to is to say that, although he is appeared to in that way, it is false that he believes—that he accepts the proposition—that he is appeared to in that way" (161). What is surprising about this remark of Chisholm's is that he seems to have said that ordinarily in seeing the objects around us we form no beliefs about how they look to us; but he has also said that in order to see a property of an object (see that it has the property) we must form a belief about how it looks to us; so he seems to have said that ordinarily in seeing the objects around us we do not notice any of their properties! Chisholm, like Dretske, pays a high price in loss of coherence for his attempts to avoid indirect realism by denying that we become conscious of our own sensing whenever we become visually conscious of something before our eyes.

3. Failure of Chisholm-Dretske Theory to Distinguish Visual from Mental Awareness of Color

I shall now ignore the fact that neither Chisholm nor Dretske achieves a position that is internally coherent. And I shall ascribe to each of them a consistent position which is in part motivated by a desire to deny that our visual awareness of objects before our eyes is mediated by a more direct awareness of something—specifically our being looked-to or sensing a certain way—which is not before our eyes.

The way it first occurs to me to do this is by assuming that, of the several beliefs which C-D ascribe to a person who sees that a surface is blue, the only one they wish to conceive as frequently conscious, so that it can constitute visual *awareness* of color, is the belief that the surface before one's eyes is blue.

The Chisholm-Dretske account of our becoming in an ordinary way visually conscious of the blue color of a surface before our eyes would now look like this: the surface looks blue to us—but this involves on our part no awareness of anything whatever; we form the belief, not, however, consciously held, that we are looked-to blue by a surface before our eyes; we form the further belief, also not consciously held, that we should not be thus looked-to blue were there not a surface before our eyes which is in fact blue (so far we have been described as conscious of nothing—if the account stopped here, no form of awareness of anything would have been ascribed to us) ; finally, as a causal result of the three states of affairs described so far, we form the consciously held belief that there is before our eyes, at a certain location, a blue surface; this belief, so held, under these conditions, comprises our being visually conscious of the blue color of the surface before our eyes.

I shall begin my appraisal of this account by asking whether or not it specifies an internal difference between being visually conscious of the blue color of a surface before our eyes, on the one hand, and, on the other, (without essential use of mental images) merely thinking, while sitting in the dark, that there is a blue surface in the same place. An internal difference between those two forms of awareness of the same thing is a difference not constituted by a difference between the causal (or other) relations which the percipient's portion of each form of awareness sustains with other things. If an analysis of visual awareness of a colored surface specifies no internal difference between the percipient's portion of this form of awareness and the thinker's portion of the *mere thought* of the colored surface, then surely this analysis is incorrect. (I speak of the percipient's (thinker's) "portion" of an awareness because one might plausibly include the external object of the awareness in the complete state of affairs comprising awareness of an object. However, I shall often let this restriction be understood and not state it.)

Does the C-D account provide an internal differentiation of visual from mental awareness of color?

Because neither Chisholm nor Dretske systematically describes what he is undertaking to do, in analyzing seeing that an object is of a certain color, as analyzing our *awareness* or *consciousness* of the object's color—each preferring to speak of either seeing or knowing or perceiving the color—one has to find one's own way to an answer to this question.

No matter how it is caused, *merely* believing that a surface is blue is the same as merely *thinking* that it is blue. If one takes the view that on the present account of vision our awareness of the color of a surface is wholly constituted of our merely believing that the surface is blue, this belief being merely caused by the object's looking blue to us, so that our awareness of the color of the surface is no more intimately connected than by this causal relation with the surface's presently looking blue to us, then one has to interpret this account of vision as specifying no internal difference between visual awareness of color and merely thinking of color. But surely there is an internal difference between these two. So the C-D account of vision, thus interpreted, turns out to be mistaken. Let us, therefore, look for another way of construing this theory of visual knowledge as an account of visual awareness.

This one suggests itself: our being visually conscious of the blue color of the surface before our eyes comprises (on our side) our consciously taking (believing) the surface to be blue, *together with* our being looked-to blue, which is happening to us at the same time that we are taking the surface to be blue. On this account of visual awareness, although our being looked-to blue does not itself constitute our being conscious of anything and although we are not conscious of our being looked-to blue, nonetheless the fact that our being looked-to blue is going on concurrently with our believing that the surface before our eyes is blue constitutes a necessary component of the fact that we are *visually* conscious of the blue color of the surface. Hence visual awareness of colors is internally distinguishable from mental awareness of colors; for the latter requires no "colored" sensing to be occurring at the same time that one is thinking of a color.

One might even go on to suggest that the visual taking (believing) a surface before our eyes to be blue consists in that (sensuous) "manner" of believing the surface is blue which is constituted by the belief's being accompanied by our sensing blue-ly. This peculiar "style" of consciously believing in colors before our eyes comprises the internal mark of visual awareness of colors which distinguishes it from the mental kind of awareness of colors that consists in merely thinking of them.

Except as a purely grammatical remark, I do not find the last suggestion intelligible (although I once made it in print myself). What I mean by viewing this suggestion as a purely grammatical remark is this: whenever it is permitted to say that doing A consists in doing B while doing C, one grammatically could always describe doing A as doing B in the C manner. One might redescribe walking while juggling as "jugglewalking", and define the latter as walking in the juggling manner. So too one might describe taking a surface to be blue while sensing blue-ly as being visually aware of blue, defining the latter as taking the surface to be blue in the blue-sensing manner. But adding this reference to "manner" adds no information we did not already have when we learned that jugglewalking is walking while juggling, or that being visually aware is believing while sensing in a certain way.

What's more, describing (the percipient's side of) visual awareness as a certain manner of believing is rather more deceptive than describing jugglewalking as a certain manner of walking. For we do understand more of how juggling is integrated with walking than merely that one person does both at the same time. Hence speaking of jugglewalking as a manner of walking has a little more significance than a merely grammatical remark. But we have no insight into how the blue-sensing is integrated into the belief that the surface is blue so as to comprise a distinctively visual form of belief in the blue surface, whereas our speaking of their mere concomitance as comprising a "manner" of believing suggests that we do have some such insight. So we risk deceiving ourselves by this way of talking.

Of course it has also been asserted that the sensing blue-ly causes our believing the surface to be blue. Since we are now supposing that visual awareness of the color of a surface includes within itself both the sensing and the believing, it can also encompass within itself the causal relation between the two. If one likes, then, one can include in the idea of the visually sensuous "manner" of believing a surface to be blue not only the idea of our "blue" sensing accompanying our believing, but also that this sensing causes the believing. This adds another element to the purported internal differentiation of visual awareness from merely mental awareness.

All talk of "manner" aside, this attempt to construct visual awareness of blue from mere belief in blue and a "blue" sensing, the latter construed either as simply concurrent with or as also causing the belief, lacks intuitive intelligibility. Let us look more closely at the difficulty.

It seems impossible conceptually to *fit* this being looked-to blue into any sensory condition answering intuitively to our idea of being visually conscious of a surface's blue color.

Because any form of awareness of a blue surface constitutes knowledge of the surface and because a belief is easily understood as the natural vehicle of knowledge of an object's properties, it is easy to understand that our being conscious of a blue surface before our eyes should take the form of our holding a belief about the surface. That visual awareness of a surface's color should include a belief (or something like a belief) about this surface's color is, therefore, easy to accept. We can go further. It is plausible to analyze our believing that a surface before our eyes is blue as our attributing to the surface the color blue. Since visual awareness is a mode of attention, we can now appreciate that our being visually conscious of a surface's blue color will require our visual attention's being held by the content of our visual attribution of this color blue to the surface. Visual attention, in turn, carries with it awareness; so our attention to the content of our visual attribution of blue involves our being aware *of* this content of our attribution. But so far we have no understanding of how our sensing blue-ly enters into our thus attending to the content of our visual attribution of blue to a surface.

According to Chisholm and Dretske, the "blue" sensing is no part of what we are conscious *of*—so it can enter in no way into what we are most directly conscious of, which is the content of our visual attribution of the color blue (to the surface before our eyes). And sensing blue-ly is itself no form of awareness of anything. We cannot make intelligible to ourselves how this "blue" sensing fits into this believing mode (this color-attrib-uting mode) of visual awareness of the blue color of the surface before our eyes. Certainly it does not help us to be told that this being looked-to blue *causes* us to visually attribute the color blue to the surface before our eyes—this is a purely external re-lationship in which the "blue" sensing stands to the belief that the surface is blue; for all the contribution this suggestion makes to understanding the internal structure of visual awareness of blue, the "blue" sensing might as well have been replaced by action of light-waves on the retina of the eye.

One finds oneself driven into concluding that what makes (our side of) the visual perception a case of *awareness of a blue* surface, according to C-D, is nothing but our consciously but merely believing—hence merely *thinking*—that the surface before our eyes is blue: there seems no alternative to supposing that the attribution of color to the surface is accomplished by the exercise of a mere *concept* of the color blue; and this is merely thinking that the color is blue. For we can find no place for the sensing blue-ly to fit *within* the visual attribution of blue to the surface.

Yet if one must resort to construing the whole visual aware-ness (of the surface before our eyes) as contained within the merely *conceptual* attribution by the visual percipient of a specific color (to this surface), with his attention held by the content of this conceptual attribution—hence held by a mere *concept* of blue—and the "blue" sensing altogether outside this process of attribution of color to the surface, then on this ac-count of visual awareness there is no genuinely internal differ-ence between our being visually conscious of the blue color of a surface and our merely thinking, while sitting in the dark, that the (blue) surface before us is blue.

I shall now attack the C-D analysis of visual awareness from a somewhat different direction. Since the distinctively visual ob-ject of awareness is color, let me attempt to get more clarity about exactly what it is that we are taking a surface before our eyes to be when we are visually taking it to be a certain color.

On an ordinary occasion of our seeing that a surface is blue we surely do not visually take the surface to be reflecting light of a certain wavelength or frequency of vibration, since we need have no understanding of the physical theory of lightwaves in order merely to see what color a surface before our eyes is. The same goes for the idea of our visually taking the surface to have an atomic structure of the kind fitted for absorbing all but light-waves vibrating with certain frequencies.

Then perhaps what we take the surface before our eyes to be in seeing that it is blue is an instance of what philosophers (and many physicists) have often proposed as the nature of visible color: we take the surface to be disposed to look a certain way. What way? No doubt, the blue way.

Let us suppose that in forming the conscious, visual belief that a surface before our eyes is blue we form the conscious, visual belief that the surface is disposed to look blue. But which way of looking is this so-called "blue" way of looking which we find ourselves believing the surface disposed to? By this question, I mean to ask how this way of looking is specified within our visual belief that the surface is disposed to this way of looking. Surely it is not, within visual perception, specified as the way of looking signified by the word 'blue'. For we do not want to say—and neither Chisholm nor Dretske ever does say—that visual per-cipients must exercise a power of using the word 'blue' in merely seeing the color of a blue surface before their eyes. And surely, also, in gaining the visual belief that the surface before our eyes is disposed to look a certain ("colored") way, the way of looking that we select is normally the ("colored") way the surface is now looking to us. But what role does the surface's presently looking a certain way play in our seeing that the surface is disposed to look that way? How does the C-D analysis answer this question?

In its briefest form it goes like this. Our presently being looked-to blue by the surface causes us to form the conscious belief that the surface is disposed (on all similar occasions) to look that very way—yet we do not become aware of our presently being looked-to in that ("blue") way! Our conscious belief about the surface's color is, therefore, the mere *thought* that the surface has a disposition to look a way we have only a mere *idea* of.

Let me now put the objection to the Chisholm-Dretske ac-count of visual awareness in the following way. On this account, our visual awareness of the blue color of the surface is wholly carried by our mere thought of a mere disposition in the surface to a way of looking which is appreciated by us through nothing but a mere thought of itself. Neither the concomitant presence nor the causal role of the "blue" sensing forces a qualification of that description; for our *present* sensing is neither itself an awareness of anything nor something we are aware of. But this merely thinking about a disposition to look in a way that we have no more than a mere idea of, this cannot constitute our *visual* awareness of the color of this surface. For on this account the sensuous dimension of visual awareness of colors—here assigned to the sensing—is left quite out of the picture. Internally, visual awareness of colors has been reduced to merely thinking of colors.

I have just considered two ways one might construe color in visually taking a surface to be blue. The first, the theoretical-physical, clearly is not how it is done. The second, dispositional way makes the C-D account inadequate. There remains sensuous blue: we might visually take the surface to be the blue it *looks* to be. This is a nondispositional ("occurrent") blue and a sensuous blue. Will the blue-sensing introduced into the C-D account now reveal the internal difference between visual and mental awareness?

No doubt "sensuous blue" is the very blue the C-D account intends to bring to mind in speaking of sensing blue-ly. But how can this sensing blue-ly, as C-D construes it, help a perceiver to be in a distinctively visual (not merely mental) way conscious of a surface as if sensuously blue? The same difficulty now recurs, because C-D denies that the visual perceiver is aware of his own sensing. Somehow one's sensing blue-ly merely *causes* one to become aware of the surface before one's eyes as if having the same, sensuous, blue quality which the sensing blue-ly "has". But this causation cannot help at all to make one's awareness of the surface's blue, as described by C-D, anything more or less than one's entertaining (with conviction of its applicability) a mere idea of sensuous blue. Merely mental awareness has not yet been internally differentiated from visual awareness.

We shall not be helped to solve our problem by filling in the full Chisholm-Dretske description of the mechanism whereby our being looked-to blue causes us to come to believe that a surface before our eyes is blue. On the full account, our being looked-to blue—our sensing blue-ly—causes us to form the unconscious belief that we are sensing blue-ly, and it also causes in us the unconscious belief that if the surface were not in fact blue then we should not now be sensing in this way. These two unconscious beliefs, in turn, cause us to form the consciously held belief that the surface before our eyes is, indeed, blue. And this latter belief, accompanied by the blue sensing that causes it, *is* our being visually conscious of the surface before our eyes.

No doubt explaining a conscious belief about the color blue as caused by two unconscious beliefs about "blue" sensing makes the connection between our belief about the color of the surface and our sensing blue-ly somewhat less opaque than it is on the shorter account. However, we continue to have no awareness of our presently sensing bluely, and our presently sensing bluely is itself no form of awareness of anything. It remains true, on this fuller account, that the only form of awareness we have of both the way of looking to which the surface is disposed and of the surface's being so disposed (its being blue), is a mere thought of each. (So too, if the surface's being blue is said to consist in its being "sensuous blue"—the blue it looks—we have no more than an idea of this blue.) So what is in fact a visually sensuous form of awareness of color is still being characterized as if it were a purely mental form of the same, which is merely caused and accompanied by a sensuous element whose presence we are unaware of and which is itself no form of awareness.

One final objection, an objection to the last recourse available to the Chisholm-Dretske account, will reveal to us the invincible ignorance of visual awareness of color into which this theory locks its adherents. The fundamental deficiency of this theory is not removed even if we allow to it what its sponsors have seemed to want to avoid: the assumption that the belief we have that the surface before us is now looking to us a certain way is a consciously held belief, so that this account now makes us conscious of how we are presently being looked-to (sensing). It is true that this assumption will constitute in one respect a move in the right direction: it will take the theory closer to indirect realism. For our conscious belief about the color of the surface before our eyes will now be mediated by our conscious belief about something *not* before our eyes, namely, by our conscious belief about how we are sensing. Nevertheless, the deep mistake of the theory remains: the visual percipient's awareness is still constituted wholly of nothing but *thoughts* of colors and of the looks of colors. For his being conscious of how he is presently sensing consists in nothing but his consciously holding the (true) belief that he is now sensing in a certain way. And this conscious belief is in no way distinguishable from a mere thought.

That this mere thought about how one is sensing is both caused and (mysteriously) justified by the sheer occurrence of the sensing cannot make it any less a mere thought about this sensing. On the present interpretation of this theory, then, our being visually conscious of the blue color of a surface before our eyes is still constituted by our having the mere thought of the surface's disposition to look blue; but now this thought is mediated by the (mere) thought that the surface is presently looking blue to us, which is to say that it is mediated by the exercise of a mere concept of being looked-to blue, a mere concept of a present blue-sensing.

Certainly one feels that this interpretation of the theory, apparently so much unwanted by its authors, brings us closer to the truth. One is almost ready to say that there is now *some* internal distinction between this visual form of awareness of color and merely thinking of color. For one notices that, in what we should ordinarily describe as "merely thinking" that a blue surface is before our eyes (as when sitting in the dark), it is not the case that we are *warranted* in thinking this by the occurrence of our "blue" sensing, since (one may suppose) we are not visually sensing at all (and do not believe we are). Certainly there is here a distinction made between the mental and the visual forms of awareness which is getting closer to what is wanted.

One has nonetheless to hold on to one crucial point. However being warranted in one's belief by a blue-sensing is to be analyzed, we must notice this: if Chisholm and Dretske are right, when we see that the surface is blue, our awareness of our blue-sensing is realized entirely by our exercising a concept of this blue-sensing; for we are conscious of this blue-sensing only as merely believing that it is occurring. What remains extraordinary and not credible in this account is its making it out that, despite our now being conscious of how we are presently being looked-to and despite the fact that our presently being so looked-to allegedly provides in some manner a justification for our visual belief in its occurrence, it remains a fact that we have no form of awareness either of this present way we are being looked-to or of the surface's blue color other than the *mere thought* of each of these. And this prevents the C-D account from providing the internal, distinguishing mark of *visual* awareness of color.

To go beyond an account of visual awareness which consigns us to merely thinking of the looks and colors of things it will be necessary to build a very different structure out of the elements provided for us by the Chisholm-Dretske analysis. It is time now to do this.

4. Indirect Realism: Sensing Blue-ly Is the
   Content of a Sensuous Attribution and
   the Direct Object of Visual Attention

First we take cognizance of the fact that visual awareness of
the colors of things before our eyes is a form of knowledge of the
"external world." It is therefore plausible to suppose that this
knowledge is carried, on the percipient's side, by something like
belief. Hence the vehicle, in the percipient, of his visual awareness of the color of a surface will be an *attribution* by him of this
color to the surface. This in turn implies that there functions
within the percipient a representation of this color, so that the
content of his attribution of the color to the surface is the content of this representation of the color. The analysis I have
credited to Chisholm and Dretske goes wrong in this: that this
representation of the color of the surface cannot be made out,
with the scheme they have given us, as anything other than a
concept of a color. Hence the visual attribution of this color to
the surface can be made out only as the mere thought that the
color belongs to the surface.

Now we take cognizance of the peculiarly sensuous item
among the elements made available to our analysis by the C-D
account: there is a sensuous "color" quality that is instantiated
within the percipient's visual experience—we may even say that
this sensuous quality is, by the intention of the theory, instantiated within the percipient's portion of the awareness of color,
but despite that intention this theory has not succeeded in
achieving an integration of sensuous quality with visual awareness. The blue-sensing is a happening in the percipient whose
character is partly specified by the sensuous quality *blue:* this
quality makes of this sensory happening the specific kind of
happening, of the generic "sensing" sort, that this sensing is.
What is wanted is that we take advantage of this sensuous quality, whose instantiation within the sensory experience gives the
latter its peculiar, visually sensuous character, and use this
quality, in our theory, to give to the visual attribution of color
to a surface *its* peculiar character as a form of attentive, visual
color-attribution (a visual form of awareness of color) that is
not a mere thought that the surface has the color blue.

How do we do this? Remember that visual awareness of a
color before the eyes is a form of attention to this color; yet this
awareness of a color is also an exercise of a representation of
this color, by way of an attribution of the content of this repre-

sentation to the surface. Visual attention to a surface's color has, then, somehow to be mediated through the visual representation by means of which the percipient attributes the color to the surface. The only plausible way to provide for this mediation of our visual attention to the surface's color is to suppose that our visual attention is given directly to the content of our attribution of the color to the surface, hence to the content of our visual representation of this color.

We do not want this content to be construed as the content of a mere concept. And as a possible content for a color-attribution we have on hand a "color" quality already instantiated somewhere within the visual experience—exactly where and how having been the mystery that baffled us in the account by Chisholm and Dretske. Let this "blue" which is said to specify the kind of sensing that is going on in the percipient be understood also to constitute the content of our visual representation of the color of the surface, which here means the content of our visual attribution of the color blue to the surface before our eyes. Hence let it be thought of as constituting the predicative content of our visual "belief" that the surface is blue. Now our visual attention to the blue color, in being mediated through our visual attribution of this color to the surface, is directly held by the "blue" content of that visual attribution.

Now our visual "belief" that the surface before our eyes is blue is no longer without an internal mark that distinguishes it from the mere thought (the *mere* belief) that the surface is blue. For the attribution of color which constitutes this "belief" has for its content not the content of a concept, but the very sensuous quality that makes the sensing going on in us the peculiar sensing it is. Let us call this quality "sensuous blue". Functioning within our visual "belief" as the content of our representation—hence of our attribution—of the surface's color, this sensuous blue represents *itself*, by the method of exemplification, as the color of the surface before our eyes. We can understand this representation-through-exemplification by analogy with the way the blue color in a painting of the sky represents itself as the color of the sky. But this mode of representation is not common in conceptual representation of properties. At most it occurs in mental imaging.

So now we have described a visual form of awareness (of the color of a surface before our eyes) which is carried by something like a mere belief, and to this extent by something like a mere thought, but which is not a mere belief or mere thought of the color before our eyes.

We also observe that, since the only way our visual attention can, on this analysis, be held by the blue color before our eyes is through being held by our *blue*-sensing—which is *not* before our eyes—we are obliged to admit that our visual attention is directly held by something *not* before our eyes. The color (and the surface) before our eyes, therefore, *indirectly* holds our visual attention. But what holds our visual attention is the same as what we are visually conscious of. So we are directly conscious of our *blue* sensing, functioning as the sensuous content of our visual attribution of a color to the surface before our eyes, and through this direct awareness we are indirectly aware of the color belonging to the surface before our eyes. But our visual awareness of any particular before our eyes is mediated and in part constituted by our visual awareness of its color—or, as in seeing regions of empty space—of the colors of other things before the eyes. So visual awareness of things before our eyes is, throughout, indirectly realistic. Is so, if this analysis is correct.

On this analysis of visual awareness, our awareness of the surface before our eyes and of its blue color is carried by something like a belief—we can call it a (visually) "sensuous belief" about the surface. But our awareness of our own blue-sensing is not carried by an *additional* belief about this sensing; awareness of our blue-sensing is an internal element within our sensuous "belief" about the surface's color. This sensuous "belief" about the surface consists in an attribution of a color to the surface and it is partly composed of a direct awareness of its own (predicative) content, the blue-sensing. Our direct awareness of the sensuous content of our sensuous belief's predicative content is no more a second belief directed upon the sensuous "belief" than is one's direct awareness of the content of one's belief about the birth date of Abraham Lincoln a second belief directed upon my one's belief about Lincoln. Our awareness of our own *blue*-sensing is not carried by an idea of this sensing; the sensing itself is directly present to us, our direct awareness of it being a component of our indirect awareness of the color of the surface before our eyes.

Our sensuous belief about the surface's color has for its content not the characteristic content of a concept but an instance of the sensuous quality *blue:* this sensuous representation of a color is like an idea, in its function within an attribution of a color; but it is not a mere idea, because of its sensuous content, which is to say, because it represents the blue color of the surface by exemplifying within itself the very quality it represents as belonging to the surface.

I have just said that the sensuous blue in us exemplifies the "quality" it represents the surface before our eyes as having. It would not quite do to say that it exemplifies the whole property it represents the surface as having, i.e., the color blue itself; for this would entail that our visual awareness of blue is itself colored, is itself blue, rather than only "colored", only *blue*. It is necessary now to become more clear about this, as well as about how what we visually attribute to the surface, in seeing that it is blue, we represent as objective blue, i.e., as the surface's disposition to look blue.

The color of the surface before our eyes is not perceived by us under the abstract rubric of a "disposition" to look a certain way. Rather, the sensuous *blue* itself, the sensuous quality that specifies the kind of being looked-to that being looked-to blue is, this sensuous quality is itself visually ascribed to the surface. Insofar as there is within mature visual perception merely of a thing's color an "object-making" function, this instantiated *blue* quality, as it is represented when visually attributed to the surface before our eyes, is doubtless assigned—now by a *conceptual* attribution—its share of the powers appropriate to an objective property of a material surface. Among these is the power to make itself manifest to our visual perception; within mature visual consciousness, we conceptually ascribe to this sensuously attributed quality the power to cause us to become visually conscious of itself whenever we open our eyes and look with attention at the surface before our eyes—and we thereby "make" this quality, *as attributed,* an objective color, blue, a possible property of a physical surface before our eyes.

This perhaps is the truth there is in the notion that what we take the surface before our eyes to be, in visually taking it to be blue, is a surface "disposed" to look blue. We sensuously attribute to the surface that nature which (we presume) accounts for how it looks, and we conceptually ascribe to this nature the power to make us aware of itself whenever (in good light) we look at the surface to which we attribute it. This nature that we sensuously attribute to the surface is the quality, sensuous *blue,* that is represented within our visual perception by an instance of itself, but it is this quality augmented by the powers we conceptually ascribe to it in representing it as inherent in the material surface before our eyes: in mature, visual perception sensuous *blue* represents itself, with the aid of *conceptual* ascription of causal powers, as objective blue.

In the end I shall conclude that the surface does not—as our visual awareness does—have sensuous *blue* as a feature. To this extent we visually misperceive surfaces' colors. However the surface does have the disposition we ascribe to it. So far our perception is realistic.

5. Direct Realism's Thesis (I) : Direct Perception of Objective Colors

The argument that I have given for an analysis of visual awareness as indirect awareness has been largely relative to another account, that of Chisholm and Dretske: I have meant to show that my analysis is better than theirs, not that it is the best. However, theirs had already a certain plausibility, all of which, I believe, is retained by the account I have offered; and mine gains the additional credibility arising from its solving the difficult problem of explaining the internal difference between visual and merely mental awareness of color, a problem any theory of visual awareness must solve.

Against the wills of its authors the Chisholm-Dretske account of vision has turned out to be closer to indirect than to direct realism. To show that visual, direct realism is false I need to examine the genuine article. To examine it I must produce it.

To be visually aware of a physical object before the eyes one must be thus aware of at least one of its features. Visually to be directly aware of such an object one must be thus directly aware of at least one of its features. The direct realist must so choose a visible feature that we *can* be directly aware of it. What feature should he choose?

He will look for a feature whose nature would be what it is were no seeing creatures so much as a possibility: a feature our actually or possibly seeing which plays no part in its being what it is. For otherwise the chosen feature is all too likely to turn out to be a disposition to *look* so and so to a viewer. And down that road, as we have discovered with other senses, lies danger for the direct realist.

Dangerous also is the choice of a feature whose nature cannot show itself to vision. The direct realist will not begin by speaking of the atomic structures of visible surfaces as a feature we directly see.

Finally he wants the feature to be one we needn't visually infer from other perceived data—for the latter will be more directly perceived than the inferred feature.

Steering away from the first danger the direct realist will initially avoid color. Shying from the third hazard he will not first choose solidity or distance or size or functional character. Trying to avoid all three dangers the direct realist will choose the shape of the facing surface of an object as the feature we directly see the object to have. When convenient I shall call this surface-shape the shape of the object. Shape is a physical feature: the definition of its nature requires no reference to how the surface looks to us. The shapes we see things to have when we succeed in seeing their shapes they would have had even if the seeing of shapes had never been dreamed of. To vision a shape reveals itself for what it is. And shape need not be inferred from another feature of the shaped object or of any object before the eyes. The direct realist begins, then, by holding that when we look with attention at the surface of an object before our eyes we become visually conscious of the surface's shape, but not in virtue of being visually conscious of another feature instantiated either before the eyes or not before them.

Surely the direct realist has made a false start. For we become visually conscious of the shapes of surfaces in virtue of becoming visually conscious of their colors and of the colors of neighboring surfaces.

If you tell me the shape of a rock slab which I cannot see, saying to me, "It is square," I become mentally conscious of its square shape. Although you may first say to me, "The slab is blue," so that I first become mentally conscious of its color, I need not become mentally aware of its shape through becoming aware of its color: your word 'blue' need play no role in your conveying to me by your words the shape of the rock slab.

However—counting black, white, and gray as colors—I cannot *see* the shape of any object except through seeing colors, I cannot become visually conscious of the shape of an object except through becoming visually conscious of a pattern of color. We see the shapes of objects by seeing boundaries. And we see boundaries by seeing demarcations between expanses of different color. Our seeing the difference in color between one region and another enables us to see a boundary, and our seeing shapes consists in our seeing boundaries. Becoming visually conscious of shapes always in part consists, therefore, in becoming visually conscious of colors. For us, becoming visually conscious of the shape of an object is becoming visually conscious of an expanse which is colored and shaped. But we see the shape in virtue of seeing the colors, not vice-versa; for it is not in virtue of seeing shapes that we see colors. Visually we are more directly aware of a surface's color than of its shape.

The direct realist holds that we become visually conscious of shaped expanses that are before our eyes, and that this visual awareness is not even in part constituted by an awareness of shaped expanses *not* before our eyes. Therefore the direct realist must affirm that the shaped expanses before our eyes of which we become visually conscious are themselves really colored; for otherwise he would have to acknowledge that our becoming visually conscious of the shaped but noncolored expanses that alone are actually before our eyes is always accomplished by our becoming visually conscious of shaped, colored expanses which would, therefore, have nowhere to be but *not* before our eyes; and it is this mediation of our visual awareness of what is before our eyes by a visual awareness of something not before our eyes which the direct realist denies.

The direct realist must, then, hold that when I look attentively at the square, rock slab before my eyes I become visually conscious of it by becoming visually conscious of its square shape, and that my becoming visually conscious of its square shape is mediated by and in part consists in my becoming visually conscious of its color. I am visually conscious of a blue expanse that has a square shape; this square-shaped, blue expanse is the surface of the slab, which surface has, therefore, as a property, the blue color that I am directly conscious of in being visually conscious of the surface's shape. According to the direct realist, the rock slab is as objectively blue as it is objectively square. I am directly aware of the slab because I am directly aware of the instance of blue color that belongs to the slab before my eyes.

The dangers the direct realist wished to avoid by avoiding color as the direct object of visual awareness he must now face.

6. Direct Realism's Thesis (II) : Directly
    Sensible, Objective Blue Is Physical Blue

To defend his claim that we *can* directly perceive a surface's blue color the direct realist must explain to us the nature of this color.

I shall use the phrase 'dispositional blue' to speak of the surface's blue color when this is conceived to consist in the surface's disposition to look blue to normal observers under normal lighting. When the objective color of a surface is not conceived as a disposition to look a certain way to a viewer, then it will be called "nondispositional color" or "occurrent color." The direct realist must conceive a rock slab's blue color to be either dispositional blue or occurrent blue. Let us first suppose that he chooses dispositional blue.

In the following discussion I shall ignore the possible case of seeing an object to be blue although it does not in the usual way look blue, because of abnormal lighting of which the observer is aware. In this case the object's looking some other color would play the role looking blue plays in the present discussion, and my argument would not be weakened, only lengthened.

If we do become visually conscious of a rock's disposition to look blue to us, then we can do so only in virtue of becoming visually conscious of the rock's presently manifesting this disposition. Anything else would not be *seeing* the rock's blue color. The rock's presently manifesting its disposition to look blue to us consists in its presently looking blue to us. Since the direct realist is now committed to our being visually conscious of the rock's presently looking blue to us when we see its color, he must explain what its presently looking blue to us consists in. In another context the direct realist might answer that the rock's looking blue to us consists in its causing us to become visually conscious of its blue color—this would be appropriate in the context of treating blue as physical blue. But this answer is no good when being blue is analyzed as being disposed to look blue. For on this analysis the suggested answer entails that becoming visually conscious of the blue color of the rock consists in becoming visually conscious of the disposition of the rock to cause us to become visually conscious of the disposition of the rock to cause us to become visually conscious of . . . *ad infinitum*.

Therefore, in the context of the present analysis of objective blue as disposition of the rock to look blue to us, the direct realist must explain the rock's manifestation of this disposition, its looking blue to us, along these lines: its causing us to have a certain sort of visual experience, which we might call "being looked-to blue"—or "sensing blue-ly." Can the direct realist plausibly hold that we are visually conscious of the causal process involved here? He could make this plausible only on the assumption that we are visually conscious of this rock's causing us to be looked-to blue in virtue of being visually conscious of the effect of this causation, that is, in virtue of being conscious of our being looked-to blue. But our being looked-to blue—or our sensing blue-ly—is an occurrence not located before our eyes (or other sense organs) ; it characterizes our subjective, sensory state. So the direct realist must admit that we are *indirectly* conscious of the blue color of the rock slab—of its disposition to look blue to us—in virtue of being *directly* conscious of our own sensory condition, being looked-to blue. His direct realism fails. He must not define objective blue as dispositional blue.

The direct realist must choose occurrent blue as constituting the nature of objective blue. (Remember that the only disposition which by definition occurrent blue cannot be is the surface's disposition to look a certain way.)

But how shall he construe the nature of occurrent blue? Again I think he has two choices: sensuous blue or physical blue.

He might say that objective blue's nature is exactly the nature that a blue thing's color directly *looks* to have under normal lighting to a normal viewer. Call this "sensuous blue".

Perhaps we cannot say that blue looks to be perfectly simple. It is said to comprise hue, saturation, and brightness. So let us focus on a certain blue hue—say robin's egg blue.

This hue's nature, now conceived as occurrent hue, does not consist in the tendency of the surface to look a certain way to a perceiver. Does it have causal efficacy? More specifically, does the surface's having this occurrent hue causally empower the surface to look that hue to us (so far as the surface can account for this experience of ours)? Suppose the direct realist says no.

In that case our seeing a surface's hue is in no way explained by the surface's having this hue. What difference does the surface's having the blue hue make to the surface's interaction with other things in the world? If the direct realist does not ascribe to the occurrent hue the power to enable the object to look that hue to us, then he surely can find no other power of the object to attribute to the object's having this hue. Nor, having denied that the hue is the object's disposition to look a certain way, can he find any plausible disposition with which to equate the hue. The object's having this hue plays no part in either explaining or specifying any of the object's interactions with other things in the world.

But in that case we cannot upon reflection have good reason to ascribe the hue to the object. The only reason we have for so ascribing it is that it looks to us to be of that blue hue. However, if we posit that the object's being that color neither consists in nor accounts for its commonly looking to us to be so, then its looking to be blue ceases to provide us with a good reason for believing it to be blue. Conceiving occurrent color as he now does, the direct realist can have no good reason for believing that a robin's egg is occurrently blue.

He might choose to be irrational and believe anyhow. To do so, however, is worse than believing without reason where a reason is wanted. If his belief is true then by hypothesis there can never be an explanation of how we succeed in seeing the colors of things exactly as they are. The direct realist will have knowingly made of this continual success a remarkable and in principle mysterious instance of pre-established harmony.

Exactly the same argument would work for saturation and brightness. So it works for color, when construed as occurrent color which does not causally empower the colored object to look a certain way to us.

Therefore the direct realist had better say that objective, occurrent blue *does* empower the surface to which it belongs to cause us to see its color. To say this is to say that occurrent blue is physical blue. What is the nature of physical blue? The direct realist has no recourse but to turn to the physicist and ask for the nature of the feature of the rock that explains—so far as the rock's surface can do so—our seeing the blue color of the rock. Set upon this inquiry, the physicist turns to studies of the selective absorption and reflection of light and to studies of the structure of the light reflected to the eye. If the physicist concentrates upon the surface of the slab he makes discoveries about the molecular and atomic structure of the surface and subsurface of the slab; if he concentrates on the reflected light, he comes up with facts about wavelength or frequency of vibration. In the one case he is talking about systems of electrons, protons, neutrons, and the like, in the other about systems of electromagnetic pulsations or streams of photons.

If the physicist finds some property of the surface of the slab or of the light reflected from its surface that accounts for our seeing blue when we look attentively at the rock slab, then this physical blue that he discovers will be a property whose nature is specifiable only in theoretical terms, a peculiarity, say, in the arrangement or behavior of the protons, electrons, and neutrons, or in the pattern of wavelengths of electromagnetic vibrations reflected by the array of protons and the like. We can be sure that the physicist's explanation of what it is in the rock slab or in the light that accounts for our visual awareness of the color we do become conscious of will specify a complex property of whose nature we do not become visually conscious. Only a scientific education can make us, and then only mentally, not visually, conscious of this complex property as the property it is.

Can the direct realist succeed in making it out that we nonetheless do become visually conscious of this physical blue *as* something or other? What plausible candidate is there for a "something or other" which we become conscious of physical blue *as?* I can think of only two plausible candidates: dispositional blue and sensuous blue.

7. Direct Realism's Thesis (III) : Physical Blue Is Identical with Sensuous Blue

The direct realist has now reached a position with which we are familiar. He must hold that the color we see is physical blue, while asserting that we do not visually perceive this color's nature. Therefore he must provide for us an account of the delineation physical blue receives for visual awareness. He cannot answer—although some have done so—that its delineation is wholly indeterminate, a mere "some feature or other", which behaviorally we separate from other properties of objects. For this belies the character of visual awareness of colors, assimilating it to the merely mental specification of colors, in which we exercise mere concepts grounded in mastery of words of general and indeterminate import, like "some feature or other." Colors are delineated for visual awareness as determinate features of surfaces.

If the direct realist chooses dispositional blue as the determinate feature that provides physical blue's delineation for visual awareness, then he holds that in seeing the blue color of a surface we become visually conscious of the disposition this surface has to look blue to us. As we have discovered, this claim will force the direct realist to concede that we can become visually aware of such a disposition only through becoming more directly aware of its manifestation. And its manifestation consists in our being looked-to blue. So we become directly conscious of being looked-to blue in becoming indirectly conscious of the surface's disposition to look blue to us. But our being looked-to blue is not a condition of something before our eyes. So direct realism fails for vision.

The direct realist is driven, therefore, to affirm that the delineation which physical blue receives for visual awareness is as sensuous blue—the blue the surface *looks* to be. Physical blue holds our visual attention in virtue of sensuous blue holding it. He cannot allow, however, that sensuous blue is a different property from physical blue. For if he does, then he will have allowed our visual awareness of physical blue to be mediated by visual awareness of another, different property: we should not be directly aware of physical blue.

Of course the direct realist might hold that sensuous blue is not a property of anything; there is no instance of it at hand; so although sensuous blue is not identical with physical blue, we are not visually conscious of physical blue through being visually conscious of an instance of some other property.

However, to take this tack is to assimilate seeing blue too closely to merely thinking of blue. The direct realist would have to hold that we visually grasp physical blue under something like a description, as "sensuous blue," where the property specified by the perceptual *concept* "sensuous blue" has no more "need" to be instantiated somewhere than the property specified by the concept "Absolute zero" has. This will not do, as argued earlier. For then there would be no internal differentiation between becoming visually conscious of the color before our eyes and merely thinking there is something blue out there.

Or the direct realist might try to make out this sensuous blue, by which physical blue is delineated for visual consciousness, to be the sensuous *manner* of our perceiving physical blue: adopt the adverbalist position. We have also earlier dispensed with this view, in discussing the Chisholm-Dretske account of visual awareness.

The sensuous blue that provides for visual awareness the delineation of physical blue must, for the direct realist, be an instantiated property that is not a different property from physical blue. The direct realist must assert that sensuous blue is identical with physical blue.

Physical blue, it will be remembered, is that feature of the surface before our eyes (or of the light reflected from it) which the physicist discovers to be the (partial) cause in that surface (or light) of our seeing the blue color of the surface. It will suffice for our purposes to suppose that this physical blue consists in the surface's reflecting electromagnetic vibrations approximately 470 millionths of a meter in length. For short, the physical blue of a surface is a feature of this sort: the surface's reflecting light-waves of length W.

This, then, is the direct realist's final articulation of his position with regard to visual perception: in becoming visually conscious of the blue color of a surface before our eyes we become directly conscious of a determinate, nondispositional color-quality—*how* the surface looks—which belongs to this surface and has as its nature (of which we do not become visually conscious) something of the following sort: this surface's reflecting light of wave-length *W*.

This last recourse of the direct realist in regard to vision is a position with which we are already quite familiar, from examination of its analogues for other senses. The direct realist is surrendering any claim to immediate intelligibility. For he recognizes that whereas in seeing a blue color we do become visually aware *that* a given surface before our eyes is a determinate blue, we do not become visually aware *that* this surface is reflecting light of a wavelength in the neighborhood of 470 millionths of a meter. Indeed these apparently two properties do not seem to have any similarity. The one is apparently very simple, the other very complex. On first consideration, the idea that these (apparently) two properties are in fact but a single property is not intelligible to us.

The direct realist justifies this position, as we know, by appealing to the precedent and authority of the scientific microreduction of such macroscopic properties as observable temperature and pressure of gases to such microstructural properties as mean kinetic energy of molecules and mean transfer of molecules' momenta to container-walls—macroscopic properties which no one can thermally or tactually discover to be the microstructural properties with which they have been theoretically identified. The visual direct realist appeals to the identities asserted by many physicists between such observable macroproperties and the theoretically articulated microproperties to which they have been reduced. Similarly, he now claims, the occurrent blue of which we become directly conscious in seeing that a rock is blue is identical with some physical property such as the relational, microstructural property of the rock consisting in the rock's reflecting from its surface electromagnetic vibrations predominantly in the region of 470 millionths of a meter in length. Nonetheless, he admits, although we can see that the rock is blue we cannot see that it is reflecting such waves.

8. Criticism of Visual Direct Realism's
   Thesis: Scientific Measurement of Color

To the direct realist's claim that to become visually aware that something is blue is to become directly aware that something has an occurrent color which is in fact (without our realizing it) identical with the relational property consisting in some surface's reflecting electromagnetic vibrations of about 470 millionths of a meter in length, I reply essentially as I did to a similar proposal in regard to the thermal qualities, warm, hot, cool, cold. The reader will recall that this latter reply was lengthy, and I shall not repeat it here.

However, there is a difference between the thermal and the visual situation which can help make an abbreviated reply more credible: there is a pure physics of heat and temperature, but there is no pure physics (as distinguished from a psychophysics) of color. In this respect color resembles loudness of sounds, and our reply can be a shortened version of part of the reply to a similar proposal in connection with loudness. For the only science of color we have—and it is quite sophisticated and venerable—has invested and still invests some resources in the "measurement" of color, an inquiry which is pursued by methods essentially like those employed in measuring sounds, in this respect: the visual perceptions of normal human percipients are as central to the subject matter of the scientific measurement of color as auditory perceptions are to the subject matter of the scientific measurement of loudness of sounds. Since colors are more like tones than like degrees of loudness, the task is more complex than the measurement of loudness (or of brightness, which corresponds to loudness), and probably should be described not as the scientific measurement of colors but as the scientific specification of colors.

The simplest way of stating how this specification of colors—called the "tristimulus specification"—works is this: it provides a systematic way of representing the color of any surface or light source by specifying a triad of quantities from which a triad of wavelengths can be derived such that light of this mixture of wavelengths, illuminating a standard surface at stated intensities, yields for a standard human percipient (defined on the basis of experimental studies of actual percipients) under standard conditions a visual perception of a color indistinguishable from the color of the given surface or light source. In brief, a colored reflector or emitter of light can be specified as to its color by a triad of quantities (the "tristimulus values") from which can be derived a specification of any number of triads of wavelengths whose mixture in stated proportions will yield either a surface or a light source which an average percipient, observing under standard conditions, will perceive as the same color as the given surface or emitter of light.

No one who reads the literature of the science of color can be left in any doubt that the effective concept of color with which it works is the concept of "same color as," and that this is the concept of patterns of reflected or emitted light which elicit from "standard" observers in "standard" conditions a visual perception of "the same color." The idea of separating the specification of color from the normal, human percipient's visual experience of reflected or emitted light no more enters into the heads of color scientists than the idea enters into the heads of scientists concerned with measuring loudness to separate this measure from the effects upon normal, auditory perception of various intensities of soundwaves. On the other hand, the scientific measurement of temperature has for several centuries now been entirely sundered from any calibration with the responses of attentive, thermal percipients. In other words, the scientific specification of color, like the scientific measurement of loudness and unlike the scientific measurement of temperature, explicitly repudiates the goal of identifying color (or loudness) with a purely physical property of things before the eyes which might be reduced to—and hence identified with—some microstructural, physical feature of surfaces or light before the eyes.

The evidence, therefore, which the direct realist would need in order to render credible his proposal that surfaces have occurrent colors of which we become directly conscious and which are identical with microstructural features of surfaces or of reflected light, is not forthcoming. All the signs suggest it will never be forthcoming, since these signs demonstrate that no color scientists are disposed to treat visible color as a purely physical property of physical things before the eyes. But the direct realist needs the same sort of evidence as that which has made credible the identification of thermometer-observed temperature with a microstructural property (mean kinetic energy) of molecules: he needs in the first place a set of macroscopic laws revealing the role that directly visible, occurrent color plays among the physical systems before the eyes of percipient organisms. Then he needs the intelligibility of the identification of this occurrent color with a microstructural feature of light (or of surfaces) to be increased for us by virtue of the explanatory role this identification plays; and this requires that the macroscopic laws of occurrent color should be explained by the microtheoretical laws, so that how directly visible color plays the role in the inanimate, physical world before our eyes which the macroscopic laws reveal that it plays is explained to us.

This necessary support for the direct realist's proposed identification of directly visible, occurrent color with microstructural wavelength of light is not forthcoming. There are no empirical laws describing the behavior of directly visible, occurrent color in the physical world before our eyes and none are forthcoming, as the color scientists' work shows; for visible color is treated by them not as a physical property of things before the eyes but as a disposition of certain classes of surfaces or of patterns of light to cause in human percipients visual perceptions of the same color. Since no physical laws governing directly visible color's interactions with physical systems before the eyes are forthcoming, the needed microtheoretical explanation of these nonexistent, physical laws cannot be forthcoming either. Hence the direct realist's proposed identification of directly visible, occurrent color with length of reflected lightwaves cannot be made intelligible to us by the only known means, the success of the explanation it facilitates of the lawfully systematized behavior of directly visible, occurrent color in the physical world before our eyes. We can, therefore, reject this last proposal of the direct realist, and conclude that there is no directly visible, occurrent color that is identical with physical color.

But the direct realist has now exhausted his alternatives. He proposed to show that we directly see objects before our eyes by showing that we directly see their shapes. But we see shapes by seeing colors. So he then proposed that we directly perceive colors. Obliged to explain how we can do this, by explaining the nature of blue color, he first tried dispositional blue. This failed. The only alternative is occurrent blue, and the next question: what is the nature of occurrent blue? He first tried to make it out to be sensuous blue, with no causal powers. This failed. The only alternative left was physical blue. But since we don't see physical blue as that, he had to describe the delineation it has for visual awareness. Here there were two alternatives: dispositional blue and sensuous blue. The first failed. And sensuous blue had either to be said to be no property of anything or identical with physical blue. If he chose the first then we only *conceive* physical blue as sensuous blue, and this is merely thinking of color, not seeing it. So he chose the second: physical blue is identical with sensuous blue. This choice has just proved untenable. No plausible alternatives remain. Direct realism, therefore, is false of vision.

Direct and indirect realism share the premise that we do, in attentively looking at surfaces before our eyes, become visually aware of the colors of these surfaces. Direct realism holds that it is false that this visual awareness occurs in virtue of our being aware of something *not* before our eyes. Since direct realism is false, I conclude that our visual awareness of the colors of surfaces *does* occur in virtue of our being aware of something *not* before our eyes. And I hold that the arguments of §2–§4, tied to the Chisholm-Dretske account, supplemented by portions of the arguments of earlier chapters, suffice to justify concluding that *what* we are directly conscious of that is not before our eyes is our sensing in a certain way—our being looked-to blue, for example; and that this sensing functions as the partial—the sensuous—content of our visual attribution of objective (dispositional) blue to a surface. Representational, indirect realism is true of vision.

Chapter Seven   # THE SENSE OF TOUCH

We feel by touch the contact other bodies make with our own. We feel the force with which other bodies press upon ours, including the resistance they offer to the pressure we exert against them.

We also feel by touch the shapes and sizes and positions of bodies in contact with our own, as well as whether what touches us is solid, liquid, or gaseous. That the surfaces of things in contact with our body are smooth or rough, hard or soft, wet or dry we feel by touch, as well as whether they are cloth or fur or hide, rock or wood or earth. We feel by touch the motion of bodies in contact with our own, and the spatial relations between them. We feel the vibrations of things laid against us. And through touch, aided by kinesthesis, we recognize a great variety of kinds of interaction with other persons: a handshake, a shove, a caress—each is perceived for what it is largely by touch.

Whatever holds our olfactory attention does so in virtue of an odor's holding it; our thermal attention can be held only insofar as an intensity of heat holds it; we cannot give our auditory attention to anything except through giving it to a sound; and colored expanses must hold our visual attention if anything more is to hold it. Furthermore, we never smell an odor through perceiving something else before our nose, we never thermally feel an intensity of heat through perceiving something else before our skin, we never hear a sound in virtue of perceiving something else before our ears, and we never see an expanse of color through perceiving something else before our eyes. In short, of all the things before our sense organs that we perceive olfactually, thermally, aurally, and visually we perceive most directly through smell, odors, through thermal perception, temperature, through audition, sounds, and through vision, colored expanses.

Is there among the things we attentively feel before our skin one thing we feel more directly than any of the others, our awareness of which mediates our tactual awareness of everything else before our skin that we notice through touch?

If there is such a thing then the direct realist must not only hold that we are more directly conscious of it than of anything else before our skin, but also that we do not become tactually

241

conscious of it through becoming conscious of something not before our skin: he must hold that we are, without qualification, directly conscious of it whenever it (and, through it, anything else) holds our tactual attention. I shall begin this inquiry into human, tactual awareness of the physical world by identifying a tactual analogue of odors, temperatures, sounds, and colored expanses. After finding the most direct object of touch before the skin, I shall ask whether or not we can be tactually conscious of it only in virtue of being more directly conscious of something not before the skin.

1. Before the Skin We Most Directly
   Feel Pressure or Stress

A preliminary inquiry concerning the organ of touch is needed. The reader will remember that in the chapter on thermal perception we concluded that we should recognize as the organ of thermal feeling not the whole skin but the sensory receptors within the skin, and should view as the most direct objects of thermal awareness before our sense organs not temperatures outside our skin but our skin's temperatures. Is there an analogous situation for touch? We can see that there is by considering how the most obvious form of the argument for indirect realism from tactual hallucination fails.

After one removes a tight hat one may for some time seem still to feel its pressure on the head. If the direct realist is right, it is argued, then when the hat is on, one is directly conscious of its pressing against one's head. But the hallucination of a hat on the head proves that it is possible with no hat on to have exactly the same tactual impression as the impression we have with a hat on. With no hat on there is, of course, nothing *before* the flesh of the head to be felt. Yet, the argument continues, in the hallucinatory situation we are directly conscious of something, and conscious of something so indistinguishable from what one feels when the hat is pressing against the flesh that we easily believe the hat to be still on the head. Since when the hat is off there is nothing before the skin of the head for one to feel, what one is then conscious of must be a subjective thing, something not before the sense organ: a "pressure image" or sense datum.

Since, the argument continues, there is no reason why the absence of the hat should cause to be created a new object of awareness that was not present when the hat was present, we should conclude that, even when the hat was on, one was *directly* conscious of that same subjective entity, a tactual pressure image or sense datum, and only indirectly aware of the hat on the head. This assumption also has the merit of explaining the hallucinatory error.

Surely, the argument concludes, if this is true of hats pressing upon heads it must be true of everything one feels pressing upon one's body. The structure of all tactual experience must be indirectly realistic.

A weakness of this form of argument which is peculiar to its application to the sense of touch shows itself in this mistaken premise: that when the hat is off, since nothing is pressing upon the skin, there is nothing *before* the organ of touch for us to feel. If the whole skin of the head were the sense organ of touch then indeed this claim would be true: once the hat is removed there is nothing whatever before the (whole) skin that is playing any part in causing one to seem to feel something pressing upon the head. However, the sensory receptors that mediate tactual experience are located within our skin. What most directly stimulates these tactual receptors within the skin is not the pressure at the surface of the skin but the resultant stress within the skin, with its concomitant deformation of the skin. The hat presses upon the skin, a stress is imparted to the skin, the skin is deformed, and the tactual sensory receptors located within the skin respond to this stress within and deformation of the skin itself. What is most directly before these tactual receptor organs within the skin is the (rest of the) skin itself, whose stresses and strains provide the immediate stimulus to these receptors' activation.

This would have no bearing upon our problem if we were never tactually conscious of the skin's displacements and stresses. But in fact we are. For we commonly feel the hat affecting our skin, pressing it down; hence we feel a change in the condition of our skin. And after a tight hat is taken off, the displacement and tension of the flesh of our head remains for some time: the flesh does not immediately spring back to its normal configuration and freedom from stress. We continue to feel this physical distortion of our flesh or the physical stress that goes with it, for as long as either condition continues after the removal of our hat.

If we continue to feel that a hat is present when it isn't, we are indeed misperceiving; but this is no hallucination. For we are correctly perceiving the distorted and stressed condition of our skin, which is before the sensory receptors within our skin and causing us, by its action upon these receptors, to remain tactually conscious of itself. And of course there is nothing subjective or mental about displaced or stressed flesh. The argument from tactual "hallucination" to indirect realism fails.

The ground for its failure which we have noticed brings to our attention that for our purposes we need to treat as the organ of touch not our surface flesh as a whole but the tactual receptors located within the flesh. The same facts provide us with a candidate for the least indirect object of tactual awareness that is located *before* our sense organs: either the displacement of our flesh or the stress within it, or both. For it has now become plausible that everything outside our body which we feel by touch we feel by feeling more directly an effect of its pressure: either the deformation of our flesh or the stress within it.

Although it is doubtless unnecessary to do so, I nonetheless do now remind the reader that if we are without qualification directly conscious of either stress within or displacement of our own flesh, whenever something outside our body holds our tactual attention, then direct realism is true of the sense of touch, since both stress in the skin and the skin's displacement are thoroughly physical quantities of an entirely physical structure located before our tactual sense organs.

Our preliminary inquiry into the organ of the sense of touch has turned out to be also a first step in seeking the analogue for touch of odors, sounds, temperatures, and color. The plausibility of the thesis that always in becoming conscious through touch of objects in contact with our body we become more directly conscious of either a stress within our flesh or a displacement of this flesh lies chiefly in this consideration: it does seem to be true that everything we feel by touch we feel by feeling that something is acting upon the surface of our body, hence by feeling something bringing about an effect upon our body's surface. This requires that we feel the effect itself; and the only two constant effects of physical contact with our body's surface that offer themselves at all plausibly as what we might feel are the stress—tension or compression or shear or torque—induced in our flesh, and the motion or displacement of our flesh. In the language of engineering, pressure upon the skin, however slight, induces both stress and strain (deformation) in the flesh. The conclusion that we feel the skin's stress or strain more directly than we feel the contact or pressure of the alien object is plausible.

Moreover, adopting that conclusion offers the direct realist more than merely an escape from the argument for indirect realism from (putative) hallucination. Let me explain what I mean.

Despite the fact that the role of direct contact with the things we perceive by touch has always, upon first thought, made this sense seem to some critics of indirect realism the latter's toughest challenge, on second thought the following consequences of this role of contact have worked, for some thinkers, in the indirect realist's favor: in order to feel the contact we have to feel its effect upon us. And perceiving its effect upon us takes the form of what we call "having a bodily sensation." I perceive an object pressing upon me by feeling a sensation as if in the flesh where that object presses. For some philosophers it has seemed a short step to conclude that I become conscious of the body pressing upon me through becoming more directly conscious *of* the sensation that I feel as if within my flesh. But everyone knows there are no sensations within our surface flesh. A sensation is a psychic entity, a phenomenon of consciousness. So, the argument concludes, the direct object of the tactual awareness we have of things before our skin is a nonphysical sensation: we are most directly conscious of *it,* and only indirectly conscious of the physical object pressing upon our flesh. In this way touch can seem to be even more susceptible to an indirectly realistic analsis than vision, since the latter offers nothing we should naturally call "sensations" to serve so vividly as the direct and physical objects of sensory awareness; neither does the sense of hearing.

But from this whole line of reasoning the direct realist is rescued if we always feel, as effects upon us of the external body's contact with us, the stress within (or the displacement of) our surface flesh. For this is a purely physical effect. The direct realist can now claim that a tactual sensation is not something we are conscious *of;* it *is* our tactual awareness—our attentive, tactual perception—of either the forces within our flesh or the deformation of our flesh caused by the object outside us pressing upon us. To become tactually conscious of an object pressing upon my skin is, the direct realist may plausibly claim, to become more directly conscious of the stress or deformation this pressure has caused within my skin and only through this latter awareness to become (indirectly) aware of the external object's pressing on the surface of my body. One perceives stress or displacement of the flesh more directly than the external body, one's doing so *is* one's having a bodily sensation (*of* the condition of one's own flesh) , and in thus perceiving one's own flesh's stress or deformation one also feels (when it is present) the pressure of the external object that induces this stress and deformation. We need not say the sensation has dropped out. It has merely revealed itself for what it is, our tactual awareness either of stress in our flesh, or of our flesh's displacement in space. Surely in these facts the direct realist finds no occasion for dismay, no reason even to suspect that tactually we are directly aware of some condition of tactual awareness itself.

I think that line of reasoning on behalf of the direct realist, in rebuttal of the argument for indirect realism from tactual sensation, is entirely sound, and I shall proceed on the assumption that what we most directly feel before our organs of touch is either the stress or the deformation of our flesh which results from the pressure of an external object on the surface of our body. Of course I concede only that this defense answers, so far, to the facts, and meets *one* argument for indirect realism. I do not concede that it also establishes as a fact that there is nothing subjective of which we are tactually still more directly conscious than of the condition of our own flesh.

The greater initial credibility which the direct realist's account of the sense of touch has, compared with his account of the other senses, is by no means yet fully present to us. To gain a nearer view of this improvement in his starting position, I need first to speak further about pressure and stress, before the skin the most direct objects of tactual awareness.

The stress on a solid may take several forms, for example, tension or compression or shear. When a string is pulled very taut at both ends the string is under tension: at every point in the string there are equal and opposite forces exerted toward the two ends of the string. When a spring attached at one end is pressed in from the other end and held, the spring is under compression: at each point in the spring there are equal and opposite forces exerted away from the ends and toward the interior of the spring. For simplification let us think of the stress induced in our flesh by objects impinging upon us as a compressive force, ignoring tension. When we remind ourselves that a compression can be conceived as a force exerted from one interior cross-sectional plane of a solid across the immediately adjoining cross-sectional plane, together with the reciprocating force in the opposite direction, this repeated throughout the interior of the solid, we realize that between the compressive force that we feel within our flesh and the pressure that we feel to be exerted at the surface of our flesh by the impinging external object there is no philosophically interesting difference in kind. For the pressure at our skin is nothing but a force exerted from the impinging object's surface, in contact with our skin, across the surface of our skin.

The similarity of these two forces, pressure and stress, may occasionally warrant simplification in discussion, provided that it is reasonable to construe pressure upon our skin as the most direct object of tactual awareness located before our *whole* skin. Let me briefly consider the case for viewing pressure in this way.

The way we perceive contact between an object and our skin is by perceiving the pressure the object exerts against our skin, a very light pressure for very light contact, a heavier pressure for heavier contact. The way we perceive the shape of things we feel by touch is by perceiving patterns of pressure exerted upon us by the objects in contact with our skin. And roughness and smoothness are merely fine-grained differences in the shapes of the surfaces of the objects in contact with our skin. A hard object exerts more pressure against us than a soft one, induces less compression in our flesh, distorts our flesh less, and yields less ground to our pressure than a soft object. This last remark introduces the perception of motion or displacement, of which I shall say more shortly.

The resistance we feel an object offer to our flesh when the latter "tries" to occupy the former's space can be thought of as the pressure the external object exerts back upon us in response to the pressure exerted by our flesh upon it. Perception of things' resistance is partially mediated by our feeling the tension in our tendons, the highly elastic tissues that join our muscles to our bones and are stretched when our muscles contract to move our bones. Liquids are distinguished from solids on the basis of differences in felt patterns of pressure, texture (smoothness and roughness), motion in response to pressure, and temperature. And wetness is characteristically simply a liquid on a solid (it's a little odd to say that water itself is wet, although it is of course even odder to say that it is not wet, since it is the common wetting agent) ; water on my hand is not what is or is felt to be wet, it is my hand that is wet and is felt to be wet when it has water on it. Finally, in the psychophysics of the sense of touch it has always been intensity of pressure that has been chosen as the relevant dimension of the object external to the skin which needs to be measured in order to establish correlations between perceived object and perceptual response.

Nevertheless this case for pressure is not conclusive. What is to be said of motion and the functions of motion—velocity, acceleration, and displacement in space? May these not be the most direct objects of tactual awareness both before the sensory receptors within the flesh and before the whole skin? It can plausibly be suggested that we feel the pressure of an external object upon our skin by feeling its movement into the space vacated by our flesh and that we feel the tension or compressive force within our flesh by feeling the deformation of our flesh, which means feeling either the motion of our flesh or the result of this motion, its displacement, both induced by the motion of the external object into our flesh.

When a portion of our body reaches a position of static equilibrium with some object pressing steadily against it, we continue to feel the pressure of the external object (and the internal stress of our flesh) after the motion of the object inward on our flesh and the resultant motion of our flesh have stopped. So we can feel pressure by touch without perceiving motion. On the other hand, there is displacement of our flesh in that circumstance, and this is commonly perceived: the positions of parts of our flesh deviate from their normal, unstressed positions, and we are tactually conscious of this deviation when our attention is held by the pressure upon our flesh.

Do we also feel motion without feeling pressure or stress? I do not think we do. Any motion I feel at the surface of my body, by touch alone, I perceive by feeling patterns of pressure. Motions of objects outside my body which I feel through feeling the motions of my own limbs are at least partially mediated through the sensory receptors in my joints. However, since the tendons are always involved in such motions, the perception of stress in them is hard to rule out. And in any event this takes us somewhat beyond what is normally taken as the sense of touch. It does appear that we do not become tactually aware of motion without tactual awareness of pressure, we do become tactually aware of pressure without tactual awareness of motion, but we do not become tactually aware of pressure (or stress) without tactual awareness of displacement. In short, pressure before the skin and stress within it turn out to be a more probable candidate for that through feeling which we feel everything we feel by touch than motion does. But pressure (or stress) and displacement seem so closely bound together as objects of tactual awareness that it is not evident that one has priority over the other as the medium through perception of which we feel the rest of the features of things we feel by touch.

Indeed through the following consideration we can appreciate how plausible the case for displacement is. Suppose that, instead of pressure and stress, displacements in space of objects at the surface of our body, felt through feeling displacements of our own flesh, are the analogues for the sense of touch of odors, sounds, intensities of heat, and colored expanses. What is peculiar to the experience of each of the other senses is conveyed to us by singling out its peculiar object of perception: whenever each of the following "objects" is what is most directly perceived before our sense organs, perceiving an odor *is* smelling, perceiving a sound *is* hearing, perceiving an intensity of heat *is* thermally feeling, and perceiving a colored expanse *is* seeing. But so is it the case that whenever displacement of our flesh is the most directly perceived object before our sense organs, perceiving motion of an object in contact with our body through perceiving a displacement of our flesh *is* feeling by touch. If the skin were anesthetized one could by vision perceive these same two phenomena, even the one through the other, but only by also seeing displacement of one's flesh through seeing colored expanses as the surfaces of the displaced portions of the skin.

Nevertheless I think that if, instead of pressure and stress, the direct realist chose displacement of our flesh for the tactual analogue of odors, sounds, colored expanses, and temperatures he would be at a disadvantage. The comparison with vision just made can help show why. According to this new account of it, the only thing that marks off the peculiar object of touch from a species of vision's peculiar object—displaced, colored expanses —is that the former need not be (cannot be) perceived to be colored. But this leaves the peculiar capability of tactual experience of the world far more negative than our experience warrants our believing it is. It is also too abstract: *what* is felt to be displaced?

Some critics will be led to believe that the reason the direct realist has produced so negative and so abstract a characterization of the peculiar nature of the experience of feeling by touch is that he has been forced by his doctrine to leave out of his account the role played by the unique, subjective quality peculiar to tactual experiences, which we might call "the feel" of displacements inward of objects at our body's surface, and the feel of displacements of our flesh. This peculiar tactual quality, construed as comprising the most direct object of tactual awareness, may seem to fill in the pure, "disembodied displacement" with the something more concrete that we seem to ourselves to feel by touch.

On the other hand, if the direct realist takes the other tack— the evidence equally supporting this analysis—and treats pressure and stress as directly felt, then the contrast with vision is no longer merely negative: for now the sense of touch is marked off by the fact that in it alone we feel most directly, among the things before our flesh, a mechanical force exerting itself against (and within) our flesh. This answers far more accurately to our experience of the positive character of the peculiarity of tactual experience, and to our reflective impression that in experience of the world through the sense of touch we achieve more directly than elsewhere sensory awareness of the action of physical forces.

Mere displacement in space, with no tactual specification of something concrete that is displaced, this thin abstraction scarcely answers to our idea of the concrete, physical reality that touch seems to open up so directly to us. But pressure certainly does answer to this idea: indeed it exemplifies what we have in mind, exactly matches, we might say, with our expectation. For what more fundamentally concrete *is* a material object for us than a something that *presses* upon us? I propose, therefore, at least for a first approximation, to choose the emphasis that seems initially favorable to the direct realist and treat pressure and stress as the primary elements (at least) in the "peculiar object" of touch: whatever we become conscious of through the sense of touch we become conscious of through becoming conscious of stress in the flesh and pressure exerted upon it, probably becoming aware of the pressure through our awareness of the stress. Later I shall briefly consider where my argument might have gone had I made the other choice, or had I given at least equal attention to displacement.

2. Superior Initial Plausibility of Tactual Direct Realism

Now we can return to our original project in the discussion of the last several pages: to get a clearer view of the comparatively stronger initial position in which the direct realist finds himself when considering touch than he starts from in treating the other senses.

If we ask ourselves what it is before our nose that most directly holds our attention when we attentively smell the things out there, we answer that it is instances of odorous qualities, such as musky, sweet, camphoraceous, putrid. When we ask the physicist what it is in the odorous emanations of things that causes us to become olfactually aware of these qualities, he tells us it is the chemical structures and perhaps shapes of the molecules composing these gaseous emanations. Whereupon many philosophers, and scientists, find themselves inclined to believe that the odorous qualities cannot be identical with the molecular structures or shapes and, hence, that what we are directly aware of in attentive olfactory perception are not properties whose instances occur before our nose.

On the other hand, if we ask ourselves what it is before our skin that most directly holds our attention when we attentively feel by touch the things before our skin, appealing to introspection, our most natural answer is that it is pressure: when pushed back from the pressure at the skin to our perception of its effect upon us, we do not seem able to find from introspection something more directly perceived than the tension or compression of our flesh. When now we ask the physicist what it is before the organs of touch that acts upon these organs and causes us to become tactually conscious of this pressure or tension or compression, he now tells us that it is—pressure and tension and compression! It is initially difficult, therefore, not to believe that what we are directly conscious of is exactly what is there before our tactual sense organs and acting upon them so as to cause us to become conscious of itself: mechanical pressure, before the skin, or mechanical stress within it. In contrast with the sense of smell, direct realism initially presents itself persuasively as the truth about the sense of touch.

When the comparison is made between the sense of touch and vision, the results are similar. When we compare the color qualities that directly hold our visual attention with the properties of light and of surfaces which the physicists discover to be the external causes of our sensing those qualities, the contrast is quite as sharp as for smell, and we find ourselves inclined to believe that neither the wavelengths or frequencies of the light nor the dispositions in surfaces selectively to absorb and reflect patterns of these, nor the atomic structures of the reflecting surfaces can be identical with the color qualities that directly hold our visual attention. For vision, direct realism looks false. Once again, and by contrast, what seems to directly hold our tactual attention is pressure of material bodies impinging upon our own flesh and stress within this flesh; but it is precisely these that the physicist tells us are there at the surface of our body and within our flesh, acting upon our tactual sense organs. In contrast with vision, direct realism initially looks true of touch.

For thermal perception the initial situation is somewhat more ambiguous. For when we ask what it is before our skin that most directly holds our thermal attention, we naturally answer, degrees of heat and cold. And when we ask the physicist what it is before our skin that causes us to feel degrees of heat and cold, he may very well answer: "degrees of heat and cold," but in any event will surely at least answer, "degrees of intensity of heat." It is by no means immediately persuasive to us that this may not coincide with our own answer; hence that we are directly conscious of what is before our skin seems quite possible.

Nevertheless we have a strong counterindication to this possibility in the qualitative disjunction between degrees of heat and degrees of cold: it is not easy to believe that the differences between, say, the thermal qualities, cool and hot, is nothing but the difference between certain molecular, kinetic energies falling below the physiological zero point of our skin and molecular, kinetic energies rising above this point, since the latter difference does not seem to us to correspond to a difference in quality of the kind we recognize in the difference between cool and hot.

Furthermore we discover upon examination that the microreduction of observable temperatures to molecular, kinetic energies cannot be equated with a similar microreduction of sensible, thermal qualities to the same molecular quantities. By contrast, again, the sense of touch does not reveal to introspection a qualitative spectrum, analogous to hot and cold, which presents itself as not plausibly identical with the spectrum of physical properties before our skin (and within it).

What is more, if there is a microreduction of pressure and stress, which is highly likely, since these are *bona fide* forces of macrophysics (mechanics), it initially appears that this *will* constitute a microreduction of the very properties we seem directly to feel by touch—pressure and stress. The initial case for direct realism in regard to the sense of touch looks, once again, strong by comparison with the situation of another one of our senses, the thermal sense.

Let me conclude this comparison by contrasting the sense of touch with the sense of hearing. Hearing is of special interest here because the "object" before our ears which offers itself as the obvious candidate for direct object of our attentive, auditory perception is a form of the very "object" that offers itself in this role for the sense of touch: pressure, but here in the form of waves of air pressure which are called "soundwaves" when audible.

The utility, for a comparison, which this feature shared between audition and touch has is the so sharply focused view it offers of the difference between an auditory attention directly held by a mere sensuous representation of pressure, and both an auditory and a tactual attention ostensibly held directly by the unvarnished physical reality, pressure itself. The relevant facts will be recalled from Chapter Five.

When waves of air pressure striking our eardrum with a frequency of less than eighteen cycles per second hold our auditory attention, we experience an auditory perception of nothing we should spontaneously call "sounds". Instead we become *aurally* conscious of waves of pressure vibrating, as it seems, within the center of the head (if the two ears receive equal stimulations) : tests prove that these experiences of pressure are not mediated by the organ of touch but by the organ of hearing. When, however, the frequency of vibration of the waves of air pressure is raised as high as 20 cps, we cease to be conscious of waves of pressure, as that, and become conscious of a distinct tonal quality and degree of loudness. It is hard to doubt that if all of our auditory perception were like our hearing of waves of air pressure of frequencies under 18 cps, then we should never have needed the words for pitch and for loudness, in short never have needed the vocabulary of sound. For hearing would have been merely another sensory organ mediating, when attentively used, sensory awareness of patterns of pressure, perceived as that. That we do have the vocabulary of sound, of tone and loudness, gives evidence that in normal, attentive listening our attention is held directly by subjective, sensuous representations of air pressure waves' physical properties (intensity and frequency) , and not by these properties themselves.

By contrast, the sense of touch, like hearing when directed to tones of less than 18 cps, generates no need for a special vocabulary specifying the qualities through feeling which we feel the pressures (and stresses) we feel: the most obvious word to use for reporting what we most directly feel before our skin is "pressure" (within our skin, "tension" or "compression") . By contrast with auditory awareness over its normal range, tactual awareness initially appears to be directly realistic in its structure.

In the works of both theoretical and applied physicists on macroscopic mechanics, in particular in those works concerned with the laws governing pressure, with the laws connecting stress and elastic and plastic strain, with the theory of static and impulsive loads on material structures, with the laws of tension, compression, torsion, and shear forces acting within solid, material structures, nowhere in these works on macroscopic, mechanical forces of the kind we feel by touch does there clearly emerge a physical conception of pressure or stress with a content so strikingly different from the apparent content of our tactual perception of these forces that one can make a persuasive inference to the conclusion that what we are directly aware of, in attentively feeling things by touch, is not pressure or stress itself, but an interior sensuous representation of these mechanical forces: at this level of physical analysis, pressure and stress are defined as force per unit area acting upon a surface; with an exception shortly to be noticed, what this force *is* is not further analyzed; and the pressure or stress we feel also appears to us, in feeling it, to be a force acting over a given area of flesh.

One mode of analysis of the action of mechanical forces may seem to provide an exception to the tendency of physical works on mechanics to support the direct realist in regard to the sense of touch. The intensity of stress on an interior plane of a solid, for example, is sometimes analyzed as the quantity of energy flowing through a unit area of the plane—the energy flux through the area. Pressure acting upon a surface can be similarly analyzed. When we assume that this energy flux is what the force's action really is, then we may think that we should not say that in feeling a certain pressure we become tactually aware that a certain quantity of energy is flowing through the surface of our skin. This is not a natural way to describe what we seem to feel when pressure on our skin holds our attention.

However, when we ask ourselves what the concept of energy, as used in physics, seems to represent as flowing through a surface the best answer seems to be: the power of doing work. Energy is the capacity for doing work. In the present instance the work in question is the displacement of our flesh. So it seems that to speak of a flux of energy across a unit area of our skin is to speak of a flux across this area of flesh of a capacity for moving this flesh inward. With this result the direct realist is justifiably encouraged. For when we have already convinced ourselves that it is a force exerted upon our skin from outside it that we feel more directly than anything else before our skin, it is not easy to be sure that it misrepresents a tactual perception so described to redescribe it as our becoming tactually aware of a flux across our skin (from without) of the power of moving our flesh inward. This redescription of what we feel seems even less off the mark when we remind ourselves of the apparently constant role played in feeling pressure by feeling the displacement of our flesh.

I am forced to conclude that we shall not find persuasive evidence from macroscopic physics that the force operating on our skin when bodies press upon it is distinguishable from what we become directly conscious of when our tactual attention is held by a body pressing upon our flesh. (Nothing is changed if this discussion is carried through entirely in terms of the stress within the flesh instead of the pressure at its surface.) These reflections have merely confirmed my original judgment that direct realism is initially more credible for the sense of touch than for the other senses.

3. Preliminary Sketch of the Argument for Indirect Realism

Macroscopic physics articulates for us the laws of the action of mechanical forces, but it does not explain this action. This explanation is provided when physics moves to the molecular level, and lower, and provides us with a microstructural analysis of macroscopic, mechanical forces. These explanations can in turn be divided into two sorts: those in which mechanical forces remain unexplained, as such, but large-scale mechanical forces are explained by reference to small-scale mechanical forces exerted by the molecular constituents of large-scale bodies; and those in which mechanical forces, as a class, are explained away, reduced to forces of another kind, which operate between smaller, constituent particles than molecules. An example of the first sort of explanation is the reduction of pressure of a gas in a container to an aggregate of impulses conveyed from individual molecules to the walls of the container. An example of the second sort of explanation is reduction of the tension in a solid to the electrostatic forces of attraction and repulsion between atoms of the solid.

Since such reductive explanations are naturally understood as telling us what the action of the macroscopic forces really consists in, we cannot be satisfied that what we feel mechanical forces as being is what they really are without examining the account of these forces which is offered to us when their action is explained through microreduction. It is possible that reflection upon these forces as they really are will convince us that it cannot be of their action that we become directly conscious in feeling things by touch. The indirect realist might hope to find grounds for an argument of the following sort.

Suppose that what actually exist before our tactual receptor organs in the way of mechanical forces such as pressure and stress, acting upon and within our flesh, are nothing but a multitude of very tiny forces, the actions of microparticles, each of which is too small for us tactually to discriminate. Consequently any mechanical force we can feel constitutes an aggregation of these minute forces. But all that this aggregation of minute forces *is* is each of the minute forces, that is to say, "every single one" of these minute forces. Therefore the only way it is possible tactually to become *directly* aware of such an aggregation of minute forces is by becoming tactually aware of each one of the minute forces: there is no other direct object of awareness offered by the aggregation, since it consists of nothing more than "every single one" of the minute forces. Since, however, we cannot feel a single, minute force of this sort, we cannot become tactually conscious of each minute force. Therefore it is impossible for us tactually to become *directly* aware of the aggregation of mechanical forces which we feel. We must be *in*directly aware of this aggregation of forces. Tactually we must be directly conscious of some *representation* of an aggregate of minute forces whenever we feel pressure upon our flesh or stress within it.

The representation of which we are in a tactual way directly aware cannot be *before* the organs of touch (or any other sense organs) ; for the "object" before our sense organs which we more directly feel than any other before these organs is the mechanical force, pressure or stress, which we have just supposed to be nothing but "every single one" of the minute forces too tiny to discriminate by touch. Therefore the representation we are directly aware of is not before our sense organs. Indirect realism is true of the sense of touch.

If an argument of this sort is to be taken seriously it is first necessary to determine the truth of its supposition concerning the nature of mechanical forces. We must therefore inquire into the microreduction of such forces, specifically pressure and stress, the forces whose action upon and within our flesh provides for us the most direct objects of tactual perception which are located before the receptor organs of touch.

The pressure exerted by a large mass of gas upon the walls of its container is much easier to analyze as an aggregate of forces exerted by constituent particles than is the pressure exerted by one solid body against another. This is true because, except for the effects of collisions with one another, the molecules of a dilute gas can be treated as acting independently of one another in their collisions with container walls, whereas the smallest parts of solids are interacting with one another in more complex ways. It would be useful, therefore, if I could use the pressure exerted by a gas upon a solid as the force whose microreduction we study, ignoring the details of the comparable microreduction for solids pressing upon solids. Would this simplification of procedure limit the generality of conclusions concerning the structure of attentive perception of pressures before our skin? Two assumptions are required to warrant a negative answer.

The first is an assumption about sense perception and its mechanisms, and is clearly reasonable: that if we perceive the pressure, say, of air in a container one of whose walls is replaced by one of our hands, if we perceive this pressure, when attentive to it, through the mechanism of becoming more directly conscious of a sensuous, subjective representation of this pressure, being only indirectly conscious of the pressure of the air, then it is so improbable as not to be credible that we should perceive the pressure of, say, a rock in our hand through so different a mechanism as an unmediated, direct awareness of this pressure. If we can only indirectly feel air pressing against our hand then surely the same will be true of a rock pressing against our hand.

The second assumption I need to make, however, cannot be allowed without the support of physical evidence. Since what we most directly feel among the things before the organs of touch is not the pressure exerted at the surface of our body but the stress within our flesh, the very strong resemblance there is between this force within our flesh and the pressure exerted by a *solid* upon the skin cannot be assumed to extend to the pressure exerted by a *gas* (such as air) upon our skin. Yet this assumption is necessary if the argument for indirect realism from the nature of the air pressure we feel *on* our skin is to be presumed applicable to the stress we more directly feel *within* our flesh. For we might feel both air pressure and solid pressure *at* our skin indirectly while feeling stress *within* our flesh directly.

Either, then, I cannot adopt the suggested simplification—examining the microreduction of pressure of gases and constructing the argument for indirect realism from it—or I must adduce the needed physical evidence that the microreduction of internal stress on the flesh would yield a result amenable to the same argument.

I shall make the simplification, first conduct the argument in connection with gas pressure, and then afterwards bring forward evidence to show that the argument works also for the stress within our flesh.

A succinct, lucid and popular statement of the molecular theory of the pressure of a gas, by the physicist, James Clerk Maxwell, will serve our purpose well enough:

Now the recent progress of molecular science began with the study of the mechanical effect of the impact of these moving molecules when they strike against any solid body. Of course these flying molecules must beat against whatever is placed among them, and the constant succession of these strokes is, according to our theory, the sole cause of what is called the pressure of air and other gases. . . .

We all know that air or any other gas placed in a vessel presses against the sides of the vessel, and against the surface of any body placed within it. On the kinetic theory this pressure is entirely due to the molecules striking against these surfaces, and thereby communicating to them a series of impulses which follow each other in such rapid succession that they produce an effect which cannot be distinguished from that of a continuous pressure.

If the velocity of the molecules is given, and the number varied, then since each molecule, on an average, strikes the sides of the vessel the same number of times, and with an impulse of the same magnitude, each will contribute an equal share to the whole pressure. The pressure in a vessel of given size is therefore proportional to the number of molecules in it, that is to the quantity of gas in it.

This is the complete dynamical explanation of the fact, discovered by Robert Boyle, that the pressure of air is proportional to its density. It shows also that of different portions of gas forced into a vessel, each produces its own part of the pressure independently of the rest, and this whether these portions be of the same gas or not.[1]

In the first paragraph Maxwell treats the "constant succession of these strokes" of the molecules against the walls as "the sole cause of what is called the pressure of the air." That the strokes are treated as one thing, the pressure another, offers us no difficulty. The same thought is expressed in the second paragraph when he writes that "this pressure is entirely due to the molecules striking against these surfaces." But when he adds to this last, "and thereby communicating to them a series of impulses which . . . produce an effect . . . of a continuous pressure," one might read this as saying the impulses communicated to the walls cause the pressure, suggesting a distinction between these impulses and the pressure. But surely this reading is unnecessary;

1. *Scientific Papers of James Clerk Maxwell,* vol. II (New York: Dover, 1965), pp. 364–5.

the natural interpretation is that the whole pressure is caused by the "strokes" of the molecules, and is an additive result of all the small impulses: the total force exerted by the gas upon the walls of its container *is* the aggregate of the small forces exerted by each molecule of the gas; and "pressure" on the walls is what we call the quotient of this whole force by the area of the walls: the force per unit area of wall surface exerted by the whole aggregate of molecules. By its blows upon the walls, each molecule of gas "produces its own part of the pressure independently of the rest," and, when the molecules are all of the same kind, hence of the same mass, "each will contribute an equal share to the whole pressure."

The indirect realist finds that this account of pressure supports his argument, already sketched: there is in fact no continuous, mechanical force actually acting upon our flesh when air presses upon it. There is only a multitude of forces which are too minute, individually, to discriminate by touch: this aggregation of forces is nothing but one molecular force, and a second molecular force, and a third molecular force, and so on, through the list of the singly imperceptible, molecular forces that compose the aggregation. Therefore the only way tactually to be *directly* conscious of this aggregation of molecular forces is to feel the action of each molecular force composing the aggregation: there is nothing else *there* to be directly aware of. Since we cannot perceive by touch the action of any one of these molecular forces, the indirect realist concludes that it is impossible for us tactually to become directly aware of every one of them, i.e., of the aggregation of these forces which constitutes the pressure we feel upon our flesh. Since, when attentive, we do become tactually conscious of this pressure, it must be that we do so in virture of becoming more directly conscious of some representation of the pressure. This representation of the aggregate of molecular forces must, furthermore, be "behind" the sense organs (and our awareness of it therefore absolutely direct), since the only candidate for direct object of tactual perception that is *before* these organs is the action on the skin of each molecule of gas.

No mention is made in this argument of tactual misperception. However, one *might* think of this argument for indirect realism as containing, as a crucial premise of fact—as a presupposition of the explicit premises—the following contention: since there is in fact no continuous pressure before our skin, in seeming tactually to perceive a continuous, mechanical force acting upon us we are misperceiving the forces acting upon us. While reserving judgment upon the question, whether or not the argument is committed to this contention, let us, for now, allow the direct realist to make this interpretation of the indirect realist's argument.

In responding to the indirect realist's argument, the direct realist may undertake to defend the veridical character of our tactual perception by defending the thesis that there are real, continuous, macroscopic, tactually discriminable, mechanical forces acting on the skin. Let us consider his defense of this position.

4. Direct Realism's First Defense of Macroscopic Mechanics, and Criticism of It

The direct realist will want to direct attention to the following sentence of Maxwell's: "On the kinetic theory this pressure is entirely due to the molecules striking against these surfaces, and thereby communicating to them a series of impulses which follow each other in such rapid succession that *they produce an effect which cannot be distinguished from that of a continuous pressure*" (my italics). Assuming that the aggregate of these impulses communicated to the container walls *is* the force whose quantity per unit area *is* the pressure, Maxwell is saying that the effect of this multitude of forces transmitted to the surfaces by individual molecules is indistinguishable from the effect of a single, large force exerted continuously in space and time over these surfaces.

The direct realist argues that, since the effect of the molecular forces is indistinguishable from the effect of a single, continuous force, tactual sense perception cannot judiciously be charged with error when it perceives pressure as a continuous force. Let us look more closely at this argument.

The direct realist's first point is that Maxwell's statement is not limited to effects upon observation. Maxwell is saying that a surface responding to the action of such an aggregate of molecular forces behaves in all respects in the same way that surface would behave were it being affected by a single, continuous force acting over its entire surface. This is a fact about the physical world, not a fact only about our observation of that world. If we imagine that the surface affected by the pressure of the gas is our skin (and the gas is air), then Maxwell is saying that our skin cannot in any way respond to this force differently than it would respond to a force of equal magnitude exercised by a continuous, material medium acting continuously in time (and space) upon our skin. For the skin, says the direct realist, the pressure of the air might as well be a continuously acting force. The same could be said of a piece of paper or a piece of tin. If, the direct realist continues, the force from the air acts upon a physical surface as if it were a continuous force, then, since a force is what it behaves like, in this context the force *is* a continuous force.

Now suppose that we imagine substituting for the skin as a surface our tactual perception of the pressure of the air; surely if this perception finds the pressure to be a continuous force, we cannot accuse it of misrepresenting the force. For we recognize that our tactual perception is "responding" to the pressure in the same way a physical surface does, in the sense that for each, as we might say, the pressure "presents itself" as a continuous action of a force. No one would say that the skin or the surface of a balloon misrepresents the pressure of the air upon it, in responding to it as continuous. Neither, concludes the direct realist, do we, in perceiving the pressure as continuous.

This rebuttal of the earlier argument of the indirect realist is unsatisfactory. Maxwell never meant to say that no matter what scale of measurement we imagine operative, no distinction can be made between the effects upon a container wall of a collection of molecules striking it and a continuous force acting upon it. Surely if we take our units of both space and time small enough, then we shall find small enough moments at which in a given, small enough region of the wall surface *no* force is acting upon the surface, because no molecule is striking there, and this bit of the wall in this moment of time is, consequently, behaving quite differently from the way it will be found to behave when a molecule is striking it at another (sufficiently small) moment later (when the pressure on the wall as a whole, however, is exactly the same) —and it will be behaving quite differently from the way a second, very small bit of the surface is at the same moment behaving nearby, because a molecule is striking this very small region when none is striking the first, small region. But none of this could be said about the behavior of the container wall in response to the action upon it of a continuous force: it would then behave in exactly the same way at any moment, no matter how small, and in every bit of its surface, no matter how small the area selected, throughout the period of time in which the macroscopic pressure remained exactly the same.

Consider the direct realist's appeal to the fact that when a physical surface behaves as a whole as if the gas pressure exerted upon it is continuous, we should not say such a surface misrepresents the force acting upon it. Of course we should not ordinarily say that such surfaces are engaged in representing or misrepresenting anything. To think of them this way is to think of them as functioning as measuring or sensing devices. So let us follow up this idea. Once we do so, we realize that such devices will have limitations analogous to the limitations in resolving power of lenses, or that they can be thought of as measuring devices which may be calibrated so as to draw, in effect, a map to a scale that leaves out a great deal of what is present in the mapped material.

Suppose we make an aerial photograph of a city block, from a considerable height above the city, and suppose the resolving power of our camera from this distance is such that houses separated by ten feet or less of grassy space are depicted in the picture as adjacent to one another. Now we could argue, following the direct realist's logic, that a certain row of houses reflects light to the film of the camera so as to affect the film in the same way a row of houses with no grass between them would do it, at least in this respect: it presents itself to the film as if it were a continuous row of houses with no intervening, grassy spaces separating them. Since, one might argue, a row of houses *is*, in a given context, what it behaves like in this context, the row of houses in question is a continuous row, with no grassy spaces between houses. However, when we descend to the ground we find ten feet of grassy space between each pair of houses, and children playing jumprope and handball on the grass. Of course the direct realist might reply that in this context the houses behave as if they make up a discontinuous row, with grassy space between each house. But surely this is nonsense. The aerial camera simply misrepresented the row of houses—although of course it got the number of houses, and which house is next to which, right.

So, too, the surface that, as a whole, responds to the molecules striking it as if it were being acted upon by a continuous force, and so, as a whole, "represents" this force as continuous, misrepresents, in this respect, the force acting upon it, which is actually a large set of very small forces acting discontinuously in space and time. Any device for measuring the pressure on the surface of a gas container will need to be responsive to a sufficiently large area of the wall for its response to be representative of the quotient of the total force acting on the surface divided by the total area. If we used a measuring device sensitive enough to detect forces acting upon areas of the surface of molecular size, we should get very different results: at a given moment some device would register no pressure at all, while others would register a much greater pressure than the macroscopic figure, since in some places no molecule would be striking, while in others a molecule would be striking over the entire (very small) area being measured. This discontinuous picture of the operation of the gas upon the container walls surely tells us how this force is actually acting; the continuous force is a kind of convenient fiction.

For the direct realist to argue as he has done is rather as if someone were to say that the demographer's report that the average population of a given region is 100 people per square mile implies that 100 persons actually live in every square mile. But if the region includes a city and an unpopulated area, then in some mile-square regions no people can be found. Yet the total population divided by the total area does come out exactly 100 —this figure for the average population is correct, and it is useful for some purposes; but the concept of the average population is also a kind of fiction, since the way the people are actually spread out within this area is not accurately represented by the concept, "100 people per square mile"; indeed if the figure 100 is taken as representing the actual distribution of people in the area, it is a misrepresentation. Just so, if the concept of the pressure of a gas on a container wall, construed as the force per unit area (however small the unit), is taken as a quantitative representation of the actual mode of action of this force over every unit area (no matter how small) of the container wall, then this concept of pressure will misrepresent the action of the force exerted by the molecules of the gas.

5. Direct Realism's Second Defense of Macroscopic Mechanics

Now I must provide a somewhat subtler development of the defense of direct realism. This defense has been based upon the way in which what we seem most directly to feel by touch coincides with what the physicist says is actually before our skin and operating upon it so as to cause us to feel its presence: we feel pressure as it is, says the direct realist. The direct realist admits that when, say, one's hand replaces a portion of the wall of a container of air under high pressure, we feel the force exerted upon our hand to be continuously exerted. Now, however, he proposes a different defense of tactual accuracy.

The direct realist now argues that the macroscopic physicist's concept of pressure is in fact a concept of a kind of "continuous force," since when the total force upon a region of surface is divided by the area of the surface, the dimensions used may be as small as you like; even molecule-sized units of measurement could be used for stating the force per unit area which constitutes the pressure the gas exerts both upon the container wall and one's hand: for the concept of the average force exerted per unit area remains valid no matter how small a unit of area is used for stating it. (The demographer's report could be stated quite as accurately as 1/100th of a person per 1/10,000th of a square mile.) Therefore, the direct realist now argues, that we feel the pressure to be in some way continuous does not entail that we feel it to be something different from what the macroscopic physicist conceives it to be.

Now, he continues, you surely cannot argue that the macroscopic physicist must be misrepresenting the reality when he employs the concept of pressure to describe the action of the gas upon the container wall. You admit that his statement of the pressure can in principle be accurate—how could you deny this, since all this requires is that the total force on the wall be accurately measured, the area of the wall be accurately measured, and the quotient of these two figures be accurately taken? As long as the physicist does not misuse the concept of pressure, he cannot be said to be misrepresenting the reality. But, concludes the direct realist, we have no reason for supposing that in our capacity as tactual perceivers of pressure we misuse some tactual representation of pressure. Indeed we scarcely need to speak of "tactual representation" of pressure. We simply become tactually aware of the pressure. The pressure, you have to admit, is a physical reality (even if not the whole physical reality) of the situation. So we have every reason to ascribe to our sense of touch, when attentively exercised, an awareness of a genuine physical reality; hence no ground can be found, in systematic tactual misrepresentation, for appealing to the analysis offered by the indirect realist. Pressure is directly felt as it is.

This argument forces me to a more careful consideration of the reasoning offered earlier in support of indirect realism.

I agree that there need be no misrepresentation of physical reality in taking seriously the idea of average force over a surface, parts of which have no force on them; nor need there be misrepresentation of demographic reality in taking seriously the idea of average population over a partially unpopulated area.

The direct realist is, therefore, justified in cautioning me about speaking of the concept of pressure as a kind of "fiction."

We need now to ask ourselves what it is in our tactual perception of a gas under pressure that justifies us in describing the object of our perception as "the pressure" of the gas, remembering that the pressure of the gas on our skin is the force per unit area exerted on our skin.

The justification for our describing the object of tactual feeling as pressure is that we feel a force always as acting over a particular area of our body. We do not feel a force as not acting on anything in particular, or feel it in independence of what it is acting upon. We feel it to be acting across a definite area, hence our perception of any total, mechanical force acting upon our skin always comprises the perception of a number of adjacent areas of skin over each of which we feel a given quantity of force to be acting. This means that over each of the smallest, perceptible areas of our skin we feel a given quantity of force to be acting, and, where the force is evenly distributed over our skin, the quantity of force we feel to be acting over each smallest, perceptible area of our skin is doubtless roughly the same quantity (ignoring any tactual errors we may make) .

Each unit of mechanical force that we feel, we might then say, we feel as acting upon a unit (perceptible) area of our skin. For tactual perception the force and the area over which its acts compose an indissoluble whole; we cannot perceive the first without perceiving the second. This is the fact about the sense of touch which justifies our thinking of it as regularly achieving the perception of force per unit area, or pressure.

Our present question has, then, to be this: Is the content of this tactual perception of force acting on a surface such as to misrepresent the reality, or is it, as the sophisticated use of the concept of pressure is for the macrophysicist, innocent of all misrepresentation?

What makes the physicist's use thus innocent? The same sort of thing that makes innocent the demographer's use of the concept of average population per square mile: he must not suppose that every bit of surface at every moment has acting upon it a force equal to the pressure (or even any force at all) , just as the demographer must not suppose that each square mile has 100 people in it, or even a single person in it, when a region's average population is 100 persons per square mile. So, too, then, our tactual perception can be acquitted of misrepresentation only if it does not take every bit of surface of skin at every moment to be suffering the action upon it of a force equal to the pressure (or even any force at all). Do we, as tactual perceivers, deserve acquittal or conviction on this charge?

If as tactual perceivers we can discriminate only areas of our skin large relative to molecular dimensions and if it is only such areas that we perceive to have acting over them a force equal to the pressure, then we are not, it would seem, guilty of misrepresentation. For the mistake arises only when one either explicitly takes areas of the skin of roughly molecular dimensions to have such a force exerted upon each of them, or makes a perceptual generalization as to all areas, without exception as to size, undergoing action from such a force. As long as the units of area are large enough to be representative of the average force—and the units of time are large relative to the time a molecule takes to strike the skin—no mistake need be involved in tactually taking the force acting over such an area (and time) to be the quantity represented by the macroscopic pressure.

But surely, argues the direct realist, in feeling pressure we neither engage in a generalization about all the regions of our skin, regardless of how small, nor explicitly take something to be true of regions of our skin too small for us tactually to discriminate. For to say these regions of the skin are too small for us tactually to discriminate is to say that we have no tactual awareness of them, hence that we presume nothing whatever about them insofar as we are at a moment merely feeling a pressure or stress. Judging from the results of psychophysical studies of tactual acuity of perception, it seems safe to suppose that we do not discriminate areas in the skin of molecular dimensions. Similar consideration of temporal dimensions would deny us the power to discriminate temporal intervals as short as those occupied by single molecules of a gas in striking the skin. So it appears that we are not capable of the kind of tactual misrepresentation here at issue. And once again the case for direct realism in regard to the sense of touch is strengthened.

6. Argument for Indirect Realism (I) : From the Mathematical Character of a Sum of Molecular Forces

The defense of direct realism just examined suggests that it is a mistake for the indirect realist to insist upon the idea that tactual perception of pressure as if of a continuous force constitutes misperception. But let us remind ourselves that this idea is in fact an interpretation by the direct realist of the indirect realist's argument. Nowhere in the argument itself, as sketched both at the opening and at the end of section 3, did the indirect realist explicitly speak of our misperceiving pressure, nor did he in any explicit way appeal to such an alleged misperception under another description. This reminder can serve to bring us back to the question that provides the point of focus of the original argument, as sketched for the indirect realist: How is it possible for a person to become tactually conscious of the total, mechanical force acting upon a given area of his skin, when this force is exerted by a gas such as air?

Relative to the areas of impact of the individual molecules of air upon his skin, the smallest areas over which a person feels the total force acting is large. If we grant that a perceiver is tactually conscious of the pressure on his skin, we must hold, as we have already observed, that he is tactually conscious of the total force acting upon certain areas of his skin, and we are now considering one such area. How is it possible for him to be tactually conscious of the total force acting there, when he cannot discriminate the action of any one of the molecular forces acting within this area? My contention is that this is possible only through his becoming directly conscious of a tactual *representation* of the total force; tactually to become *directly* conscious of the action of this total force upon an area of the skin, when one cannot perceive the individual molecular forces, is impossible.

In the science of mechanics, of course, the total force is the (what I shall for simplicity's sake speak of as *arithmetical*) sum of the individual molecular forces. Now we need to remind ourselves that the sum of the molecular forces acting on a given area is not the same thing as all the molecular forces acting on this area. If, say, there were 26 molecules striking the given area, then to speak of all the molecular forces acting on this area would be nothing more than to say that molecular force A and molecular force B and molecular force C and . . . molecular force Z are acting on this area, and no others. But to say this, alone, is not yet to have specified the *sum* of these forces. To do this one has to assign a number to $A, B, C, \ldots, Z$, representing the quantity of each force, and arithmetically add these numbers. The result is the sum of the forces. And it is this that the physicists define as the total force acting on the given area.

It is not plausible that feeling pressure on our skin presupposes mathematical training. But let us for the moment suppose that we possess some tactual mechanism capable of performing arithmetical summing operations upon molecular forces we cannot individually perceive. Then we are supposing that what most directly holds our tactual attention is the sum of the individual molecular forces' quantities. In this event, that our tactual attention can be directly held only by a representation of this sum suggests itself from consideration of the nature of a sum. If we assume for ourselves unlimited acuity of tactual perception, unlimited power of discriminating the very small, then there is nothing in the nature of a single molecule striking our skin with a certain intensity that forces us to suppose we could feel this intensity only by giving our attention to a representation of it. And if we imagine ourselves having the power of noticing a great many particulars at once, nothing in the nature of all the intensities of impact of all of the molecules entails that we could not feel them all, each individually and hence all of them, without giving our attention more directly to a representation of them.

However, if we now consider that not only is each molecule striking with a certain intensity, not only are all of them striking, each with its intensity, but it is also the case that all these intensities have an arithmetical sum, then we have described something whose nature does seem to suggest to us that we could perceive it only through giving our attention directly to a representation of it. For that these quantities of force have a sum, and that this sum is S, is an arithmetical fact about these molecular forces; i.e., it is a fact about the result of performing certain arithmetical operations upon the several numbers that give the quantities of the several molecular forces. And it is not easy to imagine, straight off, any way in which a person can apprehend the result of an arithmetical operation upon numbers except through giving his attention to a representation of this result, ordinarily to a representation of a number, as, for example, in saying to oneself, or writing down, or looking at the numeral '26', and thereby thinking that the sum is 26.

It seems, therefore, probable that if, as is unlikely, we did subconsciously perform arithmetical summing operations, in perceiving the total force acting upon a given area of our skin, then our tactual attention would be most directly held by some form of representation of the result of this summing operation. But since, on our present hypothesis, there is nothing else before the skin which we perceive more directly than the total force acting on a given area of skin, this representation of the sum of molecular forces would need to be "behind" the skin. And direct realism would be false. (It will be remembered that, for simplicity's sake, we are for the moment supposing that nothing essential would change in our argument if we were conducting it with regard to the stress within our skin instead of the gas pressure upon its surface.) Consider, now, this simple argument, in rebuttal. Suppose an array of three, easily visible, black dots on a white sheet of paper. Almost anyone can see how many dots there are without doing any arithmetical operation, not even counting. There is nothing in the nature of what we here imagine someone seeing that forces us to suppose that the perceiver can give his attention directly only to some representation of the number of dots. Yet the number of dots is the sum of the dots. So your argument fails.

One answer is that perceiving the number of dots in an array is not the same as perceiving a sum. An array of dots has a number. It does not have a sum. A sum can be formed, or got, by taking the number of dots that each single dot is (i.e., 1), and adding these numbers together. A sum must be a sum of numbers and therefore presupposes a mathematical operation in its generation. A number is a number of items of any kind, not ordinarily numbers, and presupposes no mathematical operation for its existence.

To my contention that a sum can be got only by adding numbers my opponent might reply that if, side by side, two arrays of three visible dots were arranged, one might *see* that the sum of these two arrays of dots is six, without either counting or adding. Surely one correct way to "add two arrays of dots" is to place the one array beside the other, count first the dots in one array, then continue to count by going on to the dots in the second array. The number you arrive at is the sum, and if you perform this operation, surely you are correctly perceiving the sum of two arrays of dots, when you finish the count, or anyhow you may be doing so. But if this is so, then why may not a person simply see that there are three dots in the first array, and then see that when the new array is joined with the first there are six dots, but all this without ever counting the dots? And why should this not qualify as seeing the sum of the two arrays of dots?

These considerations do, I think, render my original argument inconclusive. In relying merely upon the idea of perceiving a sum I left myself open to a counterexample in which the elements to be counted were each individually perceptible (to vision). However, in feeling the pressure of the air upon the flesh, we cannot achieve awareness of the individual forces the sum of whose numerical measures is the measure of the total force acting upon a given area. So let us return to a consideration of this fact, and now ask this question: How is it possible to become tactually conscious of this sum when we cannot perceive the action of the individual forces whose sum is wanted?

Now I contend that the only way we might give our tactual attention to the sum of the forces without attending more directly to a representation of the forces is by becoming tactually conscious of the action of each one of the individual forces with such distinctness that—as with the dots—we are able to become tactually conscious of their sum, as it were, *in* the perceptible plurality of these forces' actions. But we cannot become tactually aware of the action of any one of these molecular forces, let alone of each one of them. There is, therefore, no way in which we can directly perceive the "array" of molecular forces' actions, so as to occupy a position from which directly to perceive "in" this array the sum of these forces. Lacking the power to feel the individual quantities whose sum is needed, we have no way to perceive this sum in virtue of directly perceiving the discrete quantities that add up to it, as we conceivably could do in *seeing* arrays of a few individually visible dots. Since we cannot feel the individual, discrete quantities whose sum is needed, we surely require, for the focusing of our tactual attention and, hence, as the direct object of our tactual awareness, some stand-in, a representation either of each individual quantity or of the sum itself of these quantities.

But we know that we not only do not feel the individual, molecular forces' actions, we do not become tactually conscious of discrete representations of each one of these molecular forces. It must be, then, that if we do become tactually conscious of the sums of these discrete forces acting upon given areas of our skin, then we do so through becoming directly conscious of tactual representations of the sums themselves.

But now I need to stop and ask whether further consideration of the idea of our "feeling sums of forces" is worth while.

7. Argument for Indirect Realism (II) : From the Nature of a Totality of Molecular Forces

It will be recalled that the reason why I have made so much effort to understand how one could tactually perceive a sum of molecular forces acting upon a given area of one's skin is this: I assume that we do become tactually aware of the pressure upon our skin; the pressure is the total force divided by the total area over which it acts; the total force is, according to mechanics, the sum of the molecular forces acting upon the skin; so if we are to become tactually conscious of the pressure we must become tactually conscious of the sum of the molecular forces acting over a given area of our skin.

But now I can allow myself the reflection, having argued that we can feel this sum only by becoming directly aware of a tactual representation of it, that it does not appear to us, upon introspection, that what we are conscious of in feeling pressure upon our skin can be a sum. What holds our tactual attention when we feel the objects around us press upon us does not appear to have a sufficiently mathematical or analytical character to answer to this description. Is there an alternative?

I think we may plausibly surmise that what we become directly conscious of in feeling, with attention, the pressure upon our skin is a representation of a putative *totality* of force which is not a sum of forces, yet which somehow roughly answers, in its tactually represented magnitude, to the sum of molecular forces acting on the area over which we tactually represent this totality of force to be acting. What we become directly aware of in feeling things pressing against us is a nonnumerical representation of a purported, unitary totality of force on a given area, a force which, as tactually represented, somehow answers to the sum of molecular forces actually acting on the area.

With this revision in its conclusion, will something similar to my latest argument cogently yield the new conclusion that direct, tactual awareness is possible only of a representation of the total force on a given area of the skin? I think it will.

It is now required that we in some way tactually perceive a totality of molecular forces on an area of skin, but not through perceiving the sum of these forces. Let me try to understand how it would be possible for us to become tactually conscious of the totality (but not the sum) of molecular forces acting upon an area of our skin without giving our attention directly to a representation of this totality—that is, without being directly conscious of some stand-in for this totality.

If our attention to this totality is not to be mediated by attention to some stand-in for the totality, then it is this totality of molecular forces itself of which we must become directly conscious. A stand-in could afford to symbolize the totality in shorthand, and distortedly, yet still represent it. But if we have nothing of this mediating sort to be directly conscious of, then we must become directly conscious of the totality itself. This totality of molecular forces acting upon an area of skin *is* nothing but a plurality of discontinuously acting, individual, molecular forces. The totality of these forces is nothing more than each one of the molecular forces acting individually upon a minute region of the skin, together with the spatial and temporal relationships of these discrete actions. Barring a mediating stand-in for this totality, therefore, there is nothing for us to be tactually aware of in the way of a totality of molecular forces except "each and every one" of these molecular forces: we should have to feel the action of all of these molecular forces by feeling the action of each of them, for this is all there is in the way of a totality of forces acting there. However, we cannot feel the action of any one of the individual molecular forces acting upon a minute area of our skin; hence we cannot become tactually aware of the action of each one of them. Therefore it is impossible for us tactually to become *directly* aware of the only totality which the actions of these molecular forces constitute.

If nonetheless we are to become tactually conscious of a purported "totality of force" upon a given area of our skin (large relative to molecular dimensions), a "totality" that does have a certain kind of objective reality, as the pressure (involving the sum of forces) has, then this can be only by becoming directly conscious either of a representation of the sum of molecular forces, the alternative I now wish to reject, or by tactually becoming directly conscious of a representation of a putative, total force acting upon a given area, where this nonmathematical "totality" so represented answers, in at least a rough way, to the mathematical sum of molecular forces, as this sum is calculated in mechanics. Since we feel pressure, it is clear that we *are* tactually conscious of a totality of force acting upon an area of our skin. I conclude that tactually we are only *in*directly aware of this totality (in fact an aggregation) of forces and that we are directly aware of some tactual representation of a totality of forces acting upon our skin.

This concludes the first, crucial stage of my argument for indirect realism with respect to the sense of touch.

However, the reader should be cautioned that we are not yet in a position to conclude that one is directly aware of a representation which is *not* located before the receptor organs within the skin and is, therefore, "behind" these organs. For there is another candidate for direct object of tactual awareness which is located before the receptor organs within the flesh, to wit, the stress within the flesh itself. Since, so far as our argument yet takes us, this stress *within* the flesh might constitute a directly felt representation of a totality of forces acting *on* the skin, I cannot yet conclude that the representation of which we are directly aware is not before the sense organs. I shall go on to argue for this conclusion in the next section. Before we turn to this task a few more words should be said about the tactual representation of a totality of force.

Exactly how the "totality of force," as specified by our tactual representation of it, manages to answer to the sum of molecular forces is a problem the detailed solution to which does not easily offer itself. However, a hint as to the solution may be found in the fact that various sorts of nonnumerical representation of quantities may "answer to" a numerical representation of these quantities. For example, the position of a pointer on a gauge may represent half a tank of gasoline, or 10 gallons of gasoline in the tank: here a spatial configuration represents a quantity which in turn answers to a precise concept of a fraction of a certain quantity, i.e., a quotient, or to a precise concept of a definite number of units of some substance. Of course—and this extends the hint—the spatial configuration (the position of the pointer on the gauge) achieves this result only because of the way in which this configuration is used by us.

Following up this hint, we may surmise that the role in guiding our behavior which is played by our tactual representation of a single "totality of force" may endow this representation with the power of specifying a quantity which is roughly equivalent, for the *practical* purposes served by the sense of touch, to the sum of the forces acting upon the same area. (Even the mathematical sum itself gets its power of representing a physical reality from the use to which it is put within applied mechanics.)

A general way of understanding how the role in guiding our behavior played by our tactual representation of a total force on an area of skin can make the force so represented answer to the sum of molecular forces is the following: if the behavior we spontaneously adopt on the basis of this tactual representation, for the purpose of dealing in practical ways with the pressure represented as acting upon the skin from without, is roughly the same behavior we would adopt as a result of making rational calculations based upon instrumental measurements of the pressure on our flesh, then the force as tactually perceived roughly answers to the mathematical sum of the molecular forces. Since the antecedent of the foregoing hypothetical proposition seems probably true, we may accept the consequent.

8. Argument for Indirect Realism (III) : From the
Sub-atomic Microreduction of Stress in Solids

I have argued that what we are tactually more directly conscious of than the air pressure on our skin is a representation of
this pressure. If it is sound, however, this argument does not yet
establish that this representation cannot be some physical state
of affairs before our sense organs. The argument could do this
only if pressure before our skin were what we feel most directly
among the things before our tactual sense organs. But I earlier
concluded that pressure before our skin does not occupy this
role; the stress within our flesh does. Therefore, so far as our
argument carries us, stress within our flesh could be what serves
for us as a directly perceived representation of the pressure acting from without upon our skin. Stress within our flesh is so
similar a physical force to the pressure one solid exerts upon
another when pushed against it that the argument I have used
could have been extended to stress within the flesh, *had* I constructed the argument in terms of a solid object pressing against
our skin.

However, I did not do this. I used a gas, air, and I did so because the discontinuous nature of the aggregate of very small
forces constituting the macroscopic pressure is so evident for
gases and because my argument relies upon this discontinuity.
For this reason, I need to satisfy myself that the argument can
be extended to stress within a solid object, such as our flesh is,
with the upshot that stress in our flesh too can be (attentively)
felt only through the mediation of a more direct awareness of
some representation of this stress. *Such* a representation could
not be before the sense organs of touch, since there is nothing
before those organs which we feel more directly than the stress
within our flesh. So if the stress within our flesh cannot be
directly felt, *in*direct realism will be true of the sense of touch.

To show that the argument against the possibility of direct,
tactual awareness of air pressure on our skin can be extended to
stress—specifically to tension and compression—within our flesh,
I need to show that there is an aggregation of tactually imperceptible, small forces that constitutes this macroscopic tension
or compression, and that this aggregation is at least as discontinuous as the one that constitutes the pressure of a gas such
as air.

Because there are no differences that could matter to us between the various forms of stress solid substances undergo, it

will be convenient to limit our discussion to tension and compression. Stress, like pressure, is defined as the force acting over a unit area of some substance. Whereas pressure on a solid is the force acting upon a unit area of the solid's surface, stress is the force acting on a unit area of an interior plane of the solid. Roughly speaking, tension is the interior force generated when a solid is stretched, compression the interior force resulting from the solid being pressed in, from without. If we think of a cubically shaped solid, the simplest tension will result from pulling outward on two opposed surfaces, the simplest compression from pushing in on two opposed surfaces. When an object is stretched, it expands along the directions of pull; when it is pushed in, it contracts in the directions of push. The stretched object will also get somewhat narrower, the compressed object somewhat fatter, but these deformations I shall ignore, for simplicity's sake, since no different physical principles enter into their analysis. The change in length, per unit of original length (the change in length divided by the original total length), which a solid undergoes as a function of the stress on it is called the "strain." For tension, the strain is a stretching, a lengthening; for compression the strain is a contracting, a shortening. Hook's law states that the strain is proportionate to the stress; this law holds within a substance's elastic limits, that is to say, for those deformations which are undone when the stress is removed, the solid returning to its normal shape and size.

Let us suppose that a solid is composed of molecules whose electron shells do not overlap and that no mechanical force is applied to its external surface (ignoring the atmospheric pressure). Imagine for the moment that the molecules are arranged in some regular way, and consider an area of a plane between arrays of molecules. At this plane there will be an attractive force between the molecules which is exactly balanced by a repulsive force between them, so that the arrays of molecules on opposite sides of the plane are in equilibrium. If a small compressive force is applied to the outside of this solid, so that it acts perpendicularly to the interior plane, the molecules will be pushed a little closer together—but let us suppose intermolecular distances remain great enough to avoid overlap of electron shells. This will cause an increase in the repulsive force between the opposed arrays of molecules facing each other across the plane, and a new equilibrium, now a stress, will be reached. The compressive forces acting on the interior plane are the same sorts of forces as those that were acting before the compression was induced by the external pressure. To understand the compressive force, therefore, is to understand the attractive and repulsive forces which keep the molecular arrays in equilibrium within the solid. In the situation imagined, an induced compression simply rearranges the equilibrium among the intermolecular binding forces. The same story would be told for a tensile force, except that now the molecules would be separated a little, and a compensating increase in the attractive forces between them would arise.

Now let the solid we are considering be, say, a portion of the skin on the back of a person's wrist. Barely tap this skin with the eraser on the end of a pencil. A slight deformation of the skin is caused for a moment, and a slight compression of the skin is caused beneath the eraser. The brief, slight inward pressure on the skin induces a brief, slight stress in the portion of skin beneath the eraser. What is the source of this stress?

More than half the skin is water. So we are not, after all, dealing with a simple solid. With a slight pressure, of the sort imagined, impressed upon the skin, water is displaced: a hydraulic pressure, in effect, has been induced in the water; the molecules of the water have been pushed a little closer together. Most of the rest of the skin is protein macromolecules, which are also pushed slightly closer together; they may also be bent or unbent slightly. The induced stress consists primarily in rearranging the balance of intermolecular forces. These forces consist in electrostatic attractions and repulsions arising from the electrons and protons of the atoms making up the molecules. The repulsions are Coulomb forces between electrons and electrons or between protons and protons. The attractions are Coulomb forces between protons and electrons. On the assumption that so slight a pressure on the skin does not implicate interatomic bonds with overlapping electron shells, Pauli exclusions "forces" can be ignored. The induced compression consists of electrostatic forces of repulsion and attraction among electrons and protons. What is needed, then, is an explanation of these forces.

On page 248 of his *Introduction to Particle Physics*,[2] Roland Omnes writes:

> It is one of the basic consequences of field theory that the Coulomb attraction or repulsion between two charged particles can be attributed to the exchange of photons emitted by the one and absorbed by the other.

2. New York: John Wiley, 1971.

On page 198 of his *The World of Elementary Particles*,[3] Kenneth W. Ford, speaking here of electron-electron repulsion, writes,

> The old idea of action at a distance . . . is completely abandoned. It is replaced by the idea of a "local interaction," of each electron interacting locally—that is, at its own location—with a photon.

On pages 196/7 he generalizes:

> All of the interactions in nature arise from acts of annihilation and creation of particles at definite points in space and time. There are two important ideas here: First, all interactions involve the creation and annihilation of particles; second, these creations and annihilations do not take place over a region of space nor over a span of time, but are instantaneous and localized at points.

And a third book connects these small interactions with the macroscopic forces in which we are interested. On page 97 of *Elementary Particles*,[4] David H. Frisch and Alan M. Thorndike write:

> Thus the $1/r^2$ force between two protons at a distance r apart arises from the virtual photons emitted by one and absorbed by the other. The virtual photons emitted by the first one make contact with the proton that gives rise to them, and then they race across and make contact with the other proton. . . . The electric force between dissimilar charged particles, such as a proton and an electron, is described in just the same way, and the electric force between large-scale objects is just the sum of such interactions.

The small stress on our skin is, therefore, nothing but the sum of the interactions between photons, on the one hand, and electrons and protons on the other. The picture is analogous to the one earlier drawn of pressure on our skin by a gas, with photons, electrons and protons now taking the place of molecules. (Of course, in the last analysis the interaction between the gas molecules and our skin would also reduce to photon exchanges.)

3. New York: Blaisdell, 1963.

4. Princton: D. Van Nostrand, 1964.

In treating the so-called "virtual photons" as real particles I follow Mary Hesse who, on page 277 of her book *Forces and Fields*,[5] writes thus:

> . . . there is apparent short-term violation of conservation of energy by spontaneous emission and subsequent absorption of, for example, a photon, by the same or another source-particle . . . it will be impossible to detect a small energy unbalance, since energy and time are complementary variables in the sense of the uncertainty principle. Hence these exchanges are called *virtual* as opposed to *real* emissions of radiation, in conformity with the quantum mechanical convention that "reality" is ascribed only to . . . radiation which can produce observable effects on photographic plates, and so on. Also, no doubt, the word 'virtual' is meant to entail that these exchanges cannot 'really' take place because they violate conservation of energy, and this is 'impossible'. But it does not seem necessary to insist on this. If the uncertainty is correct and ultimate, we cannot know that energy is conserved in detail because in order to measure it accurately we need a correspondingly long time, and in dynamic process this may not be available. Its apparent conservation may be connected with the value of the constant h which sets a lower limit to observability.

I conclude that the macroscopic, tactually perceptible, yet very small stress on the skin, induced by a very light tap of a pencil eraser, is nothing but an aggregation of the spatiotemporally discontinuous actions of discrete, singly imperceptible, subatomic particles.

Therefore my earlier argument in §7 against the possibility of *direct* tactual awareness of aggregations of molecular actions, in the form of pressure of a gas, also works against direct tactual awareness of a very slight but perceptible stress in the skin. The interactions of molecules with the surface of the skin, in the original argument for gas, is replaced, in the new argument for stress on the skin, by the interactions of photons with electrons and protons.

I should remark that it is not clear that the argument would go through if one began with much heavier pressure on the skin, and a correspondingly larger stress within the skin. For at some point it is to be expected that an applied pressure begins to work

5. Totowa, N.J.: Littlefield Adams, 1965.

against interatomic bonds involving overlapping electron shells. When this happens attractive and repulsive "forces" which are not additive forces, not vectoral forces, and not an upshot of particle interactions, come into play. These are the so-called "exchange forces" ("exchange energies"), arising from the Pauli exclusion principle, which account not only for the binding energy of covalent bonds but for most of that of ionic bonds. However, the following considerations seem entirely reasonable.

On the one hand, we have the conclusion that it is impossible directly to perceive very slight but perceptible stresses in the skin. Therefore these stresses must be perceived indirectly, which means that we perceive them in virtue of becoming more directly aware of something else. But there is nothing else before the tactual sense organs which we (attentively) feel more directly than stress within the skin. Therefore in feeling a very slight stress in the skin we are directly aware of something not before the skin. Assuming that the argument of earlier chapters for moving from this weak form of indirect realism to the stronger form holds up for the sense of touch, I shall be able to conclude that we are directly aware of a sensuous quality belonging to tactual consciousness itself. It is clear that this conclusion entails the operation of a central-neurological mechanism of tactual perception which is quite different from the mechanism that would operate for direct tactual perception of the stress on the skin.

If it is now suggested that when a heavy pressure on the skin induces a large stress in the skin, direct tactual perception of this stress must be allowed, since the physical character of the stress does not rule it out, I offer this reply. It is not plausible that an entirely different central-neurological mechanism of perception should be brought into play when the transition is made from feeling a light pressure on the skin to feeling a very strong pressure on the skin. Since the mechanism for feeling a slight pressure *must* be the one needed to accommodate *direct* awareness of a "central state" (a sensuous quality of tactual consciousness), it is only reasonable to believe that the same mechanism will operate for perception of heavy pressures and, hence, that our tactual awareness of induced, strong stress in the skin is also *in*direct awareness. The same reasoning would yield the same conclusion for stresses that reach beneath the skin to the deeper flesh of our body surface.

I conclude that tactually we cannot become directly aware of the stresses our flesh sustains under pressure from objects at the surface of our body. Yet when tactually attentive we do become conscious of these stresses. Therefore tactually we always become more directly conscious of something that represents these stresses for us. But this representation cannot be something *before* our tactual sense organs, since nothing before these organs is more directly felt than stress within our flesh. Therefore this representation of stress in the flesh is *behind* our tactual sense organs; hence we are directly conscious of it, only indirectly aware of the stress in our flesh. Indirect realism is true of the sense of touch.

9. Recapitulation and Conclusion

Let me now briefly review the argument I have offered for the conclusion that always in attentively feeling something press upon our body from without we are directly conscious of a representation of the stress induced within our flesh by the pressing object and that this representation is located "behind" the receptor organs within our flesh. I shall then simply remind the reader of the sorts of consideration, so frequently adduced earlier in this book, that warrant us in going on to conclude that this representation behind our sense organs takes the form (in part) of a sensuous quality (or pattern of qualities) partially constituting our conscious state itself.

I first argued that the most directly perceived object before the organs of touch is stress within our own flesh. It follows that if this stress is not directly felt then the direct object of tactual awareness is not before the sense organs.

Because my argument for the conclusion that stress is not directly felt depends upon the microanalysis of stress and because this microanalysis is more difficult to grasp than the microanalysis of pressure by gases, I first carried through the argument under the fiction that the direct object of tactual perception is the pressure upon our skin of a gas such as air.

The argument against the possibility of becoming directly conscious of the pressure of air upon our skin (under the fiction that this pressure is the most direct object of tactual perception which is located before the skin) is, in brief, as follows. Pressure on the skin is totality of force exerted per unit area of skin. This totality of force is in fact nothing but an aggregate of the forces singly exerted by each molecule of the gas. There is nothing more that constitutes this totality of force upon an area of skin than something to be described in this way: the action of this single molecule's force and the action of that single molecule's force and the action of . . . , and so on, mentioning each molecule that hits the given area of the skin. Therefore if tactually we were directly conscious of this totality of force we should have nothing to be directly conscious of but of each molecular action singly; there *is* nothing else there, to be directly conscious of. However, we cannot tactually discriminate even one such single molecular action. Therefore we cannot tactually perceive each single molecular action. Therefore tactually we cannot become *directly* aware of the totality of forces acting upon a given area of our skin. However, we do become tactually aware of this pressure. Therefore it must be that tactually we become only indirectly conscious of this totality of force, through becoming directly conscious of some representation of this totality.

So far, this representation of which we are directly conscious may be *before* the receptor organs within the skin. For it was only a fiction that it is pressure on the skin that we most directly feel before these sense organs; in fact stress within our flesh has this place—it, therefore, might be the directly felt representation of pressure on the skin. To prove that it is not, we need only satisfy ourselves that a light stress on the skin is like pressure in a gas, in this way: the totality of stress acting upon an interior plane of the skin is nothing but an aggregation of tactually imperceptible, minute actions of minute particles composing the skin.

I argued in §8 that the nature of light stress is as just described. Consequently the argument against the possibility of our becoming directly conscious in a tactual way of pressure upon our skin becomes effective with respect to light stress within our flesh. Therefore we can be tactually aware of this stress only in virtue of being more directly aware of a representation of this stress. *This* representation, however, cannot be before the sense organs. For stress is the most directly felt object before the receptor organs within the flesh. Therefore this representation of light stress in our flesh, of which we are always directly aware, is not before the sense organs. I then argued that what holds for light stress should hold for heavy stress. Therefore, the weaker form of indirect realism is true for the sense of touch. Always in attentively feeling things outside us press upon us, we do so through becoming directly aware of a representation, *not* before our sense organs, of the stress induced within our flesh by the pressure of the external body upon our skin.

It remains to draw the conclusion that, if the representation (situated "behind" our organs of touch) of which we are most directly conscious, in feeling the mechanical forces that play upon us from the external world, were a merely conceptual representation, then we should not be feeling these forces but merely thinking of them and that, therefore, it must be an at least partly sensuous representation of these forces which most directly engages our tactual attention: a sensuous, tactual quality is instantiated within tactual consciousness where it represents itself, by the method of exemplification, as constituting at least in part the action of a force upon and within that portion of our flesh upon which an external body impinges.

This sensuous quality (or pattern of qualities) functions within our tactual consciousness as the sensuous content of a tactual *attribution* by us of the action of forces within and upon the surface of our body. What directly engages our tactual attention, then,—hence what we are directly conscious of—when our attention is indirectly given to the objects that press upon us from outside, is a sensuous, tactual quality, partially constituting our conscious state, and functioning as the sensuous content of our tactual attribution of action by forces upon and within our flesh.

No doubt this sensuous content of our tactual attribution of forces to regions of our body, the most direct object of our tactual awareness of bodies, is what is sometimes called "the feel" of bodies pressing upon our flesh.

And no doubt, too, where the property represented (action of a force) is so fully causal in its character, we may suppose that the conceptual component in our tactual representation of pressure and stress is indispensable, and perhaps more central than its conceptual analogues within the sensory representation of the peculiar and external perceptual objects of the other senses. Nonetheless, if the conceptual content of our tactual representation of pressure and stress were the whole of this content, then we should have only the thought of these forces; we should never feel them.

Chapter Eight   THE STRUCTURE
OF SENSORY
CONSCIOUSNESS

By the account I have given of sensory consciousness, our attention to public objects is held by their sensible qualities partly in virtue of being more directly held by sensuous qualities belonging to consciousness itself. Within consciousness sensuous qualities function as the contents of our attributions of them to public objects. Perceptual attribution, sensory attention, and an interior instance of a sensuous quality together constitute a complex state of consciousness whose indirect object is before the sense organs and whose direct object is the interior, sensuous, quality-instance.

1. Objection to an Interior Sensuous Object of Attention

It will seem to some philosophers an objection to my account that the direct object of sensory consciousness is internal to itself. They argue that being conscious of a thing in a sensory way—attending to it—puts us in a relationship with the thing; but talk of this relation becomes incoherent if what we are related to is included within the relating action, process, or state itself. For example, the argument continues, a person's kicking a football involves an action of his that grounds a relation between the person and something distinct from his action, a football. However, if we describe a person as kicking a kick we understand that no second term for the relation generated by the kicking action is specified by the term 'a kick'. To speak of the kick is merely to mention twice the kicking action itself, something we never do unless we mean to characterize further or emphasize or comment upon the action. It is a confusion to believe that "a kick" is an object to which a person is related by virtue of his kicking, as a football is.

It is a similar confusion, some argue against my analysis, to think that the sensuous quality instantiated within an "action" of sensory attention can be an "object" to which a person is related in virtue of his attending. What he is related to by his attention is the public object before his sense organs and the publicly sensible quality instantiated in this object. That public

283

object is analogous to the football: it is as separate from the "act" of attending as a football is from the leg motion involved in kicking. But speaking of attending to a sensuous "color" or "tone" internal to one's attention is like speaking of kicking a kick; or better, it is like speaking of kicking a "quick-kick." The latter expression serves, not to specify an object to which the kicking relates the kicker, but further to describe the action of kicking: "He kicked a quick-kick" is a way of saying, "He kicked (a football) quickly."

So too, the argument continues, the statement, "He attends to the sensuous quality, *green*, which is internal to his attending," can be made intelligible only if it is taken to mean, "He attends *green-ly* (to something before his eyes)." Expressing this by reference to consciousness: to say that in seeing the grass a person is conscious of an instance of sensuous *green*, which belongs to his consciousness, can be coherent only if it means, "He is *greenly* conscious of the grass before his eyes."

A man may *greenly* attend to the grass before his eyes; he may be *greenly* conscious of the grass before his eyes. And we should expect this to be so, my opponent continues, whenever (the light and his eyes being normal) the grass he sees is green. Here we understand that the sensuous quality specifies a manner in which he attends to what is before his eyes, or we may say that it specifies the kind of consciousness he has of the grass before his eyes. Recognizing this is like recognizing that to speak of a man as kicking a quick-kick is to speak of the manner of his kicking or of the kind of kick he performed, and not, as it might appear from its surface grammar, to characterize some object distinct from his kicking with which his kicking puts him into relationship.

This objection needs to be answered. Before answering it, however, a few remarks are wanted concerning the preferred form of speaking of the sensuous dimension of consciousness which "adverbalists" press upon us.

I can find nothing in my analysis of the role of this dimension of consciousness which precludes my saying that a sensuous quality, say *red*, specifies (in part) the kind of consciousness (or attention) that connects us with an object before our sense organs: I have no objection to speaking of a *red* consciousness (or attention). Anything that figures in any way whatever in making an object or event or state or action or process the sort of thing it is classified as being may be chosen as specifying the kind of thing under discussion: a peculiar cause of the thing can be used in this way, a peculiar effect of it, a peculiar relation of some other kind to something else, a peculiar duration or speed it has, a peculiar composition of elements—anything that can be used to mark a thing as like some other things and unlike still others can be used to specify the thing as of a certain kind. Therefore, agreeing to describe a given conscious state as of the *green* kind tells us nothing whatever about the form of connection an instance of *green* has with that conscious state: so far, it can as well be the sort of connection I suggest as any of an indefinite number of other sorts.

What is more, very nearly the same remark can be made in regard to speaking of the sensuous quality as specifying the manner in which an action or process or event proceeds. Speaking in this way does perhaps imply that our attention is an attending, our being sensuously conscious is something in the nature of a happening or process—because of the adverbial form. I have no objection to this implication. Beyond this exclusion of individual substances, or substantial objects, from possession of the quality, saying that the sensuous quality specifies the manner in which an action or process or event proceeds puts no limitations upon the form of connection the sensuous quality has with the action or event or process: anything whatever that can truly be said to figure in some central way in making some event distinctive can be used to specify that event as taking place in *that* manner.

Traveling, for example, is an action whose manner can be specified as "by air" quite as informatively as it can be specified as "fast." Yet the airborne manner of traveling is analyzable (in part) into a causal relationship between the person who travels and something quite separate from himself, an airplane. What has this mode of characterization of the person's manner of traveling in common with its characterization as "swift"? Only that both specify the manner of traveling.

The distinction between manner of acting and kind of action makes no important difference in the information conveyed. Dancing slowly is dancing in a certain manner; yet for some persons the most important classification of kinds of dancing specifies them as slow dances and fast dances. A waltz is a kind of dance, as a polka is; but—as anyone learning these dances will testify—so is waltzing an instance of dancing in one manner, doing a polka an instance of dancing in another manner.

For these reasons it matters not at all to me whether or not we speak of ourselves as *greenly* attending to—or having our *green* attention held by—the publicly green grass before our eyes. What it is important to do, having agreed that instances of sensuous qualities figure within our conscious states (or states of attention), is to settle upon the role these qualities play within these interesting states (or processes or events).

2. The Idea of an Internal Sensuous Object of Attention

Clarification of the terms of my analysis is needed, especially of the idea of an instance of a quality being interior to sensory consciousness or attention. For ease of comparison with similar structures, let us speak of our giving our sensory attention to something as a form of action we engage in. Since our being sensuously conscious of something is the form our attention takes when it is sensory attention, I shall also treat our being in this way conscious of something as a form of action we engage in. In the present context, all this way of speaking is meant to entail is that there is an activity or process occurring within us (attending to or being conscious) which grounds a relationship between us and something else—what we attend to or are conscious of.

Transitive actions found relationships between the agent of the action and a second thing which we may call the "object" of the action. And one kind of internality of object to action is so common that it is evidently not the kind I mean to speak of. An athlete cannot make a kick without a ball, indeed without contact of his foot with a ball. One could say that the ball's presence in contact with the foot is internal to the action of kicking. The action of kicking, so construed, cannot be distinguished or separated from the ball. We can nonetheless easily distinguish the agent's contribution to this action, his bringing his foot into contact with the ball, and contrast his contribution with the ball's, its being present and responding to contact with the foot.

The kind of internality that a football has to a kick, an object before our sense organs has to our attention to this object. I cannot give my attention to the grass before my eyes unless the grass is there. One could therefore say that the grass's being before my eyes is a state of affairs that is internal to my action of giving my attention to the grass. So construed, my attention cannot be separated from the grass. We can nonetheless distinguish my contribution to this action, some state of myself, from the grass's contribution, its being present before my eyes and reflecting light into them.

It is evident, if the argument of this book is correct, that sensuous qualities are more internal to our sensory attention or consciousness than things before our sense organs can be. In what does this greater internality consist?

First: the agent's contribution to his being conscious of the grass lies wholly within himself. One respect in which the instance of sensuous *green* is more internal than the grass (and the grass's instance of public green) is that it is located within the agent's contribution to the consciousness of the grass, hence within the agent; it does not qualify the grass (although he ascribes it to the grass).

Second, and probably most troublesome to critics, whereas the grass (with its public green) exists when no one is conscious of it, and the football exists when no one is kicking it, no sensuous quality has an instance except when someone is conscious of it and thus giving some degree of attention to it. Our consciousness of the sensuous quality at most helps generate the instance of this quality, at the least helps sustain it in existence: formally speaking, attention, consciousness is at least necessary to the existence of the sensuous quality-instance.

Third, although sensory consciousness can occur (in the form of hallucination) without there being something before our sense organs of which we are conscious, it is indispensable to the occurrence of sensory consciousness that there be a sensuous quality-instance within the agent's contribution to this consciousness and that he be conscious *of* this quality-instance. A fake kick (what appears to be a kick) can occur without a ball, but even a seeming sensory perception requires consciousness of an interior sensuous quality.

The most troublesome of these three respects in which sensuous qualities are more internal to consciousness than are things before our sense organs is the second one: that the action creates its object. This idea needs further examination.

3. How Sensory Consciousness Can
   Create Its Internal Sensuous Object

Further analysis of verbs of action reveals that an action's creating its object is a common occurrence. A baseball player's hitting a baseball consists not merely in his making contact with the ball by means of his bat but in his causing the ball to move away from the bat. His hitting the ball does not create the ball, but his "hitting the ball away" does create the ball's moving away. The player's own contribution to hitting the ball is his swinging his bat. When he succeeds in what his swinging his bat is an attempt to do—he hits the ball—his swinging his bat in the particular way he swings it causes the ball to move away from his bat: his swinging his bat creates what his hitting the ball (away) consists in achieving.

The ball's trajectory away from the bat may be such as to make the hit a "line drive" to short center field. The player hit a line drive. This motion of the ball, this line drive, was created by the hitter. The action of his which consisted in hitting the ball did not create the ball, but it did create the line drive, which can also be said to be "what he hit." So too did his swinging the bat in the way he did, thereby attempting to hit the ball, succeed, and create the line drive. The line drive is what he hit, and he created the line drive by hitting it, that is to say, by swinging his bat in such a way as to make contact with the ball and cause the ball to follow a fairly low trajectory into center field, where it dropped to the ground.

Despite the internal relationship of "what he hit" to his hitting (he would not have hit as he did without the ball's trajectory away from his moving bat being what it was), he created what he hit (the line drive) by hitting it, that is to say, he created it by virtue or his own contribution to his hitting (his swinging his bat in the way he swung it); and what he thus created is quite distinct from the action whereby he created it.

Not only happenings such as balls flying through the air to the ground, but also substantial things—objects, properly speaking—can be both "objects" of transitive actions and objects created by these actions—they can be caused to exist by the agent's contribution to the action. For example, a painter's painting a painting causes the painting to come into existence. Without the painting (the object), the painter's action of painting could not occur: the object is in this way internal to the action. (We may for the moment suppose that a painting exists from the moment anything is put on canvas by the painter.) And the action creates the object: the painter's contribution to the action (his applying paint to canvas) creates the object (the painting); the object is in this way even more internal to the action. Yet the object is distinguishable from the painter's contribution to the action.

With such analogues in mind we may return to the analysis of the internal relationship of sensuous qualities to our sensory attention to things before our sense organs.

Initially the most helpful analogy is that between a person's directly attending to an instance of, say, sensuous *green,* as a component within his attending, indirectly, to the publicly green grass before his eyes, on the one hand, and a baseball player's swinging his bat in hitting a ball. (If I wanted to take into account the fact that almost everyone's seeing *greenly* the grass before his eyes does make a contribution to the nature of the grass, i.e., to its color, hence does partly create its object, I should emphasize the analogy with hitting a line drive, where the ball is not created by the player's action but its motion is. By choosing "hitting the ball" I emphasize the independent reality—relative to a single perceiver—both of the grass and of its publicly sensible, green color).

The analogue of the instance of sensuous *green* is the motion of the bat. The comparison, then, is between a player's swinging his bat as part of his hitting the ball and a perceiver's attending to an instance of sensuous *green* (being conscious of it) as part of his attending to (being conscious of) the publicly green grass before his eyes.

The player's contribution to the action, hitting the ball, is his swinging his bat—more exactly, his swinging his bat into a position of contact with the ball. (The manufacturer of baseballs—and the pitcher—provide the moving ball.) The perceiver's contribution to the action, attending to the green grass, is the perceiver's attending to the instance of sensuous *green* (and, what I here neglect, his making of this *green* the content of a perceptual attribution of public green to the grass). Within the player's swinging the bat we can make a distinction between the process and its product: between the player's exerting his muscular force against the bat, and the motion of the bat; it is the distinction between the player's generating and sustaining the motion of the bat, and the bat's moving across the plate. The analogue within the visual perceiver is the distinction between the action of the perceiver's attention in sustaining the instantiation of *green,* and *green*'s being instantiated. Ignoring the player's initiation of the motion of the bat, we may speak of his actions as sustaining the motion of the bat once it has been initiated.

So too we may speak of the perceiver's attention to *green* as sustaining the instantiation of *green,* ignoring for the moment the initial source of this instantiation. The motion of the bat is doubly internal to the player's moving the bat: it is part of his moving the bat, and it is the product of the process constituted by the player's causing it to continue. So too the instantiation of sensuous *green* is doubly internal to the perceiver's attending to this *green:* it is part of his attending, and it is the product of the process constituted by his causing its continued instantiation. The reader will by now be all too acutely aware of the crucial weakness in the analogy. In bringing about and sustaining the motion of the bat the player has a bat to act upon. But instantiation of *green* is different from motion of a bat, in this crucial way: there is no *green* to be acted upon until it has been instantiated. And if the attention of the perceiver cannot generate the instance of *green* to which attention is given—for how could there be attention to *green* before *green* existed?—then what does? Moreover, since the distinction between generating and sustaining the motion of the bat is but a distinction between the first moment of generating a succession of movements and the later moments of generating later movements in this succession, must not attention's sustaining the instantiation of *green* also comprise merely later "acts" of generation of instances of *green* which are successors to the initial instance? And if attention to *green* cannot generate the first instance of *green,* how can it generate ("sustain in existence") later instances of this sensuous quality?

This problem requires a solution. Let me for a time change the analogy. The perceptual situation we have just characterized as posing a problem can be likened to the situation painting would present to us if in performing the action of painting the painter's movements with his hands were executed in the air and the painting appeared in otherwise empty space, with no discernible medium and, hence, through no discernible mechanism whereby the motion of the painter's hands acted upon something to produce the painting. If this were how painting appeared to us, then we should not be able to say that the painter's action had as a component part his applying paint to canvas: the action would seem to generate the painting directly, without consisting in part of an acting upon something which is not yet the painting and which becomes the painting only as a result of this action upon it by the painter. What the painter would seem to act upon would be the very painting itself, which he would also seem to create by, impossibly, acting upon it. To make this process intelligible to ourselves we should need to discover (or postulate) some medium upon which the painter's hand is operating and also discover (or postulate) a transformation in this medium caused by the painter's hands' motion, and constituting the emergent painting. Yet even if we developed a satisfactory theory of the medium and of the mediating action of the painter upon the medium, we might still, in ordinary life, think of the painter's transitive action of painting as having for its immediate and sole object—what it is an action upon— the very painting that it creates.

Somewhat analogously, in order to make intelligible to ourselves the role of visual attention in creating the direct object of this attention—the instance of sensuous *green*—we need also to discover, or just now to postulate, an intermediate action analogous to the painter's applying paint to a canvas. Let me now, in continuing to use my analogy with ordinary painting, using oil and canvas, suppose that a portrait is being painted: this will eliminate verbal confusion between the name of the action and that of its object and also make it possible now to require that a certain standard be reached, in the product achieved by applying paint to canvas, before we shall acknowledge that the agent is painting, rather than merely daubing paint on canvas. Furthermore, let me call the canvas, before paint is applied to it and also after this but before the result of this application has achieved the standard necessary to qualify the canvas as a portrait, a "proto-portrait"—something not yet a portrait but on the way to being one. And let me call the act of applying paint to the canvas "proto-painting." When the painter proto-paints the proto-portrait up to a certain standard, the proto-portrait is transformed into a portrait, and the action of proto-painting a proto-portrait is, we may say, transformed into painting a portrait.

Now let me postulate the most probable sort of medium upon which attention might act in generating sensuous *green* and also the most probable constituent of the "action" of attending which is likely to be capable of acting upon such a medium so as to produce in it an instance of *green*. It will be remembered that our sensuous conscious states are merely the forms our sensory attention takes. So let me suppose that our sensory conscious states, with their internal sensuous objects, are states or processes or actions of the brain. Sensory attention, therefore, is to be considered in this same way.

Suppose, then, that visual stimulation of the retina of the eye, transmitted from the grass before our eyes, generates in the visual cortex of the brain, a sensory cortical state; I shall call this state an instance of "proto-*green*"—something not yet an instance of *green* but on the way to becoming one.

Now let us suppose that this sensory cortical process generates in another portion of the brain another process which I shall call "proto-attention," something not yet attention but on the way to becoming attention. Or rather, for a reason immediately to appear, call this state "pre-proto-attention."

Now suppose that this second cortical state, this pre-proto-attention, reacts back upon the sensory cortical state that generated it. The moment that this second cortical state reacts back upon the first, the second state becomes proto-attention to the first, it becomes proto-attention to the sensory cortical state that is the instance of proto-*green*. Consciousness is not yet present here; hence I speak of both proto-*green* and proto-attention. (The entire discussion could go forward with 'consciousness' taking the place of 'attention', but the analogies with forms of action are somewhat more grammatical for attending than for being conscious.)

After the proto-attention brain process has acted upon the proto-*green* brain process with effects upon the latter that come "up to a certain standard," the proto-*green* cortical state has been transformed into an instance of sensuous *green*. Further, we may suppose that in the course of this last interaction the proto-*green*, as it undergoes transformation into *green*, under the action of proto-attention, is reacting back upon the latter, with the effect that, simultaneously with proto-*green*'s becoming *green*, proto-attention becomes attention: attention to the instance of *green*. Consciousness of sensuous *green* is born simultaneously with the birth of *green* itself, from an interaction between proto-consciousness and proto-*green*.

The transformation of the proto-*green* cortical state into a *green* cortical state is sustained, after its initial generation, by that component of the attention process which is the continuing presence within this attention of the proto-attention—just as it is the continuation, within the painter's painting-a-portrait action, of his proto-painting action (his applying paint to a canvas) which accounts for the power of his action of painting a portrait to create the portrait. We can understand how the object of the painter's action of painting can be created by this action only by recognizing that contained within this action is the action of proto-painting and that the latter action, when its product reaches a certain standard, has so transformed the canvas as to generate a portrait.

So too, we can understand how the act of attending to sensuous *green* can create this *green* only if we recognize that contained within this action is the action of proto-attending, directed upon the proto-*green* state, and that it is the latter action, when its effect upon the proto-*green* cortical state has "reached a certain standard," which transforms the cortical state so as to generate from it sensuous *green*.

It will be noticed that the instance of sensuous *green* can also be said to generate ("attract") the attention to itself: a component of the *green* cortical state, the proto-*green*, generates, through its interaction with proto-attention, the attention, which comes into existence simultaneously with the instance of *green*. In this way the *green* and the attention to it—the consciousness of it—compose a mutually dependent interaction of two cortical processes that can be distinguished from each other. And it is as important, and correct, to distinguish the attending—the being conscious of—component from the sensuously *green* component, what is directly attended to—what we are directly conscious of— as it is to distinguish the painter's contribution to the portrait from the portrait itself.

We can make this latter distinction clearly because we can easily distinguish, within the process of painting the portrait, the painter's applying paint to the canvas from the emerging portrait. This distinction is marked by our capacity to interfere, from two different directions, with the portrait's being painted: we can stop the painter from applying paint, by binding his arms, or we can remove the canvas.

So too, we can interfere with the occurrence of sensuous *green*'s being attended to from two different directions, by cutting off the sensory process, or by cutting off the attending: by stopping the external stimulation to the retina, we can stop the occurrence of the sensory process in the visual cortex, the proto-*green*, and thereby cut off simultaneously the instance of sensuous *green*, the proto-attention to the proto-*green*, and the attention to the sensuous *green*.

Or, on the other hand, we can distract a person's attention, even while the proto-*green* process continues to be activated within his brain—by stimulating him in some striking way, say, through another sensory modality; the proto-attention process will disconnect from the proto-*green*, will cease to act upon the latter, and the instance of sensuous *green* will be transformed back into mere proto-*green*: the proto-attention will no longer be acting upon the proto-*green* sensory cortical process so as to "bring it up to the standard" that transforms it into *green*.

In the latter circumstance, the sensory cortical process will continue to be activated, as proto-*green*, but will no longer be an element within a conscious state, will not be present to attention or consciousness: the instance of sensuous *green* will have been destroyed, the senuously *green* state of consciousness, which is an interaction between attention and sensuous *green*, will have been ended. Thus consciousness of *green*—attention to *green*—can be ended either by independently interfering with the occurrence of *green* or by independently interfering with the direction of attention.

Notice that the visual perceiver's attending to an instance of sensuous *green* is internal to his attending to the public green of the grass before his eyes, and so could naturally be described as his manner of attending to the grass. Then note that the latter fact provides no reason to deny that the instance of sensuous *green* is something to which he attends and which is distinct from his attending.

I have here said little about what is needed in order that our attention to sensuous qualities internal to our attention should also figure within our attention to objects before our sense organs. A part of what is needed is, of course, expressed in the idea of these qualities' figuring as the sensuous contents of sensuous *attributions* of features to objects before our sense organs. This idea will receive further clarification later.

It is equally clear that part of what is needed for attention to reach out to the objects before our sense organs is some orientation of the entire organism to those external objects to which attention is directed. Certainly our own contribution to the relationship in which we stand to those objects before our sense organs to which our attention is given must be conceived as comprising more than processes going on in our brain and must include a publicly discernible posture of the body whereby our interaction with the object before us is in various ways facilitated.

I have now given the best answer I can produce to the charge that the indirectly realistic account of sensory consciousness which I have presented in this book is incoherent because of incoherence in the idea that what we are directly conscious of is a quality belonging to this consciousness. In answering this charge I have found it necessary to adopt the hypothesis that conscious states are states of (or processes within) the brain. I do not know how to make intelligible to myself the structure that sensory consciousness does appear to have without adopting this hypothesis. If it is possible that the hypothesis is true, then it is certainly false that the idea I have been defending concerning the interior position of the direct object of sensory consciousness is, in virtue alone of the relational structure it affirms, incoherent. Whether or not there are in this idea other sources of incoherence, grounded more directly in the epistemic character of sensory consciousness, remains to be investigated. I have not wanted to adopt the materialistic hypothesis concerning sensory states of consciousness unless forced to do so in order to make intelligible other assumptions required by the facts about this consciousness and its objects. That one is forced to adopt this hypothesis is significant. We can no longer expect to understand the structure of consciousness if we entirely ignore its probable identity with states and processes, and interactions among states and processes, of the brain.

4. The Speckled Hen: Sensuous Attribution of Sensuous Qualities and Conceptual Attribution of Physical Properties

I turn now to another problem philosophers have thought insoluble for any account of sensuous qualities as internal objects of our awareness of external things, the problem variously labeled the "problem of the speckled hen" or the "problem of the striped tiger." This is an instance of a more general problem: how epistemically to characterize the relationship of direct awareness to its internal sensuous object. Because its alleged insolubility has seemed to many philosophers a major objection to an indirectly realistic theory, I shall use the problem of the speckled hen as a starting point in the project of clarifying the epistemic nature of direct sensory awareness.

The problem is this. I see a speckled hen. Let the part of the surface of the hen which I see have 27 speckles on it. Does the hen look to me to have 27 speckles on it? According to those who pose the problem, if my glance is casual and my training unexceptional the answer is "no." In regard to number of speckles, how does the hen look to me? The suggested answer is that the speckles of the hen look numerous; nothing more definite than this can be said.

According to the account offered in this book, in this sort of experience—assuming that the hen's visible surface even momentarily holds some of one's visual attention—one becomes conscious of a pattern of sensuous *colors* which it is not too misleading to call a "visual image." However, nothing I have so far said makes inevitable that I must explain our visual awareness of number primarily by reference to this visual image, rather than by reference to conceptual elements present in the visual experience. However, for the moment I leave this thought on one side.

The objection continues: "How the hen looks, the visual image must be; the explanation, on your account, of the hen's speckles looking numerous but not looking to be a definite number might be that the visual image has numerous sensuous *speckles* but no definite number of them. But an image with *speckles* must have a definite number. So this explanation will not do.

"If, on the other hand, you say that the visual image has a definite number of *speckles*, but the person who has this image is not conscious of this definite number, then the visual image is no longer doing the job it was introduced to do: constitute the sensuous content of our visual experience. For now the image has one content—27 *speckles*—and the visual experience has another (sensuous) content—numerous *speckles* but no definite number of them. So this resolution of the problem is also ruled out. And there seems to be no third solution."

There is an ambiguity in the notion of the hen's speckles not looking to be of any specific number, or, as it is sometimes expressed, our not experiencing any definite number of speckles.

Suppose there are only seven speckles, and suppose that a normal viewer visually discriminates each one of them from each of the others and from its background, but does not perceive *that* the number of speckles is seven. We might satisfy ourselves that he discriminates each of the speckles in this way: each speckle is a different color; we ask him to name for us the different colors of speckles he saw; he answers, "A red speckle, a green one, a purple one, an orange one, a brown one, a black one, a yellow one, and no others." And we ask him how many speckles he saw, to which he answers, "I don't know—let me count the colors I just named."

Did he have an experience of seven speckles? In one important sense of this question he did: he became visually conscious of each one of seven different speckles; each speckle looked to him in some way different from the others and from its background. In *this* sense of the words, the hen looked to have seven speckles.

In another sense of the question, "Did he have an experience of seven speckles?" he did not; he did not perceive *that* the number of speckles was seven.

Those who pose this problem usually have in mind a larger number of speckles than seven. Suppose there are 27. It is possible to discriminate 27 different items in a single glance. Yet probably no one of normal visual powers who has not developed a special skill would perceive *that* there are exactly 27 speckles on the visible surface of the hen.

Here is an analogy. There are 27 checkers on a board. A person picks up the checkers one by one, making out loud, each time he picks up a checker, the statement, "Here is a checker," until he has made 27 judgments of this kind. But he does not keep track of the number of judgments he makes. Does he have an experience of 27 checkers? Yes, in one important sense of this question: he affirms the existence of 27 checkers by affirming the existence of a distinct checker 27 distinct times. No, in another important sense of this question: he is unable to affirm the number of checkers he has experienced.

In visually discriminating 27 speckles we perhaps simultaneously "affirm" the existence of 27 distinct speckles; yet we do not know that the number of speckles we have affirmed to exist is 27.

An instructor stands before a classroom and visually discriminates each of the 27 persons seated before him; but he does not perceive *that* there are 27 persons seated before him.

Now we return to the visual image of the speckled hen. This image has 27 sensuous *speckles*. What is more, the person looking at the hen is directly conscious of each of the 27 sensuous *speckles* in his visual image; and he discriminates in the hen each of her 27 speckles; in *this* sense of the words, the hen looks to him to have 27 speckles. The match between (a) the look to him of the hen, (b) what is in his visual image, and (c) what he is conscious of in the visual image seems to be perfect. In the sense that I have explained, the hen looks to have 27 speckles, the visual image has 27 *speckles*, the person is directly conscious of 27 *speckles* in his visual image.

In another sense of the words, since he does not see *that* there are 27 speckles, nor is he aware *that* there are 27 sensuous *speckles* in his visual image, he is not aware of the number of *speckles* in his visual image and the hen does not look to him to have 27 speckles.

What is left of the problem after this ambiguity has been made explicit? The objection could now be phrased in the following way.

"When you remarked that the "match between what is in the visual image and what we are conscious of in this image" seems to be perfect, you were mistaken. You must identify "what is in the visual image" with the properties the visual image has. One of these properties consists in having 27 sensuous *speckles*. By your account, throughout this book, to be aware of a property of a thing is to be aware *that* something has this property. You cannot, therefore, say that a person is aware of the number of sensuous *speckles* in his visual image if he is not aware that the image has 27 *speckles*. So here is a property of the visual image of which the person who has the image is not conscious. The match between what is in the visual image and what we are conscious of is not perfect."

Fair enough. What removing the ambiguity in the idea of having a visual experience of a precise number of *speckles* achieves is to narrow the question posed by this problem down to this one: what sort of properties belonging to the image figuring in visual awareness is it required that the percipient be conscious of? That it is evident that not all the properties of the visual image belong in this category is easy to appreciate. Consider certain relational properties: for example, that the image is caused by some neurological process or that it resembles an image some other person is having at the same time. No one would suggest we need to be conscious of these properties of our visual images in order that the indirectly realistic theory that invokes such images be coherent.

Neither would anyone suggest that awareness of properties of the following sort is required: that the number of *speckles* in a given portion of the image, plus eleven, equals the number of speckles in the remainder of the image; or, that the number of *speckles* in the image is (or is not) a prime number. I think that bringing out the sense in which we *are* conscious of a determinate number of speckles and *speckles,* i.e., we distinguish each from all the others, can make it easier to accept the idea that in the sense in which we are *not* conscious of a determinate number of speckles or *speckles* there is failure to be conscious of a *non*sensuous property of the visual image (and of a "nonsensible" property of the hen) .

I am suggesting that the property consisting in the number of *speckles* belonging to the visual image is like the property consisting in the number of *speckles* in one portion of the visual image being equal to eleven more than the number in the remainder of the image: these are properties of the visual image, but they are not sensuous properties of it. The role that the visual image has been introduced to play, on my indirectly realistic analysis of visual awareness, is not, therefore, being abandoned when I stipulate that one is not required to be conscious of the number of *speckles* in the visual image of the speckled hen.

Exactly what it is about numbers which makes them non-sensuous properties of the sets of sensuous items they characterize is not evident. I have suggested that certain sorts of relational properties clearly qualify as nonsensuous: for example, a causal relation to an item of which we have no present sensory awareness, or a relation of resemblance to such an item. Also similar relations to items of which we are presently aware in a sensory way but through another modality: for example, an auditory "image" being caused by a vibration of which I am only tactually aware would not be a sensuous property of the auditory image.

It is plausible to hold that being a certain number is a relational property of a set of items. That a set of items has a certain number of members, say three, can plausibly be held to consist in this set's standing in a relationship of structural isomorphism (one-to-one correspondence between members) with a horde of other sets of varied sorts of items, where each set in this horde is such that there is an x, y, and z (neither identical with either of the others) which are members of it and anything belonging to it is identical with either x or y or z. So construed, three-memberedness is clearly a relational property of the set to which it pertains.

However, being relational does not entail that a property escapes the reach of a single gaze. Surely it is possible for arrays of dots, for example, each array containing three dots, to come within a single field of view, and for a person to see that the dots in one array stand in one-to-one correspondence with the dots in the other array. Indeed it does not seem clearly impossible for a person also to see that a third array of dots (with only two dots in it) needs one more dot in order to be similar to the other two, and even to see that a single dot, standing alone, needs the third array added to it in order to be similar to the other two arrays of dots. Surely it would be plausible to say that a person who sees all this sees that the two three-membered arrays of dots each have three dots in them. But if he can do this then, it might be held, he should be capable of becoming directly conscious of the number of sensuous *dots* in the sensuous arrays of *dots* (within his visual image) which correspond to the arrays of physical dots he is perceiving before his eyes.

Of course, if we can be visually conscious of the number of sensuous items in sensuous arrays of a small number of items, the indirect realist could hold that numbers are sensuous properties when small enough, otherwise nonsensuous. This position would leave us, however, with little understanding of the basis for the division of properties into sensuous and nonsensuous. And the line of the separation would vary as a function of individual differences in percipients' skills at detecting rather quickly the numbers of items in perceptible arrays. (But how quickly must "rather quickly" be?)

The intuitive basis of my disposition not to view even small numbers as sensuous properties is my inclination to believe that even the feat described just above requires something too near to thinking for it to count as sensuous attribution. Perhaps this idea can be made clearer by contrasting that perceptual achievement with a lesser one. Imagine someone who is capable of only one sort of response to objects that is clearly a function of their number: he can, on the basis of seeing collections of various sorts of items, match the sets with the same number, up to twelve-membered sets. And he can do this on the basis of very quick glimpses. By "matching" sets I mean that he can produce a recognizably similar response to all sets of a given number, and a recognizably different similar response to all sets of a different number from the given number, for sets numbering one to twelve items. But this is all that he can do.

For example, if he needs to cap three bottles, he will always bring one cap at a time; he will never bring three caps to the three bottles he needs to cap. If he wants to put on a glove he will only by chance select from gloves having anywhere from one to twelve fingers the glove with five fingers. Yet he can be trained to push a button when what he sees is a three-itemed set, pull a rope for five-itemed sets, turn a somersault when he sees a two-itemed set, and so on. I think that nearly everyone would agree that this person cannot see *that* there are five fingers on his hand or two hands before his eyes. What is it that he can see in regard to number? I think the most plausible answer is that he can tell the *look* of sets of visible items having the same number of items, for numbers from one to twelve (and no doubt for a limited range of kinds of items). Three-membered sets look different to him from four-membered or two-membered sets of visible items. And that is the end of the story of his visual achievement in regard to number.

We certainly cannot say of this person what we said of the person considered just before him: that he can see that the members of one set stand in a relationship of one-to-one correspondence with the members of another, or that he can see that if the members of one set were to be added to another set then the new set would be similar to a certain third set. It does, I hope, now appear that being able to see this latter sort of thing does require some thought, does in fact presuppose something it is natural to call the "concept of number." If this is correct, then it will be reasonable to believe that the visual perception of the number of a set of items requires a conceptual attribution of the number to the set. Hence the number of items in a visible array of items will not be a property that is sensuously attributed to these arrays. And therefore there is no requirement, on my theory, that we be aware of the number of sensuous items in the visual image; for the visual image is nothing but the sensuous content of the visual attribution made within a visual perception. I think this is the correct view.

However, it does not appear that the basis of the distinction between sensuously and conceptually attributed properties will turn out to be the difference between relational and nonrelational properties. For what our less accomplished visual percipient could do, become visually aware of the specific looks of arrays with determinate numbers of visible items, does at least suggest this: first, that how an array of items with a given number looks can be a sensuous property; second (and therefore), that this property is sensuously attributed; and third that a relationship between sensuous items is sensuously attributed when "the looks of numbers" are recognized.

What does present itself, from this brief discussion, as the basis for characterizing the perceptual attribution of number as a conceptual attribution? I think something of this sort: that becoming visually conscious of the number of items in a sensuously presented array requires the use of knowledge of facts not fully exemplified within the visual perception in which this array is presented. For example, one does not perceive the number of bottles in an array of seven bottles in virtue merely of being able to perceive the resemblance between the look of these bottles and the look of an also visible array of seven bottle caps; one must also realize that if one wishes to cap all the bottles in this array, then the perceived array of bottle caps will exactly suffice to do the job. And this is practical knowledge presupposing earlier experience in working at the coordination of collections of items on the basis of their cardinal numbers.

This knowledge is also a kind of causal knowledge: one must have learned the general sorts of causal powers attached to sets having definite numbers of members, in order to become visually conscious on a given occasion of the number of items in a presented array. A single sensory experience cannot alone provide sufficient data for this knowledge, nor exhaust its content. Our understanding of the sorts of things that can be done with sets of a given number and whose numbers match, and done in virtue of this specific match, is represented, within a given visual experience of some set of items, by a *concept* of number which can be used to enable us to perceive the number of items in the presented set. In consequence, our visual awareness of number, when it occurs, involves not merely the sensuous attribution to the array before us of the sensuous content of our conscious state but a conceptual attribution as well.

If I am right in this account, then it follows that even though a given sensuous content of a perception, say, a given visual image, has in fact a determinate number of sensuous items—such as *speckles*—within it, we are not required to be conscious of this number insofar as we are directly conscious of the purely sensuous content of the visual perception in which this image figures. A fuller explanation of this idea must await the more careful articulation of the differences between sensuous and conceptual attribution, to which I shall turn shortly. In the meantime I think that enough has been said to provide the solution of the problem of the speckled hen, as this problem has generally been understood.

There is, however, a closely connected problem which has not generally been included within the problem of the speckled hen, which yet seems sometimes to hover, rather obscurely, in the minds of those who raise that problem. We might label this the "problem of the striped tiger," but without meaning to imply that those who have spoken of striped tigers instead of speckled hens have clearly demarcated a separate problem. I shall use the striped tiger to do this, by emphasizing one thing we might sooner expect of a tiger than a hen: terrific speed.

Suppose a tiger flashes by you so fast that you do not discriminate any distinct stripes at all. Hence you are not in any sense visually conscious of a determinate number of stripes. No single stripe of the tiger manages to look distinctly different from any other; no single stripe is visually differentiated by you from any other stripe. There is instead a rather blurred mixture of orange and black color that presents itself to you; you nonetheless report that you saw a tiger with numerous stripes. So the tiger did look to you to have numerous stripes. It had—if one must—a numerous-striped look.

Therefore, argues my critic, the visual image must have numerous *stripes* but not a determinate number of *stripes*. And this time there is no question of a possibly determinate number of *stripes* in the visual image, without awareness of this specific number. For it is admitted from the start that no stripes whatever are actually differentiated as distinct stripes, because of the speed of the tiger and the resultant blurred visual impression that we experience: the visual image itself will be blurred, and will have no determinate number of *stripes* in it. However, the objection goes, whereas a tiger can look to have an indeterminate number of stripes and yet have a determinate number, a visual image can no more have an indeterminate number of sensuous *stripes* than a tiger can have an indeterminate number of physical stripes. So the representative analysis of visual perception is committed to an impossible sort of entity—a visual image with numerous sensuous *stripes* but no determinate number of them.

I hope that it is evident, once this "problem" is made quite clear, that the "solution" is to be found in the fact that there are no sensuous *stripes* whatever in the visual image. There is a pattern of orange and black—rather of sensuous *orange* and *black*—instantiated within this visual image; but this pattern is not a striated pattern. It is perhaps rather like the pattern a painter might make, of colored pigments, if he tried to represent the look of a tiger in rapid motion and at close range, in which colors "run together" in ways not describable as constituting regular pigment-stripes, but yet which viewers might interpret as representing a (rapidly moving) tiger with numerous stripes.

How, then, it will be asked, does the perceptual content, "numerous stripes," figure in the visual experience of the rapidly moving tiger? Again I should hope it is obvious that the answer has to be of the sort Berkeley would have made: the idea of numerous stripes is "suggested to the mind" by this flashing blur of orange and black—and this occurs, so far as we can tell, instantaneously, so that it is natural to report that we saw a tiger with numerous stripes, or one who looked to have numerous stripes. And the tiger did look the way tigers with numerous stripes look when moving by at great speed. But this is something we must learn from experience, and not only from visual experience but from tactual experience as well. The attribution of stripedness to the tiger is conceptual, on our part, not sensuous. So, too, is the attribution of numerosity of stripes conceptual and not sensuous. That we should make this conceptual attribution is suggested to us by the blurred orange and black look of the tiger, because just such looks, we have learned from experience, are regularly associated with striped objects moving very fast before us. The concept of stripes which we exercise in the present experience is the representative of this knowledge gathered in earlier experiences.

Of course the sensuous and the conceptual attributions within the visual experience are so closely integrated that we are not ordinarily aware of a distinction between the two. However, upon reflection we can distinguish between the purely sensuous (nonstriped) pattern of *orange* and *black,* and the idea of a striped tiger which is instantaneously suggested to us. I shall return shortly to this distinction between the sensuous and the conceptual attributions within our sensory awareness of things.

In fact we need not imagine a swift tiger, in order to generate the kind of problem he was intended to exemplify. This problem is available in every moment of visual consciousness, in the content of peripheral vision. In this region of the field of vision indeterminacy reigns; not only do we fail to experience definite numbers of items of every sort, it is even arguable that colors themselves are experienced as indeterminate. Hence, even if numerosity of stripes requires conceptualization, the problem can be generated for the purely sensuous content of visual awareness.

What are we to believe if the sensuous *colors* in the periphery of our visual image are indeterminate as to hue? Are we to reject the indirectly realistic scheme, or merely use this insight to inform us about the character of the sensuous attribution? Surely the latter is the reasonable choice. We are made to realize that it is in some respects an unwarranted generalization, arising from too exclusively considering the content of our focused visual attention, to maintain that always we are, in all regions of our visual image directly conscious of *colors,* meaning distinct and determinate *hues,* corresponding to the distinct and determinate hues visible in the public objects visually focused before our eyes.

It is, therefore, also a mistake to believe, on the same evidence, that the simple qualities instantiated within visual consciousness are limited to what we think of as determinate *hues.* Of course, the qualities that are instantiated there do need to be determinate qualities; the point is that they do not need to be those (or the interior sensuous correlatives of those) we come reflectively to acknowledge as the determinate hues belonging to publicly visible objects, our concepts of which are formed from focally visual experience. And the qualities that are instantiated in the periphery of the visual image may have just that relation of resemblance to the determinate *hues* (of the center of the visual field) which makes it appropriate for us to report our experience of the periphery, such as it is, as an experience of indeterminate *hues,* meaning by this way of speaking no more than that what we are barely conscious of (barely attentive to) suggests but does not altogether realize *hue.*

It needs also to be remarked that what is barely present in the periphery of the visual image is also barely attributed to the world before our eyes: the sensuous attribution involved here is barely enough to provide a kind of sense of (sensuous affirmation of) the continuing reality of the world before our eyes, as it fades out of our sight. It is not merely that what we sensuously attribute is plausibly describable as indeterminate with regard to hue; the very notion of our attributing what is in the periphery of our visual image needs to be qualified—it is a very weak attributing that is here involved, something like a very weak belief.

5. Believing and Being Directly Conscious: Corrigible and Incorrigible Sensuous Belief

The questions generated by speckles and stripes are parts of a general question concerning the epistemic content of the indirectly realistic analysis. If sensory awareness of public objects is conceived as containing something so much like belief, i.e., sensuous attribution of qualities, that its analysis gives comfort, so far, to those philosophers who hold that all forms of knowledge, of which sensory consciousness is one, are instances of belief, this comfort turns to discomfort when awareness of the external object is said to be indirect in virtue of including within itself direct awareness of sensuous qualities belonging to the belieflike state. For surely this *direct* awareness cannot be analyzed as involving a second-order attribution of a quality— to the perceptual belief about a public object. It is implausible that in order visually to attribute objective green to the grass before one's eyes one must (mentally) attribute sensuous *green* to the visual attribution. And wouldn't this second attribution require a mental awareness of its own content? And wouldn't this in turn require a third attribution of a property to the second attribution? And so on?

On the other hand, since awareness is a form of knowledge, it can appear to these same philosophers that it is impossible to analyze (hence, impossible to understand) direct awareness of interior sensuous qualities if this awareness does not consist in a belief about *its* object: such awareness, it is held, would be an inscrutable form of knowledge without belief. For the moment let me call the sensuous attribution of qualities to external things a "sensuous belief" about something before one's sense organs. And let me first remark that if we should conclude that direct awareness of the sensuous content of sensuous beliefs involves a second belief, about this content, we should not thereby be committed to adding a third belief about the second one. For sensuous awareness is unique, among the forms awareness may take, in representing qualities by the method of exemplification of these qualities. We could hold that it is only because the qualities represented within this awareness are instantiated there that this form of awareness requires a second belief directed upon it. The second belief would be merely mental awareness, in which what is represented through the belief is not exemplified within it; so no third belief need be directed at this second belief. The threatened infinite regress of beliefs about beliefs would not develop.

Nevertheless I entirely concur in the view that it is implausible that one's being sensuously conscious of the green color of a lawn entails one's having a belief about one's sensuous belief about the grass. However, my objection to this iteration of beliefs goes beyond its intrinsic implausibility. I hope that I made my objection clear in discussing the adverbial analysis of visual awareness in Chapter Six. However, I shall now briefly review the difficulty.

What is wanted is that our visual awareness of the green color of the grass before our eyes not turn out, according to the analysis offered of it, to be merely mental awareness of this color: it must not be merely thinking that the grass is green. Yet this visual awareness is partly constituted of something very like what goes on in merely thinking that the grass is green: we attribute green to the grass.

This visual attribution is internally distinguished from a merely mental attribution by virtue of the fact that the representation within visual awareness of the property attributed is constituted, at least in part, of an interior instance of the sensuous quality, *green*. Within the "act" of visual attribution the color attributed is represented by exemplification of (the sensuous portion of) itself. Only thus does the visual attribution distinguish itself from a merely mental one. To be visually conscious of the green of the grass is to be conscious of the *green* of one's visual sensory state as the green of the grass, one's attention to the interior, sensuous *green* comprising, as it were, the first moment of one's attention to the public green of the grass. One's awareness of the internal *green*—one's attention to it—becomes awareness of (attention to) the public green in virtue of its figuring within an attribution to the grass of objective green, the latter partially represented by interior sensuous *green*.

If, however, our (direct) awareness of the sensuous *green* is made out to be itself another belief, about this *green,* this belief will be purely mental, a thinking about *green.* So this direct mental awareness of *green* cannot comprise the first moment of *visual* awareness of the green of the grass; it cannot, that is to say, *be* the visual awareness of the grass, incompletely described: for then the latter would be a purely mental awareness, a mere *thinking* that the grass has a sensuous *green* one has only the *thought* of. On this view the sensuous *green* has ceased to be itself the content of a sensuous attribution of green to the grass and has become merely a quality in some way (allegedly) instantiated within our sensory state, where it "provides" nothing but a subject matter for a mere thought of itself, a thought by means of which we are enabled only conceptually to attribute this quality to the grass before our eyes.

I therefore do not want to say that our direct awareness of instances of sensuous qualities that are interior to our awareness consists in a second belief about these qualities, a belief which is distinct from and about the "sensuous belief" within which these qualities function as the sensuous contents of attributions of colors to public objects.

In turning now to try to make more intelligible the nature of direct awareness of interior sensuous qualities, I begin with a question which the approach just rejected suggests: is it possible that the "sensuous belief" (about, say, grass before the eyes) , for which sensuous qualities provide predicative content, can be understood as in some way itself a belief about these interior qualities? Can the sensuous attribution of green to the grass comprise in any way a "sensuous belief" about the sensuous *green* instantiated within itself? In a way it can. This needs explaining.

Some clarification is needed of the idea of a belief about a property. One can have a belief about a property without believing anything about a particular instance of this property: for example, believing that, in gases of constant volume, pressure and temperature are proportional to each other. This is a belief about the properties, pressure and temperature, but not a belief about any particular instance of either of these properties.

A belief about particular instances of properties commonly—perhaps always—takes the form of a belief that some particular object or event had, has, or will have a certain property. Let us limit ourselves to the present tense. A way to have a belief about a particular instance of the property, being humble, is to believe that a particular person is humble. A way to have a belief about an instance of the property, being cubical, is to believe that a particular box is cubical. A way to have a belief about an instance of the public property, being green, is to believe that a particular patch of grass is green. So the belief expressed by the words, "This grass is green," is not only a belief about the property, green, it is a belief about an instance of this property, the instance present in a particular patch of grass. Attributing green to the grass is holding a belief about an instance of green. If the attribution of green is entirely conceptual, then this is a purely mental belief about an instance of public green. If the attribution of green is sensuous, then this is a "sensuous belief" about an instance of public green.

Our present question now takes this form: does the visually sensuous attribution of public green to the grass before one's eyes comprise not only a belief about a publicly visible instance of green but also a belief about the instance of sensuous *green* which is internal to this attribution?

Here we need to remark that it is not quite enough to warrant an affirmative answer to this question that we attribute to the grass the quality instantiated within us. For the question is whether our sensuous belief is about the quality-*instance* that is within us. We may illustrate this distinction by considering a person looking at a life-size photograph of a man. Looking at the photograph one may believe, "His face is *thus*." But—assuming one is aware that it is a photograph one is looking at—one does not believe that the *instance* of a certain (facial) configuration that is now before one's eyes is the very instance occurring in the person the photograph pictures. The present instance of *thus* is not believed to be the instance existing in the person himself.

However, in ordinary, nonreflective, visual perception there is no assumption, not even an implicit one, that there are two instances of a given color, the sensuous *green* belonging to us and the public green belonging to the grass. The very instance of sensuous *green* that is in fact internal to our visual state we attribute to the grass before our eyes. It is somewhat as if the person looking at the photograph assumed he was looking at the person. No doubt in conceptual attributions of properties—in merely thinking that things have these properties—the properties attributed commonly have no instances within our mental consciousness itself; so there is no opportunity to ascribe to things outside of us instances of properties interior to our thought. But in sensuous attributions the properties attributed are exemplified within our attributions, and it is these instances which we attribute to the things before our sense organs.

The fact that in ordinary, nonproblematic sensory perception of things before our sense organs, we do not realize even that we are attributing the quality that holds our attention, this fact carries with it the consequence that we do not realize that the instance of this quality which directly holds our attention belongs to our own consciousness: we experience this instance as if it were a quality already belonging to the grass, i.e., as if it were an ingredient in the grass. Hence it does seem correct to say that the quality-instance that we sensuously attribute to the grass is the quality-instance belonging to our visual state, the sensuous quality-instance, *green*.

I have already concluded that to attribute a quality to some particular object is to have a belief about an instance of this quality; more specifically it is to have a belief about the instance that does occur in case the quality attributed is in fact instantiated. We must therefore conclude that our sensuous attribution of a color to the grass does constitute our holding a (sensuous) belief about the instance of sensuous *green* which occurs within this very attribution—within consciousness. (In the case of sensuous attribution the quality attributed is always instantiated.)

In this very special way our direct awareness of the sensuous *green* that is instantiated within our consciousness does constitute a sensuous belief about this very instance of *green*. We might express the upshot in this way: (In virtue of its place in the larger perceptual structure consisting in our visual awareness of the grass before our eyes, wherein it partially constitutes our awareness of the public color of the grass), our direct awareness of sensuous *green* constitutes that portion of our sensuous belief about a sensuous *green*-instance which consists in (the sensuous part of) our belief about what the public color is which we (mistakenly) believe the grass before our eyes to have. Our direct awareness of interior sensuous quality-instances is in this special way a sensuous belief about these quality-instances.

The conclusion just reached opens the way to understanding how we can be mistaken in our direct awareness of sensuous qualities. If the grass does not have as a property this sensuous *green,* then our sensuous belief about this *green*—that it belongs to the grass—is mistaken. In fact the grass does not have this property; so we are, so far, commonly mistaken in our visual, sensuous beliefs about sensuous *colors.* An analogous story holds true, of course, for the sensuous attributions characteristic of each of the other sensory modalities.

On the other hand, if we abstract from the sensuous belief that *green* belongs to the grass the weaker sensuous belief, that something or other is *green,* then I do not see how we can be mistaken in this sensuous belief. For its truth is entailed by the requirement that we should know what it is that we (sensuously) believe about the grass; it is entailed, rather, by this requirement taken together with the fact that in regard to sensuous belief (only), what we believe to belong to the grass, or rather the purely sensuous part of what we believe to belong to it, always belongs to something, i.e., to our sensory consciousness. Thus fully explained, this sort of incorrigibility with regard to the occurrence of instances of sensuous qualities does not seem difficult to understand and accept.

6. Behavioral-conceptual Attribution of Causal
   Properties Contrasted with Sensuous
   Attribution of Noncausal Qualities

Leaving to one side those ontological puzzles with which instances of sensuous qualities bristle, the deepest puzzle in the concept of a sensuous attribution of qualities to things before our sense organs is this: what plausible analysis of sensuous attribution reveals the latter's character *as* attribution? Why this seems a puzzle I can make clear only by sketching the kind of analysis that reveals—or at least shows promise of revealing—the character, *as* attribution, of purely conceptual attributions of properties to things; the fact that this approach fails to get off the ground when attempted for sensuous attribution generates the puzzle.

When, concerning something that exists, occurs, or obtains in the world, a person thinks that it has a certain character, there is a (mental) state of this person (his thinking what he thinks) which is responsible for establishing between him and that thing in the world a certain connection. This connection is of the peculiar generic kind that marks every thought that something in the world has some character, and it is also of the peculiar, specific kind that distinguishes each distinct thought from every other thought about some part of the world.

Even if we knew exactly the internal character of that mental state, if we did not also know the nature of the connection it makes between the person whose state it is and the things in the world the thought is about, we should have little understanding of what makes this state a thought or of what makes it the particular thought it is. For it is central to this state's being a thought that it is about something; and its being about something in the world is constituted by the afore-mentioned connection it causes to be established between the person and that something in the world.

This connection can ordinarily be divided into two components: some particular object, event, or situation (or set of them) is singled out; and some character is attributed to what has thus been singled out. The person—or his thought—refers to something and also attributes something to what it thus refers to. To understand what it is to think, concerning something in the world, that it is of a certain kind requires, above all, understanding the nature of this twofold connection—referring and attributing—which a person's having such a thought establishes between him and that thing his thought is about.

Thinking, concerning something in the world, that it has a certain character, is believing that the thing has this character. So we can also say that understanding what a belief is requires, above all, understanding how the belief establishes between the person and the thing the connection consisting in his referring to this thing and attributing some character to it. If the belief is not a sensuous belief, then the element in the belief or thought which is associated with attributing a character to the thing the belief is about I call a "concept"; and I call this kind of attribution "conceptual attribution." That is to say, a concept, as I speak of it, is an abstraction from a nonsensuous belief: it is that aspect of the belief in virtue of which *what* the belief accomplishes an attribution *of* is some specific character.

The only promising way of understanding the connection between a person and the world which is established by his thought about the world construes the thought as a guide to action, and finds the connection between thought and what the thought is about to be constituted by a mode of action toward the object of the thought. That a person's belief is about a particular thing (or set of things) in the world, this consists in the person's being disposed, in virtue of having this belief, to single out in some way, by his action toward it, this particular thing. That he attributes, through his belief, a character to the thing, this too is achieved by his belief's disposing him to behave in a special way toward the thing his belief is about. Any way of acting that singles out one thing (or set of things) from another, if this action depends upon the presence in the agent of a given belief, will suffice to accomplish reference of the belief to this thing (or set of things) . (For simplicity's sake I shall not keep repeating "or set of things"; let this complication be understood.)

However, the mode of acting toward the thing a disposition to which makes the belief a form of attribution of a particular character to the thing, this form of action must display *what* character is attributed to the thing by the belief; so the requirements upon it are more complex. Expressing them roughly and simply, they have this general form: where a person S believes that a particular b has the character $C,$ then, when S has as a goal $G,$ if action in relation to b is relevant to achieving G and if action A in relation to b would be appropriate to S's achieving G *in case b has the character C,* S's believing that b is C (as well as his believing that if b is C then A will help get him to G) will in part consist in S's being disposed, in advance of actually encountering b along his path to $G,$ to behave toward b by acting in manner $A,$ a disposition which will show itself perhaps partly in the way S organizes his behavior in advance of encountering $b.$

For example, if S wants to fill a certain hole in a wall and if he thinks that the hole is square, then before going to the hole to fill it he will get himself a square peg, which he will carry with him to the hole and then place in the hole. His bringing the square peg is caused by and expresses his thought (belief) that the hole is square. And the mental state in S which constitutes his belief that this hole is square *is* this belief in virtue of the role it plays in disposing S to the entire set of actions toward b which S would adopt in varying circumstances and when pursuing varying purposes, all these actions having it in common that they are particularly appropriate to achieving some purpose only if the hole is square.

Many of these ways of behaving toward the hole in the wall S will in fact never have occasion to adopt; but his belief constitutes a mental state that would cause him to adopt them (and organize them in advance) if the appropriate circumstances and purposes were to obtain. To have such a mental state is mentally to attribute to the hole the character of being square. It should be evident from this simple example that a single belief alone would have no behavioral manifestation; always further beliefs are presupposed in order that a particular form of action manifest a given belief.

Ideally, from the total pattern of behavior to which the thought that b is C disposes a person, together with knowledge of the circumstances—including the person's goals—we should be able to read off not only what particular thing his belief is about but what character he attributes to this particular, in believing what he believes.

Introducing into the picture beliefs that require mastery of the use of words does not change the basic form of explanation of what it is to have a belief. Of course the sorts of belief a creature can have are profoundly different when words figure in them. And the sort of action that manifests the belief now comes to include in a central place the use of words. Hence this action includes mastery by the believer of complex forms of linguistic behavior defined by the social practices of the entire community of those who use his language.

Indeed, some of the patterns of action which give to a believer's words the power of reference and attribution may be within the repertory of only a part of the community that shares with him the language he uses, as when only experts in a certain area of knowledge can be said to have full mastery of the defining uses of certain technical words.[1] Nevertheless there must be larger community, patterns (or dispositions to patterns) of action, in association with the words which express his belief, which succeed (or would succeed) in converging upon the thing his belief is about in such a way as to single it out as what his sentence is about and imply, by the pattern they compose, what it is that his words attribute to the thing they are about.

Certainly great difficulties confront the project of spelling out the patterns of communal action in association with words which empower the utterance of words with reference and attribution. And the more theoretical the sort of utterance whose reference and attribution we attempt to account for in this way,

---

1. See Hilary Putnam, *Mind, Language and Reality:* Philosophical Papers, Volume 2 (Cambridge: Cambridge University Press, 1975), pp. 227–229.

the greater the difficulty. Yet the project is barely under way; so it is too soon to be pessimistic about its chances, especially in view of the absence of promising alternative programs for taking the mystery out of thinking's power to be about the world.

In any event, the more evident it is that a belief has a practical role in the lives of the believers, the more promising this mode of analysis is. And the nonsensuous beliefs that figure in informing sensory perception, as this perception occurs in ordinary people engaged in carrying out the ordinary (as distinguished from sophisticatedly technological) business of getting around in the world, these beliefs are most plausibly viewed as eminently practical in their intent and function. Since it is primarily with such beliefs that I need to be concerned in trying to understand the structure of sensory consciousness, it will not be necessary for me to attempt to do justice to the difficulties of analyzing the action content of highly theoretical concepts.

Indeed even to attempt to do justice to the behavioral analysis of the content of evidently practical beliefs, of the sort contained within sensory perception, would require another book. It is only to the outline of the sort of analysis such beliefs appear to be susceptible to that I shall now turn, so as to pinpoint the peculiar difficulty one encounters in trying to understand a form of attribution one would expect to be equally practical in its nature, the sensuous attribution of sensuous qualities, which figures in all sensory awareness of the world.

Let me now contrast two persons each of whom sees (in a wall) a hole which is square, i.e., whose shape as a break in the plane of the wall surface is square, and which, for anyone capable of seeing that something is square, is visibly square. Person *A* passes certain tests we devise, of the following sort. When told to plug the hole, he picks up from a tray of assorted objects a square peg and uses it to plug the hole. When carried in an automobile around several city blocks, one at a time, at a speed he is told is constant, and asked to decide which block has the same shape as the hole in the wall, he uses a watch and selects the block each of whose sides takes the same time to traverse. He also devises a method for comparing the sizes of the angles at each corner of a block and selects the block that, in addition to passing the first test, also has angles at the corners all equal to one another. Given the necessary equipment (a ruler and a protractor), he is able to draw a figure whose shape is the same as the hole in the wall. And when presented with objects merely to be looked at, he picks those with square (or approximately square) surfaces. When presented with objects to be judged by the sense of touch, he achieves a similar result, with somewhat more judgments only approximately right. And so on.

Person *B*, on the other hand, passes only one test: he recognizes, when he views them visually, those surfaces which have the same shape as the hole.

From this evidence it seems reasonable to conclude that person *A* sees *that* the hole has a square shape. It seems reasonable to conclude that person *B* does not perceive that the hole is square. Why is this? *A*'s behavior manifests an understanding of what one might call the causal—or perhaps the physical—significance of an object's having a square shape, whereas *B*'s behavior does not manifest such an understanding. And we consider this physical significance of shape to be part of what shape is.

Person *A* shows by his behavior that he understands that objects of the same shape are congruent, that is, they do, under certain physical circumstances, fit together. He also shows that he understands the kinds of practical operation that will generate an object of square shape. And he shows that he understands the analysis of this complex property into certain relationships between sides (and angles) and that he understands certain physical consequences of these relationships: that applied protactors will show certain results, that objects traversing the sides at constant velocities will use equal times for each side. That a surface and its parts will sustain with each other and with other physical objects relationships of this sort is what we mean in saying that it has a square shape. Person *A*'s behavior manifests his understanding of these relationships, and it manifests his attribution of them, hence it manifests his exercise of the concept of a square shape, more specifically his visual attribution of this shape to the surface and his visual belief that the surface is square.

Person *B*'s behavior, on the other hand, which consists in nothing but singling out as one group all objects visible to him whose surfaces have square shapes, manifests no understanding on his part of the physical—or practical—significance of a surface's having a square shape.

Do we wish to say that nonetheless person *B* becomes visually conscious of the shape of the hole, although he does not perceive *that* this shape is square? The question may be considered merely verbal, in this way. We may believe that there is an ambiguity in the idea of becoming visually conscious of a shape which is like the ambiguity I suggested in the notion of becoming visually conscious of a determinate number of items in an array. If we mean by 'conscious of the shape' conscious *that* something or other has a certain shape, then B is not conscious of the shape of the hole. If we mean by 'conscious of the shape' visually discriminating this shape from other shapes, B is visually conscious of the shape of the hole in the wall. I concluded that it is probably least misleading not to say that a person becomes conscious of the number of items in an array when he does not know *that* the number is n, for example, 27. Similarly I think it will be least misleading if we follow the practice of denying that a person becomes visually conscious of a shape when he does not know anything of what it is to be the shape of a surface (or opening in a surface) except how it looks. What shall we say of B's visual achievement? I think that the most we can say is that he recognizes, and distinguishes from others, the look of square shapes, but without knowing the shape this look is the look of.

Retrospectively, on the basis of this discussion of the visual experience of shape, we can now say of the visual achievement mentioned earlier, in connection with the problem of the speckled hen, the seeing *that* there are three dots on some surface (the number of dots now being quite small), that the sensuous component of the visual attribution—as distinguished from the conceptual component—accounts only for the specific look of three dots, and not for the content, "three dots." The person considered in that earlier discussion who was able only to match visible sets of the same number of items (the number being 12 or less), and do nothing else, cannot be said to perceive that the members of two three-membered sets stand in a relationship of one-to-one correspondence because he had not learned how to utilize this relationship by actively connecting up members of such sets in the pursuit of his practical ends: never having learned that a set of three bottle caps is exactly what is needed to cap three bottles, he lacks the concept of one-to-one correspondence between the members of sets of visible items and, consequently, is unable to see that a set has three members.

What he is able to do—which not every sentient being is necessarily capable of doing—is sensuously to attribute what *we* can call "the look of three-memberedness" to all sets of three visible items (wherever he can distinguish the items). No doubt, how sets of the same number of items look to such a percipient is a certain property, and a sensuous property. The visual attribution of determinate numbers and determinate shapes is conceptual attribution; only how numbers and shapes look is sensuously attributed. We should now be in a position to provide a more perspicuous description of the difference between A's and B's visual achievements in regard to shape.

First, however, because description of the way patterns of color determine the visible shapes of regions of empty space is more complicated than description of the similar role of such patterns in regard to material surfaces, let us now imagine that it is a "square peg", rather than a square opening, which *A* and *B* are looking at. Similar tests would in a similar way distinguish *A*'s visual achievement from *B*'s.

Now we can describe *B*'s visual achievement in this way: *B* sensuously attributes to the visible surface of the peg a certain, determinate pattern of color. Let's suppose the surface of the peg is blue, and, to further simplify description, let us suppose the blue peg is actually plugged into a square hole in a red wall. Then *B*'s visual achievement is more accurately described thus: he sensuously attributes to a surface in front of him a certain determinate pattern of blue and red color. *We* should describe this pattern that he sensuously attributes to the wall as a square patch of blue, surrounded by red. Saying this will convey to others the determinate pattern of color that *B* sensuously attributes to the surface before him. Yet we must not say that *B* attributes to the blue patch a square shape, for the reasons already explained. Therefore it may seem appropriate to describe *B* as sensuously attributing to the surface this: "*thus* color-patterned."

A, on the other hand, does the same thing *B* does, and more. By means of an exercise of a concept that *A* has but *B* does not have, the concept of a square-shaped surface or region, *A* conceptually attributes to the surface, to which he has sensuously attributed the color pattern *thus,* the shape, square. What is more, it is because *A* sensuously attributes to the surface the color pattern *thus* that he conceptually attributes to the surface the shape, square.

Indeed, the union in *A* of sensuous and conceptual attribution is even more intimate than this. It is rather as if *A* makes out the pattern of color that both he and *B* sensuously attribute to the surface, more specifically the boundary between the blue and the red, a boundary both he and *B* sensuously attribute to the surface, *A* makes out this boundary to *be* the shape of the peg. Perhaps *A*'s visual attribution to the peg could be represented in this way:

Being *thus* is being square.

Or more completely:

Thus this peg, and its being *thus* is its being square.

The sensuous attribution is contained within the 'thus', whereas the attribution of "peg-ness" (here assumed but not analyzed) and the attribution of squareness is conceptual.

This still does not quite get all of the complexity before us. The sensuous attribution actually consists of two components: the attribution of color and the attribution of a pattern of color. So *A*'s visual achievement looks more like this:

> *Thus* (red) and *such* (blue) and *so* (pattern of red and blue) the peg and the wall, and being so (boundary the color pattern determines) *is* the peg's (and the hole's) being square.

Being a peg, being a hole, and being square are all conceptually attributed. Being *thus* and *such* and *so* (what *we* should describe as being red and blue and being a square boundary the two colors make where they meet) , these are sensuously attributed.

Of course, when I say that for *A* there is the visual "assertion", "Being *so* IS being square," I mean this to constitute not an impoverishment of the concept of being square, but rather an enrichment of the sensuous content *so,* which has for *B* no further content—or implications—than being a certain pattern of blue and red.

7. Behavioral Analysis of Sensuous
   Attribution Appears to Be Impossible

I am now in position to explain what I meant in speaking of a puzzle about what makes a sensuous attribution an attribution.

We explain what it is for a person conceptually to attribute to a surface before his eyes a square shape by mentioning a state of the person, which is presently activated in some way and whose causal role in his behavior consists in its determining, for a wide variety of circumstances in which square surfaces might present themselves and of goals the person might have, a variety of forms of behavior (in relation to surfaces) which would be appropriate, given the circumstances and the person's goals, if the surfaces were square.

It is especially to be noted that we do not merely ascribe to this mental state the capacity to elicit some behavior uniquely associated with square things; the behavior is more interesting.

In principle, if we contemplated the whole pattern of behavior that the person's having the concept of a square shape potentially elicits from him and contemplated the circumstances, including the operative goals of the person at the time, then we could infer what the property is that is attributed by exercise of this concept, even if we did not have independent knowledge of the possession of this property by the object to which he attributes it. Thus we could infer from a full knowledge of the behavior he is disposed to that A is treating a certain surface as square in shape, even if we had no independent knowledge of the shape of the surface he was dealing with. The sensory or mental state of A which is responsible for this treatment we may therefore consider to be an attribution by A of square shape to the surface.

Now we come back to person B. The only test he passes is that which shows him capable of visually matching the peg with objects of similar shape which are visually presented to him, where matching means not inserting a square peg in a square hole, but merely giving *some* identical response to all visible objects with visible, square surfaces.

If our knowledge of B's behavior is complete except that we do not know the shape of the peg itself, we can certainly infer that B is in some way peculiarly affected by the peg in virtue of the peg's having a square surface, since all the other objects (we may imagine) have in common as a notable visible feature only their square shape. But we certainly cannot infer—even after we gain the knowledge of the shape of the peg—that B is attributing to the surface of this peg a square shape, that he believes or takes the peg to have a square shape. For there is nothing in this way of treating the peg that shows he knows what it is for a surface to be square. Nothing in his behavior manifests a taking account of the physical consequences of a surface's being specifically square in shape. But being square is a physical property whose nature consists in the relations among an object's parts and with other physical objects which are entailed by a given object's surface being square.

It might be objected that we can infer that B attributes to the peg some likeness to the other objects he matches with the peg and that this likeness is somehow connected with visible squareness of shape. But for the surface of the peg to be like a group of square surfaces in some respect that is associated with their being square in shape and associated with this shape's being visible to anyone capable of seeing shapes is, at best, for this peg to have a property so indeterminate that it scarcely counts as a property. It is for this reason that I describe *B*'s situation as one in which his behavior does not manifest the attribution by him of any determinate property to the peg.

It is true that I have said of *B* that he is visually conscious only of the peculiar look of a square shape. But this does not mean that he attributes to the surfaces a peculiar "look." For this would imply that he is exercising the concept of a look, and I do not mean to suggest this. What I hold that he sensuously attributes to the surfaces is rather a pair of colors and a certain pattern of these colors, and nothing more. Nor do I infer even this from his matching behavior. Rather, I have started out with the idea in mind of someone who is visually conscious of the look of a square shape but not of the shape itself, and I have then described the sort of behavior we might expect of such a person in regard to square surfaces.

A similar account holds good for the person described earlier who can only visually match arrays of the same (small) number of items. Nothing in his behavior shows that he understands the practical consequences of two sets having the same number of items. But the number of items in a visible array of items is a property whose nature is constituted by the physical relationships with other arrays of items which this number makes possible: for example, that a set of three bottle caps exactly suffices to cap all the members of a set of three bottles is the sort of thing that constitutes the nature of what it is for these two sets to have the name number of items. This number's being 3 is a property whose nature is constituted by this sort of fact: that if you start with *a* cap, then you have to fetch another cap, and then still another cap, in order to have in hand a group of caps exactly capable of capping all the bottles. Nothing in the behavior of the person who—as I describe him—recognizes only the looks of numbers manifests his treating a given pair of sets as having the same number of items or one set as having some determinate number of items.

If nonetheless we suppose, as I think we must, that he is aware of a peculiar look, then we must suppose that he does sensuously attribute to arrays of a small number of items a specific sensuous property. Yet his behavior cannot manifest this attribution. This attribution does not comprise any state of the person which organizes his behavior in such a way as to enable him to treat the surfaces of objects as if they had *this* sensuous property. It seems that there is no way to treat objects as if they had the sensuous properties of which we are conscious in being visually conscious of the peculiar looks of shapes and numbers of objects.

A few moments' reflection will reveal that what I have here shown concerning how shapes of objects and numbers of items in arrays of objects look holds even more evidently for sensuous colors. There is no way to treat objects which manifests our understanding of the nature of the sensuous colors that we sensuously attribute to objects insofar as we are visually conscious of their colors. No doubt there are things we can do in the way of arranging colored surfaces in relation to each other which manifest our attributions of degrees of similarity and difference in color, or harmony and disharmony; there are also uses to which we can put colored surfaces which may manifest our atttributions of emotional differences among colors. Yet none of these behaviorally expressible attributions comes at all near to specifying the determinate nature of each distinct hue of which we are in fact visually conscious.

Here I think we can say, as we cannot of the look of a shape or a specific number of items, that it is precisely because hues are nonrelational properties that there is no way of behaving toward them which can manifest an understanding of what it is to be a particular hue. This is so because the only way we can behave toward an object is either by putting our own body into a certain relationship to the object or by putting some other object(s) into a certain relationship with the given object. And where an attributed property of the given object has as no part of its nature that some relationship purportedly holds between the object and others in virtue of the object's purportedly having this property, then there is no way that our putting either our body or other objects into a certain relationship with the object to which this property is attributed can reflect the attributed nature of this property.

I should remark that the case of the attributed looks of shapes and numbers of objects shows that although being a nonrelational property, such as hue, is enough to preclude a behavioral manifestation of our attribution of such a property, being a relational property is not enough to make such a manifestation possible. For if the relationship attributed—as in attributing the sensuous pattern of sensuous colors that comprises the look of a square shape—has no attributed causal powers, then our behavior is still incapable of manifesting this attribution. For our behavior toward an object can manifest our belief about the nature of some property of the object only insofar as this nature enables or precludes certain relationships with other objects (including our own body) and only insofar as our way of putting our own body or other objects into specific relationships with the given object shows that we are relying upon this enabling or precluding power of the object in order to achieve an objective of ours. But it is precisely the failure of a person to appreciate the causal powers of a given shape of an object or number of an array of items that led us to describe him as making only a sensuous attribution of a sensuous pattern of sensuous items, and not attributing either number or shape themselves to things or sets of things.

Sensuously attributed properties, it appears, are either non-relational altogether—like hues—and therefore, of course, also noncausal, or else relational but without attributed causal powers. Since the natures of all conceptually attributed properties can be reflected in our behavior, they must be not only relational properties but properties whose natures include causal powers: their possession by objects or sets of objects must enable and preclude certain relationships with other objects or sets of objects.

The elements of the puzzle that I need to attempt to solve in connection with sensuous attributions should now be before us. If the argument of this book has been sound, then in all of our sensory experience our awareness of the sensible properties of objects before our sense organs is in part constituted of a purely sensuous attribution to these objects of purely sensuous qualities instantiated within our consciousness. On the other hand, the only feasible way of explaining what it is to attribute a property to an object before our sense organs seems to consist in describing the state in which this attribution is realized as a state that enables us to organize our behavior so as to treat objects before our sense organs as if they had the attributed property. And we discover that there is no repertory of behavior which comprises our treating objects before our sense organs as if they had the properties we sensuously attribute to them. Our purely sensuous attributions (as judged by the visual attribution of colors and the looks of shapes and of numbers of items in arrays) do not have a behavioral manifestation.

We cannot, therefore, analyze what it is to sensuously attribute colors and patterns of color to objects before our eyes by appealing to the behavior that this attribution enables us to organize and enact in relation to the objects to which we attribute these qualities. We are left unable to explain what it is to sensuously attribute qualities to objects before our sense organs—and so far unable to suggest even the direction in which we might look for an explanation of what this form of attribution consists in.

I have argued for this puzzle only in connection with sensuous colors and what one might call the "visually sensuous analogue" of shape and number. But the same conclusion will also readily be reached concerning the aurally sensuous attribution of tonal qualities, the olfactually sensuous attribution of most odors, and the sensuously gustatory attribution of most tastes. The situation may not seem so clear for the sensuous attribution that figures in the tactual perception of pressure, in the thermal perception of heat and cold, and even in the sensory perception of some tastes and odors, for example, offensive ones. Consideration of these forms of sensory experience is, therefore, required. But before turning to them, let me be clearer about the criterion I have employed in distinguishing the sensuous from the conceptual component in the perceptual attributions so far considered.

Conceptual attributions of properties enable us to organize our behavior in advance so as to treat objects as if they possessed the attributed properties. Only properties whose natures involve causal powers possessed by objects in virtue of possessing these properties are susceptible to having these natures manifested by the behavior of ours which attributions by us of these properties organize in us. This is true because we can treat an object as if it has a certain property only by bringing either our body or other objects into relationships with the given object which facilitate our achieving our goals in virtue of outcomes that the given object's having the given property either enables (or facilitates) or precludes (or hinders). But causal powers of objects never exhaust themselves in a single incident and can never be discovered by us in a single sensory experience. We must bring into any single sensory experience in which we attribute to some object some causal power knowledge gained from earlier experiences.

It is this feature that provides perhaps the best intuitive grasp of why attributions of causal powers need to be thought of as conceptual rather than sensuous: to carry over from previous experience into a present experience some representation of the lore gathered in the earlier experience and to apply this representation within the present experience is to do something we commonly recognize as bringing to the present experience some idea gained from earlier experience and applying it to the present one. Application of this idea within a present sensory experience I describe as the conceptual attribution within this sensory experience.

Sensuous attributions of sensuous qualities, on the other hand, ascribe no causal powers to things before our sense organs, fail to organize behavior that manifests the content of our attribution (the nature of the property attributed), and in themselves introduce into the sensory experience in which they figure no representation of lore gained from earlier experience.

8. Further Comparisons of Conceptual and Sensuous Attribution within Perception

Even for the rather simple concepts that figure at the primitive level of perception with which I have been here concerned, the notion of behavior manifesting the nature of a conceptually attributed property is not so free of difficulty as I have tried to make it appear.

I have suggested that from the behavior associated with a purely sensuous attribution (only matching behavior has been so treated) one cannot infer the attributed property without independent knowledge that the objects toward which the behavior is directed do have this property. This is not strictly true. For example, from observation of the treatment native automobile drivers in the United States give to traffic lights one could determine which lights are red without looking at the lights: the lights the drivers stop for are the red ones. But here we are relying, in making the inference from behavior to color of traffic light, upon our knowledge of a conventional connection between stopping a motor vehicle and a traffic light's being red. The behavior of stopping, itself, no more reflects the nature of the color red than the word 'red' does: each is associated by a mere convention with the color red.

On the other hand, it is no convention that associates picking up a square peg with perceiving a hole to be square, or picking up three bottle caps with perceiving the number of bottles one wishes to cap to be 3. These sorts of behavior do seem to manifest the nature of the property perceptually attributed in a way that stopping before red lights does not manifest the color of light.

The kind of knowledge we are relying upon in inferring from behavior the nature of the attributed property might not need to be more precisely specified here if there were no sorts of cases that raise a question for us other than those in which knowledge of conventional connections between behavior and perceived property is invoked. Unfortunately there are other sorts of cases.

Consider the thermoperceptual attribution of thermal qualities to things before our skin. We certainly believe that we can infer from characteristic patterns of behavior associated with the perception of cold what property is being perceived, and this without either independent knowledge of the property or knowledge of any conventional associations between behavior and perceived property. If a person puts on heavy clothing, or turns up the furnace, or builds a fire and holds his hands before it, we conclude that his flesh feels cold to him. But does this behavior reflect the nature of the property perceived in the same way that the behavior described as reflecting the nature of a particular shape or number does? One is inclined to say that it does not, and then to go on to remark that our inference from behavior to perceptually attributed property here depends upon knowledge of merely contingent connections of this sort: that human beings suffer from cold and that heavy clothing reduces the effects upon them of cold air; fire does the same, partly by warming the air, partly by warming the people. On the other hand, one is inclined to say, the connection between square holes and square pegs, or between three bottle caps and three bottles is not contingent.

The interpretation of any behavior requires knowledge of the behaving person's current goals—we have to know that a person wants to fill a hole or cap some bottles. So too we have to know that a person wants to stay warm; it merely happens that we can pretty well count on most persons' having this goal. Given this knowledge of motivation, I think the connection between fire and temperature of the air and skin, as well as that between heavy clothing and insulation is quite as close as we could want in describing behavior as reflecting the nature of the perceptually attributed property. Shapes and numbers are perhaps exceptional in ways we do not here need to develop fully.

There are nonetheless further questions raised by thermal perception. Is being cold a relational property? If so, what is it that we sensuously attribute in thermal perception of cold? If not, how is it that we can reflect in our behavior our perceptual attribution of it to the air?

Being cold is a mongrel sort of property. It is definable as being a temperature below the normal temperature of the human skin, but only by ignoring the sensuous content of our thermal perception of cold. By that definition, cold is a relational property. Yet it is surely implausible that in thermally perceiving cold we attribute the property, "temperature below the normal temperature of our skin." We are, for one thing, conscious of no reference to the normal (or any other) temperature of our skin—many of us are not even aware that there is a normal temperature of our skin. For another, to say we attribute this property within our thermal perception leaves unexplained how the attribution of "a temperature" and being "below" a certain standard temperature is to be understood as specified within the sensory perception of cold. Certainly the capacity for thermoperceptual attribution of cold precedes knowledge of molecular kinetic energies and even knowledge of thermometers. So no concept of temperature involving these ideas operates in perceptual attribution of cold.

Far more plausible as an analysis of the content of our thermoperceptual attribution of cold to things before our skin, like the wind, is an analysis that resembles the account I gave of the visual perception of a square shape. We sensuously attribute the occurrent—that is to say nondispositional—sensuous quality *cold*, and we conceptually attribute certain causal powers: the power to freeze things, to make some pliable things stiff, to cause us to shiver and "feel cold." What is more, what we conceptually invest with these causal powers is the sensuously attributed quality *cold* itself. The visual perception of shape I suggested has this content:

This is *thus* (red) and *such* (blue) and *so* (boundary between blue and red), and being *so* is being square.

The two colors and the boundary they make are sensuously attributed, the attribution of a square shape is conceptual. The content of our thermal perception of cold has a similar composition.

This is *thus* (sensuous quality, *cold*), and being *thus* is being capable of making pliable things stiff, freezing things, making other things cold, making us feel itself. . . .

The thermal quality, *cold*, is sensuously attributed. The causal powers, relational features, are conceptually attributed.

Some odors are offensive to us, and this fact about them can certainly reflect itself in our behavior. However, if we distinguish, as we should, between the odorous quality we are conscious of and the offensiveness to us of this quality, then the correct account of this situation would seem to be the following. Our behavior reflects our own reaction to the odorous quality—it expresses and partly constitutes this reaction—but it does not reflect the nature of the odorous quality itself. The odorous quality is sensuously attributed and involves no relational component. The conceptual component of the olfactory attribution of an odorous quality is limited to whatever dispositions or causal powers we invest—within olfactory perception—in this quality: perhaps often no more than the power the quality has to make us aware of its presence. A similar story applies to tastes.

Tonal qualities perceived through the sense of hearing resemble colors perceived by vision. I shall return to these after completing my account of the difference between sensuous and conceptual attribution. For the present it will suffice to say that the perceptual attribution of tonal quality and color seems closely to resemble the state of affairs just sketched for odorous qualities: sensuous attribution of occurrent color and tonal quality, with rather minimal conceptual attribution of causal powers to these qualities.

On the other hand, loudness, like brightness, does raise questions calling for immediate answers. For it does seem that our behavior can reflect degrees of loudness and brightness. Is there a nonrelational component of loudness and brightness? What is sensuously attributed in the perception of these qualities? What is the relational content, and what is conceptually attributed?

Let us focus on loudness. If a sound is not loud enough for us to hear we bring our ear very close to its source; if it is too loud we move farther away or hold our hands over our ears. If we can control the sound-making process, we may "turn the volume up" or turn it down and thereby manifest by our behavior how loud we perceive a sound to be. That loudness is a matter of degree suggests that it is a relational property: a given sound is relatively louder or less loud than some standard sound, or it contains so many degrees of some unit of loudness. But what is the standard sound? Or what is a unit of loudness to be analyzed as a unit of? A unit of pressure is a unit of force per unit area, or a unit of energy flow per unit time and area. A unit of energy is a unit of work-capacity. On the other hand, a unit of length is simply a standard length, which cannot be further analyzed as a unit of something else. How are we to analyze what it is we perceive in perceiving degrees of loudness in sounds?

I should dearly like to avoid taking on the task of mastering and clarifying the technical subject of "measurement of sensations." I hope that a rather simple-minded, quasi-phenomenological approach to our present problem will suffice. I shall assume that the arguments of Chapter Five suffice to prove that we are not, in making auditory assessments of loudness, judging how intense the pressure of the airwaves (which are the sounds) is.

What is the common, practical import of loudness in sounds? Primarily, audible discriminability. To find a sound not loud enough—as evidenced by our "cupping our ears"—is to find what we wish to discriminate, to make out in the sound, not discriminable. To find a sound too loud may be to find it audible to persons or animals whom we do not wish to hear it. So far, we may say that auditory attributions of loudness may involve perceptual judgments of degree of audible discriminability. Clearly, our behavior can manifest our attributions of this character, where definite goals are ascribed to auditory perceivers. There are also hedonic and emotional effects of high degrees of loudness to which our behavioral adjustments to sound may be responsive; seeking and avoiding some of these effects may be sufficiently similar to seeking to avoid extremes of cold and heat to allow us to treat behavior adapted to these ends as manifesting auditory attributions of higher degrees of loudness. So far, loudness would be a relational property, and attributions of degrees of this quantity could plausibly be construed as conceptual attributions.

However, if one is to escape an analysis that entails that in hearing sounds we have only the thought of their loudness, then one must acknowledge that we also make sensuous attributions of "intensive magnitude" which do not have a relational content for us: in these sensuous attributions we neither make one of the practical sort of judgments just described nor affirm a relationship in which the presently heard sound stands to sounds not presently heard (or not still "reverberating" in our immediate, auditory memory). This sort of attribution is, if you will, a sensuous attribution of degree of "absolute" loudness. That a scale of loudness, and a unit of loudness, can be constructed by psychologists and, under instruction, even employed by subjects in experiments is nothing to the point. In the ordinary, simple hearing of loudness of sounds the sensuous attribution of sensuous degree of sensuous loudness is not an operation in which a scale is actually employed or any relationship with items not now sensuously present (or present in immediate "sensuous memory") is attributed to the sound we are hearing. This sort of attribution is the purely sensuous attribution within our auditory awareness of the loudness of sounds before our ears, to be distinguished from the conceptual attribution of degrees of auditory discriminability and of hedonic and emotional effects upon us.

I shall assume, also, that a similar story is true of our visual awareness of degrees of brightness of colors, lights, and surfaces. Finally, it seems not wholly implausible that the sensuous and conceptual attributions are related in the sort of way already suggested for other forms of sensory consciousness; we perhaps identify the sensuous loudness with, say, the degree of audible discriminability: "being *thus* IS being (aurally) discriminable (in the degree now experienced) ."

In the preceding chapter I argued that what we are directly conscious of when attentively exercising the sense of touch is not the actual pressure exerted upon our flesh (nor the actual stress within it) but a tactually sensuous representation of a force exerted upon or within our flesh. Can we distinguish here also a sensuous from a conceptual attribution? Not, I think, by inspection of the contents of tactual experience. For this inspection does not appear to reveal anything simpler than apparent pressure or stress, the apparent action of a force upon or within our flesh. And such content is of the sort which, on my view, should be conceptual rather than sensuous.

We are nonetheless quite certain that feeling a pressure is internally as different from merely thinking that something is pressing upon us as feeling one's face turn cold is internally different from merely thinking that someone else's skin temperature is below normal. For the reasons developed throughout this book, I believe that this internal difference must consist in a difference in the contents of the two sorts of attribution, here attribution of mechanical force. However, there is no vocabulary available with which to mark this difference by giving the name of the sensuous tactual quality an instance of which functions as the internal sensuous content of our tactual attributions of pressure and stress. One can only point to this sensuous content of our tactual attributions of pressure and stress by mentioning the difference between the content of our mere thought of mechanical forces—as when working, say, with the Boyle-Charles law, connecting pressure, temperature, and volume, or Hooke's Law, connecting stress with strain, wherein we achieve a purely mental form of awareness of pressure and stress—and the content of our tactual awareness of mechanical forces when we feel them acting upon and within our flesh. Reflectively realizing this difference is, if you will, turning the mind's attention to the distinctively sensuous content of our tactual affirmations of the action upon our flesh of so-called "mechanical" forces (whose actual nature, as pointed out in the last chapter, is ultimately electrostatic and quantum-mechanical) .

Beyond this I do not find it possible to go in eliciting the sensuous content of tactual awareness of pressure and stress. I have no doubt that the reason for the difficulty in elucidating the nature of the difference between the sensuous and the conceptual components of tactual consciousness is the extraordinarily intimate character of the fusion these two attributions undergo in tactual perception. And the reason for this, in turn, is doubtless the extreme practical urgency that attends tactual awareness of the mechanical action of neighboring bodies upon our own, action either offering immediate support or threatening immediate damage.

Between the sensuous content of our tactual awareness of something pressing upon our body and what we perceive to be the actual deforming action upon our flesh we cannot achieve so much as an intimation of a difference: conceptual and sensuous contents of tactual attributions of pressure and stress are inextricably fused together. Nonetheless, to avoid the absurd theory that in feeling objects press upon us we have only the thought of this pressure, I postulate a tactually sensuous *thus* and hypothesize that our tactual experience has the structure: "This being *thus* is (identical with) its being a pressing, there." The sensuous component is the *thus;* the conceptual component is the idea of something's pressing upon us.

It is certainly possible that not only the sensuous component but also the conceptual component of our tactual attributions of mechanical force should be innate. If it is, no doubt the (evolutionary) reason why it is innate is, again, the practical urgency of knowledge of the mechanical action of bodies actually impinging upon us. Of course, if the tactual concept of pressure is innate, then part of my reason for calling it a concept is removed: it is not a representative of knowledge acquired through experience. However, its role in organizing behavior that manifests its content remains—and many tactual concepts in which it figures as a component, for example, concepts of various shapes, perhaps of sizes and of textures, are probably acquired through experience.

9. Explaining Sensuous Attribution (I):
Necessary for the Presence of a World

I return now to the problem of explaining how a sensuous attribution can be an attribution.

We understand how a conceptual attribution of a property *P* can be just that by appreciating its role in disposing the person in whom it occurs to treat the object to which *P* is attributed as if it had the property *P*.

However, the purely sensuous contents of our perceptual attributions do not lend themselves to that sort of analysis. The features we sensuously attribute are endowed through our sensuous attributions with no causal powers. So we cannot think of the sensory states in which these attributions figure as readying their possessors to behave in ways that specifically manifest the character of the attributed properties: there is no way of behaving which constitutes treating a surface as if it were red; by contrast, there are ways of treating a surface as if it were square or pressing upon one's back. My question, therefore, is this: What is it about the relationship between ourselves (or our sensory state) and an object before our sense organs which makes of our sensory state a sensuous *attribution* of a sensuous quality to that object?

I shall proceed by two stages to make such headway as I can in answering this question. In the first I shall try to produce a "deduction" of the necessity for purely sensuous attributions, more directly, of the necessity for direct awareness of purely sensuous qualities, if we are to have experience of the *presence* of a world. Such a "deduction," however, fails to show how what is necessary is possible. In the second stage, therefore, I shall try to make at least a beginning in understanding how sensuous attributions achieve the character of attributions. First, the "deduction."

Suppose that one has a purely mental belief about a nearby object. This belief is analyzable into a set of purely conceptual attributions. Suppose the belief is, "In that wall, there, there is a square hole." One is conceptually attributing a wall to a place—or a place to a wall—and a hole to the wall and a shape to the hole, thus:

(a) In that place there is a wall.

(b) In that wall there is a hole.

(c) That hole is square.

One is exercising, let us say, the concepts, "that place," "a wall," "in (a place)," "a hole," "in (a wall)," "there is," (i.e., "exists"), and "is square." I am not sure what to say about the concept, "exists," but I shall try this: if one genuinely attributes to a place a wall and to this same wall a hole and to this same hole a shape, then one has affirmed—one believes—that there exists in that place a wall with a square hole in it. Whether or not the affirmation is genuine is settled by whether or not one is genuinely disposed to act, when pursuing certain goals, in ways that constitute treating a certain place as filled with a wall and this wall as having in it a hole and this hole as having a square shape.

For example, if one wants to fill the hole then one looks for a square peg, and, having found it, one goes to a certain place with the peg, finds the wall there (if the belief is true), looks for the hole, finds it, and puts the square peg into the square hole. That one is exercising the concept of a certain place is manifested by one's going to this place after one has got the square peg; that one is exercising the concept of a wall (and of a wall in the aforesaid place) is manifested by one's slowing one's gait as one approaches the wall in the given place, by one's reaching out one's hands and feeling for the wall, by one's running one's hands over a part of the wall feeling for the hole. That one is exercising the concept of a hole (in the wall) is manifested by one's feeling for the hole by running one's hands over the wall, stopping the search when the hole is found, and putting a peg into the hole—and also by one's initial search for and retrieval of a square peg.

That one is exercising the concept of a square hole is manifested by the search for and selection of a square peg and by the placing the square peg in the hole. And the sort of exercise of each of these concepts which each of these bits of behavior manifest is the attribution of the content of each concept to something or other. Of course the attribution of place to the wall is a matter of attributing relationships between the wall and other objects, including one's own body. I am suggesting that when all these concepts have been attributed in some way then the existence of a square hole in a wall in a certain place has been affirmed, or is believed in.

I have said nothing about the internal character of the states of the person which comprise the conceptual attributions; I have merely specified them as readying the person for the kind of behavior just described. I shall not say more about the internal character of these states. The important point for our present purposes is that the contents of these conceptual attributions are to be understood as specified by the behavior to which each disposes or for which each readies the person making these attributions: what is being attributed is specified by this behavior, taken together, of course, with what in the environment of the person the behavior constitutes an interaction with.

In order to appreciate the necessity of sensuous attributions if experience of the presence of a world is to be achieved, it will be useful to construct this fiction: imagine that all forms of sensory consciousness of things before our sense organs are replaced by purely mental beliefs about these things, beliefs whose contents are specified, like the belief just sketched, entirely by patterns of prospective behavior, so that the sensuous dimension of ordinary sensory awareness of the world has been eliminated. This may seem impossible to conceive, for this reason: purely mental beliefs require, for their analysis, behavior adopted in the pursuit of goals and adapted to fulfilling these goals. This instrumental behavior in turn requires sensory perception of one's environment and of one's own body. So, it may be argued, we cannot conceive purely mental beliefs wholly replacing sensuous beliefs.

I reply that we can do this by imagining that each sensory perception is replaced by a purely mental belief whose content comprises the conceptual attributions present in the sensory perception and by supposing that these purely conceptual attributions are caused to occur through the usual stimulation of organs that resemble our sense organs in every respect except one: they generate no sensuous quality-instances—hence no sensuous attributions—in us.

For example, the belief whose conceptual content I just now partially sketched could be thought of as replacing the visual experience of a square hole in a wall five yards ahead of one, hence as caused by the action of light reflected from this wall to our eyes, the eyes now thought of as so modified that nothing but the conceptual content of ordinary visual perception of a square hole in a nearby wall is caused in us by the action of light upon them. Then, in turn, the full, tactual experience associated with feeling for the hole in the wall and locating it by touch we imagine reduced to a sequence of purely conceptual attributions of properties to the wall, attributions caused to occur in us by contact of the wall with the "sensory" receptors within our flesh. The content of these purely mental but tactually generated beliefs will, in turn, be analyzable wholly in behavioral terms and, therefore, will share with the content of the belief just partially analyzed its character as entirely prospective. Every sensory modality is to be imagined undergoing a similar metamorphosis. Behavior can, in principle, still be guided by something playing a role like the role of our sensory perception, a set of purely mental beliefs generated by the usual stimuli acting upon modified receptor organs located in the usual places.

But now all of our consciousness of the world around us is prospective in its content at every moment, in the same sort of way in which the belief just now analyzed, about the square hole in the wall at a nearby place, is entirely prospective in its content. For when all attributions are conceptual, all have their content specified by the behavior they prepare us for; and such behavior is necessarily yet to happen: all our awareness of the world now directs our attention to situations that have not yet occurred, which is to say, away from our immediately present situation.

Thus, if we imagine that the purely mental belief about the hole in the wall is a replacement for a visual perception of the hole in the wall six yards away, this means that light from this wall striking our eyes elicits in us a mental awareness of the wall that has this sort of content: to get to it, walk six paces straight ahead; before doing this, in order to keep the poisonous gas in the next room from seeping into this room, find a square peg; take the peg six paces forward, insert it (at a place also behaviorally specified) ; and so on, for other behavioral repertories involved in these conceptual attributions.

Of course, all of this is in some way abbreviated within our present, conscious state. If one has words, the abbreviation may be through a sentence uttered silently "within the mind." If one has not the words, and perhaps often even if one has, there is very little I can say about the form of this abbreviation; it will remain true, however, that what is abbreviated is entirely prospective, concerning how one would interact with one's environment if acting with certain purposes or how one will perform and be affected under present motivations.

From within such an "experience"—a consciousness of objects which is composed entirely of the mere thought of the objects— such experience of a world as we could be said to have would be of an entirely future world, of a world that has not yet happened. No objects or happenings would be *present* for us. And we should therefore not experience ourselves as present to a world, as present in a world. If we are not in the presence of a world of objects and happenings then we are not present in such a world.

Indeed the very "we" to which I am referring—the "I" I am presupposing as somehow experienced but not experienced as present in a world—this "I" itself comes in question, when we reflect upon such a purely mental "experience." For the reader is likely, so far, to be supposing that the prospective behavior and interaction with things which constitutes the content of present awareness of them is somehow anchored to a present self from which action is understood to originate—as when one is said to think, "Move six steps forward. . . . "

However, our experience of our own body must be conceived to be also entirely mental. All bodily sensations are now replaced by purely mental beliefs in which only the purely conceptual attributions present in normal bodily sensation (perception of the body) remain, the sensuous attributions having been eliminated. Feeling toothache, for example, is replaced by having the thought (mental conviction) that something is wrong with one's tooth. Feeling a tingle in the skin of one's arm is replaced by having the mental conviction that a pencil is brushing one's arm and is causing a disturbance in the skin. And each of these thoughts about one's body is caused by the same bodily stimulation that used to cause the corresponding sensation. But this replacement of sensuous by mental beliefs about our own body has the effect that awareness of our body is also entirely prospective. For the contents of our mental beliefs about, say, a tooth or an area of skin on the arm are constituted by dispositions or powers these beliefs ground in us to *treat* the tooth or skin in an appropriate way. And this is future behavior. By the same reasoning, therefore, even our own body fails to be present to us. Consequently we do not experience ourselves as present in our own bodies.

Not only, then, is there no world in which we experience ourselves as present, there is no bodily self we experience ourselves as present in and through our presence in which we might be a point of origin from which to relate to a prospective world. Not even the experience of a prospective world is clearly possible for such a purely mental consciousness. Stripping human experience of sensuous attributions denies us experience of presence in a world, presence in a body, and possibly therefore even denies us experience of the very prospective world which mental beliefs normally provide for us.

If, therefore, we are to experience our bodies as present to us, ourselves as present in our bodies, a world as present to us, and ourselves as present in a world, it is necessary that we become conscious of our bodies and of objects outside our bodies through becoming conscious of qualities they at least appear to have which we can grasp only by some nonconceptual mode of apprehending them, a mode therefore whose content is not behaviorally specified and hence need not be entirely prospective.

But the only properties we know of this kind—and so far as I can determine the only kind of property we can conceive which meets this test—are properties of the purely sensuous sort, sensuous qualities. But I have argued throughout this book that sensuous qualities do not belong to things before our sense organs. However, if our awareness of sensuous qualities does mediate awareness of properties genuinely belonging to our bodies and to objects in the neighborhood of our bodies, then awareness of the sensuous qualities as *apparent* properties (appearances) of our bodies and of objects around us does constitute awareness of the presence of our bodies, of the presence of the world of objects external to our body, and of ourselves as present in our bodies and as present in a world of objects external to our bodies.

Again, as I have argued throughout: these sensuous qualities do not in fact belong to our bodies nor to the objects external to our bodies. Since this is so, and since our awareness of these qualities is not mediated by our awareness of anything else, and since we are conscious of them as if they were properties of objects before our sense organs, and because this consciousness is internally different from a purely mental consciousness of these qualities, the best hypothesis, as I have also argued throughout the book, is that these qualities are actually instantiated within our conscious states and function there as the sensuous contents of our sensuous attributions of themselves to our own bodies and to objects external to our bodies.

It follows that what is necessary in order that we should experience ourselves as present in our bodies and in a world of objects external to our bodies is that we should not only conceptually attribute properties to our bodies and to other bodies external to ours, but that we should also sensuously attribute to bodies sensuous qualities that are, as attributed, either altogether nonrelational or if relational without causal powers.

What I have tried to make it plain that we do, I have now tried to make it plain that it is necessary that we should do if we are to have, as we obviously do have, experience of ourselves as *present* in a world of physical bodies and happenings.

However, it is precisely what is required of our sensuous attributions in order that we should experience ourselves as present in a world which makes it so difficult to understand how these attributions of properties can be *attributions*. For the very fact that in ascribing these qualities we commit ourselves to no relationship whatever between what is now present to us and what is not now present to us means that there is nothing in what we affirm through these sensuous ascriptions whose presumed truth would entail some specific adaptation of our future behavior. The content of these sensuous attributions therefore cannot be explained by reference to the role they play in so organizing our behavior as to prepare us for the world's answering to these attributions. What makes these sensuous attributions attributions remains a puzzle even after we appreciate why they are necessary.

10. Explaining Sensuous Attribution (II) : The Sensuous Content Is a Model for the Conceptual Content

The puzzle takes two forms. There are simple sensuous attributions and complex, or structural sensuous attributions. An example of the latter we have already encountered: the sensuous attribution of a certain pattern of colors which those of us who understand what squares are would call a square pattern but which, as sensuously attributed, is better described as merely the look of a square. What is in question here is explanation of the attributional character of the attribution of relationships between sensuous elements, for example, that two *"lines"*—boundaries between two pairs of *color expanses*—meet *thus* (what the sophisticate would call "at right angles") .

Obscure though the suggestion may be, I think a glimmer of light is offered on the solution to this puzzle by the suggestion that mastering this form of attribution may coincide with and be somehow "caught up in" learning to make conceptual attributions of, say, edges of surfaces of material objects' meeting at certain angles. If the conceptual attributions of such causally empowered properties is primary, introducing into our experience the attributional structure, and if at the same time this mode of attribution can use a kind of sensuous stuff or model around which or about which or through which to organize itself, then it may be that the conceptual mode of awareness generates for the sensuous material a place within an attributional structure.

The relationship between the conceptual attribution of square shape and the sensuous attribution of the mere look of a square shape may be in some way analogous to the relationship between an incompletely interpreted theoretical structure and a model for this theory. But here we must imagine that although the model has some predisposition to take on a specific structure it does not actually acquire this structure until organized by the "theory" to be the latter's model: the sensuous "complex" of *colors* becomes the look of a square in virtue of our learning to conceptually attribute squareness to actual surfaces, a feat in which we are helped by having available the sensuous material for a "pictorial model" for squareness. And to say that the complex of sensuous *colors* becomes a determinately structured pattern that comprises the look of a square is to say that we now sensuously attribute to the boundaries of two pairs of *color* expanses (two *"lines"*) a specific mode of interaction. But we do this only as one "moment" of a total sense-perceptual attribution of physical shape to material surface, in which the conceptual mode of attribution has invested the sensuous mode with attributional form by the use it makes of the latter as a sensuous modeling of its own more abstract (ultimately practical) content.

I wish that I knew how to give this suggestion a more adequate articulation. Some help may be found in at least moving toward the realization of this hope if something useful can be said about the other form of this puzzle.

The second form of the puzzle concerns the attribution of simple sensuous qualities: sensuous color, tone, odor, pain, tingle, and the like. Let us consider color.

For vision colors are characteristically the colors of material surfaces. Even the sky is for vision a blue dome. We may go further and believe that for vision colors are the very stuff of material surfaces. But if the stuff of material surfaces, then presumably colors are for vision the material stuff of surfaces. Of course this thought requires that a surface be very thin—but for vision how thick need a surface be? But being a surface *is* being the stuff of a surface, and having certain boundaries or edges, and constituting a "boundary" of a solid object. Assuming, then, that the visual attribution of "surface" to a solid must be in part a conceptual attribution, certainly the possibility again presents itself that the attribution of the abstraction—the "theoretical" content—"surface" (which is ultimately practical and hence prospective in content) requires for its visual sensory form integration with a sensuous attribution of color which provides a kind of sensuous model for the more abstract (and practical) structure, so that the whole content of the perception becomes this: "being *thus* (blue) *is* being the stuff of this surface." And again it seems a possibility that the conceptual attribution provides the primary attributional structure, into which the sensuous color-content is integrated in such a way that it too acquires the role of content of an attribution of a property to a solid object, but now a sensuous property, a sensuous quality, a color.

Since we probably need to learn from experience about surfaces' existence, experience in which the deliverances of the sense of touch are coordinated with those of vision, and since we probably need even to develop through this experience the concept of a surface, my present hypothesis entails that we should not sensuously attribute colors until we had developed the concept of a material surface. This in turn suggests that in some, possibly primordial experience of color, before the coordination of vision and touch, color, since not attributed, would not be experienced as a property. How it would be experienced passes, I confess, my understanding; but perhaps this is as it should be.

My hypothesis also entails that there is a constant error in visual perception. For sensuous, occurrent (nondispositional) color is not the stuff of material surfaces. But then models are generally only partially true, anyhow. And there is surely a partial truth in the visual belief that the surface is *thus* (where the word *'thus'* represents on this page the actual instance of sensuous color present within visual experience). For as sensuously attributed to a solid, color is spread out, it is an expanse; and so is the surface. The sensuous expanse of *color* has boundaries, as the material surface has edges. Here is the truth in the sensuous model offered by the sensuous attribution of color.

Even if we suppose that the line of attack just suggested should succeed in explaining what it aspires to explain, it seems clear that there remains an unanalyzed residue of sensuous attribution. The difference between, for example, attributing a brown surface to an object and attributing a blue surface to an object remains unaccounted for. What it is to attribute *what* we attribute, insofar as we attribute something different in sensuously attributing a brown surface to an object from what we attribute in sensuously attributing a blue surface to it, this remains unanalyzed. And we may expect a similar residue of unanalyzed attribution to be found when this approach is carried through with each of the sensory modalities.

The behavioral content of the visual attribution of a surface to a solid it is conceivable one could spell out; even the behavioral content of the visual attribution of a surface's stuff we might be able to articulate; but the behavioral content of the sensuous, visual attribution to a surface of blue—as distinct from

brown—promises still to stymie us. A similar residue would undoubtedly remain to puzzle us in connection with pains, tingles,
itches, sensuous thermal qualities, tones, tastes, and odors, and if
we could isolate them, with tactual qualities as well. A deeper
probe is needed.

11. Explaining Sensuous Attribution (III) :
    Presenting a World to Ourselves

If within sensory experience conceptually to attribute a property to an object is to be in a state that prepares one to behave
toward the object as if it had this property, but sensuously to
attribute a quality to an object cannot prepare us to behave
toward the object as if it had this quality, our puzzle is how to
conceive the function that is performed by this purely sensuous
moment in our perceptual attributions. We have only this clue:
conceptual attribution takes us away from the present, away
from the presented world; sensuous attribution creates for us
the presence of a world of objects and happenings, it is what
makes us present in a world. What makes a sensuous attribution
of a quality an attribution must be discovered somewhere in
how we make objects present to ourselves, in how we create between an object and us that peculiar bond that is its presence
for us.

But this can be a maddening recommendation. For the general idea of presence seems to be clarified for us by the specific
idea of sensuous attribution, but to offer very little handle for
grasping more firmly the latter idea.

Let me move away from this sort of "making present" to some
better understood sort, and ask whether any of the elements in
the latter can help me to analyze the sort constituted of sensuous
attribution.

Suppose that a person wants to convey to us what it is to be
present at night at a specific place on the shore of a certain lake
with which he is familiar. We could say that he wants to convey
to us the presence of the lake from that position on its shore
and at that time. Suppose that this person has some skill as a
painter. He paints us a picture of a blue-black-gray-white lake,
sky, moon, clouds, further shore, mountains beyond. Take this
painter at the moment he is putting on paper white paint to
represent the moon. Within an expanse of black, blue, and gray
he is now making an expanse of white. He is attributing to the
moon he is representing in his painting a white color. How is

he accomplishing this attribution? Not alone by creating a new expanse of white, nor even by doing this on a paper that already has a pattern of other colors on it.

It is only in virtue of his making this new expanse of white within a human context in which such expanses are *treated* as representations of objects—as pictures of objects—that the painter's making this particular new expanse of white color can constitute his attributing to the moon in a certain situation a white color.

Now we notice a division of labor within the process of attribution of white to the moon. That the white is being *attributed* to an object depends upon the painter and others participating in the practice of treating paintings as representations of objects. That they do so treat the painting must show up in forms of behavior external to the painter's action of putting paint on paper; for example, that after viewing the painting they now speak to others about how a certain lake looks on certain nights from a certain position. But that *what* is being attributed is the color white depends entirely upon the painter's putting white paint on the paper, hence upon the existence of this particular bit of white paint. The color of the paint represents itself as the color of the moon. The actual existence of this bit of white paint is an indispensable part of the mechanism of attribution of the color white to the moon. Now let us return to the sensuous attribution of color which occurs within visual consciousness of things before our eyes.

Now it is the task of a single person—or rather, of certain processes within each person, over which he has no deliberate control—to make present to himself a physical object before his eyes. Let us, for simplicity of expression's sake, not distinguish between the person's deliberate actions and processes occurring more or less automatically within his visual consciousness, speaking of both as things the person does. Somewhat like the painter, the person creates a bit of color. Rather, since he does not make a visible expanse, he creates a bit of *color;* there is realized within a visually conscious state of his an instance of sensuous *brown,* let us say. The sheer existence (in its particular place) of this instance of sensuous *brown* determines what quality the desk before his eyes is going to be represented by him as having. But its mere existence is not enough to make it a representation of a property. It must be treated by the person in whom it is instantiated as a representation of something.

However, just as (let us suppose) the painter and the viewers of his painting are not free to determine by their behavior what property the white on the paper is to represent if it represents anything (it must represent the color white, which is to say, itself), so too it is not to be settled by the perceiving person's actual or potential behavior what property the instance of sensuous *brown* is to represent: if it represents anything it must represent itself (made objective), i.e., the color brown. What the perceiver's "treatment" of this instance within himself of sensuous *brown* can determine is only that this bit of *brown* shall represent something—and what particular physical object shall be selected for the represented property to be a property of. (For the moment I ignore the way in which the property represented by the sensuous *brown* must be in some ways enriched— as by the conceptual ascription of a disposition or a causal power—in order that it shall represent the objective color, brown, an enrichment which, since conceptual, *is* generated by the person's behavioral dispositions.)

It is, I hope, helpful to recognize that there is some reduction in our remaining explanatory task: we no longer need to explain how it is that *what* is sensuously attributed is the color *brown;* we need only explain how it is that this color is *attributed.* We need only describe what the behavioral evidence is that the person does attribute to an object before his eyes a property that could be the color brown; we do not need to provide behavioral evidence that settles it that brown is indeed what is attributed; for this latter is settled, as analogously by the white paint in the case of the painting, by the bit of sensuous *color* actually instantiated within the visual perceiver.

The behavioral evidence of attribution must constitute also a way in which the person is, as it were, "treating" the instance of sensuous *brown* within himself; which is to say, this behavior must at least in part constitute a way in which the sensuous *brown* instantiated in the person is functioning in this person's behavior. It is necessary, in other words, to understand the idea of the whole person "treating" in a certain way these involuntary, sensory processes within himself as the idea of how these processes function within this person to organize his behavior in certain ways. This is like saying, for example, that a man treats a judgment of duty he makes as a prescription for action provided that this judgment functions in his conduct to organize his action into an attempt to perform this duty.

We do not need to work hard over the question, What behavior is it that manifests the attribution of properties which it is possible are sensuous colors? The patterns of discriminatory, matching behavior that I have associated with attributing what is in fact the look of an objective property (for other modalities, the sound, the feel, the smell, and so on) provide the answer.

Using the extended argument of this book, then, as warrant for the assertion that we do make sensuous attributions of *colors* and other sensuous qualities and that this involves the instantiation within our sensory state of these same qualities, we are entitled to view matching behavior as being organized in part through the instantiation within our conscious states of these sensuous qualities. These interior, sensuous quality-instances—or rather, the similarities between some of them—may be considered as functioning to help organize in us the treatment of all green lawns as similar in appearance and as doing the same for all chessboard squares, three-columned ranks of marching soldiers, cool breezes, sandpaper surfaces, vaporous emanations of blossoming linden trees, whistling quail, tingling bodily parts, and so on.

That the same sensuous quality or pattern of qualities is caused to be instantiated in our sensory state by the members of a given one of these sets of perceptible items enables us to match up, by our behavior, the members of this set; and our so matching them, in turn, helps to make of this quality (or quality-pattern) the content of a sensuous attribution of itself to each perceived member of the set. This matching-up way of "treating" these interior instances of sensuous qualities partially constitutes our so employing them in our behavior as to effect an attribution of them to objects and events before our sense organs, somewhat as the viewers of the painting of the lake so treat the white expanse of pigment on the canvas as to help make of it an attribution of white to the moon over the lake. (I say only "helps to make" and only "partially constitutes" because the story needs to be completed by reference to the already-remarked contribution of conceptual attribution of causal powers—to which I shall shortly return.)

I am suggesting that the particular, sensuous quality instantiated within our conscious state functions in somewhat the same manner as the white in the painting does to specify what it is that we sensuously attribute to something before our sense organs. That we sensuously *attribute* is to be accounted for by the matching behavior our sensory state organizes; but *what* we sensuously attribute is not accounted for by the content of our behavior (as it is when attribution is conceptual) but only by the presence within our sensory state of a particular instance of a sensuous quality (or pattern of such qualities) ; and that we sensuously attribute exactly what we do attribute—that the sensuous character attributed and the "act" of attribution are brought together as they are—this is accounted for by a class of similar, sensuous quality-instances or pattern-instances—of similar sensuous "images"—functioning within our sensory state to help organize in us the behavior of matching with each other the members of one class of objects before our sense organs.

As we are constituted, we require that our sensory states be partially composed of actual instances of sensuous colors and of patterns of sensuous color in order that we become visually conscious of the similarity in the looks of square surfaces, three-membered arrays of items, and green things. And we require that the sensory states associated with our other senses be partially composed of actual instances of the sensuous qualities and patterns of such qualities peculiar to those senses in order that we achieve sensory awareness, in the various modalities, of the similarities in the sound, feel, smell, and taste of sets of objects perceptible through those senses.

Our sensory awareness of the appearances of things—our sensuous attribution of sensuous qualities—provides also a condition and occasion of our achieving sensory awareness of some of the causal powers of the appearing things, since it provides the occasion of our making, within our attentive sensory perception, conceptual attributions of these causal powers to objects before our sense organs. However, if some of my earlier hypotheses have been correct, there is a reciprocal interdependence between sensuous and conceptual attribution. For I have earlier suggested that simple matching behavior would not be sufficient to generate for the sensuous quality-instances within our sensory states their role as contents of sensuous attributions; we need also to be developing, more or less simultaneously, the habit of making conceptual attributions of dispositions or causal powers to the objects before our sense organs.

For example, sensuously to attribute a color to a surface requires that we apply to an object the concept of a surface and of a stuff for the surface. Sensuously to attribute a color-pattern constituting the look of what is in fact a square-shaped surface may require that we conceptually attribute at least some of the physical features that compose the shape of the surface. And conceptual attribution of physical properties presupposes a more complex behavioral expression than simple matching behavior: for conceptual attribution we must be disposed to treat an object as if it has the specific property attributed, whereas matching behavior does not require this. So it would appear that in order conceptually to attribute, within sensory perception, a square shape to a surface, one must have available the interior, sensuous model—the pattern of sensuous qualities—which, in turn, we can experience as the look of something (for the case of vision) only if we sensuously attribute it to the thing; and yet this sensuous attribution, in its turn, presupposes not only behavioral matching up of those objects which, in being perceived, cause instances of the same sensuous quality (or quality-pattern) to occur within our sensory state, but also some measure of conceptual attribution of causal powers.

One way to think of this interdependence is the following. Before the interior, sensuous quality-instances figure for us as contents of attributions, they occur within our sensory states. The matching behavior these qualities help make possible, and whose occurrence provides part of the foundation of these qualities' functioning as contents of sensuous attributions, commonly develops only in conjunction with the development in us of the power to make conceptual attributions of those physical properties whose sensible manifestations are the appearance to us of the objects that possess these properties. Conceptual attribution of a causal feature uses the sensuous quality instantiated within our sensory state as a model for the causal feature, even identifying the two, and in doing this, conceptual attribution helps to transform the sensuous quality into the sensuous content of a perceptual attribution, making possible the quality's role in helping us match up objects of similar appearance, which are also usually objects having a shared physical property causally connected with their similar appearance. Sensuous attribution of sensuous quality, matching behavior, and the behavior which manifests our conceptual attribution of causal powers to the matched objects before our sense organs, these three activities develop in the closest coordination with each other.

To illustrate: a certain pattern of sensuous *color* is caused to be instantiated within our sensory state by each one a set of light-reflecting, square surfaces; we develop the power to use this internal *color*-pattern in treating such surfaces as surfaces, and even as square, and thus develop the power conceptually to attribute to these surfaces their character as surfaces and as square; and the sensory state in us that helps organize this behavior consists in part of a conceptual attribution to the surfaces of these physical characteristics (these causal powers). As this power of conceptual attribution is developing, however, there is developing, hand in hand with it, the power to match up all visible surfaces having a square shape, and, as part of the basis of this power, the power sensuously to attribute to these same surfaces the sensuous *color*-pattern they cause—through reflecting certain patterns of light to our eyes—to belong to our sensory state, a sensuous *color*-pattern whose mere presence within our sensory state enabled this entire process to get started. In the end, we visually identify the sensuously attributed boundaries of the sensuously attributed expanses of color with conceptually ascribed physical edges of physical surfaces and with the latter's conceptually attributed, physically square shape.

Through all these complications, it remains true that *what* sensuous quality or quality-pattern we sensuously attribute is determined by the actual instance of sensuous quality or pattern occurring within our own conscious state. That we *attribute* this sensuous quality to some object before our sense organs (and thus, that this quality-instance *represents* something) is determined by the role this sensuous quality belonging to our conscious state plays in helping to organize within us both our simple matching behavior and the more complex behavior comprising our treating objects as if they have those causal powers which we ascribe to them as partly inhering in the sensuous quality we sensuously attribute to them.

In giving this account of the sensuous attribution of sensuous qualities, have I contradicted my earlier assertion that sensuous attribution of these qualities entails no specific adaptation of our possible behavior to the presumed possession of these qualities by objects before our sense organs? Certainly I ought not to have done so. Since a sensuously attributed property has, purely as such, no attributed causal powers or dispositional content, its presumed possession by any single "object" to which in perception we sensuously attribute it would not entail help or hindrance for any behavior of ours. When the full content of the present explanation is understood, I do not think it will appear that I have contradicted myself.

First we should notice that it is never a sensuous attribution of a quality to a single thing which enables us to behave in some way toward this thing. What gives us this power is always our sensuously attributing the same quality or pattern of qualities to two or more things, and our taking account of the similarity in content of these two attributions: this enables us to match up, in our behavior, the two or more things to which these similar sensuous attributions pertain.

Second, the matching behavior associated with these similar sensuous attributions does not constitute our treating the things to which a sensuous quality has been attributed as if they have *this* quality. Mere matching does not go so far. It entails only that we give some identical response to each object to which we sensuously attribute the same quality: for example, we might nod our head sideways in response to every surface that has the look which is in fact peculiar to square surfaces (although we're not attributing a square shape). This is quite a different response from, for example, fetcthing a square peg and placing it in a square hole—whereby we do treat the hole as square and, thus, manifest a conceptual attribution of shape. In merely matching up objects, we do not treat the objects as if they have the property we have sensuously attributed, we treat them only as if they have *some* property in common.

Third, as remarked much earlier, neither the conceptual identification of a sensuous quality, e.g., *brown*, with a physical feature, e.g., the stuff of a surface, whereby the sensuous quality, as perceptually attributed, is "transformed" into an (ascribed) objective feature of a public object, nor the ascription of the quality as thus "transformed" quite coincides with the purely sensuous attribution, although here behavior in which objects are treated as having a feature is figuring. For the purely sensuous attribution settles what quality it is that is identified with the stuff of a surface rather than what it would be for this quality to be the stuff of a surface. No behavioral treating a color as stuff of a surface (behavior manifesting a visual perception) can determine the nature of the quality thus treated— none can make it brown, as distinguished from blue, that the surface is treated as having for its stuff. This can be done only by the presence of the purely sensuous content-attribution, which merely as such has no behavioral expression. To be sure, I have said that the behavioral manifestation of the conceptual attribution of the "transformed" quality (the sensuous quality identified with an objective feature) does play a crucial role in helping make a sensuous attribution an *attribution*. Nonetheless the unique, sensuous content of the perceptual attribution of sensuous *brown* as the stuff of a surface is altogether undetermined and unmanifested by the attribution-manifesting behavior.

If my account is correct, our sensuous attributions do, as attributions, offer some slight prospective outlook: they ready us to encounter something similar to what we are now experiencing, providing intimations of continuity, of kinship between what is present and what is absent. But the contents of our sensuous attributions are not prospective; these patterns of sensuous quality comprise nothing more—nor less—than how the physical world is presently appearing to us: through the unfailing hold they have upon our attention, the world becomes for us a presence, we are present in a world.

NAME INDEX

Aiken, Henry David, v
Amoore, John E., 80–82,
    passim, 85
Armstrong, D.M., 1, 4, 8, 9, 40,
    129
Austin, John, 1

Beets, M.G.J., 83n
Bekesy, George von, 199–202,
    passim
Berkeley, George, 1, 303
Boltzmann, Ludwig, 121, 135
Boyle, Robert, 111, 112, 258
Bridgman, Percy, 110
Brown, A.I., 118n

Carnot, Sadi, 112, 119, 120
Causey, Robert, 9, 86
Charles, Jacques A.C., 112
Chisholm, Roderick, ii, 2, 4, 9,
    208–223, passim, 239

Cook, Linda, 10
Cornman, James, 2, 9

Davis, Hallowell, 200
Deutscher, Max, 183–189,
    passim
Di Carlo, Frances, 10
Dretske, Fred, ii, 2, 9, 208–223,
    passim, 239

Eisenstadt, Melvin M., 185,
    186, 187

Ford, Kenneth W., 277
Fourier, Joseph, 112, 116–119,
    passim, 197

Frisch, David H., 277

Gibbs, Willard, 111, 112
Gibson, J. J., i, 59–63, passim,
    79
Goodman, Nelson, 39n
Gorovitz, Samuel, 10
Griffith, A.A., 186

Helm, Richard, 81n
Henning, H., 60
Hesse, Mary, 278

Jackson, Frank, 4, 8
James, William, 138
Johnson Jr., James W., 81n

Kelvin, Lord, 112, 119, 120,
    135

Leutkemeyer, Mary, 10
Lincoln, Abraham, 225
Locke, John, 1

Marco, S., 118n
Martin, Raymond, 10
Maxwell, James Clerk, 111,
    112, 257–261, passim
Moncrief, R.W., 80
Morgan, Sheila, 10

Omnes, Roland, 276

Paden, Debra, 10
Perkins, Desirée W., 10
Perkins, Moreland, 69n
Place, U.T., 9
Presley, C.F., 183n

DATE DUE	
DEC 13 2013	